STUDIES IN THE STRUCTURE OF POWER

DECISION-MAKING IN CANADA

The series 'Studies in the Structure of Power: Decision-Making in Canada' is sponsored by the Social Science Research Council of Canada for the purpose of encouraging and assisting research concerned with the manner and setting in which important decisions are made in fields affecting the general public in Canada. The launching of the series was made possible by a grant from the Canada Council.

The studies included in the series are not confined to any one of the disciplines comprising the social sciences. The books explore the ways in which social power is exercised in this country: it will encompass studies done within a number of different conceptual frameworks, utilizing both traditional methods of analysis and those prompted by the social, political, and technological changes following the Second World War.

In establishing the series, the Social Science Research Council has sought to encourage scholars already embarked on relevant studies by providing financial and editorial assistance and similarly to induce others to undertake research in areas of decision-making so far neglected in Canada.

STUDIES IN THE STRUCTURE OF POWER

DECISION-MAKING IN CANADA

EDITOR: JOHN MEISEL

J.E. HODGETTS

The Canadian Public Service

A Physiology of Government

1867-1970

UNIVERSITY OF TORONTO PRESS

© University of Toronto Press 1973
Toronto and Buffalo
Reprinted in paperback 1974, 1976

Printed in Canada

ISBN 0-8020-1863-7 (cloth)
ISBN 0-8020-6260-1 (paper)
LC 72-90738

Foreword

The reader whose appetite has been aroused by the title of the series of which this book is a part may be disappointed in discovering that the volume in his hands is not concerned particularly with decision-making as such but with 'laying bare the structures within which decisions affecting every citizen and every public servant are taken daily.' The disillusion is certain to be short-lived, however, for one of the central points which emerges from this work is that an inescapably close connection exists between the nature and quality of decisions taken and the ecological, temporal, and structural contexts in which they are reached. Professor Hodgetts emphasizes the latter and demonstrates to those who have come to admire his earlier studies of public administration that he has once again succeeded in blending the theoretical and conceptual preoccupations of contemporary social science with a solidly based and vast knowledge of the empirical setting of the problem he explores. Social science, in its praiseworthy and generally successful efforts to become more exact, comparative, and predictive, has nevertheless often failed, even when making important theoretical advances, to link its abstractions to the real world of events. Professor Hodgetts, while fully cognizant of – and ever ready to draw on – the insights and benefits provided by organization theory, systems analysis, functionalism-structuralism, and most of the other props which have enriched our studies of society, remains closely attached to the historical and environmental parameters within which the public service performs its tasks. He has therefore provided a reliable and realistic analysis of many of the conditions in which governments generally, and the Canadian government in particular, make their decisions, of the circumstances which have affected these decisions in the past, and of the conditions which will likely have to be met in coping with the exciting and exacting demands yet to come.

In the course of his 'historical-analytical survey, mapping the profile and physiology of the public service,' he has also written a comprehensive catalogue of, and guidebook to, the administrative forms and formations with which Canada has dotted its administrative landscape over the years. He has, furthermore, produced along the way a handbook in which the alert administrator – both in the government and outside – will find numerous situations parallel to his own. These can be highly instructive in a variety of settings – some as models to be followed and others as errors to be avoided.

There is a widespread view that studies of mass behaviour, of confrontations and revolutions, or of decision-making at the politico-economic command-posts of society – to name only a few – are much more fascinating and 'relevant' than what is often assumed to be the inevitably plodding examination of the stodgy, remote, and grey public service. The present volume is a vibrant example giving the lie to this mistaken notion. Professor Hodgetts' well-known skill in synthesizing and organizing complex data, his vigorous style, and his unerring eye for the colourful phrase and telling illustration have produced a compelling, lively, encyclopaedic, yet easily followed study of the public service set in the context of Canada's most persistent problems.

The volume, particularly in its final pages, also addresses itself to the implications for the public service of current criticism which sees 'a mounting array of social, economic and ecological issues crowding the public agenda, the solutions to which require more rapid response than can be expected from the piecemeal, time-consuming procedures of the liberal's consensual politics.' The analysis which follows has convinced its author that, by comparison with most other political institutions, the public service has proven itself quite unusually flexible, adaptable, and even innovative in response to societal changes. He therefore concludes that, far from necessarily being a conservative force as is often asserted, the public service may well come to play a positive and creative role in helping society adjust to the new demands which are being voiced with increasing frequency and stridency. No one, as this study shows, could be more aware of the issues and problems raised by this possibility than Professor Hodgetts, but it is a significant contribution of this book that, in addition to providing an informed insight into the past and the present, it applies the fruits of retrospection to a daring speculation about the future. We are provided with an indispensable, fully annotated work of reference and, by implication, with a challenging call to arms, addressed both to researchers and activists.

J.M.

Preface

The gestation period preceding the appearance of this study has extended well beyond the time span of twenty months required for the birth of such large mammals as the elephant. The lesson to be drawn from this biological fact by the student of public administration is that the physical bulk of his brain child is likely to vary in inverse proportion to the time spent on creation. The reason for this paradox is to be found in the changing, even evanescent, nature of the data with which the researcher has to deal. This book was originally conceived as a much bulkier, definitive, and detailed analysis of the federal public service of Canada. But, with the passage of time, the attempt to incorporate all relevant details into the study was constantly frustrated by changes in organizational structure and management practices that rendered much of the factual data obsolete before it could be enshrined in print. Part Two of this study, which is the most technical and detailed, has had to concede most to the rapid obsolescence of data and, although every effort has been made to capture all relevant changes up to the end of 1970, use of factual detail is designed to be illustrative rather than exhaustive.

The abandonment of the initial intention in favour of a more generalized and historically oriented study should, perhaps, be defended on grounds other than the sheer impracticality of the more exhaustive treatment. In 1966 one of the most far-reaching series of organizational changes in the public departments was inaugurated, and in 1967 three statutes were passed which marked the culmination of many years of agitation for reform of the management functions, even as they set in motion new mechanisms for performing these functions. Accordingly, Part Three of this volume is devoted to presenting four essays that provide the background against which the new measures can be assessed and the likely course of their future development appraised.

The conviction that the past is prologue for the contemporary public service has also coloured the approach taken in the first part of the study. The public service, both in the tasks it is required to perform and in the ways it is organized to accomplish these tasks, is a reflection of the community it exists to serve. The verification of this hypothesis is attempted in the first four chapters. While this so-called 'ecological approach' to public organizations is in keeping with contemporary academic fashions, other portions of this book may be viewed by many students as wedded too closely to the classical school of public administration theorists who enjoyed their heyday in the 1930s. There is a simple, straightforward defence that can be mustered in favour of the procedures used for analysing the allocation of programmes to departments and agencies and for exploring the internal division of labour: it has not yet been done and it should be done before we fly off to the esoteric realms inhabited by modern-day organizational theorists and administrative behaviouralists. The failure to adopt these exciting contemporary tools of analysis is not a mark of disapproval or disagreement: the preference for more pedestrian modes of inquiry is simply based on an old-fashioned notion that we must first learn to walk before we can fly. In this respect, such weaknesses as this study exposes are reflections of the comparative neglect of the subject by students of Canadian public administration and the retarded stage of development in which it still languishes.

The immaturity of our formal study of public administration also explains the omissions which are frankly conceded throughout the following pages. The opening chapter, for example, develops what amounts to a research prospectus, lengthy enough to enlist the vigorous attentions of many students for years to come. This volume, for the most part, pursues the limited objective of laying bare the structures within which decisions affecting every citizen and every public servant are taken daily. The nature of the decision-taking processes awaits a multitude of case studies and a synthesis from such studies. We know virtually nothing about the process of 'exchange' that enters into the transactions between the bureaucracy, its clients, and the general environment. We know even less about the internal adaptive processes that contribute to the preservation of a 'steady state' for the bureaucracy. And we have barely probed the surface of the fundamental issue of bureaucratic accountability, in an era when the balance of effective power tends more and more to be tipped in favour of the submerged part of the governmental iceberg that constitutes our permanent administrative branch.

Issues of this magnitude and others that will be found scattered throughout these pages cry out urgently for documentation and penetrating analysis. The major part of this book, relying on relatively straightforward techniques of analysis, is directed to an attempt to open up the subject, to dissect and describe the anatomy and physiology of the federal public service. If it provides the incentive for others to launch studies to fill the many obvious gaps, using more sophisticated research techniques, this volume will have attained the limited objectives imposed by the prevailing state of our studies.

Countless former students and practising public servants have given generously of their comments, experience, and material over the years during which this manuscript was in preparation. Because it would be invidious to single out any of these persons and, in any case, would violate the traditions of the Anonymous Service to which so many of them have devoted their careers, they shall remain nameless. Also in the true spirit of the public service, since they remain nameless they shall also remain blameless for any misstatements of fact or personal biases expressed in the following pages. Nevertheless, in token of appreciation for friendly encouragement and help, this book is respectfully dedicated to those devoted members of the Canadian public service upon whose integrity and impartiality we all increasingly rely for the protection of our purse and person.

The work has been published with the aid of a grant from the Social Science Research Council of Canada, using funds provided by the Canada Council.

Contents

Chronological perspective of Canadian Public Departments, 1867-1972

This chart follows the five-fold functional division employed in the text and is designed as a convenient visual guide for the reader who wishes to follow the intricacies of a century of department building in the federal public service. In compiling the chart heavy reliance was placed on the *Guide to Canadian Ministries since Confederation*, with a Supplement to 1 August 1965, compiled by the Public Archives of Canada.

A heavy black line boxes in the full departments; lighter boxes are used to identify functional units that had less than cabinet status; dotted boxes highlight major features, while dotted lines indicate movement of a segment of an existing department into a separate department, for example, Railways and Canals out of Public Works.

It should be noted that the Department of Justice in Category I has evolved to a service department more approximately placed in Category III, just as Public Works in Category II is now best located in Category III, Similarly, in Category III, the Registrar General moves to Category V with its transformation into the Department of Consumer and Corporate Affairs. Finally, the mix of human and physical resource administration still necessitates the location of the contemporary Department of Indian and Northern Affairs in both Category IV and Category V.

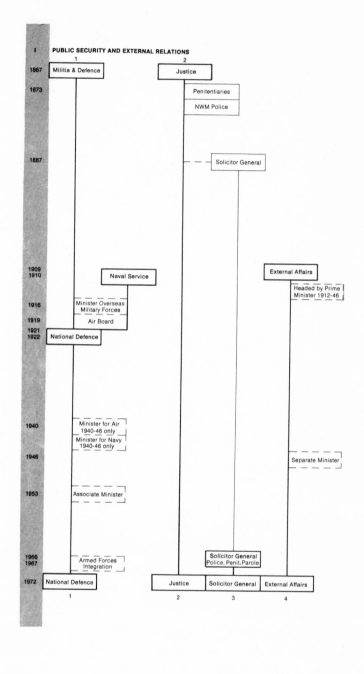

I   **PUBLIC SECURITY AND EXTERNAL RELATIONS**

                    1   2

1867 | Militia & Defence | | Justice |

1873 | Penitentiaries |

                                                  | NWM Police |

1887   - - - | Solicitor General |

1909
1910 | Naval Service | | External Affairs |

                                                                  | Headed by Prime
                                                                    Minister 1912-46 |
1916 | Minister Overseas
          Military Forces |

1919 | Air Board |

1921
1922 | National Defence |

1940 | Minister for Air
          1940-46 only |

        | Minister for Navy
          1940-46 only |

1946 | Separate Minister |

1953 | Associate Minister |

1966 | Armed Forces | Solicitor General
1967   Integration | Police, Penit, Parole |

1972 | National Defence | | Justice | | Solicitor General | | External Affairs |

                    1   2   3   4

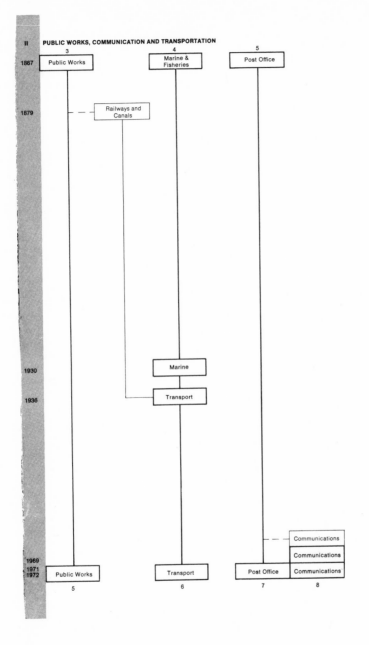

II   **PUBLIC WORKS, COMMUNICATION AND TRANSPORTATION**

3	4	5
1867	Public Works	Marine & Fisheries	Post Office

1879   Railways and Canals

1930   Marine

1936   Transport

Communications
Communications

1969
1971
1972   Public Works   Transport   Post Office   Communications

   5   6   7   8

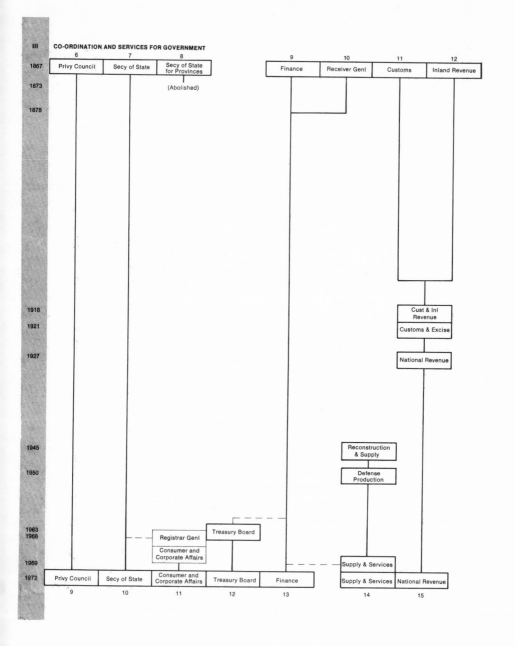

III CO-ORDINATION AND SERVICES FOR GOVERNMENT

	6	7	8		9	10	11	12
1867	Privy Council	Secy of State	Secy of State for Provinces		Finance	Receiver Genl	Customs	Inland Revenue
1873			(Abolished)					
1878								
1918							Cust & Inl Revenue	
1921							Customs & Excise	
1927							National Revenue	
1945					Reconstruction & Supply			
1950					Defense Production			
1963 1966			Registrar Genl	Treasury Board				
			Consumer and Corporate Affairs					
1969							Supply & Services	
1972	Privy Council	Secy of State	Consumer and Corporate Affairs	Treasury Board	Finance		Supply & Services	National Revenue
	9	10	11	12	13		14	15

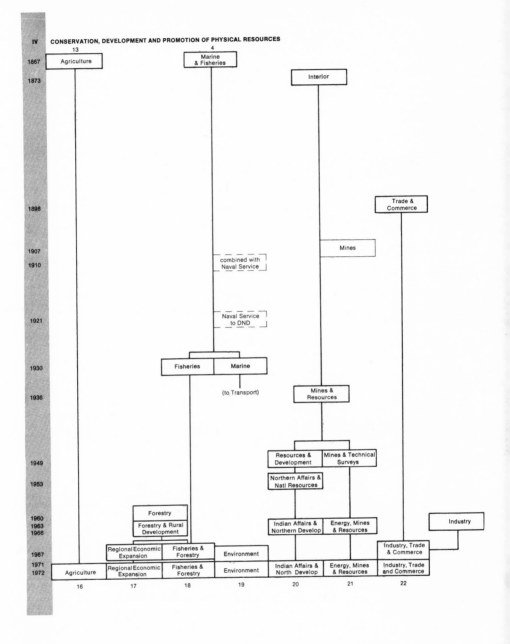

IV **CONSERVATION, DEVELOPMENT AND PROMOTION OF PHYSICAL RESOURCES**

	13			4					

1867 — Agriculture | Marine & Fisheries

1873 — Interior

1898 — Trade & Commerce

1907 — Mines

1910 — combined with Naval Service

1921 — Naval Service to DND

1930 — Fisheries | Marine

1936 — (to Transport) | Mines & Resources

1949 — Resources & Development | Mines & Technical Surveys

1953 — Northern Affairs & Nat'l Resources

1960 — Forestry
1963 — Forestry & Rural Development
1966 — Indian Affairs & Northern Develop | Energy, Mines & Resources | Industry

1967 — Regional Economic Expansion | Fisheries & Forestry | Environment | Industry, Trade & Commerce

1971 —
1972 — Agriculture | Regional Economic Expansion | Fisheries & Forestry | Environment | Indian Affairs & North Develop | Energy, Mines & Resources | Industry, Trade and Commerce

16	17	18	19	20	21	22

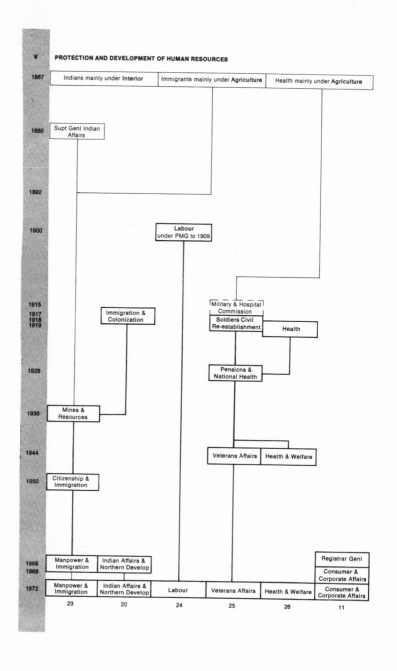

V   PROTECTION AND DEVELOPMENT OF HUMAN RESOURCES

1867	Indians mainly under **Interior**	Immigrants mainly under **Agriculture**	Health mainly under **Agriculture**	
1880	Supt Genl Indian Affairs			
1892				
1900		Labour under PMG to 1909		
1915			Military & Hospital Commission	
1917 1918 1919		Immigration & Colonization	Soldiers Civil Re-establishment	Health
1928			Pensions & National Health	
1936	Mines & Resources			
1944			Veterans Affairs	Health & Welfare
1950	Citizenship & Immigration			
1966 1968	Manpower & Immigration	Indian Affairs & Northern Develop		Registrar Genl / Consumer & Corporate Affairs
1972	Manpower & Immigration	Indian Affairs & Northern Develop	Labour	Veterans Affairs	Health & Welfare	Consumer & Corporate Affairs

23   20   24   25   26   11

PART ONE

Environment and Structure

... an organism must adjust its activities
in such a way as to take into account
the nature of and changes in its environment ... [The phenomena of
adaptation] consist of all the changes
in position, activity and structure which
an organism undergoes so that it can
better survive ... Under extreme conditions an organism may be forced to
alter its environment ... or to remove
itself to a new and more favourable
environment. Adaptations are made
not only to external situations but to
changes within the organism ...

'Physiology,' *Encyclopædia Britannica*

CHAPTER ONE

Social purpose and structural response

The citizens of Canada pursue a multitude of objectives; many of these are strictly personal and private in nature but an increasing number have to be sought through some sort of collaborative effort. Such effort entails organization, sometimes quite simple and rudimentary but more often these days highly developed and elaborate. The greater part of these joint undertakings in a pluralistic society is sponsored by voluntary, private associations, but to an increasing extent the joint pursuit of social objectives is being conducted through public organizations – that is to say, agencies of the state. This study is devoted to the latter type of organization and is confined in fact to the description and analysis of only one important segment, the federal public service of Canada.

Broadly speaking, what we shall here refer to as 'public organizations' are deliberately brought into being to perform two vital tasks. First, the goals which the community seeks to implement through governmental bodies have themselves to be defined by means of an organized effort. This is what 'politics' is all about: mobilizing, focusing, and articulating the scattered individual wills by means of political parties and interest groups. In the initial stages both public and private organizations are involved, but at certain intervals a rather crude measuring stick of free public elections is used to settle the fundamental question whose party will prevail and thus be entitled to initiate the measures deemed consistent with the social purposes sought. Thus, this crucial making of choices is conducted by means of a mechanism that provides an opportunity for alternatives to be tested in the public arena by competing organizations. Preferences developed at this broad public level are usually couched in such general terms that much more concrete definition of public objectives has to be given by means of a refining process carried out in parliament. Organization, in this broad context, exists to pool individual wills into a reservoir of community power which will provide the motive force for politics. Politicians in parliament draw on this reservoir of power to further social objectives.

Another set of structures is required to translate the declarations and definitions of public policy into action. This is the task of the public service. However, it should be obvious that the two elements of public organization mentioned above, even though they may differ greatly in their structure and primary function, interact with one another. Much of the initiative for redefining or elaborating the social purposes of a community does in fact spring from the practical experience of those in the public service. Parliament then becomes an instrument for validating the choices made within the public service and ensuring that implementation is in accord with the declared purposes of the majority party, as upheld by the cabinet.[1]

It should also be noted that all organizations – whether directed towards articulating the purposes to which community effort should be applied or to executing these purposes – are means, not ends in themselves. Admittedly, for those who make a life or career within an institution there is a strong tendency to lose sight of the instrumental quality of the organization and to assume that its unchanging existence is an end in itself.[2] It follows, therefore, that an organization tends to be shaped not only by the special purposes which it has been designed to fulfil but also by the attitudes of its working members. Not unexpectedly, these factors produce bodies such as parties, parliament, and the public service whose organizational contours and working ethos are quite dissimilar. These differences make it reasonable for students of government to segregate the several components of public organizations and to write separate treatises on each.

1 At the turn of the century Frank J. Goodnow established this dichotomy in the very title of a book: *Politics and Administration* (New York, 1900). This led to an artificial separation of what are essentially two elements of a seamless web. The analysis here should not be interpreted as an effort to revitalize this thesis in which administration is purely the slave of the politicians' policy lamp. The distinction is made here in purely formal, legal terms.
2 The sociologists' distinctions between function and dysfunction and latent versus manifest functions are valuable in this context. For one of the most perceptive treatments, see R.K. Merton *et al.*, eds., *Reader in Bureaucracy* (Glencoe, Ill., 1952), pp. 361–71. See also 'Informal Organization,' by Harvey C. Mansfield and Fritz Morstein Marx, in *Elements of Public Administration*, ed. F.M. Marx (2nd ed., Englewood Cliffs, NJ, 1959).

On the other hand, the fact that the functions of the separate entities often intersect or overlap means that even the most exacting description of each will be incomplete if the interrelationships are neglected. This study focuses specifically on the public service, but at the same time tries to take into account the larger environment to which it must constantly relate.

Theoretically, it should be possible to make a fairly accurate assessment of the appropriateness of the public service organization simply by determining how well it fulfils its assigned functions. Unfortunately, the public service is not organized, nor does it operate, in a social vacuum: it is shaped not only by the particular nature of the purpose for which it has been created but also by the physical, social, and institutional features of the community it serves. In a quite literal sense it is a part of all that it has met. Moreover, the public service is also shaped by the need to adapt to certain internal pressures stemming from the competitive struggle between each of the organizational components to survive or expand, as well as by the compulsion to redefine its own role in relation to changing goals.[3]

It may well be that in adapting itself to these inescapable environmental factors the public service becomes less satisfactory as an instrument for fulfilling its assigned objectives. Utopians, intuitively and sometimes explicitly, have been aware of this phenomenon for centuries. Characteristically all Utopians begin with a criticism of existing social institutions; their next step is to reconstruct society itself (if not human nature as well) to fit their image of the ideal; Utopia is then made possible by recasting the institutions of that society in their newly created mould, from whence they emerge to bring about a brave new world.

The student of contemporary organizations – thinking as a practical realist and not an Utopian idealist – is compelled to look at things as they are. He can judge an organization and find it wanting when he compares its performance with the function it was intended to perform, but it would be premature to seek reform until the entire environmental context has also been thoroughly examined: only in this way is it possible to discover that there may be valid social, economic, legal, or political reasons why the organization appears to be less than satisfactory for the purposes it was designed to serve. In short, organizations are organisms that share many of the features of birth, growth, adaptation, and decay which

3 Herbert A. Simon, Donald W. Smithburg, and Victor A. Thompson, *Public Administration* (New York, 1950), chap. 5, has a stimulating analysis of organizational struggle and strategy for survival; see also Philip Selznick, *Leadership in Administration* (Evanston, Ill., 1957).

characterize the evolution of plants or humans: in tampering with one part of an organization it is therefore necessary to be aware of the likely repercussions on the operations of the whole organism.

The foregoing comments are based on a biological analogy which, if carried to extremes as the German organic theorists did, can be misleading; but, treated as an analogue only, it serves to emphasize the dynamic, responsive, and adaptative qualities of human organizations. The contemporary school of 'systemic politics,' using the analogue of mechanics or physics, can also be overdrawn, thereby imparting a conception of an automatically self-balancing organization. In their terms[4] the political system comprises a set of institutions – all acting in an agency capacity for the community – whose function is to refine the demands entering the system from the environment (the inputs) and then make and implement the decisions (the outputs) which will satisfy or placate the demands. The system's success in performing this task is measured by the extent to which the environment's demands are satisfied – the satisfaction being registered through continuing support of the system. The end result is an equilibrium model which corresponds roughly to the concept of homeostasis (that is, the maintenance of relative constancy of conditions in the organism) in the biological or physiological analogue.

The public service organization, as one essential element in the political system, is obviously compelled to respond to the 'input' from the environment, particularly as articulated and aggregated through interest groups and political parties, but it is equally clear that the public service is triggered to action by internally generated demands which have been aptly designated 'withinputs.' This being true, it is possible to conceive of the public service organization as a subsystem within the larger political system, working somewhat independently within its own frame of reference as well as responding to the other elements and the inputs from the surrounding environment.

The mode of analysis prompted by the physiological and systemic approaches (both of which recognize the importance of environment to the organism) has inspired the attempt which is made in chapters 2, 3, and 4 to sketch what appear to be the most important of the environmental and 'systemic' influences that have helped to shape the Canadian public service. Nothing short of a full-scale history of the public service could do adequate

4 David Easton's *The Political System* (New York, 1953) provided an influential stimulus to the systemic approach which scholars interested in comparative government have found particularly useful in analysing developing nations: see, for example, Gabriel A. Almond's 'A Developmental Approach to Political Systems,' *World Politics* 17 (Jan. 1965), pp. 183–214.

justice to this theme, and these chapters are intended to provide only a suggestive outline.

Once the public service has been fixed in its social setting and its legal foundations established, attention can be directed (as in Part Two) to exploring the vital elements of the organization itself, that is, to the public service as a subsystem. For this purpose it becomes necessary to view the subsystem as if it has an autonomous existence, responding only to the inner dictates of logic – usually expressed in terms of greater or lesser efficiency.[5] In broad terms there are three major elements involved in any complex organization of a subsystem:

1 A goal and an operating plan
2 The means for activating and implementing the plan, including:
    (a) an allocation of work or the assignment of jurisdictions
    (b) an arrangement of offices or a division of labour
    (c) appropriate personnel to staff the offices
    (d) money to finance operations
    (e) supporting services to meet 'housekeeping' needs
    (f) direction and co-ordination of all the foregoing components
3 The means for evaluating performance and revising the plan

Where the purposes are comprehensive, far-reaching, and enduring an organization must become formal and stabilized. For example, the state, with perhaps the most complex and multiple purpose organization, is given a constitution which makes provision for the allocation of work, arrangement of offices, the staffing, financing, supplying, and co-ordination of the whole operation.

The public service portion of the state is in a strict constitutional sense an agent for executing purposes set in broad terms by other elements. According to this view we must assume that its purposes are given: it is an organization for implementing goals, not for setting them. Nevertheless, as has been previously noted, a more realistic approach is to view the public service as operating within a broad parliamentary charter, but assigned an ever-widening area of discretion within which it plays a far from neutral role in making vague purposes more explicit and concrete. Much of what goes on under the name of administrative planning in the

5 There has been much controversy among students of public administration concerning the acceptance of efficiency as *the* value or ultimate goal, and indeed much disagreement about a definition of efficiency. See Simon *et al.*, *Public Administration*, chap. 23; and John M. Pfiffner and Robert V. Presthus, *Public Administration* (4th ed., New York, 1960), chap. 6 and literature cited.

public sector is related to this process, and the annual preparation of a budget affords the main opportunity for reassessing and establishing anew the various priorities among the goals to be implemented, as well as re-defining the goals and the means used to achieve them.

Constitutions normally have little to say about the structures of the public service for the state, and this we shall find to be particularly true for Canada. Their main concern is with the goal-setting and adjudicative organizations – and even here they often remain surprisingly silent about some of the real components of the political structure, such as parties and interest groups. The failure of the constitution to make explicit provisions for the public service immediately raises a problem that has been surpris-ingly neglected in the literature of public administration. If, indeed, the public service legally is an agent responsible for implementing public purposes declared by others, then to what other body does it stand in this servant capacity? The usual response is that an official in the public service is an agent of the state or an agent of the Crown. But, does this mean that the public service is an instrument of the executive (that is, the institu-tionalized version of the Crown) or of the legislature? In the one case the political executive, the cabinet, is monopolized by the majority party and in the other case the party dominates the legislature. Does this mean then that we are simply saying that the public service is, for all practical pur-poses, the agency of the party which for the time being, because of its parliamentary majority, is in a position to declare the goals which the state shall pursue?

Generally, the public service is held to be an extension of the political executive arm (in practice, the cabinet) of the state. Nevertheless, it is the legislative branch which in the final analysis determines the broad allocation of work and whether it shall be conducted by a department or some other form of administrative entity. Parliament's traditional control of the purse also gives it grounds for asserting that the public service is its agency – although in actual practice the raising and spending of public funds has fallen more and more into the hands of the executive branch. Clearly, the subdivision of labour within the non-political administrative sector and the recruitment of people to fill public offices are primarily matters for the political executive's decision, but even here there has been a sustained battle between the executive and legislative branches parti-cularly over the right to recruit public service personnel. Chapter 4 at-tempts to unravel some of the confusing features bound up in the legal status of the public service.

Returning to the other elements of organization listed above and begin-ning with the allocation of work, we encounter yet another array of problems which it will be the purpose of subsequent chapters to examine. The universal and conventional method of allocating the manifold tasks assigned to the public service is to group them in departments. Is there any agreement on the procedure to be followed in setting up departments or the limitations on their number? Even to the apparently simple preliminary question 'what is a department?' we cannot really get a clear-cut answer. Why are some activities which are obviously of a lower order of importance to the community at large (for example, insurance) set up in a 'department' all of their own, while others, which involve a much larger staff and affect more people (for example, the Meteorological Service), are relegated to the position of one of several branches in a larger department? What is the consequence of placing a function in one department rather than another? Do we have adequate devices for reallocating work when a department becomes overburdened or overextended? Are the departments adaptable to the changing needs or social circumstances of the nation – the dramatic introduction of atomic energy as a new instrument for meeting social purposes, the rapid erosion of a long-standing function such as tuberculosis treatment, the attrition of functions caused, for example, by the gradual decline of the veteran population today serviced by the Department of Veterans Affairs, or the rapid expansion of the provincial health services to supplant federally provided services?

The departmental method of allocating work in all modern jurisdictions has to an increasing extent been supplemented by the use of a bewildering variety of public corporations, crown companies, boards, and commission. What defects in the department system, if any, have accentuated this development? Considering the complications they create for those concerned with preserving conventional forms of control and an informed public understanding of the public service, are such departures warranted?

The third subordinate element of organization is an arrangement of offices which customarily takes the form of a pyramidal or hierarchical pattern. The objective is to ensure that authority can be focused at the top of the pyramid by grouping offices at successive levels in the hierarchy on the basis of the authority, discretion, and abilities located at each level. A structure of subordination and command, familiar to military organizations, is the end result. It provides, ideally, a means of keeping minor issues of detail from piling up on the desks of superior officers; it ensures that each officer knows the area in which he can act alone, to whom he can issue commands, and to whom he must refer matters up the 'line.' In short, the hierarchy is expected to provide a formal communication system for a large structure, permitting the orderly flow of information upward and decisions or orders downward.

The 'line' organization is an inevitable consequence of the growing size and complexity of the public service. It should necessarily be kept under constant review. Where should this review be undertaken and by what means? The public service in recent years has answered this query by setting apart certain sections of the organization whose sole purpose is to service the line function. The 'care and feeding' of the line operations therefore entail the creation of ancillary or auxiliary agencies that make no direct contribution to implementing the purposes of the organization but exist rather to ensure that those so concerned are equipped with pencils, paper, typewriters, desks, office space, light, heat, and so on. Since these are common requirements of all administrative bodies, the question naturally arises whether it may not be more economical and efficient to place housekeeping activities undertaken on behalf of all departments in a single agency set up for this purpose alone. Can one supradepartmental agency meet all these requirements or must there be several auxiliary agencies? How can one offset the natural tendency of such service agencies to impose controls along with the services they are expected to render to the client departments?

While the growth of public service organizations focuses attention on the specialized services required to keep them in operating trim, the increasing complexity of the programmes they are called upon to develop places heavy burdens on the shoulders of the senior cadre of policy-formers. Belated recognition of this fact is now beginning to be evidenced in the emergence of 'staff' services, acting as the *alter ego* to these senior administrative and political officials by processing data, preparing position papers, and tendering advice. It is possible that our traditional reliance on the cabinet as the supreme collegial planning body has engendered a reluctance to provide comparable supporting staff functions at lower levels in the public service. Yet, even in its collective capacity the cabinet has needed staff services of its own and these have appeared late in the day. As for individual ministers and their deputies, they have been even slower to recognize a similar need. Consequently, we are still in the early stages of resolving the problems that attend any effort to associate a 'pure' staff function with the line policy-makers. Indeed, there is a very real question whether staff services detached from the line can be influential or useful. And there is also a question whether these services should be organized from internal resources or whether it is best to 'import' the advice by relying on royal commissions, task forces, or experts temporarily attached to the public service.

Even as the hierarchical pattern of arranging offices is affected by the need to create special servicing agencies, so too the problems of administering across a continental domain introduce a geographical factor that must be faced. Wherever the fulfilment of a department's objectives necessitates a widespread dispersion of offices the hierarchical pattern must be adapted to meet the geographic challenge. Can the formal lines of communication and command, which it is the purpose of hierarchy to provide, be preserved in the face of extensive physical decentralization? What are the most effective ways of structuring the headquarters-to-field relationship so as to preserve unity of command at the top and the free flow of information and instruction between units physically separated by thousands of miles?

The questions raised in the immediately preceding paragraphs are examined in considerable detail in the chapters grouped under Part Two of this volume. Part Three directs attention to the last four elements of a complex organization – staffing, financing, servicing, and co-ordinating. These elements constitute the hard core of the management function. Volumes could be written on each but this study focuses only on the organization, role, and interrelationship of the central agencies and the departmental management teams, together with the emerging opportunities for employee participation in management decisions.

In the past students of public administration have tended to focus on personnel management almost to the virtual exclusion of the other components of public service management. The emphasis is natural for, after all, people are the most important elements; their mode of selection has been a matter of long-standing controversy between legislature and executive dating back to colonial rule in Canada; there are always the lurking skeletons of patronage to be dragged into the open; and the problems of managing human resources can never be settled once and for all. Furthermore, governments today are by all odds the most important employers, something like 12.5 per cent of the total labour force in Canada being in the employ of federal, provincial, or municipal governments.[6]

In Canada, the locus of managerial authority over personnel has shifted and has never really come to rest in one single place. Today, this historical uncertainty has resulted in a division of authority between the Public Service Commission, the Treasury Board, and department or agency. Is this division inevitable or desirable? Should the move be towards comprehensive dispersal of this authority to individual departments or towards a more centralized and unified personnel management agency? This broad

6 J.E. Hodgetts and O.P. Dwivedi, 'The Growth of Government Employment in Canada,' *Canadian Public Administration* 12 (Summer 1969), pp. 224–38. In 1966 the total labour force was 7.4 million, of which government employees accounted for over 710,000.

issue lies at the heart of much of the material in Part Three and no attempt has been made to embark on the manifold technical problems associated with selection, training, promotion, and the many other conditions of service (most notably classification and pay) that have to be regulated.

Even a superficial acquaintance with the composition of the public service is enough to indicate that it contains not only a large share of the labour market but embraces within its ranks an infinite variety of skills and training.[7] In particular the increasing need for professional, scientific, and technical personnel ('high level manpower' as current jargon has it) reflects a transformation in the Canadian work force that is mirrored within the public service. It is the dimension of this task and the need to respond to the qualitative changes produced by rapid technological advance that justifies the special attention directed in Part Three to the significant transformations that have been taking place in the organization for managing public service personnel.

Marching in step with these organizational adjustments is another and virtually universal phenomenon, namely, the rise of employee organizations and the recognition of their plea to be considered as essential contributors to all policies connected with their own terms of employment. The means by which belated and oft-times grudging recognition of this pervasive pressure has been reflected in the Canadian public service provides the closing chapter for Part Three. This issue is tied in with the regulations and conventions governing the right of civil servants as citizens to employ conventional political pressures to rectify alleged injustices. Here, a judicious balance must be found that will not make civil servants politically underprivileged citizens and yet will not jeopardize their permanency in office by forcing them to become publicly partisan.

A relatively new factor has beclouded the relationship of the public servant to his employer: this is the loyalty issue with its accompaniment of security checks. On the one hand, the traditional code of behaviour is based on the assumption that the public servant should not have – openly at least – any politics; on the other hand, security regulations insist that he openly identify himself with the political consensus which sustains the democratic state and which in effect the civil servant himself has sworn to uphold. Although the security issue is no longer a significant bone of contention, in recent times it has re-emerged in a more subtle form, largely associated with programmes for development. The new breed of civil

---

7 On the civilian side of the Department of National Defence, for example, the list of trades and professions runs the alphabetical gamut: architects, bricklayers, butchers, chauffeurs, chimney sweeeps, doctors, dentists, editors, firefighters, greasers, librarians, lawyers, map-makers, photographers, professors, sail-makers, welders, and x-ray technicians – to name a selected sample.

servant involved in the so-called war on poverty or crusading to help underprivileged minority groups, like the Indians, to help themselves, is creating an anti-establishment ethic *within* the establishment ethos. Where such a group is set apart from the conventional agencies of government, as is the case with the Company of Young Canadians, the confrontation is as dramatically visible as is the uncertainty of the establishment in knowing quite what to do about its obstreperous creation. Less visible and less dramatic are the confrontations between officials in the 'old bureaucracy,' many pursuing the paternalistic welfare practices of the past, others committed to the policy of self-help for the underprivileged which leads to the engineering of dissent against their traditionalist fellow employees. Whether management will be able to live with such officially sanctioned internal 'oppositions' is still far from clear.[8] What is clear is that this issue, together with others of which a selective sample has been presented, will continue to exact from senior management concerned with personnel matters their unflagging attention and most ingenious initiatives.

The fourth subordinate element of organization has been listed as money. Financial resources are needed to meet the cost of setting up whatever administrative apparatus may be necessary to produce the goods or provide the grants and services which constitute the raison d'être of the organization. The source of an organization's funds provides a useful key to its actual membership, and the nature of the membership may in turn have a pronounced influence on the methods of allocating or spending the funds. In a professional organization or an interest group money comes from membership fees and services are restricted to the members. A political party is in rather a unique position for the number of actual 'members,' so adjudged because they pay dues, is small in proportion to the number who show their support by voting for the party. A business organization conveys certificates of 'membership' on those who purchase its shares. Those who purchase its products are to be regarded much as the voters who support a party or as fans who support the home football team: their dollar votes or their cheers rather than their political votes reflect the degree of support for the organization.

Viewing the state as a public organization we observe at once several important differences. Membership is compulsory and universal, not voluntary and limited as in all other cases. Its services, for this reason, also tend to be available to a much wider public. In turn, revenues are

8 A further commentary on this feature is to be found in my 'Social Goals from the Perspective of Political Science,' in McGill University School of Social Work, *Social Goals: Fiftieth Anniversary Colloquium, November, 1968* (Montreal, 1969), pp. 5–6.

derived from generalized levies of a compulsory nature that cannot be evaded by any of the members. This means that the members are much more conscious of the fact that the state organization is using 'their' money; this is less true of other organizations from which people can withdraw membership or even their support. It is this psychological attitude on the part of the members of the state which helps to explain the amount of attention devoted to the raising and even more particularly the spending of the members' contributions. In practice, these decisions are made by members' proxies assembled in parliament[9] and by the public service organization itself through whose hands nearly all the revenue so provided will ultimately flow. And within the public service the number of purely internal checks and controls on the handling and disposal of funds accounts for much of the paper work and cumbersome procedures which are constantly laid accusingly at the doorstep of bureaucracy by the very people whose interests these procedures are designed to protect.

The fact that the funds are provided by one segment of the state organization, that is to say, parliament, and generally spent by the other segment, the public service, introduces a further complication. It means, in effect, that the public service in its agency capacity has no formal control over the amount of money it will have to spend. Indeed, in broad terms, parliament reinforces this master-servant relationship by voting the money for specific objects so that the public service will have no discretion to spend its allotment in support of alternative activities of its own choice. Nevertheless, it is within the public service that the detailed plans for expenditures are annually formulated, and it may be this segregation of money-raising proposals from the expenditure-planning proposals that gives rise to Professor Parkinson's second famous law, that is, 'expenditure rises to meet income.'[10] In other words governments do not normally proceed by taking stock of their expected income and then tailoring expenditures to fit this income; they proceed rather by concentrating on the expenditure side and then, in the parliamentary phrase, find 'ways and means' to meet these expenditures.

However great the complexities and apparent contradictions in the procedures used to finance the public service, in the last analysis it is the budgetary process through which social goals are established, priorities granted, and co-ordination of effort achieved. The consideration of this element of organization then must extend beyond the sheer mechanics of

9 An analysis of the 1961 session of parliament – probably quite typical – reveals that of the 146 sitting days one-third were devoted to plans for raising or spending money (much more on the latter than the former).
10 C. Northcote Parkinson, *The Law and the Profits* (London, 1963), chap. 1.

financial and accounting operations to a more basic concern with the use of the budget as a planning, co-ordinating, reviewing, and revising device.

The proposition that the public service is an agent to implement the goals set by other parts of the governmental organization should logically lead to an examination of the mechanisms for preserving responsibility of the agent to the master. This study deals only marginally with this subject; its importance warrants a separate full-scale analysis which cannot be attempted here. It is clear that achieving the accountability of an organization as large and complex as the public service of Canada is not a matter of relying entirely on the political representatives of the citizen in cabinet or parliament to maintain a watchful vigilance over the activities of all servants of the state. Consequently, it is important to explore, as this study seeks to do, the hierarchical structure of the organization and the many rigorous internal checks and controls which are designed to provide a species of self-regulation and self-evaluation. Ideally, a complete picture could be obtained only by a thorough account of the legislature's techniques for preserving a responsible bureaucracy; a careful survey of the unwritten code of behaviour for public servants which inspires a growing self-respect for honest, efficient administration; a description of the external controls imposed by an impartial judiciary over the enlarged areas of discretionary action now available to public servants; and an examination of the increasing contacts between civil servants and representatives of organized groups with whom they have dealings; all of which provide further incentive to be responsible and responsive in the daily tasks of administration.

Undoubtedly, within the public service there is need to improve the machinery of top management and co-ordination not so that it may impose a stultifying negative control but rather that it may inspire a co-operative partnership throughout the public service in the search for more efficient ways of releasing the energies of the capable people who man public offices. The political executive as a board of management responsible for an ever-enlarging administrative machine also needs to improve its 'general staff' if it is to meet successfully the challenge of the administrative state.

In particular, management will have to devote more attention to measuring the results stemming from the means it has mustered for meeting planned objectives, and also refine its techniques for revising plans and making the necessary adjustment of means in order to adapt to the fluid forces of change. These are the features we have suggested as the third key component of any large organization pursuing complex goals, requiring the co-ordination of many resources. And it is this component of organization that is designed to evaluate the 'feed-back' from the operating front and to propose appropriate adaptations of organizational response to change of goals and programmes, which has been most neglected.

Parliament, too, must be given more help in exercising its role as shareholders' trustee. Basically this means some significant change in the present methods used by the executive to report on their stewardship of the public funds with whose expenditure parliament has entrusted them. But there may be another area where parliament could make a contribution: the administrative powers conferred on public officials are large and growing, the lone citizen with a grievance is increasingly likely to be submerged and neglected. Continuous parliamentary scrutiny of the characteristics of these delegated powers and the uses to which they may be put by public servants would appear to be vitally important in preserving the citizens' rights. Whether the appendage of a 'parliamentary commissioner' or 'ombudsman' would be essential to the performance of this function may be debatable but that there is a need for increased attention to be devoted to this problem is beyond question.

Regrettably, most of these problems associated with the preservation of a responsible and responsive public service must be set aside in this study in order to preserve the primary focus on the internal problems of organization for operations and management. There has been remarkably little work done on either the accountability of the Canadian bureaucracy or the ways and means of making it efficient. This study makes a modest start on exploring the second theme, that of bureaucratic organization and management with a view to achieving efficiency. The other theme, bureaucratic accountability, must be placed high on the agenda for the current generation of students of public administration.

No apology is required for emphasizing the theme of efficiency. This preliminary chapter, a sort of conspectus for the material that follows, projects a sufficiently substantial bill of fare to warrant the detailed attention which the following chapters will devote to each item. The drama and excitement that attends the periodic efforts of political parties to rally support behind their leaders and the social goals which they espouse seem superficially more important and intrinsically more interesting than a mundane consideration of the public service. But unless we devote thought and study to organizing the means required for implementing social goals the best laid plans of princes and principalities may well 'gang aft a-gley.'

CHAPTER TWO

The public service and the powerful persuaders

John Donne's comment that 'no man is an island' could be applied with equal relevance to organizations created by men. However important the internal physiological laws of an administrative organ may be in regulating its growth and physical features, it is equally shaped by the environment in which it operates.[1] Once organizations are brought into being they begin to create a network of linkages essential to survival and growth: they compete with other organizations for scarce financial and manpower resources; they seek public acceptance and prestige by cultivating their clientele and generally creating an environment congenial to their ongoing functions. In short, the laws of organizational survival compel organizations to enter into transactions with the environment and with other components of the political system. In the resulting mutual exchange an organization may reshape the environment even as it may itself be moulded by its surroundings. In this chapter only one side of this complicated exchange will be examined, that is, the impact on the public service of the most persistent environmental features of Canadian society, namely, the geographical and economic settings, technological change, and culture. In the following chapter we explore the interplay between the public service, viewed as a subsystem, and selected elements of the political system, such as the federal framework and the political conventions surrounding our parliamentary system of responsible government.

1 Much of the matter in this chapter has appeared in foreshortened form in my 'Challenge and Response: A Retrospective View of the Public Service of Canada,' *Canadian Public Administration* 7 (Dec. 1964), pp. 409–21.

GEOGRAPHY

Sir Ernest Barker, commenting on the significant influence of geography on a nation's development, observed that the history of Egypt could be best understood by reference to the impact of the Nile and that English history for centuries was similarly conditioned by the isolation it enjoyed as an island.[2] In the case of Egypt, the Nile could be utilized only by means of expensive irrigation works which in turn necessitated a large centralized bureaucracy. In the case of England, physical isolation made for security against invasion; hence a large standing army, so necessary to western European powers, was not required, and a large central bureaucracy of tax gatherers to maintain the army was slow to develop.

The illustrations are suggestive when one comes to consider the impact of geography on the Canadian public service. To read the first thirty or forty annual reports of Canadian government departments is to hold up a mirror reflecting an almost frenetic organizational response to the problems of nation-building across an expanding continental domain. As late as 1926 the Minister of the Interior, whose department had presided at the centre of these activities, remarked that his annual report was 'the barometer of western conditions.'[3] The 'barometer departments' were those concerned with opening up and populating western land, and providing the water and rail transportation that could link several thousands of miles of continent extending from the Atlantic to the Pacific. Geography not only dictated the goals of the public service, it imposed the conditions which governed the ways in which the tasks themselves had to be performed. If administrative apoplexy was to be avoided at the centre, the factors of space, time, and communication insisted that organization had to be carried to the sparsely populated hinterland.

Even at the beginning of the new federation the geographical factors were reflected in a widespread dispersion of government employees which found barely a quarter of them working at headquarters. Apart from a far-flung network of customs ports, the major administrative tasks of the federal government basically involved preparing the way for the expected flood of settlers who were to colonize the newly opened territories. In essence, this preparation consisted in providing police or protective services, surveying and mapping the terrain, and servicing the needs of the transportation facilities which were counted on to bind the new nation together. A federal policing agency, the Royal North West Mounted Police, along with more traditional protective officers such as the fisheries

2 See chapter 1 of Barker's *The Development of Public Services in Western Europe, 1660–1930* (Oxford, 1944) for a brief treatment of this theme.
3 See Department of the Interior *Annual Report, 1926.*

overseers and the Indian agents, were all involved in on-the-spot administration, often in the most remote areas. The Geological Survey, whose headquarters in Montreal were not shifted to Ottawa until 1881, also of necessity conducted a highly decentralized operation. In the case of land administration, the land agents moved westward with new settlement, and indeed, in 1881, as the transactions in federal land nearly doubled, a Dominion Land Board operating out of Winnipeg became the hub and centre for land and timber agencies, land guides, and homestead inspectors operating in Manitoba and the Northwest Territories. Not until 1897 was it possible to return the board to Ottawa headquarters. Similarly, immigration and colonization services required the presence of agents not only throughout Canada but scattered at strategic points across Europe and Great Britain. In like fashion, the construction and maintenance of the public canal system, the provision of aids to navigation including dredging, beacons, and buoys, as well as the mounting direct governmental involvement in railway construction could only be handled by widely dispersed engineers, technicians, and labourers in a Public Works Department and in a Department of Railways and Canals that was soon to be split off from it.

It is clear, then, that geography set its mark on the early public service of Canada, first by posing the major social goals explicitly identified with meeting the challenge of continental development and second by forcing an extensive physical decentralization of the major operating tasks of the public departments. Vast improvements in the means of communication have alleviated some of the problems of carrying on administration in isolated outposts: the telegraph, telephone, and aeroplane have provided substitutes for the millions of letters that were the chief administrative bugbear of the old Department of the Interior, just as the typewriter and more recent electronic equipment have been substituted for the handwritten letter and the hordes of copyists who prepared the inevitable duplicates for record purposes. Nevertheless, the harsh facts of geography still pose essentially the same problems today and the price tag for preserving such a continental union (whose discrete parts were physically more naturally related to a north-south rather than an east-west connection) has become one of the most critical contemporary issues for Canadian nationalists. The price has had to be paid indirectly through tariffs and directly by means of government involvement through enormous public investment and the assumption of operating responsibilities for railways, airlines, broadcasting, and the like.

Direct governmental participation has necessitated the continuation of an extensively dispersed administrative operation. Nor is that involvement today restricted primarily to the material and physical side of the nation's development; increasingly, welfare and regulatory activities have become characteristic features of the state's concern for the health and well-being, security and protection, of the general citizenry. While a major share of such activities is assumed by provincial governments, the federal government has a prominent role to play in distributing grants, ensuring minimum standards, or in outright provision of services including research. In all these matters the local tentacles of the central administration touch the lives of citizens, bringing restrictions or benefits that were not thought of in earlier times.

Dispersion of the administrative forces of a nation across a continent, even when they are dealing with negative policing functions or such physical tasks as canal building or surveying, brings many problems in its wake. But when one adds to these typical nineteenth century duties the tasks of making personal contact with millions of citizens and of dealing with matters which often involve their health or livelihood, decentralized administration is certain to produce even more serious problems. It is not enough, in these new circumstances, to effect merely a physical deployment of officials in the field; it is equally important to accompany this with a genuine devolution of the authority possessed by those at head office to those in the field so that they may use their discretion in determining individual cases or in adapting the general regulations to the peculiar circumstances prevailing in one locality. Adaptability and flexibility are impossible to achieve in administration if all matters have to be routed back to a remote headquarters for final decision. Consequently, a physical decentralization of the work force, which took its roots as a logical response to the challenge of administering across a continent, continues in being as a vital necessity to provide the adaptability required for so many of the state's contemporary positive welfare functions. Decentralization, then, is as much a solution to demands for democratic responsiveness of the administrative machine as it is a logical outcome of the original geographic challenge of governing a continent. A later chapter is concerned with describing the structures and analysing the procedures that have evolved in the effort to resolve the many problems that derive from this most important physical characteristic of the Canadian public service.

THE ECONOMIC SETTING

Economic historians have traced the history of Canada by pursuing the fruitful path of the staple products approach.[4] Economic development has

---

4 This approach was most fully developed in the earlier works of Harold A. Innis; significant contributions were also made by A.R.M. Lower, W.A. Mackintosh, and D.G. Creighton.

been associated with the rise (and sometimes the relative decline) of such important staples as fish, fur, timber, minerals, wheat, and pulpwood. These are all extractive industries based on the exploitation of a great wealth of natural resources and the marketing abroad of such products. The provision of adequate transportation facilities to get access to relatively remote sources of supply and for export purposes is an obvious prerequisite for this type of economic development. Indeed, as the historians have shown, in the process of breaking new ground for the railways and settlers some of the mineral treasures themselves were discovered.[5]

None of these developments took place in an Adam Smith type of economy. The government was heavily committed from the outset, first in canal building, then in construction and ultimate operation of railways, latterly in the provision of air transport. The Geological Survey and the land surveyors mapped the terrain and revealed where natural wealth might most profitably be searched for and exploited. Gradually the government also assumed a protective function to ensure a steady source of supply from such extractive industries as the fisheries and forests which, without such regulation, would have been threatened with extinction. Promotional activities were soon added: the Canadian trade commissioner service was established in the 1890s; agriculture research stations came into being in 1886, from which such discoveries of governmental biologists as rust resistant wheat were to revolutionize farming in the west; government assay offices and ore testing facilities were made freely available to mining interests; government initiative sponsored the first association of livestock producers in 1906 and of dairy farmers in 1922; and so the list could be extended.

Four of the original public departments – all of them with the heaviest operating responsibilities – emerged in conjunction with these economic factors. Today, at least five of the two dozen departmental portfolios are still primarily concerned with problems pertaining to the production, transportation, and trade in these various staples.

But the impact of the economic setting on the Canadian public service extends beyond the direct influence of staple production on the creation of departmental portfolios. Government was early drawn into business, originally through the ownership and operation of railways but more recently and rapidly by means of a tremendous variety of state undertakings. The chief feature of all these undertakings is that they fit the pattern of the 'mixed economy' which has been evolving for many years in Canada. Characteristically, federal government monopolies have been avoided: a great state system of railways is run in-parallel (almost liter-

5 See D.G. Creighton, *Dominion of the North* (New ed., Toronto, 1957), pp. 474–5.

ally, in a physical sense) with a great private system; broadcasting is conducted by both state and private enterprises; a central bank and its governmental adjunct, an industrial development bank, supplement the services provided by private banks; a similar parallel is found in the mortgage-lending field; public telegraph services parallel private services; the same is now true of air transport; the ability to produce electricity from atomic-powered generators is a result of a partnership consisting of the federal government, a provincially owned utility, and private companies.[6]

Practically all of this growth in state, industrial, financial, and business activities has been absorbed by non-departmental forms of administrative organization. A point has now been reached where the number of people employed in this sector of the public service is almost as large as the number employed in the departmental system proper.[7]

It is not surprising that in devising the non-departmental forms the organizational model used has largely been the industrial or commercial counterpart found in private economic organizations. In short, the mixed economy has produced a corresponding organizational 'mix' in the public service and has raised issues concerning the propriety of grafting a heterogeneous collection of administrative entities on to the conventional departmental system. This practice warrants detailed consideration at a later stage.

Finally, a brief word may be said about a relatively recent influence on the public service that also derives from the economic environment. This has to do with the movement in the world of private business which was inspired in the early part of this century by the so-called 'father' of 'scientific management,' Frederick Winslow Taylor, and has culminated in the emergence of a new type of 'efficiency expert' found in management consultant firms.

Modest evidence of what might be termed the 'businessman's approach' to the public service can be traced back even to pre-Confederation times in Canada. It took the form, usually, of a diatribe against rule by lawyers.

6 For a general catalogue of these undertakings, see my 'The Public Corporation in Canada,' in *Government Enterprise: A Comparative Study*, ed. W. Friedmann and J.F. Garner (London, 1970), pp. 205–6. One of the most recent illustrations of the 'mixed enterprise' partnership is the federal government's investment in 1966 in Panarctic Oils Limited of Calgary – an investment which gives 45 per cent ownership to the government. See *Globe and Mail*, Toronto, 5 Feb. 1970.

7 In the most accurate and detailed breakdown available of government employee statistics provided by the Royal Commission on Government Organization, for the year 1960, there were 345,946 civilian employees, of which 150,396 were employed by crown corporations. *Report*, I, *Management of the Public Service* (Ottawa, 1962), report no 3: 'Personnel Management,' pp. 308–9.

William Hamilton Merritt, a prominent businessman in the cabinet, confided to his diary that as long as lawyers dominated the cabinet one could never expect to instil business-like procedures into the public service.[8] And, in 1878, Peter Mitchell complained publicly in parliament that 'members of the legal profession had too much Parliamentary influence in the country ... when he looked round and saw the amount of influence possessed by the lawyers in the house, and the way legal gentlemen monopolized positions, and desired to extend that monopoly to every emolument and office in the country, he could not but consider this as another effort of the government to swamp the independent layman of the country ...'[9]

This latent antipathy of the business community towards lawyers in the public service never took the organized form that developed, for example, for a brief period in England in the mid-nineteenth century. There the Economical Reform Associations, inspired entirely by business interests, constituted a critical pressure group which sought to destroy the myth of administration by amateur gentlemen which had been so badly shaken by the disasters in the Crimea and the revelations of inefficiency in the War Office.[10]

The only other early indication of the pressure to introduce 'business principles' into public administration is found in the few agencies which were providing services at a fee to identifiable groups of beneficiaries. This was notably the case in the Department of Marine where the steamboat inspection service was expected to pay its own way and in the financing of the Trinity Houses at Quebec and Montreal which, like their quasi-public counterparts in England, for years really administered aids to navigation.[11] But scattered examples of this type were far from representing a concerted or uniform response to firmly declared principles. Two questions were really at issue: should the consumers of government services pay for them; and, if the charge was to be levied, should it cover the full cost of providing the service? Over the years the expansion of the servicing functions of government was so great that these two questions were never properly answered. By the 1960s dozens of these services had emerged and were directed to particular beneficiaries rather than to the

8 See my *Pioneer Public Service: An Administrative History of the United Canadas, 1841–1867* (Toronto, 1955), p. 68.
9 *Can. H. of C. Debates*, 1878, p. 1585.
10 The activities of these associations can be traced in the pages of *The Times*, London, between 1855 and 1857, perhaps the most notable being the occasion when Charles Dickens made a brilliant critical speech before a large audience (perhaps a warm-up for his satire of the Circumlocution Office in *Little Dorrit?*).
11 For a full description of these borderline public agencies, see 'Annual Report of the Department of Marine and Fisheries,' *Sessional Papers*, 1869, no 12.

public at large: sometimes they have been provided at no charge to the consumer; in other instances there have been charges which may not cover costs or may even exceed the costs.[12] The Royal (Glassco) Commission on Government Organization – whose work it will be apparent has an important bearing on nearly every aspect of this book – recommended that this particular aspect of the public service be put in order. The commissioners provide a logical restatement of the old claim that sound business principles should be injected into public organization. Indeed, the commission went one step further when it suggested that some of these services might well be contracted out to private concerns – again, a far from revolutionary proposal when one looks at the prototypes mentioned above for providing the navigation aids at the time of Confederation.

One must move on well into the twentieth century to find the most impressive evidence of the impact of the 'business management' movement which began to gather momentum in the early 1900s and was much consulted by private organizations. When the Civil Service Act was virtually rewritten at the end of the First World War, Arthur Young and Company, an American firm of consultants, was brought in to help reorganize the public service of Canada.[13] Its report left a lasting imprint on the classification of public offices, for the detailed classification plan which it proposed was built up over the ensuing years into a highly complex system. This direct inheritance from the world of private industrial organization has been criticized – even ridiculed – by some observers who, with the apparently much simpler British classification plan in view, have considered the Canadian plan to be an administrative incubus. That the critics oversimplified the British pattern and that the ingenuity of administrators has been capable of making the Canadian system work are not relevant at this point. What is clear is that the variety of occupations which a public service classification plan must comprehend is infinitely greater than any to be found in the larger private organizations. Consequently, the direct importation of plans and procedures which have been found to be satisfactory for private organizations cannot be achieved without making allowances for the greater size and complexity of the public service. It is probable, also, that the original decision to adopt the detailed classification plan was inspired as much by its value in eliminating patronage ('the right man for the right classified job') as by the confidence of laymen in the wisdom of management consultants.

12 See *Report*, II, *Supporting Services for Government* (Ottawa, 1962), report no 10: 'The "Make or Buy" Problem.'
13 R. MacGregor Dawson's *The Civil Service of Canada* (London, 1929) gives a highly critical analysis of the work and contributions of this outside team of management consultants.

Clearly, this first and most prominent assault of the outside management expert on the barricades of the public service has not diminished the confidence of the layman in the advice proffered from such sources.[14] Management consultant firms have grown apace in recent years – often as adjuncts to well-established firms of accountants – and a substantial portion of their business is provided by federal, provincial, and municipal governments seeking their assistance.[15] The management expert-cum-accountant is prepared to offer highly specialized services going well beyond traditional job analyses and extending to financial and accounting procedures, systems analyses, paper work flow and disposition, the installation of electronic equipment – in short all the paraphernalia and processes involved in operating any large-scale organization.

By far the most impressive demonstration of the influence of this new profession is to be found in the staffing of the Royal (Glassco) Commission on Government Organization, established in September 1960 – well over half of the staff of some 170 investigating officers were associated with management consultant firms and most of the remainder were drawn from executive positions in private industry. Over the decade of the sixties the commission's reports have had a profound impact on the Canadian public service, having been used as a source of argument (if not inspiration) for any conceivable administrative alteration in structure and procedures. Not only in their underlying principles but in their many detailed proposals the reports reflect the thinking of the business-oriented community on problems of managing and organizing large enterprises. We find the accountants' concern for identifying 'real' costs; we observe the businessman's concern for relating revenues from services to charges for services, for accrual accounting, and for the need to 'contract out' many operations now being undertaken within the public departments; we see the claim for the energetic adoption of systems analyses and other management techniques that have now proven their effectiveness in private

14 However, this confidence was shaken so badly by the first efforts of management consultants that the principles of efficiency they fostered did not really gain acceptance in the public service until after the Second World War. Anti-American attitudes, coupled with dissatisfaction with the pay scales attached to the new classifications, aborted all the reorganization proposals of the first consultants and induced the Civil Service Commission for nearly thirty years to play down its statutory responsibility for reorganizing departments.

15 S. Rajagopal (unpublished paper prepared for the author's graduate seminar) has surveyed the members of the Canadian Association of Management Consultants and shows growth from 306 staff members and gross billings of $6.5 million in 1964 to a staff of 651 and billings of $15 million in 1968. The number of annual assignments increased in the same period from 963 to 2677. In 1967, 8 per cent of all assignments were for various levels of government in Canada.

business and in the provision of which the public service has lagged behind. Above all, we find a pervasive assumption that the differences between private and public organizations are not so substantial as to prevent the incorporation of the best practices and principles from the realms of private business management into the public service.[16] Thus may one epitomize the tone and tenor of this monumental study. These reports have constituted points of departure for reform of the public service during the 1960s, but it is already apparent that, in the course of implementation, these obviously business-oriented proposals have been adapted to meet the other environmental factors which in this chapter are regarded as of equal importance in shaping the public service organization.

TECHNOLOGICAL CHANGE

Changes in technology have a twofold impact on the public service. In the broadest sense they influence the substance of administrative activity, either in compelling the state itself to sponsor the development of the technique or to grapple with the social and other problems posed by the widespread adoption of the technique. In a narrower sense new techniques have an important influence on the administrative procedures employed by the public service: we live in an age of gadgetry, and public servants are no more immune to the charm of applying gadgets to their daily labours than is any other group of employees.

Taking a long view of the Canadian public service we observe that its history embraces a century in which technological changes have probably been greater and more revolutionary in their social impact than in all of the previous centuries combined. For example, the ships with which Nelson defeated the French at Trafalgar were much the same wood-wind-sail vessels which his Elizabethan compatriots used to destroy the Spanish Armada several centuries earlier. But the important technological innovations that revolutionized transportation and communication and that provided new ways of exploiting physical energy have basically come into full being in the last century. Thus the Canadian public service began in the early steamboat and railway age, witnessed the emergence of the telegraph and telephone, saw the origin and growing onslaught of the automobile age; and, while still adjusting to these technological developments, has had to make its peace with the new air age, the electronics revolution, the atom, and, most recently, outer space.

16 See, particularly, Royal Commission on Government Organization, *Report*, I, passim. Strong criticism of these biases is expressed by T.H. McLeod, 'Glassco Commission Report,' *Canadian Public Administration* 6 (Dec. 1963), pp. 386–406.

The federal public service could not but be affected by these momentous changes. It responded to the steamboat and railway age by assuming full responsibility for maintaining the major navigation system of the nation – the first St Lawrence waterway – culminating a century later in its joint assumption with the United States of the construction and operation of major works required to adapt the seaway to the needs of the mid-twentieth century. In addition, the operation of several 'national' harbours and a host of smaller inland ports has necessitated direct state action and/or support. Government took an even more positive role in response to the costly challenge of the railways, beginning with the provision of capital and such additional support as land grants to finance railway construction, moving on to regulation, and ending up by operation of a vast network of lines. The telegraph and telephone provided, in the main, regulatory problems for the state apparatus, although in the case of telegraphs public ownership of that part which was associated with the government-owned railways was also entailed. The automobile age left its greatest mark on provincial public services, in highway construction, regulation of traffic and licensing, and in grappling with the social and economic problems of urban concentration, tourist facilities, and the like – all of which sprang essentially from the introduction of this new technique. Only in more recent times has the federal administration become involved in such projects as the Trans-Canada Highway, though largely in the capacity of financial supporter for provincial efforts.

In 1932 two important judicial decisions resolved the question of jurisdiction over radio broadcasting and aeronautics in favour of the federal government and set the stage for another series of adaptations of the public service to meet these new developments. Again, the state entered these fields both as an operator and a regulator, virtual national monopolies in both fields being gradually abandoned as private enterprise expanded to pluck the fruits of pioneer cultivation which had developed under state auspices.

In the last twenty years Canada has been party to the energy revolution which has affected the whole world. In part, this has been generated by new techniques for the long-range transmission of conventional energy sources such as oil and natural gas, but in the forefront are the applied scientists' breathtaking applications of the awesome potential locked in the atom. The more conventional components of the energy revolution have been handled by federal regulatory action and some financial assistance in the construction of pipelines – rather like the early situation in the railway age. But the enormous costs and immense complexity of the operations required to release and harness nuclear energy, as well as the national security implications, have compelled the state to assume practically the whole burden of research and development associated with the atomic energy programme. The full implications of this latter development are only now beginning to become apparent. It is clear that direct state involvement has given an enormous boost to the research and developmental efforts which the state has for many years been applying to the conventional fields of agriculture, mining, fisheries, or chemistry, physics, and other pure or applied sciences. This new and rapid expansion makes the federal government establishment the largest research organization in the country and raises certain general issues such as the relation between traditional research in universities and of science in government which have been urgently studied over the past four or five years.[17]

It is also important to observe that many technological changes have transformed the means of communication and transportation; such transformations have affected trade and have opened hitherto inaccessible areas for development. The expense of introducing these technical innovations was such that the state had to become an active partner if not an outright owner, developer, and operator of these new systems. In turn, the new systems fostered the extension of an interdependent economy which brought new regulatory problems capable of being met only on a nationwide scale by federal government action. These changes were not confined to Canada, for worldwide application of new techniques has shrunk the world and produced fresh problems of international trade and communication which fall naturally within the orbit of the federal government: the proliferation of the trade commissioners of the Department of Trade and Commerce and of Canadian legations abroad, the emergence of the Overseas Telecommunications Corporation and the Export Credits Insurance Corporation are but a few of the many easily identified responses to the indirect consequences of revolutionary changes in technology. Moreover, without the new technology, programmes such as those promoted by the Department of Indian Affairs and Northern Development in the remoter regions of Canada's north would be inconceivable.

Apart from these broader repercussions of technological changes on the public service there are the products or gadgets which derive from them and whose application affects the procedures used by the public service

17 Two such studies that will have much influence on future relationships in this area are Special Study no 7, *The Role of the Federal Government in Support of Research in Canadian Universities*, prepared by John B. Macdonald *et al.* for the Science Council of Canada and the Canada Council (Ottawa, 1969); and the report of the Special Senate Committee on Science Policy, *A Science Policy for Canada*, I, *A Critical Review: Past and Present* (Ottawa, 1970).

itself. The telephone, for example, must have had a tremendous impact on a bureaucracy oriented to paper as the medium of communication. The typewriter and its subsequent camp followers, each more ingenious than its predecessors in multiplying papers, have given rise to a new problem of records management. Historically, the mechanics of producing paper, filing it, or otherwise disposing of it have been characterized unflatteringly as the 'donkey work' in the civil service. There is more than a shadow of a home truth in the designation of the first women in the British public service as 'female typewriters.' And yet it is the low status accorded this type of work which has concealed the fact that paper constitutes not only the bloodstream of an organization but also its 'memory.' Only as one ponders the costs of filing cabinets, storage facilities, and space is the importance of proper records management brought home. The Royal Commission on Government Organization painted a forbidding picture of the present state of the art of paper management in the public service, observing that failure to catch up with the consequences of gadget innovation will doom the public service, like the sorcerer's apprentice, to drowning in a flood of its own creation.[18]

Yet even as technical innovation produces new gadgets that increase the production of paper, more refined and expensive equipment emerges from the electronics revolution which is capable of recording, analysing, and even memorizing the information conveyed on paper. The utilization of computers and automatic data processing machinery in the public service is progressing rapidly and one can confidently predict that their immediate impact deserves to be enshrined in a 'neo-Parkinsonian law': the quantity of paper will rise to meet the capacity of the machines available for processing it! The long-term consequences of automation have been variously forecast. Pessimists contend that the machine will displace humans – probably in large numbers where, as is the case in the civil service, there is much routine and repetitive work which lends itself to being programmed and fed into capacious electronic memory banks. The other and probably more realistic prognosis is that little displacement of the human will occur but that there will be a need for new types of skill and a substantial retraining programme to meet this need.

In the foreseeable future the enormous capacity and costliness of such equipment suggest that a high degree of concentration of data processing in a few large electronic machine shops is the sensible outcome of this development. But, while the mechanics of processing should be highly centralized – or at least located in a very few strategic centres – it does

18 See, especially, *Report*, I, report no 4: 'Paperwork and Systems Management.'

not necessarily follow that the trend towards decentralized administration, so desirable from other points of view, should be reversed. New media such as Telex and tape can communicate the information quickly and accurately to the processing centres. An 'executive' computer can instruct the machines to produce the information in any one of a multitude of desired formulae and transmit it back to the desk in an outlying district for decision and action. At the same time, it is conceivable that the machines can also be used to help headquarters' offices exercise an informed surveillance over the actions taken in the field by simplifying and speeding up reporting procedures.[19]

It is probably too early to present more than this general and speculative assessment of the likely impact of the new age of gadgetry on the public service. At one extreme it is possible to forecast a gloomy future in which the machines play havoc with the public service: suffocating it in the burden of paper products; displacing large numbers of the lower grade clerical and technical personnel; and substituting for the humanized, across-the-counter dealings with the public a species of 'numbers game' in which every citizen, equipped with coded punch cards as identification, simply feeds his card into the electronic brain and receives his birth or marriage or death certificates, his cheques for children's allowances, old age pension or unemployment insurance benefits, the income tax department requests for payment of back taxes, an approved patent document, or his passport. Even the venerable Post Office might become redundant as electronic media of communication make letter writing obsolete and doom philatelists to the collection of outmoded postage stamps. At the other extreme we can visualize the machine taking over much of the less interesting and stimulating work which stultifies and deadens so many people performing routine operations in the public service; we can envisage the machines speeding up the processes of bureaucracy, resulting in improved service from officials vested with more authority to make decisions on the spot and yet held accountable by the machines' capacity to improve reporting procedures; and, finally, we might see the machine performing wonders with assembling and interpreting social data from which economists, statisticians, scientists, and others could with more confidence and accuracy plan the future goals of society.

19 A most interesting example is the development within the Public Service Commission of a programme whereby an extensive sample of decisions made on personnel issues by departmental managers, exercising powers devolved by the commission, is monitored by computers. In the same area of personnel management the commission is also pioneering a computerized personnel data flow system which will provide almost instantaneous retrieval of information on all personnel at headquarters and in the field.

THE CULTURAL SETTING

With the emergence of Canada as an independent middle-weight in the international league of states, it has been customary to ascribe to her the role of intermediary between the United Kingdom and the United States. Whether this be simply a rationalization for cautious middle-of-the-road policies and a preference for leaving the initiative to the larger powers between which Canada is expected to mediate, is at least debatable; but there can be no doubt that the impact of these two great nations on the general cultural setting in Canada has been continuous and significant.

During the period when English-speaking Canadians could respond without embarrassment to Macdonald's cry, 'a British subject I was born, a British subject I will die,' the historical British 'connexion' served to commend the mother country's governmental institutions as the most appropriate models for Canada to follow. Opposing this traditional attachment, from early times, has been the continuing, pervasive, and inescapable counter pressures of 'American' culture. Towards this vital, pulsating influence Canadians have reacted ambivalently, swinging between hypnotic attraction and fearful revulsion. Economically and militarily (and today, it is strongly claimed, intellectually) Canadians have been drawn into a vortex of continentalism dominated by the larger partner. These facts of life today encourage not so much the invoking of the British tradition (for that harbours too many overtones of colonial dependency of another order) but the assertion of a stubbornly held conception of some vague but unique Canadian identity – an identity that is more difficult to penetrate because of the resurgence of the 'French fact' and the concept of 'two nations.'

Canadian policies, despite all the rhetoric of after-dinner speakers concerning the 'undefended boundary,' have strongly reflected a nationalistic defensiveness, even as they have wavered between practices and precepts borrowed from Britain or the United States. Closer inspection reveals that the boundary in fact bristles with defences, most of them of the Canadian governments' own making. Since the abandonment of reciprocity and the emergence in 1878 of Macdonald's National Policy, the tariff has been one line of defence and has led to the proliferation of customs ports, complex legislation, and equally cumbersome administration. The insistence on constructing an 'all Canadian' transcontinental railway is another costly expression of the do-it-yourself drive, inspired by strong national pride and the reluctance to be beholden to the United States. When the aeroplane and radio arrived, the government monopolies with which the era began were deliberately conceived as instruments of national policy and, in the case of broadcasting, as an exciting new means of developing national self-consciousness and establishing national cultural links. The creation of the Canada Council in 1957 was inspired by the Royal Commission on National Development in the Arts, Letters and Sciences which was greatly concerned to foster and strengthen indigenous culture as the best way of counteracting the mounting cultural tide from the south.[20] The Canada Council was a governmental surrogate for private American foundations on whose paternal beneficence a generation of Canadian scholars had depended. A recommendation from the Royal (O'Leary) Commission on Publications even approved state action to redirect the flow of Canadian advertisers' dollars from American journals to Canadian periodicals that find it difficult to keep afloat in competition with them.[21] Another defensive barrier was erected when the Board of Broadcast Governors (now replaced by the Canadian Radio-Television Commission), which regulated both private and public broadcasting, prescribed a 55 per cent quota of 'Canadian content' for all programmes.[22]

Direct involvement of the federal government in these cultural enterprises cannot be attributed solely to the positive desire to adopt a strongly defensive national posture in the face of possible American cultural hegemony. Nevertheless, there are strong grounds for thinking that the heavy commitments assumed by the state, just as in the various fields of transportation, would not have been nearly so great were it not for the existence of the cultural magnet of the United States. In other areas, where the question of cultural self-defence does not arise, the federal government has not extended its activities beyond conventional frontiers. A Public Archives appeared on the scene as early as 1872, a National Gallery in 1913, a National Museum in 1927, a National Library in 1953, and, most recently, in 1968, authorization for the National Museums of Canada.[23] Some of these state-run amenities were probably prompted as much by the desire to find permanent storage space for records, specimens, or pictures as by any definite conception of the state's positive obligation to foster Canadian culture. Over time, it is true, their repository and storage functions have been expanded to display and educational functions, represent-

20 *Report* (Ottawa, 1951), especially section IV.
21 *Report* (Ottawa, 1961), part III.
22 The Canadian Radio-Television Commission, in February 1970, reiterated this emphasis on Canadian content and is grappling with regulations to restrain cable companies from flooding Canadian households with imported programmes.
23 The merger of several of these 'cultural' agencies into a species of holding corporation took place in 1968 (Stats Can. 1967–8, c. 21) and included the National Gallery and three segments of the original National Museum – Human History (Man), Natural History (both dating from 1957), and Science and Technology (1966).

ing a significant contribution to scholarly research and Canadian culture generally.

If a number of the federal government's most important cultural activities have evolved in response to Canada's sensitivity to the pressure of American culture, it is equally the case that the organization of the public service itself bears marks of the constant borrowing from somewhat contradictory British and American traditions. Early Canadian reformers, for example, looked to Britain as the model to be emulated in their efforts to introduce the principle of open competitive examinations.[24] In 1878, in defending the legislation that converted the Auditor General into an independent officer serving parliament, Sir John A. Macdonald relied successfully on the precedent set in Britain in 1866 when the Exchequer and Audit Act effected the same change.[25]

Despite such constant references to Britain, whenever proposals affecting the civil service were before the legislature, actual Canadian practice has followed a pendulum swing, at one stage quite consciously in the direction of the British pattern and at another stage, less consciously, towards American practices.[26] In the early preference for regulating the civil service by statute rather than by executive decree as in Britain we find the first identification with the American pattern – although this may have occurred on the erroneous assumption entertained by some Canadians that there was, in fact, a civil service act in Britain. The next parallel to American developments came in 1908 when a Civil Service Commission was given statutory powers that extended well beyond those granted to its British counterpart and much more comparable to those enjoyed by the US Civil Service Commission. But the most pronounced swing of the pendulum came in 1918–19 when a new Civil Service Act not only confirmed and extended the powers of the commission over all personnel matters but, borrowing directly from the United States (indeed, anticipating developments there), incorporated a system of detailed classification of the public offices. Until this plan was introduced, classifications had tended to follow the British system of a small 'officer' class and a

24 The indefatigable reformer in the House of Commons was George Elliott Casey who constantly appealed to British studies and practices in promoting his own private members bills for civil service reform. For illustrations, see *Can. H. of C. Debates*, 1875, p. 708 ff.; 1877, p. 196 ff.; and 1878, pp. 1673–4. Most of the royal commissions on the civil service leaned heavily on British experience in their surveys: see especially 'First Report of the Civil Service Commission,' *Sessional Papers*, 1881, no 113, appendices F and G.

25 *Can. H. of C. Debates*, 1878, p. 1626.

26 A more detailed commentary on the pendulum swing between British and American practices may be found in my 'Canadian Administration Faces the Fifth Decade,' *Journal of Politics* 11 (Nov. 1949), pp. 715–35.

larger, graded, clerical class for performing more routine operations. A modest restoration of this pattern was sought in the mid-thirties when the Civil Service Commission introduced a scheme for recruiting university graduates directly into junior administrative offices, obviously modelled on the British method of recruiting personnel for the élite administrative cadre. The pendulum swung even further towards the British pattern with the report of the Royal (Gordon) Commission on Administrative Classifications in 1946. A prominent British civil servant, Sir Thomas Gardiner, clearly left the imprint of British 'Treasury thinking' on that report, just as, in 1912, Sir George Murray imported a similar point of view in his report on the Canadian public service. In fact, the Canadian pattern proved as resistant to the later proposal for modelling central personnel management on British practices as it had in toning down most of the Murray recommendations that expressed the same bias. The recommendations of the latest and most far-reaching inquiry into the public service, found particularly in the management reports of the Royal Commission on Government Organization, also inclined towards the British pattern of personnel management, although the same amalgam of American management practices and British institutions adapted to the Canadian environment is still present.

Apart from the significant and continuing pressure from these external cultural influences, the Canadian public service has had to adapt to a unique, indigenous cultural factor. Section 133 of the British North America Act guarantees the right to use either the French or English language in the parliament of Canada and the legislature of Quebec. The records, journals, and acts of these legislative chambers must also use both languages. Either language may be used in pleadings before any court of Canada or Quebec. These features, which have their cultural and constitutional counterpart in countries like Belgium, Switzerland, and South Africa, were most prominently and practically recognized in the period from 1841 to 1867 when the two cultural groups were almost evenly divided in what was then known as Canada East and Canada West. A hyphenated premiership was coupled with double-headed ministries and double-barrelled administrative units for several public departments. Even the headquarters of the union was rotated between the capitals of the two sections making up the union of that time.[27]

Between 1841 and 1867 French Canada was evenly balanced with its partner. This parity position provided the political leverage with which

27 For a more extensive treatment of these features of administrative dualism, see my *Pioneer Public Service*; see also 'Our Early Peripatetic Government,' *Queen's Quarterly* 59 (Autumn 1952), pp. 316–22.

political dualism could be maintained, even though in formal terms the separate components labelled Canada East and Canada West were merged in a legislative union known as the Province of Canada.[28] After 1867 the larger Confederation with its subsequent accession of new provinces progressively reduced the French-speaking element from its former position of equality to one of a political minority. The situation was akin to that which had developed a generation or more earlier in the United States where the slave-owning southern states lost their position of political parity in the enlarging American Union. Lacking the political leverage provided by equal numbers, French Canada was unable to insist on the maintenance of the old administrative patterns of dualism – just as the southern states saw themselves deprived of the necessary leverage to maintain one of their cultural and economic mainstays, the institution of slavery. The response of the American South was the decision to secede from the Union – a decision that was countermanded by resort to arms and the ultimate victory of the North in the Civil War.

French Canada's response was of a totally different order, for separatist agitation assumed significant proportions only a century later in the 1960s. In effect, as its minority position worsened in political terms, French Canada elected to use the federal framework to retreat into the enclave of provincial rights, there to concentrate on becoming *maîtres chez nous*. (The American South after the trauma of post–Civil War reconstruction, in like fashion withdrew to lick its wounds and nurse its romantic visions of the past.)

The success of this strategy of withdrawal depended on Quebec being able to find in its assigned fields of jurisdiction sufficient elbow room within which it could cope with its problems in its own style. This strategy was doomed from the outset by the very objectives for which the wider federal union had been explicitly created, that is, the achievement of a continent-wide transportation and postal system, a nation-wide customs and taxation union, and the like. In short, there were many significant areas affecting each province, not excluding Quebec, that would have to be managed by a federal bureaucracy – a bureaucracy, however, which no longer preserved the features of administrative dualism previously found in the Province of Canada.

It is significant that the maritime provinces, rather than Quebec, were the first to appreciate the significance of this point: the early years after

28 Sensitivity to this point is demonstrated in Emile Gosselin's contribution to a symposium of the Institute of Public Administration of Canada on 'L'administration publique dans un pays bilingue et biculturel': see his 'Perspective historique,' *Canadian Public Administration* 6 (Dec. 1963), p. 407 ff.

their entry into the broader union are filled with their complaints about the unrepresentative character of the bureaucracy and their demands for positions in the headquarters of the new federal departments.[29] Obviously, the Maritimers accepted the realistic strategy: if you can't lick 'em, join 'em (and make sure you get a fair share when the appointments are being made!). Quebec did not join this lobby, partly because of its strategy of withdrawal but possibly because the new federal bureaucracy in Ottawa at the outset was virtually a complete carry-over from the old Province of Canada, where the French-Canadian representation had been tolerable and, more importantly, administrative dualism had existed. But that pattern dissolved rapidly after Confederation because most of the agencies which had the dual administrative apparatus were operating in jurisdictions that in whole or in part were transferred to the provinces and thus became provincial departments. Since acceptable representation of French Canada depended on organizational dualism, the rapid dissolution of this pattern led to a progressive diminution of French-Canadian representatives in the federal bureaucracy, particularly in the senior, higher-paid posts at headquarters.

Viewed from this perspective, the recommendations in 1969 of the Royal Commission on Bilingualism and Biculturalism which called for the creation of unilingual enclaves for both French and English in the federal bureaucracy – including particularly headquarters' establishments – may be viewed as attempts to reinstate the old pattern of administrative dualism.[30] And, to the extent that the old pattern provided an incentive for French-speaking Canadians to join the central bureaucracy, the royal commission presumably anticipated its recommendations would have the same effect.

Up to this point the implications of the two cultures have been confined to organizational features of the public service; inextricably entwined with organization is the issue of communication among civil servants as well as between the civil servant and the public.

29 A good example is to be found in *Can. H. of C. Debates*, 1870: 'Mr. Burpee objected that the Civil Service was almost altogether in the hands of people from Ontario and Quebec, and in the Lower Provinces this would be felt to be an injustice' (col. 1061); or, again, E.M. Macdonald (at col. 1062) complained that Nova Scotia got only $1000 in salaries and New Brunswick got $10,500 (that is, 'ten representatives' in the Ottawa bureaucracy) out of a total salary bill of $306,000. Prince Edward Island, as a later entrant to the union, had even more difficulty in asserting its claims for recognition, particularly because, as Senator Heath Haviland remarked in a debate in 1873, 'the smaller the pit the more fiercely the rats fight.' *Can. Senate Debates*, 1873, p. 192.
30 *Report*, Book III: *The Work World*, vol. 3A, part 2: 'The Federal Administration' (Ottawa, 1969), p. 265 ff.

For the first fifty years after Confederation the language of communication between bureaucrats and the public was left to fate (since section 133 of the BNA Act was silent on this point), and such was the continental dominance of the English language that it gravitated by default into the position of being the operating language of the federal public service.[31] Not until 1938 was the Civil Service Act of 1918 amended to make the first formal concession to French as a language of communication with the public. This was an extremely belated concession to the fact that the Civil Service Commission had, since 1918, jurisdiction over the 'Outside Service,' in addition to the 'Inside (Headquarters) Service.' Thus, as the 1938 act stated, 'no appointment ... shall be made to a local position within a province, and no employee shall be transferred ... until and unless the candidate or employee has qualified, by examination, in the knowledge and use of the language, being the French or the English language, of the majority of the persons with whom he is required to do business.'[32] By regulation the commission amplified this provision to require a knowledge of both English and French for a locality where both languages were spoken.[33] The Civil Service Act of 1961 followed the same formula, placing the stress on qualifications in either or both languages sufficient 'to enable the department or local office to perform its functions adequately and to give effective service to the public.'[34] Not until the major revisions in the Public Service Employment Act of 1967 was a new stress placed on comparable language requirements at headquarters.[35] No doubt anticipating recommendations from the Royal Commission on Bilingualism and Biculturalism, the Civil Service Commission in the mid-

31 It is interesting to discover that the provincial civil servants of Quebec were bilingual at the outset. See 'Premier rapport des commissaires du Service Civil de la province de Québec sur les bureaux des départements au siège du gouvernement,' *Documents de le Session*, no 12, 1869–70, para. 78. Even so, according to Richard J. Joy, *Languages in Conflict: The Canadian Experience* (Ottawa, 1967), 'even the provincial Civil Service of Quebec used English as the language of work during the nineteenth century' (p. 10). I am indebted to Professors Iain Gow and Guy Bouthillier for these citations which appear in a draft manuscript of a study they are preparing on the history of the Quebec civil service.
32 Stats Can. 1938, c.7, s.1.
33 *Civil Service Regulations: Office Consolidation* (Ottawa, 1954).
34 Stats Can. 1961, c.57, s.47.
35 Stats Can. 1967, c.72, s.20, fully amplified in 'Statutory Orders and Regulations,' no 129, *Canada Gazette*, part II (1967), regulations 4, 5, and 6. Where 40 to 60 per cent of the public to be served have English or French as mother tongue, officers must be bilingual and supervisors shall be sufficiently proficient in one or both languages to permit effective direction to be given the persons supervised. The regulations also envisage bilingualism to be 'desirable' (though not essential) for headquarters' units where 10 per cent or more of the public served (meaning all of Canada in this instance) has French or English as its mother tongue. The degree of bilingual proficiency is also spelled out in four gradations.

sixties launched a massive language training programme for civil servants which, given sufficient time, should enable it to administer realistically the complex and rather drastic requirements now spelled out in the act of 1967.

While the developments outlined in the immediately preceding paragraphs have been directed to coping with the problem of communications between public servants and the public, a more intractable problem is that of developing bilingual communications within the public service – again, especially at headquarters. As noted, section 133 of the British North America Act entrenches the equality of French and English as the official languages of communication, both verbal and printed, for the legislature and the relevant courts.[36] Indeed, in the absence of any corresponding constitutional guarantee of the pattern of organizational dualism, this section was the only remnant of parity left for French Canada at the national level, after the broader union was proclaimed. Even here, however, parity was restricted, and nothing was said about the language of communication to be used by or among public servants in the executive branch.

Once again, then, as was the case for so long with communications between the bureaucracy and the public, internal transactions were left to fate. And, as in the former case, the tendency to restrict communications to English-language users prevailed.[37] The French-speaking officer, especially at headquarters, confronted a unilingual communication system in which he was the only person who had to be bilingual. Beyond this immediate disadvantage he found himself located in a city whose pervasive English culture was alien to his own. Added to these two strong disincentives, for many years, was the traditional orientation of the Quebec educational system towards classics and law. This tradition did not fit into the post–First World War reforms in recruitment for the federal service which stressed 'the merit system' and a detailed job specification calling for more specific educational or technical skills than the Quebec educa-

36 This section is just as much a protection for the English-speaking minority in Quebec as it is for the French-speaking minority in the rest of Canada, and in practice the English minority has probably been better done by than has the French minority.
37 Extended commentary on this feature and those that follow in the text is to be found in the symposium on public administration referred to in note 28 above. Anticipating the Royal Commission on Bilingualism and Biculturalism, Professor Gilles Lalande spoke of his preference for administrative dualism through unilingual enclaves as 'dédoublement des organismes partout où il sera possible de faire.' A more recent contribution is to be found in E.A. Côté, 'The Public Service in a Bicultural Community,' *Canadian Public Administration* 11 (Fall 1968), pp. 280–90.

tional system was prepared to provide. When this system did respond belatedly to the market requirements, Quebec itself was in the throes of rapid secularization, industrialization, and bureaucratization. The province's own demands for skilled manpower give every evidence of being able to absorb the bulk of its own qualified residents, so that even with the recent positive measures and recommendations for further measures to inculcate the equal use of French with English as a means of communicating within the bureaucracy, the attainment of a federal public service truly representative of the two cultures will not be easily or quickly realized. In short, the crash programme currently contemplated[38] or already in being cannot be expected all at once to remedy the deficiencies or heal the wounds left by a century of neglect of the bicultural features of Canada.

38 The director general, language division, of the Public Service Commission, G.A. Blackburn, has given a good account of this programme in his 'A Bilingual and Bicultural Public Service,' *ibid.* 12 (Spring 1969), pp. 36–44.

CHAPTER THREE

The political system

The Canadian public service has been shaped not only by environmental factors but also by special features of the political system of which it is a part. Of the numerous aspects of this system which have had a pronounced influence on the public service only two will be considered here: the federal framework and certain major political conventions which have evolved in the course of adapting British parliamentary government to a continental setting.

THE FEDERAL FRAMEWORK

While geography, as we have seen, establishes certain physical determinants for the performance of administrative services (and, to an important extent in early days, determined the administrative goals as well) the constitution sets the legal terms that bind the public service. The constitutional framework of a country is, in many respects, simply the product of social necessity. In the case of Canada, the prime objective was the union of separate provincial units varying greatly in size and with an unusually wide range of economic and cultural differences. The constitution therefore sought, by asserting the principle of federalism, to provide a formal arrangement for allocating or zoning out the duties of the state. The subdivision of labour between provincial units and the central government has had two important repercussions on the public service. First, the federal public service remained smaller than it otherwise would have been if provincial public services had not been available to assume some of the burden of state activities. Second, the existence of parallel provincial and federal services has necessitated the development of complex mechanisms for reducing duplication and friction and for positive co-ordination when these services are required jointly to pursue related goals.

It is clear that the federal constitutional arrangement has helped to alleviate the burdens of administering a continental domain, but it is equally apparent that it brings other problems in its wake that are not found in a state organized along unitary lines. No constitutional allocation of functions – particularly one made one hundred years ago – can demarcate zones of jurisdiction so precisely that jurisdictional disputes will never arise. Adaptation to meet changing conditions or to remove areas of doubt can be only partially achieved by formal processes of amendment or by the more commonly used device of judicial interpretation of the constitution. For much of the adaptation to meet emergent problems a variety of 'administrative expedients' must be found.[1] These range across a broad spectrum of possibilities: the sporadic assembling of a diplomatic conference between dominion and provincial leaders; the annual convening for more limited purposes of a conference of ministers, often in conjunction with officials from national interest groups (as happens in the case of labour and agriculture, for example); formal agreements, rather like treaties, setting out the respective responsibilities and duties, for example in the field of health insurance; the device of joint advisory committees (a recent listing recorded some 125 of these, embracing fields that involved practically all departments and representing relatively permanent instruments for ironing out dominion-provincial problems);[2] the use of federal officers to perform provincial tasks or vice versa; and the use of federal funds to finance numerous provincial activities.

It is interesting to observe that departmental records in earlier years show surprisingly few examples of administrative conflicts arising from the division of jurisdictions.[3] Only as the activities of the state expanded

1 For an early description of these expedients, see J.A. Corry, 'Difficulties of Divided Jurisdiction,' a special study prepared for the Royal Commission on Dominion-Provincial Relations (1940), appendix 7. A more recent survey, somewhat critical of the Corry report, is to be found in Donald V. Smiley, 'Public Administration and Canadian Federalism,' Canadian Public Administration 7 (Sept. 1964), pp. 371–88.
2 See Edgar Gallant, 'The Machinery of Federal-Provincial Relations,' Canadian Public Administration 8 (Dec. 1965), pp. 515–26. Eight years before, a listing of such co-ordinating committees showed only half the number mentioned by Gallant: see K.W. Taylor, 'Co-ordination in Administration,' in Institute of Public Administration of Canada, Ninth Annual Conference, Proceedings, 1957, pp. 253–73.
3 In the areas of concurrent jurisdiction (agriculture and immigration) the central government paused a long time before becoming actively involved in agriculture, just as the provinces were inclined – for a much longer period – to leave immi-

and as both the provinces and the central administration began to press outward on the specific powers conferred on each did signs of administrative friction develop. Both provinces and dominion, in the formative years, found quite enough to occupy their limited administrative resources without trespassing on the other's preserves. But as matters affecting fisheries, resources, labour and industrial relations, health and welfare, and interprovincial or international trade began to come to the fore, the administrative boundaries set by the constitution proved to be less and less satisfactory. Basically, the provinces could be expected to assume the main burden of administering these programmes, but increasingly the limitations on and unevenness of provincial revenues required action on a broader front. The administrative response of the federal public service tended to make headway in stages: first it acted as a central fact-gathering agency; then it embarked on expensive research operations, the results of which were disseminated to provincial governments and individuals; next it moved to the provision of grants to assist provincial programmes in specific fields of health and welfare, the conditions attached to these grants being 'policed' by federal officials; finally, in cases where provincial governments were unable to mount programmes of an appropriate standard or for financial reasons could not undertake some of the programmes, the dominion created its own operating administrative units.

The cumulative results of this step-by-step evolution are that for the newer social service and scientific activities of the state the federal public service operates extensive fact-gathering services, conducts a broadly based research operation in both applied and basic sciences, and in association with these activities has developed elaborate publication, promotional, and educational programmes of an unprecedented nature. In addition, about one-quarter of the federal budget passes through the hands of such federal departments to be spent directly on individuals and another 20 per cent is distributed to other levels of government to support related programmes.[4]

Two factors contribute to the perpetuation and even the continued expansion of the federal public service's involvement in the new areas. First,

gration, in the main, to the central government. Fisheries involved international negotiations which produced a lengthy struggle on the part of the federal government to wrest independent negotiating powers from Britain, and subsequently led to difficult jurisdictional problems with the provinces for such fish as the salmon whose spawning habits showed no respect for the refinements of international law or federal distribution of functions.

4 See Canadian Tax Foundation, *The National Finances, 1969–70*, p. xx, and Dominion Bureau of Statistics, *Provincial Government Finance, Revenue and Expenditure, 1969*, Nov. 1969, tables 1 and 5. Latest estimates are to be found in *Can. H. of C. Debates*, 1970, p. 4748.

there is the natural reluctance of federal officials to give up an operating programme which they were forced to pioneer because provincial public services failed to respond to obvious social needs. An easy rationalization for continuing the programme, even in the face of an obvious resurgence of provincial intentions to take up the slack, is that the provincial administrative apparatus is less than adequate to the task – a supposition that may have had substantial evidence to support it a generation ago but in the face of rapid improvements in the provincial public services is growing increasingly less tenable. The other factor is that, confronted by the amplitude and ready availability of the federally provided services, the poorer provinces at least have had little incentive to assume operating responsibilities. When it is realized that for several of the provinces over half of their budgeted revenues come from the federal treasury,[5] one can understand this reluctance, even though it may place an unnecessarily heavy operating burden on the federal public service.

On the basis of this brief survey it is perhaps surprising to reach the conclusion that the constitutional frame of reference within which the federal public service has had to operate has imparted not a static but a particularly dynamic quality to that service. Working in parallel, the federal and provincial public services had to evolve a variety of expedients for securing co-operative action, eliminating administrative 'no man's lands,' and reducing friction wherever possible. In the course of working out these arrangements, more particularly as the state embarked on wide-scale social welfare measures, many of the federal government departments have assumed new tasks, such as fact-gathering, research, promotional, and grant-dispensing responsibilities. Until very recently the provinces have concentrated much more on administering programmes. Thus, new types of professional personnel, such as statisticians, accountants, economists, scientists and technicians of every species, public information officers, and the like, emerged much sooner in the federal public service than in the provincial services.

There is room and need for a full-scale study of both the provincial public services and of the administrative interrelations that have developed between provincial and federal public departments. In addition, we need assessments of the personnel problems associated with the emergence and expansion of those particular groups of employees which are placed in today's public service to meet the requirements of two sets of administrative authorities. Here, however, attention must be limited to the foregoing

5 See *ibid., Provincial Government Finance*. The provinces of Newfoundland and Prince Edward Island derive over 56 per cent of their revenues from the central government, Ontario about 16 per cent, and British Columbia nearly 15 per cent.

generalized comments on the significant impact which the adoption of a federal constitution has had in shaping the national public service.

THE POLITICAL TRADITION

The public service organization is 'public' precisely because it implements the goals set by politically responsible organs of the state. It is, therefore, natural to find that some of the characteristic features of the public service are directly attributable to the political institutions and to the conventions that have been built up around them. In Canada there are three important political institutions that have left an indelible imprint on the public service: the cabinet system, the doctrine of ministerial responsibility, and the patronage system which has been the handmaiden of the party system.

The cabinet

The cabinet system, which has been borrowed directly from Britain, has evolved in response to a long-standing political convention that has an important bearing on the organization of the public service. The convention itself arose out of the political necessities of federation: all of the separate political units had to be represented in the cabinet and nothing less than cabinet status could satisfy this claim for representation.

Edward Blake, speaking from the opposition benches in 1878, reminded the House of Commons of the origin of the doctrine which in less than a decade had become a convention that could be disregarded by a prime minister only at his peril:

... the hon. gentleman [Sir John A. Macdonald] then laid down the principle of sectional representation. He alleged that there must be two members of the cabinet from each province ... that the smallest province, therefore, should have two members in the cabinet. He pointed out, further, that there being two for the least Province, there should for the larger and important Province of Quebec, be double that number, and Ontario, being still larger, the least number she would be content with would be 5; and he thus summed up the number of 13 as the minimum number of Cabinet Ministers for four Provinces, and that was the statement upon which he defended that organization.[6]

Macdonald, in rebuttal, claimed that he had 'repudiated the idea that that should be a permanent necessity. Eventually, when the Provinces had become more intimately united, the system would be that the only question would be to choose the best man to come into the Government.'[7] Never-

6 *Can. H. of C. Debates*, 1878, pp. 1601–2.
7 *Ibid.*, p. 1618.

theless, in 1893, one of his successors, Sir John Thompson, answering a complaint about the increasing size of the cabinet, commented: '[We] must remember that in this country we have still the system of provincial representation in the Cabinet. That system was founded in 1867 ... I doubt very much, indeed, if any of the provinces will be willing to give up the share of representation which it had at the time of the union.'[8] There was even a note of fatalistic acceptance sounded by Sir Richard Cartwright, an opposition spokesman, in the same debate: 'The whole thing is an unfortunate business and a great mistake – even under the necessity of meeting political exigencies and supplying his [the prime minister's] political menagerie, even with the temptation, which I admit to be great, of seeing the Protestant lion munch his provender contentedly as the very last joint in the tail of the Catholic lamb.'[9]

The convention still persists, applied perhaps with a little more flexibility than one might infer from the comments of these early cabinet-builders. It helps to explain why the size of the cabinet – and hence the number of public departments – can vary only slightly today, ranging around a normal figure of two dozen members.

Another relevant convention arose from the reaction of Canadian leaders to the two more fully matured administrative models to which they looked for inspiration – the British and United States patterns of organization. In Britain a large number of administrative departments had evolved without making the cabinet so large as to be unmanageable: the practice of appointing 'junior' ministers to head many of these departments provided a means of keeping the cabinet proper quite small by seating only a select group of ministerial heads representing the departments whose activities were of major importance to the state; the remainder were in the ministry but not in the cabinet.[10] Despite numerous favourable references to the British system of 'junior' ministers, it was never adopted in Canada. The most significant experiment with the device was of short duration: between 1892 and 1895 the commissioners of customs and of inland revenue were not accorded cabinet status, although they held ministerial office.[11] After a brief trial, in which the newly created Minister of Trade and Commerce was expected to speak in cabinet for these two ministers,

8 *Ibid.*, 1893, pp. 301–2.
9 *Ibid.*, p. 302.
10 For a detailed analysis and comparison of Canadian and British practices, see Margaret A. Banks, 'Privy Council, Cabinet, and Ministry in Britain and Canada: A Story of Confusion,' *Canadian Journal of Economics and Political Science* 31 (May 1965), pp. 193–205.
11 See the invaluable source, Public Archives of Canada, *Guide to Canadian Ministries since Confederation, July 1, 1867–January 1, 1957* (Ottawa, 1957), p. 20; also *Can. H. of C. Debates*, 1887, p. 882 ff.

they were restored to the cabinet, and throughout the years the only other ministerial appointment that might be viewed as a species of junior minister has been the Solicitor General (though he, too, has recently been assigned specific programmes and is sworn to the Privy Council).[12]

Failure to adopt the British model meant that all political heads of public departments in Canada had to be in the cabinet; and, if the cabinet was not to become monstrously cumbersome, this decision imposed a practical outside limit to the number of departments.

In the United States, the other exemplar upon which the businessman-type of politician was more inclined to rely, an entirely different organizational pattern had developed. Many early Canadian observers, particularly the economy conscious Liberals in opposition, were inclined to praise a system by which 'forty millions, instead of four, were ably governed by an administration of seven members instead of fourteen.'[13] Critics of the American model characterized it as 'the bureau system,' by which they meant that the number of departments was kept small only because each embraced a large number of relatively autonomous operating bureaux. For reasons which were never clearly articulated, the official position in Canada was that the system was antagonistic to the doctrine of ministerial responsibility and of cabinet government. Thus, the alternative of preserving a small cabinet by appointing ministers to head a few comprehensive departments, exercising authority over a large number of bureaus, never commended itself to Canadian cabinet-makers. They may have rationalized their decision on the theoretical grounds that the system conflicted with the spirit of responsible cabinet government, but quite clearly the primary consideration was the federal imperative of cabinet-building which set the minimal limit for adequate provincial representation at twice the number required for the United States cabinet of the time.

The early entrenchment of the convention governing the representative quality of the cabinet, together with a rejection of both the British practice of appointing junior ministers and the American practice of employing a

12 Stats Can. 1887, c.14. The Solicitor General was 'to assist the Minister of Justice in the counsel work of the Department of Justice, and shall be charged with such other duties as are at any time assigned to him by the Governor in Council.' Ten years before, while in opposition, John A. Macdonald had suggested this arrangement (*Debates* 1878, p. 1590), adding: 'let him [the Solicitor General] be a member of the Government if they liked.' In practice, the Solicitor General was seldom in the cabinet, but by order in council 1966, confirmed in the Government Organization Act of the same year (Stats Can. 1966, c.25), he was given a real portfolio that included the penitentiaries, correctional services, and the police.

13 *Can. H. of C. Debates*, 1878, p. 1592. The statement was made by Sir Charles Tupper but he was attributing the comment to the Liberals while in opposition.

few 'holding-company departments,' left little room for manœuvring when new functions were undertaken by the state. In the circumstances, only two options were available: either the new functions had to be absorbed into the existing and relatively stable departmental framework or else they had to be undertaken outside the walls of the departmental system altogether.

In practice, the record reveals that both options were used. The departments themselves, with surprisingly moderate increase in their numbers, have steadily swollen in size. But, it is interesting to observe in view of the criticisms directed at the American 'bureau system,' a good deal of the expansion has in fact been achieved by resorting to bureaux or branches which are genuine 'departments' in their own right.[14] With the passage of time, the rigidities of the departmental framework have often made it difficult to find an obviously appropriate home for particular functions. In the event, some departments have come to embrace a variety of ill-assorted functions simply as a means of housing what otherwise might become administrative orphans. The top-level co-ordination of this organizational motley has always been a problem in American administration and in the Canadian context of ministerial responsibility the problem is so accentuated as to confirm that antagonism of early Canadian observers to which reference has previously been made.

The other option – a resort to non-departmental administrative forms of organization – has been increasingly adopted in the effort to supplement and even evade the rigidity of the old departmental system. Admittedly, Canadian practice in this respect is by no means unique. In the United Kingdom, even with the larger number of departments to fall back on, Sir Ivor Jennings identified the presence of a host of these non-departmental 'outriders' and 'camp followers.'[15] And, in the late 1930s, the president's Committee on Administrative Management spoke of their counterparts in the United States as having grown up like 'the barns, shacks and silos' that attach themselves to the original farmstead.[16]

The bewildering variety and profusion of these non-departmental administrative entities reflects the somewhat haphazard organizational response to the growing burden of state activities. In a subsequent chapter special attention is directed to the current justifications for such departures

14 See below, chaps. 5 and 7.
15 *Cabinet Government* (3rd ed., Cambridge, 1965), p. 102: 'The ministers are not leaders of columns marching behind them in organised ranks, for the columns have outriders on their flanks, and a relatively unorganised mass of camp followers trailing behind.'
16 President's Committee on Administrative Management, *Report, with Special Studies* (Washington, 1939), p. 36.

from the departmental norm and to the peculiar problems of fitting them comfortably into the system of ministerial responsibility.

Ministerial responsibility

This doctrine is the second feature of the political setting whose implications for the public service require elaboration. It is central to the whole system of Canadian government and the British system from which it was borrowed intact. Reverting to the concept of public organizations for setting and implementing goals, it may be seen that the principle of ministerial responsibility is the device for bridging the gap between parliament (the goal setter) and the public service organization (the implementer of goals): it not only establishes a bridge across which most of the traffic between parliament and the public service is routed but, applied collectively to the ministers in the cabinet, it ensures a unity of purpose and a co-ordinating of direction at the very top. The individual minister in compliance with the doctrine is required to assume a Janus-like posture. Facing towards parliament the minister is required to convey the public service's requests for money and to defend it against all criticism as the sole public spokesman. Parliament benefits by being able to 'home in' on an identifiable target rather than experience the frustration of trying to locate a responsible spokesman in the serried ranks of the public service. The public servant benefits because he is not forced out into the open to debate the challenge to his political overlords. His anonymity preserves the constitutional fiction of his political non-commitment, without which he would be unable to remain in office whenever a change in political party control occurred at the top.[17]

Facing towards the public service, always conscious of his obligation to defend every action of the lowliest official when he confronts parliament, the minister must play an active role as administrative chief in his own departmental domain. Until the quite recent introduction of parliamentary secretaries, the minister was expected to carry out his parliamentary duties unassisted. But, from the very beginning, his role as administrative chief has been buttressed by the appointment of a permanent deputy minister. The title, whose origins are not very clear, is extremely misleading. Even a casual consideration indicates that the permanent head in no way 'deputizes' for the minister when he acts in his parliamentary capacity. It

17 For a more detailed analysis, see my 'The Civil Service and Policy Formation,' *Canadian Journal of Economics and Political Science* 23 (Nov. 1957), pp. 467–79. A thorough historical examination and contemporary critique of the doctrine in its native British setting is contained in Henry Parris, *Constitutional Bureaucracy* (London, 1969), chap. 3.

can only mean that in the implementation of certain goals – a power usually conferred by statute specifically on the minister – the deputy is authorized to execute the function in his stead.

It is inappropriate at this point to embark on a lengthy analysis of the complex relationship between the deputy and the minister.[18] But it is clear that the growth in the size and functions of the departments over which ministers now have to preside has substantially altered the relationship and, indeed, placed the whole conception of ministerial responsibility under enormous strain.

In the formative years departments were small enough to enable energetic ministerial heads to attend personally to much of the day-to-day business. Somewhat indirect evidence that this was the case is to be found in the early practice whereby the prime minister himself assumed charge of a particularly active department: Macdonald chose the Department of Justice; his successor, Alexander Mackenzie, chose Public Works – which in his time was also responsible for railways; later, Macdonald presided over the Department of the Interior – at that time, by all odds, the largest and most heavily burdened agency. Further evidence of this direct personal concern of ministers in the detailed management of their departments is provided in the records of the Privy Council in which we find lengthy memoranda dealing with proposed reorganization, right down to the last low-grade clerk. Again, when the Liberal government in 1878 decided that the Department of Justice was overworked, their solution was to create an Attorney General as a second and separate ministerial head rather than appoint a second deputy minister.[19]

But even at this early stage of development, an alternative and obviously more realistic view of the minister's proper role was developed. Indeed, it found expression in the debate on the previously mentioned proposal to divide the work of the Department of Justice. As one critic logically contended:

... if he understood it rightly, the Government of this country had proceeded in the principle of each one of the heads being responsible to Government for its own Department. Now, if this Act passed, they would have that plain rule entirely overcome. They would have repeated what has been seen over and over again this Session. When a Minister came down to justify an act he simply said someone in the Department, some engineer, or some deputy-head recommended it, and, therefore, the Government did it. Instead of one head and a

18 But see below, chap. 9.
19 See debate on the Receiver General and Attorney General Bill, *Can. H. of C. Debates*, 1878, p. 1584 ff.

single Department with somebody responsible for it, the responsibility would be shifted from one Minister to another ... Surely, if the deputy was the person who ought to do the executive, the actual work, it could not be expected the Minister to do more than direct the work to be done. It could not possibly require two to direct the work of one ... one head ought to be able to direct as much as another man could do.[20]

Sir John A. Macdonald, contributing to the same debate, had contended that the only reason why the Justice Department's work had been increased was that a 'circumlocution system' of references to the department had been introduced because the new Liberal ministers were 'inexperienced men in the practical working of the administration of affairs.' Countering this claim, R. Laflamme for the government observed 'that the deputy heads of the Departments, who were naturally their advising officers, had not been changed; and these were men accustomed to the work, and who, notwithstanding the experience of the former Ministers, were those who had advised them, and upon whom those Ministers had relied for the good administration of their Departments.' Macdonald's rejoinder was that 'although political heads were inexperienced ... no man, no permanent officer could supply the want of knowledge on the part of the political head; he alone was responsible to the country and to Parliament. He must be informed, and should study for himself the subjects that came within his departmental scope. It was false in theory and reprehensible in practice, that the political heads were to throw themselves on the deputy heads and make them the measure of their consciences, their judgments and their responsibilities.'[21]

The contradictory tone of this debate serves to illustrate the point that, even in the relatively small-scale administrative operation of those days, it was scarcely possible for the ministerial head to do more than exercise a general surveillance over the execution of programmes. What was becoming clear even in the early post-Confederation years has been made even more apparent with the passage of time and the tremendous expansion in the size and labours of the departments.

Nevertheless, there was one significant feature of the cabinet system which imposed on ministers a continuing obligation to take personal charge of the detailed execution of policy – the need to preserve the collective responsibility of ministers. It is true that the same doctrine of collective responsibility in Britain did not have the same results, for there ministerial heads have tended generally to adopt the role of directors

20 *Ibid.*, p. 1604 (Edward Palmer).
21 *Ibid.*, pp. 1588, 1610, 1614–15.

rather than managers. But there were two factors present in Canada that were not nearly so significant in Britain which helped to account for the perpetuation of the 'managing' role of ministers, even in the face of growing size and complexity of the administrative machine. First, the convention that the cabinet should provide adequate regional representation could make sense only if most matters were brought before the cabinet for final decision. Thus, while in England the statutes generally confer powers on the minister to act, in Canada the statutes much more commonly provide for a determination by the 'Governor General in Council' – that is, the cabinet. The necessity of obtaining collegial decisions on a wide range of relatively unimportant matters has, in a sense, forced the Canadian cabinet, like the individual minister, to concern itself with detailed problems of management often at the expense of its broader task of acting as a co-ordinating board of directors in settling the main policy goals of the nation.

If to this peculiar feature of the Canadian cabinet we add the prevalence of political patronage, we can understand more clearly why ministers, individually and in their collective capacity, were unable to extricate themselves from direct involvement in the management of their departments. Sir George Murray, the commissioner brought over from Britain in 1912 to investigate the public service, saw this as perhaps the most unique and, from his British perspective, the most undesirable characteristic of the Canadian service. 'Ministers,' he concluded, 'both have too much to do and try to do too much.'[22] In the years since the Murray report efforts have been made to expunge this epitaph which so pithily and accurately described the predicament into which the doctrine of ministerial responsibility had fallen at the outbreak of the First World War. The real expansion of the federal public service has occurred primarily since 1939, and the machinery of management which has been devised to bring the doctrine of collective cabinet responsibility and individual ministerial responsibility into line with present-day administrative realities will occupy our attention at a later stage in this study.

Patronage

Reference has been made to the importance of patronage – a third aspect of the political system to leave its significant mark on the public service. As British and American experience amply demonstrates, political patronage is by no means a monopoly of one country: it is the natural con-

22 'Report on the Organization of the Public Service of Canada,' *Sessional Papers*, 1912, no 57a, p. 7.

comitant of the emergence of parties competing for votes and power. It is true that patronage was used, for example, by the British monarchs or the British colonial governors to attract a loyal personal following, but it reached its height when the modern party system evolved in the nineteenth century. Its significance for present purposes is that a positive act of self-denial is required if its obviously deleterious influence on the quality of the public service organization is to be removed. The timing of such a decision depends in part on how long a nation can afford the waste and inefficiency that inevitably accompany the widespread use of patronage.

In the United States and Canada natural wealth in land and resources and the relatively low order of skills required in early public administration delayed the taking of the necessary decision. It is no accident that the first European country to attack patronage was Prussia – a state with limited endowments from nature and an oppressive burden of administrative costs deriving from its desire to become a foremost military power. In North America a pervasive philosophy of egalitarianism acted as a deterrent and delayed the positive action required to remove patronage. Indeed, in the United States, particularly under the influence of Jacksonian democracy, this philosophy provided a rationalization for the retention of patronage by making a virtue out of the partisan necessity of turning out the old guard with each change of the party in power – liberty of the subject could best be preserved by denying public officers permanent tenure. In any case the duties of office were thought to be simple enough to enable any citizen to qualify. Everyone should, therefore, have equal access to public office, just as no one should expect to hold such office in perpetuity.

The Jacksonian philosophy in Canada received no such open acknowledgment as it did, for example, in the series of Tenure of Office Acts (which set limits to the number of years a public office could be held) in the United States. Nevertheless, the egalitarian assumptions of the philosophy were as congenial to Canadians as to Americans, and the procedures used for recruiting Canadian public servants still reflect to some extent the persistence and prevalence of these assumptions.[23]

However, the real significance of patronage is that the measures taken to eradicate it have left their mark on the public service. The implicit self-denying ordinance accepted by the politicians, in the case of Canada (as well as the United States), had to be confirmed by statute. In Britain, significantly, patronage was removed by executive decree, and the public

23 They are seen, for example, in the advertisements of positions which permit the substitution of practical experience for specific academic degrees – an acknowledgment that opportunities for advanced formal academic training were far from equal. Extensive reliance on nationwide competitions stresses the same philosophy of open access to the bureaucracy.

service – with the exception of pensions and the prohibitions on holding political office – continues to this day to be regulated by executive decrees. This procedure is consistent with the antique conception of the civil servant as a servant of Her Majesty, or the servant of the Crown (which, for practical purposes today is the minister of the Crown in cabinet). It is suggested that the use of a general civil service act to regulate the Canadian public service – a practice which in fact antedates Confederation – relates to the peculiar tensions that developed in the colonial period between the emergent popularly elected legislature and a political executive that was still suspected of being a minion of the imperial government.[24] Whether or not this is the true historical explanation, the fact is that the precedent once established was continued thereafter without question by means of successive civil service acts culminating in the last thorough overhaul in 1967. The significance of such legislation is that it reflects an underlying ambivalence in the legal status of the Canadian public service which it is the purpose of the next chapter to elaborate. The ambivalence arises from the apparently dual subservience of the public service to both the legislature and the executive. In the American system of divided powers this duality is not unexpected, but in Canada, which adheres to the British system of the union of powers, it raises constant doubts about the appropriate relationship of the administrative branch to the executive and legislature which, surprisingly, seldom emerged as an issue in the United Kingdom.

While the use of a statute to eliminate patronage gives parliament a stronger legal basis for claiming ampler jurisdiction over the public service than is true in Britain, a more definite repercussion on the public service has been the negative philosophy of control that has characterized the application of the legislation. Patronage could only be eliminated by imposing a rigorous mechanism of control, and this primary concern of the Civil Service Act – to regulate rather than service or facilitate – has, until quite recent times, dominated its administration. The desired result of preventing the unfit from gaining admission to the public service was achieved at the expense of a failure to take positive measures to attract the most highly qualified candidates available. But, even more important, the act conferred on the Civil Service Commission not only the responsibility for vetting candidates seeking admission but also comprehensive managerial responsibilities over the entire range of personnel tasks. The orientation towards control, generated by its primary function as patronage eliminator, has tended to rub off on to the other personnel management responsibilities which clearly demand a more positive, service-

24 See my *Pioneer Public Service* (Toronto, 1955), chap. 2.

minded approach. Only in recent years has this heritage been counteracted by a conscious effort to assert the servicing and developmental responsibilities.[25]

Nor is the negative control attitude, deriving originally from the fear of patronage, restricted to the central personnel agency – although it has its most obvious repercussion in matters of staffing. The whole expenditure process is riddled with control mechanisms which again mirror the historical and admittedly legitimate concern to guarantee honesty in the expenditure of the public's money.[26] But, as in the field of personnel so in matters of expenditure, the negative prohibitions tended to overshadow the sensible use of the machinery to foster the efficient application of resources. At the same time, departmental managers caught in the pincers of centralized agencies have had to operate in an atmosphere of distrust which gave rise to the imposition of control in the first place. In the circumstances, departmental managers have had small incentive to take the initiative in seeking ways to improve efficiency or in assuming responsibility for matters over which in the last analysis they have no right to make the final decision.

No one observing the conditions in the public service which gave rise to the centralized control agencies could argue that the controls ought never to have been introduced. But, as in colonial rule there comes a time when the period of tutelage gives way to responsible self-rule, so in the life of the public service central control agencies should be prepared to admit that their success is to be measured by the degree of independence they can afford to grant the departments under their jurisdiction. However, control agencies are as loath as imperial administrators to give up their powers; it is difficult for them to see that their raison d'être is not really threatened by the proposal to devolve their powers to departments; all that happens is a reorientation away from a negative régime to a more productive co-operative relationship with their erstwhile wards. The Canadian public service has undoubtedly now reached this stage of maturity and must face a readjustment which will make heavier calls on the initiative and ability of departmental managers and will require the centralized agencies of co-ordination to think less of control and more of guidance, service, and setting standards for the departments. This theme is only introduced at this point; since it connects the several chapters in Part Three where the managerial agencies of the public service are examined, we shall have occasion later to explore it at considerable length.

25 See below, chap. 12.
26 Detailed evidence on this matter is to be found in Royal Commission on Government Organization, *Report*, I, *Management of the Public Service* (Ottawa, 1962), report no 2: 'Financial Management,' passim.

CHAPTER FOUR

The legal foundations

Organizations, once established, become so much a part of the scheme of things, such accepted objects in a familiar landscape, that there is a natural tendency to overlook the foundations upon which they were built and to which they must refer to secure authority for their current functions in society. The habit of taking organizations for granted results in a failure to come to grips with such basic questions as the following: Under what legal authority has a particular organization been brought into being? How far does the law determine its specific structure? What is the legal basis for effecting changes in structure or function? From whence does it derive the capacity to act? How, legally, does it obtain the resources in money, facilities, and personnel requisite to the performance of its tasks? Such questions are especially pertinent in considering the public service, which, acting as an agent for other public organizations, is legally dependent on external authority for the delineation of its structure and purposes.

No attempt will be made here to provide an answer to the fundamental question: what is the fountainhead of legal authority from whence the public service organization derives its capacity to act on our behalf? The quest for an answer would necessitate a careful back-tracking along a confused constitutional trail on which so many historians have lovingly lingered – back, indeed, along the perplexing paths pondered by the great political philosophers of ancient times.

For present purposes there is no need to retrace our steps farther than the period of absolute monarchy, avoiding as we do so the vexed question of where absolute monarchs derived *their* authority. At a time when the monarch combined in his person the role of landlord-in-chief, military commander, chief justice, legislator, and executor, the question of the legal foundation of public administration was readily answered. Only as a functional separation and specialization of organs for the performance of each function emerged did the question become more difficult to answer. In the case of British public service organizations, whose history is obviously most relevant to Canadian developments, the earliest evolution was from a single office in the Royal Household – the King's Secretary or Secretary of State. In theory, the incumbents of the modern secretaryships, such as Foreign Affairs, War, Home Affairs, Scottish Affairs, etc., all hold the same office, and each is capable, in general terms, of exercising the functions of any or all of the others. This group of departments may be characterized as emanations of the Royal Household.[1]

A second group of departments began as administrative committees or boards of the King's Privy Council. These departments reflected the gradual transition of 'the Crown' from a personal to an institutionalized concept in which the royal prerogative increasingly came to be asserted by ministerial advisers. Throughout the nineteenth and on into the twentieth century such areas as local government, education, and housing evolved in this fashion, preceded by their eighteenth century prototype, the Board of Trade. Some of these have today become 'ministries' and even where the title 'board' is still retained for a department it has long since ceased to use the collegial form of top direction and control.

The third transformation came with the evolution of an Executive Council of ministers which owed its power to the capacity to maintain the political support of parliament. The tortuous complexities of this long evolution produced a situation where all new departments of state were founded on statute and where, as the royal prerogative was whittled away by statutory enactments, even the older group of 'prerogative departments' tended to be re-established and confirmed by positive parliamentary action.[2]

The end result of a process which might be described as parliament's taming of the royal prerogative is that today the British public service organizations, however they may differ in historical origin, by and large exist by virtue of the declared will of parliament and perform functions which parliament has deemed it appropriate for them to undertake. Nevertheless, the carry-over from the early days of uninhibited prerogative still finds expression in the legal status of the British public servant as a servant

1 Frederick Austin Ogg, *English Government and Politics* (2nd ed., New York, 1936), contains a well-documented description of this evolution; for a brief account, see W.J.M. MacKenzie and J.W. Grove, *Central Administration in Britain* (London, 1957), pp. 163–77, and references there cited.
2 Ogg, *English Government and Politics*, passim.

of the Crown. The conditions he faces in seeking admission to the public service as well as his terms of service – including his tenure 'at pleasure' – are practically all imposed by the executive acting in the name of the Crown, rather than by parliament.

The legal foundations of public administration in Canada were erected during the third stage of British development mentioned above. The colonial period was marked by the same disputes between Crown and parliament which had characterized several centuries of British constitutional evolution. The battles between royal governor acting in the name of the Crown and colonial assemblies increasingly representative of the populace were direct counterparts of similar and much more drawn-out controversies in the mother country. The final settlement of the Civil List question in Britain took place on the accession of Queen Victoria to the throne in 1837: in effect, the monarch was no longer able personally to dispose of any portion of the public revenues and was henceforth limited to a fixed grant in support of the personal household of the monarch.

In the colonies, the period of the 1830s also witnessed the climax of this controversy which was resolved in the 1840s in favour of the representative and responsible legislature.[3] Indeed, it would appear that the antagonism between the 'alien' representative of the Crown and indigenous local legislative bodies resulted in an assertion of legislative supremacy over the executive branch – and with it the permanent public service – which went further in establishing the formal claims of parliament than did the British development. In the Province of Canada a measure, passed as early as 1843, to secure the independence of parliament, proscribed the seating of any office holders in the legislature – with the important exception of those holding specified positions as ministerial heads of departments.[4] This legislation took its inspiration from a long list of so-called Place Acts, beginning in 1705 in Britain, and was intended to achieve the same purposes, namely, to establish a clear-cut dividing line between permanent and political office holders and eliminate executive influence over place holders in the legislature. But colonial parliaments went further, as was noted in the previous chapter, in passing civil service legislation which was to ensure that the patronage of the Crown now dispensed by ministers should be subjected to detailed parliamentary control. The British parliament never sought this power and, as a result, in legal form at least, the old conception of public officers being servants of the Crown has survived.

3 See my *Pioneer Public Service* (Toronto, 1955), chap. 3.
4 Stats Prov. Can. 7 Vict., c.65 (1844). This act was approved in 1843 by the provincial assembly and, after being reserved by the governor, was accepted in 1844 by the imperial authorities.

At the time of Confederation, then, the tension between executive and legislature during the period of colonial rule inclined the Canadian parliament to adopt a more proprietary attitude towards the public service. In the years to come this attitude was often reflected in the disposition to intervene in matters of administrative detail and to assume a much more possessive air towards public servants. In short, Canadians fostered the view that the civil service was indeed the public's service and, for all practical purposes, parliament was to act as the agent of the public in maintaining a close control over the affairs of the public service.

It is probable that this view received additional support from the fact that Canada's constitution leaned heavily on a major legislative enactment and that changes in its provisions required legislative action. If one examines, for example, the few sections in the British North America Act bearing on the public service, one discovers the repeated use of the standard phrase: 'until the Parliament of Canada (or the provincial legislature) otherwise provides.' Section 12 of the act declares that 'All Powers, Authorities, and Functions ... shall, as far as the same continue in existence and capable of being exercised after the Union in relation to the Government of Canada, be vested in and exerciseable by the Governor General, with the Advice or with the Advice and Consent of [the respective executive councils thereof] ... subject nevertheless ... to be abolished or altered by the Parliament of Canada.' Section 65 makes the same provision for subsequent action by the provincial legislatures. Or, again, section 130 reads in part: 'Until the Parliament of Canada otherwise provides, all Officers of the several Provinces having Duties to discharge ... shall continue to discharge the Duties of their respective Offices ...' By section 131 the Governor General in Council is empowered to 'appoint such Officers as [it] deems necessary or proper for the effectual Execution of this Act' – until the parliament of Canada 'otherwise provides.'

The phraseology of the British North America Act is in complete accord with the constitutional doctrine of parliamentary supremacy. Thus, the locus of *ultimate* authority over the public service seems to be clearly settled in parliament. What needs further exploration is how parliament – applying the phrase so consistently used in the BNA Act – 'otherwise provides' for three fundamental features of the public service: (1) the organizational form, (2) the functions and powers, and (3) the responsibility for managing and 'provisioning' the public service. The following examination of these three areas will serve to demonstrate how far we can realistically expect the sovereign reach of parliament to extend when confronted by the inevitable need for strong initiatives from the executive branch of government.

THE ORGANIZATIONAL FORM

Canada's administrative entities arrived comparatively late on the scene and hence did not originate as prerogative creations from the Royal Household. When Lord Sydenham – whom one may fairly credit with the founding of the system of public departments in 1841 – set about the task of administrative organization for his new Province of Canada, he secured legislative enactments to found all his new or reorganized administrative agencies.[5] Many of these were carried forward virtually intact in title, function, and personnel into the wider union of 1867. In any case, the parliament of the new Canada quickly reconfirmed the statutory foundation of the departmental system by approving separate enactments for each of the major departments of state. There was one important exception: the Privy Council Office was never given formal statutory recognition and must, therefore, be assumed to be the lone Canadian counterpart to the ancient prerogative departments in Britain – a situation that still persists.[6]

With this single exception, parliament has repeatedly and unvaryingly clung to the early practice of requiring special authorizing legislation for every additional department. Nevertheless, the executive has always been the source of inspiration for all such organizational changes and its primary concern for the machinery of administration has been demonstrated in at least three positive ways.

First, while it is clear that parliament must authorize the creation of a department, it is equally clear that the executive determines when the department shall, in fact, begin to function. The clearest illustration of this power is to be found in the surprisingly lengthy period that elapsed between parliamentary approval of the Department of Trade and Commerce Act, consented to on 23 June 1887, and the measures taken by the executive to bring that department into physical being which were not completed until more than five years later on 3 December 1892.[7]

The second and much more important indication of executive initiative with respect to all organizational questions is to be found in a short law entitled the Public Service Rearrangement and Transfer of Duties Act.

5 See *Pioneer Public Service*, chap. 3.
6 It may be said that the statutory base for the Privy Council Office is to be found in the British North America Act itself, in which section 11 provides for the constitution of the Privy Council for Canada and section 130 (as noted previously) provides for the continuance of public officers in their positions until parliament declares otherwise.
7 *Can. H. of C. Debates*, 1893, p. 300. A private bill, sponsored in 1890 to rescind the legislation of 1887 (50 and 51 Vict., c.11) because it had not been implemented, received only first reading.

This act, which dates back to 1918, as subsequently expanded in 1925,[8] provides that the Governor in Council 'may transfer any powers, duties or functions or the control or supervision of any part of the public service from one Minister of the Crown to any other Minister of the Crown, or from one department or portion of the public service.' Similarly, the Governor in Council may 'amalgamate and combine any two or more departments under one Minister of the Crown and under one deputy minister.' A final section of the act significantly attaches a proviso: all orders made under the authority of the act must be tabled in the House of Commons.

It is worth examining the history of this legislation in more detail for in effect parliament appears to have given carte blanche to the executive to initiate major organizational changes, subject only to a rather ineffectual *ex post facto* control by way of insisting that any orders issued under the act after tabling can be debated and theoretically reversed. When the legislation was introduced in 1918 it was clearly intended to give the executive a relatively free hand to reconstruct an administrative service temporarily swollen and disoriented by wartime exigencies. Parliament expressed no antagonism to the move: in fact, the only query was whether provisions in the laws which created existing departments did not make the proposed enactment superfluous. Prime Minister Robert L. Borden replied that one or two acts, such as the Department of Agriculture Act, did in fact authorize the executive to take the action contemplated, 'but,' he continued, 'there is no general provision of this kind.' He reassured the House that the new act 'does not permit an increase of the number of departments, but it does permit the transfer of a department or of a branch thereof from one minister to another. It permits also an amalgamation of two departments under one minister.'[9]

While the House was surprisingly complacent in registering no demurrer to Borden's general legislation, it was most critical of a related financial resolution proposed by Borden which, after enumerating three new ministerial appointments for whom salaries were requested, went on to ask parliament to give blanket approval 'during the present war and for one year thereafter [for] one or more other ministers, not exceeding three members of the King's Privy Council for Canada, who may be named by the Governor in Council, may be paid such salaries or other remuneration as Parliament may provide ...' From the opposition benches Ernest Lapointe contended: 'Parliament must remain supreme in a matter of this kind. Departments must be created by Parliament; the business which will

8 Stats Can. 1918, c.6; 1925, c.23.
9 *Can. H. of C. Debates*, 1918, p. 83. Parliament's lack of interest in this measure is demonstrated by the short, perfunctory discussion.

be transacted by these departments must be provided for by Parliament, and surely we should not deprive ourselves of our rights in that respect and appoint the Prime Minister as the real dictator of the country.'[10]

In registering this conception of the proper role of parliament Lapointe was echoing the views expressed by Sir Wilfrid Laurier in 1892, in a debate over a section in a bill designed to give the Governor in Council discretion to transfer the Geological Survey from the Department of the Interior to some other (unnamed) department. Stressing the general issue raised by this specific request for such a discretionary executive power, David Mills enlarged on his chief's criticism:

There may be some manipulation going on, there may be jealousies and disputes in the Cabinet, there may be a disposition on the part of some Minister to grasp more authority than he is now given, and so branches are taken from the department to which they properly belong and are given to another Minister. I do not think that is satisfactory. They ought to be properly organized, appropriately designated, and they should be under the Minister of the Crown whose name will indicate the duties he is called upon to perform. We ought not to have to look up Orders in Council to see whether a branch is under the control of the Department of the Interior, the Department of Justice, the Secretary of State, or the Minister of Marine and Fisheries.[11]

These comments illuminate parliament's perpetual concern for what, even then, Sir William Mulock could characterize as the attempt 'to aggrandize the Executive at the expense of the legislature.'[12] Clearly, if the executive were to take unlimited advantage of the discretion conferred on it to shift branches from department to department, both parliament and the public would be even more confused than they oft-times are in seeking to track their way through the bureaucracy. Nevertheless, it is interesting to observe that parliament itself, in allowing the Transfer of Duties Act to go through with scarcely a comment in 1925, was presumably acknowledging the inevitable. The public service, even at that time, had become so large and complex that it would appear that only the executive was disposed to make all-important decisions concerning the reallocation of organizational units made necessary by growth and change of functions. Moreover, the executive showed scant respect for the legislature's ability to contribute to such decisions, since parliament was effectively confronted by a *fait accompli*.

An examination of the orders in council issued under the powers con-

10 *Ibid.*, p. 845. For the terms of the financial resolution, see p. 76 ff.
11 *Ibid.*, 1892, p. 1650.
12 *Ibid.*, p. 1652.

ferred by the Transfer of Duties Act provides reassuring evidence that, in earlier years, the executive did not take undue advantage of the liberal discretion conferred on it. In normal years, two or three such orders were passed; while in a period of change or crisis the value of this flexible power was demonstrated by much more frequent use of it; for example, in the first wartime session of parliament (1940) eleven orders for organizational changes were made, and in the immediate post-war reconstruction period the organizational adaptation to new functions and the absorption or elimination of purely wartime functions was accomplished largely by means of applying the powers from five to ten times a year. Since the early 1950s it has been impossible to trace from the published records the executive's use of this discretionary power, for orders in council under this act that effect organizational changes are no longer required to be tabled in the House.[13]

The fact is that in the early 1960s the organizational shuffling that occurred in the wake of the reports from the Royal Commission on Government Organization were accomplished by what appears to have been a far too free-and-easy use of the Transfer of Duties Act by the executive.[14] Under the circumstances the earlier minimal requirement of tabling these orders in the House should surely have been restored.

It should be observed, however, that parliament has not always been excluded from considering more important organizational adaptations. In the decades of the 1930s and 1940s reallocations of functions and a shuffling of departmental nomenclature took place, and were confirmed by statute.[15] Such legislative action appears to have been required in order to confirm a set formula designed in each instance to clarify or protect the status of the people and powers transferred from the bits and pieces of the predecessors of these newer organizations.[16] However, in the major reorganization of 1966, and again in 1968, and almost annually thereafter, parliament has been left in the position of having to confirm belatedly decisions which were taken in considerable secrecy either by a small

13 Up to 1949 the *Journals* of the House of Commons religiously listed the orders in council approved under the terms of the Transfer of Duties Act. With the passage in 1950 of the Regulations Act (c.50, s.10 + Schedule) the requirement for tabling such orders (contained in the 1925 act) was eliminated. I am indebted to officers in the Privy Council Office for supplying me with selected lists of orders issued under this legislation since 1950.
14 On this point, see G.V. Tunnoch, 'The Bureau of Government Organization: Improvement by Order-in-Council, Committee, and Anomaly,' *Canadian Public Administration* 8 (Dec. 1965), pp. 558–68.
15 Major instances occurred in 1930 and particularly in 1936. See *Can. H. of C. Debates*, 1930, pp. 1730, 1778–81; 1936, beginning at p. 1815.
16 The typical formula is in the Department of Transport Act, Stats Can. 1936, c.34, s.8.

coterie of senior officials working with the prime minister or by the prime minister acting of his own accord. In the latter situation even the internal specialists on organization matters were not brought in to work out the details until after the executive had announced its reorganization proposals. Thus, not only was parliamentary opinion not sought but the views of experts in the public service, including many senior officials, were never consulted.[17] Admittedly, then, parliamentary consideration and approval of major organizational changes is largely a matter of *ex post facto* consent to purely executive initiatives, and these initiatives, in turn, seem to have become more and more the prerogative of the prime minister.

A closer inspection of the legislation which authorizes the creation of departments provides even less evidence of parliamentary intention to assert control by inserting detailed prescriptions concerning the actual form of organization. Nearly all the departmental statutes are exceedingly short – normally seven or eight sections, covering only two or three pages. With few exceptions they contain a standard declaration that there shall be a department (bearing a particular title) over which a minister shall preside and over which he has 'the management and direction'; the Governor in Council may appoint a deputy minister who, like his minister, shall hold office during pleasure; then there customarily follows the authority to appoint such clerks and subordinates as the departmental business may require in the manner prescribed by law (that is, in accordance with the terms of the Public Service Employment Act). In a very few instances statutory provision has been made for the appointment of a second deputy minister (Health and Welfare, for example) or for one or more associate deputy ministers (Department of Defence Production) or for more than one minister and deputies to correspond (prior to integration, the Department of National Defence, in an 'emergency').

Three departments appear to be unique in retaining in their statutes organizational prescriptions which date back to an earlier period and which extend below this senior level of direction: the Public Works Act, for example, specifically provides for a secretary, one or more chief engineers, and a chief architect; the Department of Transport Act provides for a secretary and two or more chief engineers; while the Department of Public Printing and Stationery Act prescribes not only a Queen's Printer but also a controller of stationery, a director and superintendent of printing, a superintendent of stationery, an accountant, and a controller of

17 Evidence for these statements is largely of the 'grapevine' nature: an official in the branch of the Civil Service Commission concerned with reorganization problems claimed that the changes occurred without any study by his branch, or, again, certain deputy ministers whose positions were definitely affected by the changes professed to read about them for the first time in the newspapers.

purchases. When one reads that among the duties imposed on the secretary of the Department of Transport is that of conducting 'under the direction of the Minister, the correspondence of the Department,'[18] the archaic quality of these surviving detailed statutory prescriptions becomes apparent. In fact, there has been a steady reduction in such detailed provisions to the point where parliament effectively has to be content with endorsing the legal existence of a particular department and permitting the vast organizational infrastructure to build up, beneath the law, like a coral island. In short, even the closest scrutiny of the legislation which brings a department into being affords few clues to this complex organizational structure under the minister and his deputy. Nor does the legislation seek to tell the minister how he should organize his department to perform the assigned tasks.

Much the same conclusion emerges from a consideration of the legislation which underpins the growing complex of non-departmental government agencies. The sections dealing with organization are, as a rule, somewhat more detailed in prescribing the makeup of the governing board and its relationship to the responsible minister. In at least four instances, in fact, parliament has conferred a general discretionary power on the executive to set up one type of non-departmental agency – the crown company. By virtue of sections in their own statutes, the National Research Council, the Atomic Energy Board, the Department of Defence Production, and the St Lawrence Seaway Authority were empowered to recommend to the Governor in Council the creation of such companies. These companies, in turn, must be shaped to meet the general requirements of the Companies Act of 1934.[19] Indeed, there is one important wartime survival, the multi-million-dollar Polymer Corporation Limited whose charter was secured on the legal base of an order in council passed under authority of the original Munitions and Supply Act – an act which is no longer on the statute books.[20]

There is one important constitutional requirement which, for all significant organizational changes such as the creation of a new department, reinforces the initiating role of the executive, even as it demands ultimate parliamentary sanction for such changes. The requirement is that all pro-

18 RSC 1970, c. T-15, s.5.
19 As of 1965 the Canada Corporations Act, Stats Can. 1964–5, c.52.
20 The author while engaged on a government survey of the public corporation thought he had inadvertently caught the government out in an error of omission: the discovery of an important crown company (Polymer) whose legal base had been pulled out from under it. Not so, claimed the legal adviser: an order in council properly issued under an empowering statute goes on like the brook, even when the statute has been repealed. (This opinion still leaves the author, for one, with a distinct sense of uneasiness.)

posals involving increases in expenditure of public funds must be recommended by the Crown, which in practice means they are initiated only by ministers of the Crown. Clearly, a proposal to set up a new organization is a 'money bill' and therefore comes under this constitutional provision.

When Jean François Pouliot, as a private member, sought in 1936 to repeal an act approved in 1935 for the creation of a central Bureau of Translations he ran afoul a Speaker's ruling which rested heavily on the constitutional prerogative of the executive to recommend all such measures. Pouliot's amendment ingeniously sought to accomplish his purpose by providing for the dismemberment of the bureau in the first section and, in the second section, providing for the transfer of the translators to the jurisdiction of individual department heads.[21] In a closely argued decision, which cited at least two other confirmatory decisions by his predecessors in 1918 and 1933, the Speaker contended that the rules of the House required each section of a bill to be considered in proper order: the adoption of the first clause would have meant that the Bureau of Translations would cease to exist and that consequently the positions of nearly all the translators in the civil service would automatically be abolished; the second clause, therefore, constituted a proposal to appoint additional civil servants, and since this would involve an increased public charge the bill could not be introduced by a private member.

The Speaker elaborated a further reason for rejecting the bill, relying on the views of Sir Wilfrid Laurier expressed in the 1911–12 session of the House: the adoption of the bill 'would mean the transfer of the authority under which appropriated money is to be spent.' After quoting Laurier's views, the Speaker concluded 'that the circumstances under which an expenditure is to be made are indivisible from that expenditure. The choice of the minister responsible for paying out the money is a material condition of an appropriation, and in order to change it the House would have to amend the principal clauses of a money bill.'[22]

This reinforcement of the executive's initiatory role by decisions of parliament's own chief spokesman should not be interpreted as an endorsement of a total exclusion of parliament from such major decisions on reorganization. The fact that these decisions must be cast in the form of money bills may prohibit all but ministers of the Crown from recommending them, but precisely because they are money bills a special parliamentary procedure for their approval must be followed by the executive. A formal resolution expressing the governor general's approval (on behalf of the Crown) of his ministers' proposals and requesting parliamentary

21 See *Can. H. of C. Journals*, 1936, pp. 61–2.
22 *Ibid.*, p. 62.

endorsement must first be submitted; and only after the financial resolution receives approval in the House can the executive introduce the bill
setting out the organizational changes for which the money will be required. Thus, when the Department of Forestry came into being in 1960
the bill for the proposed department was preceded by a financial resolution;[23] and it is at this stage, as Laurier observed, when objections to the
purposes of the expenditure should be urged. In a constitutional sense,
then, parliament retains the right to reject the executive's reorganization
proposals by using its ultimate power to refuse to grant the necessary
funds. In practice, however, the executive's determination to effect major
reorganizations involving new charges on public funds is never thwarted
by parliament's capacity to refuse approval of such funds. Moreover, an
executive that commands a safe party majority in the House can assume
with some confidence that its capacity to hold the allegiance of its supporters is not likely to be challenged on decisions affecting organization.[24]

Thus, the discretion conferred by the Transfer of Duties Act tends to
make the executive completely responsible for reorganization at the
secondary or lower levels within departments and the constitutional requirements for initiating money bills effectively place responsibility on
the executive for all major reorganizations such as the creation of a new
department and the amalgamation or reconstruction of existing departments.

The third indication of executive domination in all matters of organization is to be found in the continuing day-to-day concern with what in
old-fashioned terminology was called 'organization and methods' and is
now known as systems analysis. Obviously, parliament has neither the
time, facilities, or expert knowledge to attend constantly to the needs of
the administrative machine. Sporadic interest and even occasional prod-
ding can be anticipated from parliamentary committees, as experience
with certain wartime commitees and with the Estimates Committee demonstrates. Yet, change, growth, and decay attack administrative organisms

23 *Can. H. of C. Debates*, 1960, p. 5415.
24 A notable illustration of this proposition is to be found in a heated editorial
   commenting on the methods employed to create a central governmental information service, following on recommendations from a special task force.
   'Information Canada was established by single executive decree. No legislation
   was drafted. No Act was passed. Prime Minister Pierre Trudeau simply
   announced that the agency would be created and by providing for it in the
   estimates recently tabled in the House it was, in fact, created. The appropriations
   in the estimates for Information Canada have not yet been voted on. If the vote
   went against the appropriation it would mean the end of the agency. But it is
   inconceivable that Liberals would bolt the party to oppose the agency.' *Globe and
   Mail*, Toronto, 2 April 1970. This editorial prognostication was subsequently
   shown to be completely accurate.

much as they do the cells of the human body. No organization can afford to remain static in the face of these natural forces, and its repair and adaptation are duties which can best be undertaken by 'organizational engineers' within the public service itself. Parliament, being remote from the working levels of the administrative machinery of government, tends to be relatively unconcerned with such details; indeed, even ministers seldom demonstrate any great predilection for occupying their already overworked lives with matters of this nature. Thus, the initiative for keeping the administrative machine in proper operating trim tends, if it exists at all, to stem from those who have to work within it. And the emergence of this internal initiative has itself been delayed by the absence of strong external pressure. On the other hand the interest of the general public and the consequent preoccupation of those within the public service for improving its staffing by eliminating patronage have tended to obscure an equally valid concern for improving civil service organization: of the numerous royal commissions appointed by the executive to report on the state of the civil service, for example, only two could be said to have looked at organizational issues – the Murray commission of 1912 and the Glassco commission of 1960–3 (and, marginally, the Gordon commission of 1946).

The Civil Service Act of 1918 had this need vaguely in mind at least when it conferred on the reconstituted Civil Service Commission the authority 'after consulting with deputy-heads, heads of branches and other chief officers [to] prepare plans for the organization of each department and each branch or portion of the Civil Service, such organization to follow, as far as possible, the same general principles in all branches of the Civil Service.'[25] All such plans, or subsequent changes in them, were to be approved by the Governor in Council. But nearly thirty years elapsed before the commission or departments employed specialists to undertake the tasks envisaged by the legislation of 1918. The Civil Service Commission took the first important step in 1946 by creating a special branch, and since then both the central group and the number of departmental or agency organization and methods units have gradually expanded. Under revisions based on statutes approved in 1967, centralized responsibility

---

25 Stats Can. 1918, c.12, s.9. Because of the antagonisms created by the first intrusion of outside management consultants in the early 1920s, the departments shied away from organizational reviews and the Civil Service Commission, then battling for survival, found it advisable not to press its own statutory authority to conduct such reviews (see above, chap. 2, n. 14). For a description of organization and methods work generally, see D.M. Lyngseth 'The Use of Organization and Methods in Canadian Government,' *Canadian Public Administration* 5 (Dec. 1962), pp. 428–93.

for laying down guidelines for such units has come to rest in a special division of the Treasury Board.[26] In turn, in 1968 central services associated with organization and methods analyses were transferred from the Public Service Commission to the Department of Defence Production.[27]

It is sufficient for present purposes merely to note the relatively recent development of internal specialized units devoted full time or part time to tending the organizational and procedural needs of an increasingly complex administrative machine, often supplemented by employing outside firms of management consultants. This development is but the latest practical illustration of the steady enhancement of the responsibility of the executive branch for such matters.

Our inquiry into the legal foundation of public service organization leads to the following conclusions:

1 Only the major units – the departments and agencies – are based on parliamentary enactments.

2 Even in these cases executive initiative predominates because all such organizations involve charges on the public funds and these, constitutionally, can be proposed on behalf of the Crown only by ministers.

3 For organizational changes of a less significant nature, parliament has virtually granted the executive full discretion to take such action as it sees fit by means of orders in council issued under authority of a general and liberally worded statute (the Rearrangement and Transfer of Duties Act).

4 All matters of procedural and organizational detail which affect the day-to-day operations of departments come entirely within the purview of organization and methods experts, partly concentrated until 1968 in a special section of the Civil Service Commission, but also located in a number of the larger departments and agencies. The shifting of general guidance and policy on such questions to Treasury Board staff and the transfer of central service aspects to a new department in 1968–9 confirms the trend to make all such matters part of management's responsibilities.

Perhaps these conclusions are to be expected. The purposes of a statute are to tell the people generally what government intends to do, to give the

26 Stats Can. 1967, c.74 (An Act to Amend the Financial Administration Act), s. 1(b), and instructions from the Management Improvement Branch of the Treasury Board to departments on criteria for employing outside firms of management consultants rather than using internal resources: 'Management Improvement Policy' no M 1-9-66, 19 Aug. 1966.

27 PC 1298, 13 July 1968, transferred the Bureau of Management Consulting Services from the Public Service Commission to the Department of Defence Production; this department, in turn, became the core of a new Department of Supply and Services in 1969 (Government Organization Act, Stats Can. 1968–9, c.28, part v).

legislature something it can fruitfully debate, and to establish limits within which government can legally act. In the legislation reviewed above, there is little prospect for the legislative process to serve any of these objectives with the exception of establishing limits – and even here, as the next section will reveal, parliament is on shaky ground, for all its alleged legal potency.

THE LEGAL SOURCE OF AUTHORITY

Parliament may have displayed little interest in seeking to prescribe by law either general organizational structure or its detailed refinements but it has been much concerned with the powers and duties to be exercised by the organization. This is as it should be because, in the absence of a precise delineation of its functions and powers, the public service might well become the master. The sovereign capacity of parliament formally to set the terms and conditions of the public servant's powers is not at issue; rather, we are concerned to discover the manner in which these powers and duties are assigned and to note the problems that emerge in the transaction. The traditional stress placed on the legal omnipotence of parliament may blind us to the realities of a parliamentary system that is dominated by a majority party and a working executive committee of that party – the cabinet. Much of our current criticism of the 'decline of parliament' is based on the assumption that its major function is to legislate and that through legislation parliament's sovereign will is made flesh amongst us. If we begin by observing the severe practical limitations on parliament's capacity to contain all things and persons within its sovereign will, we shall more quickly arrive at a realistic appraisal of what can be properly expected of it.

This observtion has a prominent bearing on the issues now under consideration. One cannot conceive of parliament, for example, attempting itself to perform the multifarious duties involved in operating the government's programmes. Parliament can and does use its unlimited capacity to legislate into being the agencies which the executive deems requisite for the tasks at hand and can, through legislation, confer on such agencies the authority to carry out the assigned tasks. It is the manner and mode by which parliament authorizes these programmes to which we may now most profitably direct attention.

A scrutiny of the statutes reveals that parliament establishes programmes to be implemented in several ways by the public service. If we look once again at the organic legislation which declares that a department shall exist or be brought into being, we invariably find one or more sections – varying in the amount of detail and precision – which set out the 'powers, duties and functions' of the minister. The description may be in most general terms, the powers and duties extending 'to the execution of the laws enacted by the Parliament of Canada and of such orders of the Governor in Council' passed in relation to these enactments. The Minister of Agriculture, for example, is assigned his powers and duties in this fashion in so far as they relate to agriculture, arts and manufactures, and experimental farms.[28] A more detailed and specific prescription is found in the Department of Health and Welfare Act where the general direction to look after all matters concerning the promotion or preservation of the health, social security, and social welfare of the people of Canada is followed up with an extensive list, including such items as investigation and research into public health, inspection and medical care of immigrants and seamen, supervision of public health on various forms of public transport, the health of civil servants, the administration of such legislation as the Food and Drugs Act, the Opium and Narcotics Act, and so on.[29] In addition to conferring powers and duties on the respective ministers, the organic acts for each department invariably assign powers to the Governor in Council, that is, the ministers in their collective capacity functioning in cabinet. Not the least important of these is the authority conferred on the Governor in Council to assign 'such other duties or powers' to the minister from time to time as may be deemed fit.

The second major source to be searched for a description of a department's task is the separate pieces of legislation that specify and assign the programmes. Most of this type of legislation is set out in considerably more detail than the generalized statements associated with the organic acts that create each department. The short statute which is the foundation for the Department of National Revenue must, for example, be read in conjunction with the Customs Act, consisting of many pages and detailed schedules. Again, the eleven-page act for the Department of Transport would have to be supplemented by a reading of the Canada Shipping Act, most of whose provisions it administers and which runs on for over three hundred pages. This act is only one of a number of pieces of specific legislation which the Minister of Transport is required to administer.

In exploring the way in which parliament outlines the job assignments for administrators, one must go beyond the departments to include the non-departmental forms of administrative entity to which an increasing proportion of the government's tasks has been assigned. The infinite variety of these agencies defies any attempt to find a general formula

28 RSC 1952, c.66, s.5.
29 RSC 1970, c.N-9, s.5.

which would embrace them all. Parliament, of course, must approve the preliminary formal decision to depart from the normal departmental form. Having stated in broad outline what the organizational form shall be, parliament then proceeds to declare the purposes and to state the powers and duties of the entity it has created. The legislative assignments to such agencies follow much the same forms as the provisions applying to ordinary departments. However, power in these instances is conferred not on the minister as such but on the board or the executive head of the agency, such powers frequently being exercised in the capacity of 'an agent of Her Majesty.' Again the organic legislation creating these non-departmental agencies varies in the degree of precision with which the powers and duties are specified.

Superficially, a review of the legislation tempts one to the reassuring conclusion that parliament has displayed much energy and resourcefulness in dotting the 'i's' and crossing the 't's' of the powers and duties allocated to ministers, boards, and chief executive officers. But, in fact, there is a mounting concern, obviously not confined to Canada, that parliament's ability to preserve the master-to-servant relationship is by no means adequately ensured through its efforts to delineate powers and duties of ministers (exercised either individually or collectively) by means of legislation. Despite the existence of the five bulky tomes of the *Revised Statutes of Canada* that appear to testify to parliament's legislative productivity, the claim is that such legislation is merely a skeleton – a bare-bones description of the powers and duties of the executive branch. Parliament is declared to be remiss in failing to prescribe more clearly and in greater detail, with the result that its legislation leaves gaps which public servants must fill by applying discretionary powers explicitly or implicitly incorporated in the statutory statements of their duties.

Broad questions concerning the accountability of administrators are raised by this process of delegation, but these must be deferred for the moment. It will be useful, however, to examine several features of the current mode of parliamentary conferral of power which help to account for contemporary criticism and misgivings.[30]

30 Public concern over executive–legislature or executive–citizen relationships has resulted in important official investigations and reports in both Britain and the United States. In Canada the province of Ontario mounted a monumental survey by the Royal (McRuer) Commission Inquiry into Civil Rights; several provinces are experimenting with an ombudsman; while the federal government has waited until 1969 to produce a relatively modest inquiry by a special committee of the House of Commons: see Special Committee on Statutory Instruments, *Third Report* (Ottawa, 1969). In May 1971 a Statutory Instruments Act was finally approved and in March 1972 a joint Committee of the Senate and House of Commons to scrutinize delegated legislation was announced.

First, it is to be observed that, no matter how precisely parliament seeks to define and delimit the powers and duties, in nearly every instance it is compelled to introduce a general clause which authorizes the Governor in Council to assign 'such other duties' to the minister as may be deemed appropriate. It is probable that the ultimate result of such general clauses is not the enlargement of the sum total of executive powers but rather an increased freedom to shuffle or reallocate specific powers and functions among the various executive agencies. It cannot be interpreted to mean that the executive has been given carte blanche to do anything it likes without first seeking parliament's approval – the need to secure the legislature's authorization for new funds to accompany the new functions would, in any event, act as a check on autonomous executive action.

However, when one adds to this general permissive power such a typical broadly worded clause as that found, for instance, in the statute setting out the duties of the minister of the Department of National Resources and Development, one can see how the area of executive discretion is enlarged.[31] Section 7(1) of the act stated: 'the minister may formulate plans for public works ... housing, research, conservation and development of the resources of Canada, and with the authority of the Governor in Council and in co-operation with other departments and agencies provide for carrying out such plans.' Similarly, the Post Office Act and the Veterans Act empower the respective heads of these departments to make regulations embracing a wide range of enumerated subjects.[32] Discretion of a different type is also conferred on a minister or the Governor in Council whenever, under the legislation, regulatory powers affecting individual rights and obligations have to be exercised; in some instances the minister makes 'the final determination' or the appeal may lie to yet another administrative tribunal.[33]

The prevalence of these broad permissive clauses and the consequent discretion accorded to make decisions or to take action, help to explain why, for most acts of parliament, there is an accompanying 'gloss' consisting of rules and regulations that dwarf in volume the legislation under which they are promulgated. Thus it happens that each departmental office retains its composite legal guidebook, a compilation made up of the organic statute that created the department, other statutes which it ad-

31 RSC 1952, c.76.
32 RSC 1970, c. P-14, s. 6 + 7 (Post Office), and RSC 1970, chap. V-1, s.6 (Veterans Affairs).
33 Powers under the Immigration Act (RSC 1952, c.145) are good illustrations of the routing of discretionary judgments through the internal hierarchy to the minister where, until 1967, such decisions were final. With the addition of an Immigration Appeal Board, provided by statute in 1967 (Stats Can. 1966–7, c.90), the appeal moved outside the department but still remained with a tribunal which is not part of the regular judiciary.

ministers, and (much bulkier) all the rules, orders, and regulations bearing on or dependent upon this legislation. If one desires to discover the duties of a government agency and how it goes about performing them, reference to the basic legislation must be supplemented by a careful inspection of this so-called subordinate legislation, that is, the decrees made by the executive but possessing none the less the force of statutory enactments. And, if we would seek to understand the way in which the powers are being used, we should have to consult the many regulations or orders which reflect the specific application by the political executive of the general powers conferred on them.

Parliament has an interest in and indeed a duty of ensuring that ministers and their officials do not go beyond the powers and duties assigned to them. But, in the broad phraseology in which characteristically contemporary legislation is phrased, parliament would find difficulty in ascertaining when, in fact, the legal boundaries it has imposed have been violated.[34] Much will then depend on the vigilance of the courts in seizing on particular instances where there is an alleged trespass by public servants. And, once again, if the statutes to which the courts must refer in making judgments are so vaguely or loosely worded or when they may even specifically exclude judicial review, the courts' task becomes correspondingly more difficult.[35]

It would require a separate volume to explore this problem in greater detail, but, for the moment, enough has been said to conclude that the conferral of power and duties on departments and other public agencies must today be done in such loose terms that there is a wide and hazy legal penumbra surrounding administrative action in which the executive enjoys substantial latitude to apply, extend, or contract its functions. Admittedly, it exercises this discretion on sufferance of the legally sovereign legislature, but the means available to the legislature for reviewing the use of discretionary powers or the decisions of public servants leave much to be desired.

A second relevant point of general significance is that the powers and

34 Such adjectives as 'just,' 'safe,' 'reasonable,' 'fair,' 'fit and proper,' which characterize the statutory guidelines for administrators in making determinations, reveal the loose fit of the legal clothing.
35 The law courts tend to interpose at points where questions of law rather than of fact are at issue, or where there has been a denial of 'natural justice.' In practice, questions of fact and of law tend to intertwine and, even where a statute specifically declares the decision of an administrative tribunal to be final and not reviewable (the so-called 'privative clause'), the courts have often managed to assume jurisdiction. For a thoughtful review of some of these issues, see the symposium 'Appeals against Administrative Decisions' in *Canadian Public Administration* 5 (March 1962), p. 46 ff. See also the useful booklet *Judicial Review of Decisions of Labour Relations Boards in Canada*, by Jan K. Wanczyak, for the Legislation Branch, Department of Labour (Ottawa, 1969).

duties set out in various parliamentary enactments are, in the main, conferred not on the department as such but on the individual minister or on the ministers in their collective capacity – that is to say, acting as the 'Governor in Council.' For reasons that have been suggested in the previous chapter, the Canadian parliament has preferred to entrust powers to the Governor in Council rather than to individual ministers. In this respect, Canadian practice has tended to diverge from its origins in Britain, where parliament has more frequently conferred powers on the individual minister. Clearly, this legal requirement is the outcome of invoking the constitutional doctrine of ministerial responsibility to parliament – whether in an individual or a collective capacity. It is not the department or the subordinate official in it who is responsible to parliament, it is the ministerial head and the cabinet as a whole.

There are exceptions to this generalization which must be immediately identified. The least important of these are the occasions – usually when powers of a judicial nature are being conferred – where the legislation specifically assigns powers and duties to particular public servants well down in the hierarchy: where, for example, a customs officer or a fisheries overseer is granted powers to enter, search, and seize or to take evidence on oath.[36] More important are the exceptions which derive from the resort to non-departmental forms of administration and where, in effect, the minister may be bypassed in good measure by the direct legislative conferral of power on a board, a statutory executive, or a regulatory tribunal. The significance of this method of conferring administrative power can best be explored by reverting to the doctrine of ministerial responsibility.

Preservation of the doctrine has two important advantages. For the representatives of the general public assembled in parliament it provides a clear-cut means of focusing responsibility on one person or a small group of persons, rather than attempting the impossible task of identifying within the ranks of the public service the responsible person or persons. The complicated process by which decisions get made and actions are taken would, for all practical purposes, make it virtually impossible to establish the identity of the alleged culprits. Second, as already noted, there is an important advantage to the member of the public service in maintaining the doctrine of ministerial responsibility, for if he could not shelter behind a minister or the cabinet he would be forced 'into the open' where he would be compelled to defend his actions and in the process lose the political neutrality and anonymity upon which his claims to per-

36 RSC 1970, chap. F-14, ss. 35–42 (Fisheries), and RSC 1970, chap. C-40, s.132 and subsequent sections (Customs).

manency in office largely depend. In short, the doctrine enables responsibility to be brought to a focus and at the same time ensures permanency and continuity of administration in the face of the transfer of political power which is implicit in any scheme of elective party government.

Nevertheless, ministerial responsibility viewed in the context of contemporary large-scale bureaucracy is seen to be a convenient legal fiction. Few, if any, ministers placed in charge of a large department could honestly profess to know everything about the actions taken by thousands of subordinates – quite probably scattered from St John's to Victoria or Inuvik. The legal requirements may compel the minister and cabinet to pretend otherwise, and the opposition in parliament will certainly insist on their adhering to the letter of the law; but, in practical terms, it can readily be seen that the burden is an impossible one to carry and that the functions, duties, and powers ostensibly vested in the minister or cabinet have to be devolved on subordinates.[37]

The Interpretation Act[38] recognizes this problem in part by stating that 'words directing or empowering a Minister of the Crown to do any act or thing ... include ... his ... deputy.' But, curiously, only the statute that set up the Department of Defence Production went out of its way to face practical administrative reality. Section 5 of this act stated that 'the minister may authorize any person, on his behalf and under his control and direction, to do any act or thing or to exercise any power that the minister may do or exercise under this Act.'[39] But, what this single act states so explicitly must be read implicitly into all other acts, and, where the minister is given 'the management and direction of the department' one must perforce mentally add some such phrase as 'or any person authorized to do these things under his control and direction.' That picture of the secretary of the Department of Transport legally required to answer all the correspondence of his department conjures up no more ludicrous visions of a bygone age than does the effort to imagine (say) the Minister of Health and Welfare personally carrying out research, inspecting immigrants, routing out drug addicts, or looking after thousands of civil servants in health centres (to take a sample from a literal reading of his many duties).

The conflict between the legal necessity of conferring powers and duties on one man and the practical impossibility of his being able to execute them obviously has to be resolved if administration is not to be brought to a full stop. The solution is to devolve the minister's assigned tasks on

37 For the British tradition, see Henry Parris, *Constitutional Bureaucracy* (London, 1969), chaps. 7 and 10.
38 Stats Can. 1967–8, c.7, s.23(2).
39 RSC 1952, c.62, s.5.

to subordinates in such a way that they will be constantly held accountable to the superior political officer and through him to the cabinet and to parliament for the way in which they use the powers or execute the functions. The organizational requirements for this sort of devolution cannot be stated by parliament, nor does it seek to proffer much guidance to the executive in achieving such organization. The details have to be worked out by the public service itself (as the previous section has suggested) and, by and large, departments have assumed a similar organizational shape moulded to the common necessity for devolution: they take on a pyramidal form, broad at the base and rapidly dwindling to a narrow apex with the political head at the top. This so-called hierarchical pattern, with its set levels of duties and delegated authority, is the almost universal method devised for resolving the problems of devolution.[40] The refinements and administrative implications of hierarchical organization are more properly dealt with in a later chapter. Here, it is sufficient to note only its close association with the doctrine of ministerial responsibility and the potentially divisive influence it may have on the attempt to confer and concentrate legal powers and duties on a single man or a single body of men assembled in a cabinet.

The pressure on the doctrine of ministerial responsibility comes not only from the practical difficulties of making one person responsible for the multifarious activities of a modern department; it also stems from the increasing reliance on non-departmental forms of administrative agencies. Immediately, we confront a paradox. On the one hand, all of these agencies must be viwed as parts of the public service in its broadest definition. As such, they cannot be relegated to a constitutional limbo of irresponsibility. On the other hand, many of them operate by virtue of a direct statutory grant of powers which, in whole or in part, bypasses the normal ministerial chain of command. In one way or another such agencies must be brought into this legal chain of command that culminates in the minister or cabinet and parliament. The Audit Office, whose head (the Auditor General) is in a very special sense a servant of parliament, is possibly the only agency that can properly and logically claim exemption from these arrangements. But with all others the character and closeness of the ministerial or cabinet connection varies widely. The conventional

40 Devolution can also be achieved by invoking the federal principle of zoning out duties to constitutionally separate and independent entities. Within any one legally separate level of government devolution is also achieved by assigning tasks to a corporation, board, or commission legally established in quasi-independence from the regular departments. Both of these solutions weaken or complicate the lines of accountability which can be more clearly maintained by the hierarchical pattern. Later chapters go into this problem at some length.

executive connection is normally preserved by leaving the power to appoint and dismiss the members of the governing body in the hands of a minister or, more commonly, the Governor in Council.[41] Equally universal is the obligation to report annually through a specified minister to parliament. Beyond these common requirements, the extent of these agencies' attachment to the political executive ranges from virtual isolated independence to a status that is indistinguishable from that of a regular branch of a department.

The permutations and combinations of these organizational relationships will require detailed consideration in a later chapter. Here, we are concerned with the consequence of a failure to resolve a paradox in which the desire to achieve independence from the normal department cannot be permitted to override the basic need to preserve accountability. Our legislative draftsmen have obviously been unable to find a single satisfactory formula; nor is this surprising, given the great difficulty of any attempt to type or categorize the varied agencies that exist. The law courts are in a similar predicament in trying to determine in specific cases what manner of administrative species they are dealing with: and, in the event, have developed parallel lines of interpretation which enable them to claim departmental status for them one day and autonomous status on the next occasion.[42] Similarly, when members of parliament seek information or an accounting from one or other of these bodies they may either procure it without reservation or be told that the agency, being independent of politics, cannot and should not be compelled to provide

41 Exceptions to the normal procedure for dismissal are most often found where agencies have a judicial role. For example, the members of the Public Service Staff Relations Board are removable by the Governor in Council 'for cause' at any time, but the chairman and vice-chairman hold offices during pleasure for a period not exceeding ten years and are removable only upon address of the Senate and the House of Commons. Stats Can. 1966–7, c.72, s.11.
   The nature of tenure 'at pleasure' of the Crown was interestingly developed by R.B. Bennett at the time when a bill to form the Department of Mines and Resources was introduced (*Can. H. of C. Debates,* 1936, p. 3540 ff). Mr Bennett found the prerogative right of the Crown to dismiss at any time was in conflict with contractual rights he asserted were granted in provisions for superannuation. This argument was strengthened in 1953 when, in fact, the superannuation act for civil servants was drastically amended, as D.C. Abbott (then minister of finance) pointed out, to ensure 'that in future the benefits under the plan will be a matter of right rather than a matter of grace. Hitherto all payments of superannuation and related benefits have, as a matter of law, been grants by the governor in council – rewards for good and faithful service. Even pensions to widows under the present Law are dependent upon their "worthiness to receive them"' (*Debates,* 1953, p. 3727).
42 For futher elaboration of the court's ambivalence, see my 'The Public Corporation in Canada,' in *Government Enterprise: A Comparative Study,* ed. W. Friedmann and J.F. Garner (London, 1970), p. 212 ff.

the answers. Small wonder, then, that parliament alternates between confusion and irritation in seeking to deal with this growing flock of administrative variants which, in fact, parliament through legislation has itself brought into being.

This section has traversed rather generally what is obviously a most difficult terrain, filled with legal pitfalls at every step and raising issues which, for the moment at least, have been laid aside for fuller development in later chapters. Though generalization is difficult where so many exceptions make their own rules, several conclusions may be drawn together at this point:

1 Parliament is the ultimate repository of the power to assign duties and functions.

2 Parliament, itself, is obviously incapable of exercising these powers or performing the duties.

3 Thus, powers and duties in the case of departments are statutorily conferred on the minister, the Governor in Council, or occasionally on specified categories of subordinates; in the case of non-departmental agencies the assignment is directly to the governing board or the chief executive officer, but all such powers are normally hedged by limitations of varying degrees of severity implicit in powers still reserved to the minister or the Governor in Council.

4 In all cases the statutory conferral of powers is seldom able to cope with all eventualities and must be either stated in broad terms or include general permissive powers which leave substantial freedom for the exercise of executive discretion. This discretion is always subject in theory if not always in practice to the ultimate sovereign capacity of parliament to rescind or amend the permissive legislation.

5 The way in which parliament is compelled to assign powers and duties and the extensive reliance on non-departmental administrative entities place great strain on the constitutional doctrine of ministerial responsibility – a doctrine that has historically been viewed as essential both to the preservation of executive accountability and the neutrality and permanence of public servants.

6 The conferral of powers and duties by parliament to a minister or a board necessitates yet a further redistribution of authority and operating responsibility within each agency. To this end and in order to preserve ultimate accountability, the familiar hierarchical arrangement of offices has evolved. In the process parliament, as the originator of the allocation, tends to become more and more remote from the points at which action

is taken, and the problem for the minister of accepting responsibility becomes much more difficult to solve.

THE LEGAL RESIDENCE OF MANAGERIAL AUTHORITY

Thus far the analysis of the legal bases of public administration has disclosed an interesting dichotomy between the acknowledged formal sovereign power of parliament and the necessities of administrative life which effectively place the politically responsible executive branch in a commanding position. This dichotomy is more pronounced when we extend the inquiry into the field of management. It has already been observed that the British North America Act explicitly acknowledges the sovereign claims of parliament by repeatedly using the words 'until the Parliament of Canada otherwise provides.' Thus, we must assume that the exercise of managerial powers over the public service is, like all substantive functions of the executive, a matter for parliamentary determination. It would be entirely within parliament's right to retract the powers which it now vests in individual ministers to have 'the management and direction of the department.' That is to say, what parliament has the power to do by statute it can readily undo by the same means. Moreover, it is parliament that determines who shall be a civil servant by inserting definitions in the Public Service Employment Act or the Superannuation Act and by providing in all departmental legislation that the employees shall be appointed in the manner provided by law, that is, in accordance with the terms of the Public Service Employment Act.

But the question of the legal status of a management function cannot be dismissed by a simple reference to the sovereign claims of parliament. If we examine the actual status of a public servant it soon becomes apparent that for all practical purposes he is not a servant of parliament but a servant of the executive. His appointment to office is not a legislative decision; the classification of the office to which he is appointed is a matter for executive determination, as would be the pay scales attached to the office; promotion, transfer, and reclassification fall outside parliament's purview, and, indeed, political lobbying or the use of parliament as a court of appeal on these managerial decisions is expressly prohibited; decisions affecting a public servant's tenure are taken by means of grievance or appeal procedures that are created by the executive. Finally, in the performance of his functions, the public servant is responsible through the hierarchy to his minister. In most instances it is the minister to whom these powers have been explicitly delegated by statute – obliged by the doctrine of ministerial responsibility to account personally to parliament for his own and his subordinates' actions.

In practical day-to-day terms, however, the most critical issue arising in the field of management is not so much the ambiguity and possible duality of a public servant's relations with his minister on the one hand and sovereign parliament on the other; rather, the problems emerge from the division of the management powers within the public service. Admittedly, this division can be partly attributed to parliament's own reluctance to sign over all responsibilities in this field to the executive branch: allocation to several executive agencies may be regarded as a reflection of parliament's uncertainty about its own status vis-à-vis the management of the public service. It may also reflect the executive's uncertainty about its own capacity to monopolize the management functions in a system of fused powers which nevertheless still carries within it the tensions of old battles between the executive and the legislature. But, in any event, the consequences are that the lines of managerial control have been badly crossed up and controls compounded.

While specific statutes assign the management and direction of a department to the minister and in turn by reference to the Interpretation Act to his 'lawful deputy,' in the Public Service Employment Act and the Financial Administration Act parliament has expressly authorized competing agencies to countermand its original intentions. Appointment, promotion, and transfer, and release from employment for incompetence, are formally in the hands of the Public Service Commission. The cabinet and its key 'management committee,' the Treasury Board, have the final word on each department's 'establishment' – that is to say, can determine the number to be employed in each category. The same body assumes authority for disciplinary dismissals, particular terms of individual pension awards, and, indeed, all salary questions and other terms and conditions of employment.

In short, the executive's need to provide central control and co-ordinating devices for management purposes has been reinforced by parliament's desire to have central supervisory control agencies of its own that exist in part to play a watch-dog role. Thus management and directing functions originally conferred on individual ministerial heads have been supplemented or supplanted by overriding powers assigned to central control agencies, primarily located in the Treasury Board. And parliament has sought guarantees for its own historical interest in an honest and efficient public service by creating such bodies as the Public Service Commission and the office of the Auditor General. One important consequence of this arrangement is that it has confused the status of the Public

Service Commission. On the one hand parliament views the commission in a very special sense as its own agency – an agency that has emerged as the result of 'the self-denying ordinance' by which members of parliament gave over their patronage to an independent body which could handle appointments and promotions in an objective, non-partisan fashion. Thus, for example, we find John Diefenbaker, then prime minister, telling the Civil Service Association in 1958 that: 'The Commission is not an arm of the government to which ministers can give direction. It derives its power and basic instructions from Parliament.'[43] In so far as parliament through the Public Service Employment Act has conferred specific statutory powers on the commission, this statement is of course true. But the problem is that parliament has also devolved other managerial powers onto the Governor in Council, powers which in practice are exercised by the Treasury Board.[44] In effect, the sharing out of these management powers has placed the Public Service Commission in an awkward position in which the implementation of decisions which it has the unquestioned legal right to take can be effectively countermanded or modified by the Treasury Board exercising its equally legitimate power to regulate public expenditures.

At least two important recent developments have accentuated the awkwardness of this duality of managerial control agencies, adding fresh heat and little additional light to the recurrent controversy. The inauguration in 1957 of a Pay Research Bureau, located in the Civil Service Commission, illustrates one aspect of the problem. The bureau, until 1967, was advisory to the commission and acted in a staff capacity in helping the commission to develop recommendations on salary revisions. But what of the report of the commission based on the bureau's findings? Is it made to parliament or to the executive – specifically the Treasury Board? Accepting Mr Diefenbaker's view, as most parliamentarians do, it would seem logical that the report be made directly to parliament. But the executive has taken the position that the report is not for the public but for its other managerial arm – the Treasury Board and the Minister of Finance – and these are the agencies that can disregard or modify the commission's report and make the final pay determination.[45]

43 Quoted by R.A. Bell in *Can. H. of C. Debates*, 1960, p. 3149.
44 It should be noted that the lines of authority are made even more complex by the power of both the Public Service Commission and the Treasury Board to delegate certain of their powers to the deputy minister – not, be it noted, to the minister – of a department, although under his own departmental act the minister is given the 'management and direction' of his department.
45 See below, chaps. 11 and 12. A heated debate on this issue occurred in July 1959. See *Can. H. of C. Debates*, 1959, especially comments of the Minister of Finance at p. 5704 f.

This managerial ambivalence is sharply delineated by a second controversy. Civil service associations, as we shall see later, have successfully pressed for the acceptance of collective bargaining and arbitration. The question is immediately raised: who represents the 'employer' in the event these rights are acknowledged? Should it be the Civil Service Commission or the Treasury Board? If it is the commission, does not this open identification with the executive completely countermand its traditional role as the impartial agency of parliament, capable of performing its statutory responsibilities for vetting appointments and promotions, hearing appeals, and so on, only because it is independent of the executive? Thus the awkward circle is completed: if parliament insists on viewing the commission as its 'own' agency for managing the civil service, how can that agency perform the task without getting involved as part of the executive branch and losing its capacity to act independently on behalf of parliament?

These problems are mentioned at this point merely to illustrate the practical difficulties that can arise because of a failure to resolve the theoretical or constitutional issue. As long as parliament claims the Public Service Commission as its 'own' agency and the executive claims to be the ultimate 'employer' of a public servant, the dual management arrangement will persist.[46] And as long as dual management exists there can never be a clear-cut resolution of such practical issues as pay determination, collective bargaining, and arbitration. In later chapters we shall see how major legislative changes made in 1967 have attempted to resolve these ambiguities.

Attention in this section has focused on the legal basis for the management function in the public service. We have not found a clear or definitive answer because of the apparently legitimate but dual claims made by parliament and the executive over the public service. For all practical purposes, few civil servants are likely to look upon themselves as 'employees of parliament'; nor, indeed, would they consider themselves to be employees of the Public Service Commission or the Treasury Board, simply because these agencies have the formal last word on their appoint-

---

46 One of the best discussions that disclosed the general dichotomy between legislative claims to pre-eminence and executive claims to independent prerogative authority – qualified only by the ability of the executive to retain its political support in the legislature – is to be found in the exchange, mainly between J.L. Ilsley and John Bracken, in the House of Commons in 1945 (*Debates*, pp. 1689 ff.). For a review of the arguments, see my 'Parliament and the Powers of the Cabinet,' *Queen's Quarterly* 52 (Winter 1945–6), pp. 465–77.

ment and terms of service. It is much more likely that they deem themselves to be employees of the government of Canada. If it makes sense to view the public service as a single entity, encouraging free transfer between the various administrative units into which it must be divided as a practical expedient, then the concept of a public servant as a servant of the government of Canada is obviously the most appropriate designation. But to be meaningful, one must find some way of determining a central focus among the many elements that make up the government of Canada for the management function – and this is where we come up against the perplexing legal ambiguities that have been built into the system. It is likely that the constitutional fusion of an executive branch with the legislative branch (to which the former is responsible) has concealed the fundamental ambivalence to which attention has been here directed. A tension (and even hostility) that was quite overt in days when colonial governors struggled with local legislatures for control of the public service has over the intervening years been ameliorated but not eliminated by an overlay of competing control agencies, each sharing an ambivalent relationship to its parent body. Recognition that there is such a legal ambivalence in the system is the first necessary step which it has been the purpose of this section to develop. The means by which, in recent years, the administrative problems created by this duality have been sorted out will be examined in later chapters.

PART TWO

Design for Operations

If it is desired to know more about how and why [an organism] does these things, it will help to know more about the parts which go to make up the machine ... When we look around us and see the vast variety of things which we are willing to accept as living organisms, the thing which almost invariably impresses us is their diversity of form and activity ... Living organisms are discrete from their environment ... They are forced to make exchange of materials with the environment but manage to maintain enough control over the exchange so as to retain their structure and composition. They metabolize, *i.e.*, burn or degrade some materials to obtain energy for growth, activity and repair of the living machinery. They reproduce themselves in kind, co-ordinate the activities of their various parts and manage to adjust to the nature of and changes in their environment.

'Physiology,' *Encyclopædia Britannica*

CHAPTER FIVE

Allocation of programmes: the departmental rubric

The organization of the Canadian public service has responded to special environmental pressures, and even at a very early stage these were sufficient to require the adoption of programmes too numerous and too complex to be performed by a single agency. The allocation of programmes to appropriate agencies, therefore, has been and is an organizational matter of the first importance.

The adoption of the federal system in Canada afforded the initial means of effecting this necessary subdivision: the responsibilities for each province and the central government were set out in considerable detail in the British North America Act. This method of allocating fields of responsibility obviously eases the burden on the several partners in the enterprise, but it is not without difficulties and defects. In the first place, no matter how detailed and specific the enumerated powers granted to each authority, the list can never be exhaustive, even for the day and age in which it was written, let alone anticipating all subsequent changes in a nation's responsibilities. In addition, the lines separating the two jurisdictions can seldom be drawn with such precision that the overlapping of interests and responsibilities will be completely avoided. And, in the event that changes in the original allocation of duties are required, resort must be had to cumbersome amending procedures or prolonged diplomatic negotiations to obtain agreement on administrative *modi vivendi* designed to overcome jurisdictional problems. Finally, where the respective authorities trespass on the other's preserves, the dispute has to be resolved by formal intervention of the courts.

The present study is concerned primarily with the national system of administration and the problem of allocating programmes *within* one level of government rather than these quite different, though vitally important, problems of assigning duties *between* two independent levels of government. It is sufficient, for present purposes, merely to take note of this method of effecting primary programme allocation through the application of the federal principle and to realize the rather special order of issues to which it gives rise.

Like most other countries Canada, at the national level, early settled on a departmental form as the most logical device for compartmentalizing the various programmes to be undertaken by the public service. For reasons that have been previously explained, the political conventions associated with cabinet-building set a limit on the number of such administrative compartments. The business of government at first could quite easily be absorbed by the available portfolios and their elastic sides were subsequently stretched to take in a vast number of new programmes. But the constant expansion of governmental responsibilities ultimately proved too much for the departmental containers and recent years have witnessed the proliferation of various non-departmental administrative entities which today stand in an uneasy and sometimes ambiguous relationship to the conventional departmental forms.

A mere skeleton description of the current roster of such departments and agencies requires a book in itself. Fortunately, such a compilation already exists under the title *Organization of the Government of Canada*,[1] which is maintained in loose-leaf to keep pace with rapid organizational change; no useful purpose would be served by attempting to condense this material here, but the interested student will find it a helpful guide for any tour of the public service. This chapter is confined to describing the ways in which the original departmental portfolios have been adjusted to accommodate expanding and changing functions of government. The following chapter seeks to discover what, if any, guiding principles underlie the allocation of government business to departments, while a subsequent chapter attempts to find order and reason in the mélange of deviations from the departmental norm by which major programmes have been allocated.

Turning, then, to the prime organizational form – the department – we face an immediate question: 'what constitutes a department?' The concept of a 'department' is imprecise because any administrative unit can be so designated by parliament or, for certain purposes, be so declared by the Governor in Council.

Two general acts illustrate the legal flexibility of the organizational

1 (Ottawa, 1966).

concept. The Financial Administration Act[2] declares that 'department' means: (*a*) any of the departments named in Schedule A (a list of twenty-nine administrative entities); (*b*) any other division or branch of the public service of Canada, including a commission appointed under the Inquiries Act, designated by the Governor in Council as a department for the purposes of this act; (*c*) the staffs of the Senate, the House of Commons, and the Library of Parliament; and (*d*) any corporation named in Schedule B (a list of fourteen 'departmental corporations'). The Public Service Employment Act of 1967[3] is no less liberal in its definition: 'department' means any body so 'named in Schedule A to the Financial Administration Act and any division or branch of the public service designated by the Governor in Council as a department for the purposes of this Act.'

These definitions have a specific purpose: each is designed to declare what portions of the public service organization shall be subjected to a particular regimen of financial or personnel controls. Neither is particularly helpful in establishing the criteria to be applied in determining when an administrative entity qualifies as a 'department' or what basis should be used for aggregating work units that make up a department.

In the following analysis, for the sake of clarity, an arbitrary definition will be used: a 'department' is an administrative unit comprising one or more organizational components over which a minister has direct management and control. This definition restricts our terms of reference to major ministerial portfolios and thereby excludes subordinate units such as Insurance and Public Printing and Stationery that in law actually carry the title 'department.' Since we are also concerned with the ways in which programmes are allocated to these units, we can disregard cabinet portfolios to which no duties are assigned: thus the customary minister without portfolio will be excluded from the list. With these excisions there were, as of 1970, twenty-four working departments among which the business of the federal government was divided. One hundred years ago just over one-half this number was more than ample to embrace the functions of central government and, it should be noted, with a total staff somewhat less than one-one-hundredth of the modern civil service.[4]

A coherent description of programme allocation can best be achieved by adopting broad functional categories for the basic responsibilities of

2 RSC 1970, chap. F-10.
3 Stats Can. 1966–7, c.71.
4 See *Pioneer Public Service* (Toronto, 1955), p. 36, where a total at Confederation of 2660 civil servants has been compiled from detailed and not always consistent figures. Against this number is the contemporary total of well over 225,000 civil servants, not counting those employed in crown corporations, etc.

government. Viewed in the abstract, there are certain duties which are common to nearly all governments; others may be a response to the peculiar needs and expectations of one particular community. In the former category we would include:

1 Public security and external relations
2 Public works, communications, and transportation
3 Co-ordination and services for the public organization

Responsibilities that are more peculiarly a response to conditions in Canada would be embraced under two further headings:

4 Conservation, development, and promotion of physical resources
5 Protection and development of human resources

The first two categories are equivalent to Adam Smith's triumvirate of functions which even as an exponent of laissez-faire he thought properly belonged to the state. The third category includes organizations whose primary tasks relate to co-ordinating and servicing the needs of the other operating departments with so-called 'line' responsibilities, although their jurisdiction often extends to include as well substantive programmes of the government. The contemporary roster of Canadian departments has representatives in all five categories. But even a century earlier the original departmental structure comprehended the same duties, some of course only in embryonic form. Using these five categories, the history of expansion and adaptation of structure to function can be briefly outlined.[5]

PUBLIC SECURITY AND EXTERNAL RELATIONS

Public security includes both internal order and external defence, and two of the original departments – Justice and Militia and Defence – were concerned with these areas of governmental responsibility. The fact that Canada in 1867 was still a colonial dependent of Great Britain so far as her external relations and most of her defence arrangements were concerned meant that Canadian responsibilities related primarily to the maintenance of internal order. Even in this sector the local protective and judicial authority conferred on the provinces tended to limit the role of a central government. Federal penitentiaries, placed under the Minister of Justice in 1867, and a special federal police force, the North West Mounted Police, created in 1873 (with a jurisdiction originally confined

5 A visual synopsis of the evolution of the departmental system is provided in the charts at the end of this chapter. Much of the detail in this chapter has been compiled from departmental reports and statutes, but in order to avoid a clutter of footnotes specific citations have been restricted.

to federally owned territory) were the main operative instruments in this category.

The gradual emergence of Canada as an independent nation necessitated the creation of a Department of External Affairs in 1909. But for three years it was treated as an adjunct to the Department of the Secretary of State, and from 1912 to 1946 was a portfolio held by the prime minister himself. The full flowering of Canada's external responsibilities did not receive complete organizational recognition until External Affairs received a minister of its own in 1946.

Similarly, Canada made slow progress in developing its own independent status as a military power. For many years it had to concern itself only with the organization of a militia force for operations on land. In 1910 the Laurier government's decision to create an independent naval force necessitated the formation of a Department of Naval Service – though the new unit was regarded as part of another department under the Minister of Marine and Fisheries. The introduction of aircraft called for a third organizational response at the close of the First World War, but in this instance an Air Board was set up rather than a special department. In 1922 all three service arms were integrated under one department and one Minister of National Defence, with each of the hitherto separated agencies tending to be run as autonomous units. The pressure of the Second World War necessitated a substantial organizational expansion, with once again separate ministers for each service, a new but temporary Ministry of National War Service (1940–8), and a Department of Munitions and Supply, which was successively renamed the Department of Reconstruction, the Department of Reconstruction and Supply, and, in part, persisted in the Department of Defence Production until it was transformed in 1968–9 into the Department of Supply and Services. The Department of National Defence in peacetime has not only reverted to its single ministerial head but has been actively involved in an extensive integration of the three historically separate service branches.

In sum, Canada's originally limited responsibilities for police, protective, and external services were met at the outset by allocating them to two departments. The Department of Justice supervised the judiciary and housed as well the federal police force – now the Royal Canadian Mounted Police – and the federal penitentiaries, until 1965–6 when both were made reporting responsibilities of the Solicitor General. The more significant responsibilities of the Department of Justice, however, developed along lines that entitle it to be placed in the third category discussed below. Meanwhile, evolution to a self-governing dominion ultimately transformed a modest Militia Department into today's integrated giant Department of National Defence. The same change in international status necessitated the addition of a third department to this group, the Department of External Affairs, which, after brief incubation in the Secretary of State's Department and a long period of personal control by the prime minister, matured into adulthood at the close of the Second World War.

PUBLIC WORKS, COMMUNICATIONS, AND TRANSPORTATION

The second category of essential government functions was obviously of particular importance in 1867 to an expanding nation which had to rely on government capital for the costly programmes involved. The Post Office Department and the Department of Public Works are the most obvious candidates for inclusion in this category, and they have remained permanent fixtures on the departmental roster from Confederation to the present. Transportation was, at the outset, primarily the responsibility of the Department of Public Works, but the boom in railway construction forced the creation of a separate department in 1879 which also took over the related transportation media of canals. The Department of Railways and Canals was able to preserve its title as a meaningful description of its major areas of concern until 1936. The advent of a new means of communication, the automobile, left only a temporary mark on this department between 1919 and 1928 in the form of a Highways Branch; in the main it was the provincial administrations that were called upon to bear the brunt of problems associated with this new mode of transportation. But by 1936 the declining significance of canals as a means of communication and the rapid emergence of civil aviation necessitated a reconstitution of the federal department and a change to the more comprehensive title, Department of Transport.

Superficially, there would appear to have been surprisingly few organizational changes since Confederation in the departmental portfolios involved with this second segment of government activity: the Post Office and Public Works existed from the beginning, and transportation earned its own separate department in 1879. This apparent stability is deceptive, for it conceals two dynamic factors: this area of state activity has witnessed perhaps the heaviest reliance on non-departmental forms, for reasons that will be examined in a later chapter; and, apart from the Post Office, there has been much shifting of various portions of these programmes reflecting an uncertainty about the appropriateness of the principles applied to allocating programes in these areas. Once Public Works had relinquished control of programmes concerned with transportation to the Department of Railways and Canals, this raised the prospect of confining its role to that of a glorified housekeeper for the government itself. Thus, Public

Works, like Justice, must make its second appearance in the third category, to which we now turn.

CO-ORDINATION AND SERVICES FOR THE PUBLIC ORGANIZATION

Under this heading several functions are merged, ranging from central recording and registering of government decisions, through special co-ordinating and planning tasks, to financial provisioning and other special services for all departments. This series of functions is difficult to associate with specific departmental portfolios, particularly in considering the early days of the public service when each department tended to be a law unto itself and where the cabinet was expected to provide all necessary co-ordination on a collegial basis.

The central registration and recording of government decisions has traditionally fallen within the purview of the Privy Council Office. Indeed, for most of its existence it has been little more than a central record office for decisions taken by the Governor in Council. The registry function still persists, but since the Second World War the inauguration of a cabinet Secretariat headed by the clerk of the Privy Council has transformed this office into an instrument of service and co-ordination, not only for the whole cabinet but for the many committees of cabinet that now exist. Moreover, in recent years the office has been further enlarged to undertake special assignments that could best be described as a modest planning operation in selected areas.

The expanded role of the Privy Council Office is reflected in the altered status of its ministerial head, the President of the Privy Council. From Confederation, the president was virtually in the position of a minister without portfolio. Gradually it became the convention – though not always invariably followed in practice – that the prime minister would assume the position. However, in recent years the presidency has been assigned as a distinctive portfolio to a separate minister and the incumbent chosen in 1968 was assigned such specific planning tasks as parliamentary procedural reform; investigation of the possibilities of strengthening parliament, its committees, and the opposition by providing research assistants; and reform of legislation dealing with electoral campaign expenditures.[6]

6 See Fred Schindeler and C. Michael Lanphier, 'Social Science Research and Participatory Democracy in Canada,' *Canadian Public Administration* 12 (Winter 1969), p. 491 ff., for Prime Minister Pierre Trudeau's reorganization of the Privy Council Office showing clearly the accretion of new functions. It should be noted that, despite the separate portfolio of President of the Privy Council, the prime minister is depicted as being the responsible minister.

The current efforts to strengthen the personal staff services of the prime minister has led to the segregation of these functions in an up-graded Prime Minister's Office.

The other department vested at the outset with a rather different set of central responsibilities for recording, registering, and state correspondence was the Department of the Secretary of State. The fact that the Great Seal of Canada (which must be imprinted on many important state documents) was placed in the custody of the Secretary of State made the department a natural centre for registering and recording vital decisions concerned with such matters as land patents, chartering of companies, and the like. The department also provided a central clearance point for assembling the departmental answers to questions raised by members of parliament.[7] These were responsibilities that existed at the time of Confederation and persisted until the reorganization in 1966 which deprived the Secretary of State of his second title, Registrar General, by creating a separate portfolio for the latter – in 1967 to be absorbed into the Department of Consumer and Corporate Affairs.[8]

The Secretary of State's Department was also made responsible in 1867 for conducting all the correspondence between the new central government and the provinces, through the federally appointed lieutenant governors. It is interesting to observe that this duty was expected to become so burdensome that, following the practice of other 'colonial powers,' the national government actually created a short-lived Department of Secretary of State for the Provinces to take over this function, along with certain operating programmes that had also been placed in the Secretary of State's Department and which were expected to generate substantial correspondence with the provinces – notably Indian Affairs and the Geological Survey. The formality of this arrangement probably reflects the view then

7 This last responsibility was transferred to the Privy Council Office in 1968.
8 The Government Organization Act (Stats Can. 1966, c.25), transferred to the separate portfolio of Registrar General not only custody of the Great Seal but also combines, mergers, monopolies; patents, copyrights, and trade marks; bankruptcy, insolvency, and corporate affairs; and custodianship of enemy property. This arrangement set the stage for the conversion of the Registrar General into the Department of Consumer and Corporate Affairs in December 1967, adding a new consumers affairs branch and by subsequent order in council transfer (PC 1968–1297) of the standards branch and gas, electricity inspection, trade marks and labelling, etc. from the Department of Trade and Commerce and from Fisheries the retail inspection service; from Agriculture its general services division of the Production and Marketing Branch. With this assemblage of functions the Department of Consumer and Corporate Affairs in large measure should be removed from this third category to the fifth functional category of departments concerned with conservation and protection of human resources.

current that the lieutenant governors were virtually proconsuls of the new 'imperial' power in Ottawa, a view that rapidly disappeared as improved communications and transportation made it possible to establish direct correspondence between headquarters and an expanding field service of federal officials. In any event, the new department was abandoned after three years and its operating responsibilities transferred to other agencies.

Apart from these two departments that have continuously performed the functions of record and registry offices since Confederation, there were two others in the original list that, in increasing measure, have acted as co-ordinating centres: the Department of Finance and the Department of Justice. The former has become essentially a policy rather than an operating department. Through its minister's pre-eminent position on the committee of the cabinet concerned with assembling the financial needs of all departments, it evolved as the centre for co-ordinating total governmental programmes. This position of pre-eminence was acknowledged by conferring on one of its branches the duty of providing secretarial and staff services for the management committee of cabinet known as the Treasury Board; while another major division, from 1932 onwards under the Comptroller of the Treasury, was vested with significant co-ordinating, servicing, and controlling powers in the field of accounting and pre-audit. The Royal Commission on Government Organization, reporting in 1962, recommended important changes that were subsequently adopted. Formal recognition of the significance of the central managerial co-ordinating role traditionally embraced within the Department of Finance was given by the decision to create a new portfolio, President of the Treasury Board. The decision was made in 1963 and was statutorily confirmed in 1966. Over the same period, again in response to the royal commission's criticisms of the Office of the Comptroller of the Treasury, steps were taken to devolve some of that office's functions to other departments and shifting the comptroller in 1969 to be one of two deputy ministers in a new Department of Supply and Services.[9]

9 The complex stages in the creation of ministerial status for the Treasury Board are described in chapter 11. The transfer of the Comptroller of the Treasury function to Supply and Services was announced on 12 July 1968 and took effect in April 1969 after approval of the Government Organization Act of 1969 and amendments to the Financial Administration Act. The Minister of Supply and Services, by section 45 of the former act, became Receiver General (the nominal second title of the Minister of Finance since 1878); the office of Comptroller of the Treasury was abolished; and the Receiver General inherited those responsibilities of the comptroller that had not been vested in departments (that is, pre-audit and commitment control), particularly the responsibility for maintenance of accounts of expenditures and revenues and other payments into and out of the Consolidated Revenue Fund.

The Department of Justice, which appears in our first category, has also evolved to a central position as legal adviser to the government, legislative draftsman, and a source of legal aid for many departments who do not employ their own lawyers.[10]

A final group of agencies, which has been included in this comprehensive third category, is concerned with providing services for the other programme-oriented departments. Chief among these – and perhaps deserving a separate category of their own – are the agencies concerned with collecting the public revenues for governmental undertakings. At Confederation there was a disproportionately large number of departments set up to provide the financial sinews for the public services. In addition to the Department of Finance (already discussed as a central policy and co-ordinating body) there was a separate Receiver General's Department which, though something of a supernumerary inherited from pre-Confederation times, was not merged with Finance until 1878. For revenue collection there were two separate departments, Customs and Inland Revenue. Apart from a short-lived attempt to convert these departments into subordinate adjuncts to the Department of Trade and Commerce in the 1890s (with two commissioners excluded from the cabinet), no change was made until 1918. In that year a single Department of Customs and Inland Revenue was formed, renamed Customs and Excise in 1921, and in 1927, after income tax collection was placed under its jurisdiction, retitled the Department of National Revenue. These mergers reduced from four to two the number of departments concerned with financing government operations.

One should also list, in this subcategory of servicing agencies, the Department of Public Works, one of whose main responsibilities has been the provision of accommodation for the public service and the construction of facilities required for executing various departmental programmes. In addition, a Department of Supply and Services emerged in 1969 out of the more restricted Department of Defence Production, seeking a consolidation comparable to that achieved in the real property service areas covered by Public Works.[11] In practice, complete centralization and co-ordination

10 See Royal Commission on Government Organization, *Report*, II, *Supporting Services for Government* (Ottawa, 1962), report no 11: 'Legal Services.'
11 On the Supply side the responsibility of the new department covered supply and provision of articles, supplies, machinery and equipment, including printing and publishing services for departments. The Services side (see n. 9 above) took in the residual functions of the Comptroller of the Treasury and added from the Public Service Commission the Bureau of Management Consulting Services and from the Treasury Board the Central Data Processing Service Bureau.

of these 'housekeeping' activities have never been achieved – a problem to which we have referred above and to which we shall later return.

Other mechanisms for centralizing records and statistics and for co-ordination and control have gradually evolved to meet the needs of an ever-growing public service, but most of these have developed outside or in semi-independence from the conventional departmental portfolios. In this category one would include such agencies as the Public Archives (1872), Public Printing and Stationery (1886), the Civil Service Commission (1908), the Dominion Bureau of Statistics (1918), the Bureau for Translations (1934), the Economic Council of Canada (1963), the Science Council of Canada (1966), and, most recently, the Official Languages Commissioner (1969).

In summary, the responsibilities for central co-ordination and servicing have greatly expanded and received special organizational recognition to keep pace with the growth in size and complexity of governmental programmes allocated to other departments. The Privy Council Office has grown from a passive registry office to a central secretariat for the co-ordinating mechanisms of the cabinet and its committees and has even begun to branch out to take on special programme-planning assignments. The need to mount central managerial services and co-ordinating machinery for an enormous bureaucracy led to the late creation of the President of the Treasury Board, to take on and expand functions performed for nearly a century by a special division within the Department of Finance. Since 1932 central accounting and pre-audit services have been centralized in the Comptroller of the Treasury, originally attached to the Department of Finance but, as of 1968, with substantially modified jurisdiction, placed in the Department of Supply and Services. Moderate flirtations with central planning are seen in the additions of the Economic Council and the Science Council of Canada. The collection of public revenues has been integrated in a single Department of National Revenue, while taxation policy and management of the Consolidated Revenue Fund is in the hands of Finance. The attempt to consolidate other common services has not been and is never likely to be complete: the Department of Justice provides a central repository of legal services for government as a whole and for some departments; Public Works consolidates much of the government's real estate and construction needs but is far from possessing a monopoly. As a result of recommendations of the Royal Commission on Government Organization, further consolidation of such common services as telecommunications and supply has occurred – the latter being concentrated, after 1968, in an expanded Department of Supply and

Services. This department assumes jurisdiction over joint procurement for all departments but there remain a number of semi-autonomous agencies – not of departmental stature – to provide centralized services for personnel selection and for archival, publication, translation, and statistical needs.

It will be observed that significant as many of these changes have been, the departmental rubric scarcely reflects them. Only two new departments, the President of Treasury Board and the Department of Supply and Services, have been created and these additions are offset by the reduction from four to two of the departments concerned with the financial provisioning of the public service. For the rest, the major adaptations have occurred through an internal transformation of the traditional functions of older departments, or more frequently by creating agencies either as adjuncts to or sometimes quite separate from the regular departments.

CONSERVATION, DEVELOPMENT, AND PROMOTION OF PHYSICAL RESOURCES

It is in the categories concerning the conserving and developing of physical and human resources that we would naturally expect to find government organization mirroring the growth and change in Canadian society as well as the significant shift of that society from an individualist to a collectivist philosophy. It is also in these fields that we find perhaps the most uncertainty about the proper bases for allocating the varied programmes and a consequent perpetual movement and shifting of functions between departments.

Beginning at Confederation, governmental programmes for protecting and developing its own citizens were spotty and were included in the physical resource departments. Over time, as the importance of protecting and fostering the life and well-being of the individual was accentuated by changing attitudes of governments towards social and welfare responsibilities, departments came to be more oriented towards a separate treatment of these two major areas. But the original combination of human and physical resources as a basis of departmental structure has left its mark on government organizations.

Two of the departments created in 1867 were primarily involved in these fields, and two others had a short-lived concern for certain aspects. The Departments of Agriculture and of Marine and Fisheries occupied most of the area, but the Departments of the Secretary of State and the Secretary of State for the Provinces had a special regard for the government's real estate holdings until in 1873 they were swept in under the newly constituted Department of the Interior. When the crown lands, the primary physical asset, assumed renewed importance for the national government as a result of the acquisition of the Territories beginning in 1870, it was decided that a new department was needed. At the same time the department fell heir to the administration of Indian Affairs – a more natural conjunction than is apparent at first glance for a department concerned with lands, since handling Indian lands and funds was a major element of the task. Ultimately the Territories; dominion, ordnance, and admiralty lands; Indian affairs; and the Geological Survey were all merged in the Department of the Interior.[12]

Throughout the period of rapid westward expansion, this department continued to claim for itself every activity that could have any conceivable bearing on the conservation and development of the new territory: topographical, geodetic, and boundary surveys; forestry protection; parks and game preserves; irrigation and water power; and so on. In the late twenties and early thirties the transfer to the western provinces of their own natural resources necessitated the consolidation and regrouping which in 1936 reduced land administration to only two major subdivisions of a newly created Department of Mines and Resources. By 1949 it became necessary to effect a further regrouping and a new Department of Resources and Development was constituted in which all the former responsibilities for land administration were once more given a departmental status of their own. In 1953 the creation of a Department of Northern Affairs and National Resources once again combined the administration of land with other resource programmes, but as the departmental title implied, with a pronounced orientation towards all developments located in the northern territories of Canada. The reorganization of 1966 divided land administration between the Departments of Indian Affairs and Northern Development and of Energy, Mines and Resources.

The administrative arrangements to take care of the second major physical resource, agriculture, followed a different and somewhat less confusing path. At the outset, in fact, the Department of Agriculture was a most inappropriate title with which to describe the multifarious activities confided to the agency; indeed, it is correct to say that it was concerned with almost everything but agriculture. Thus, the history of its development is really a story of how the irrelevant programmes came to be reassigned and room made for duties that were genuinely identified with the

12 Joseph Howe, after briefly holding the presidency of the Privy Council, assumed the short-lived portfolio of Secretary of State for the Provinces as well as superintendent general of Indian Affairs; he then became head of the Interior Department. All of this suggests the government was feeling its way towards the most suitable departmental structure to administer the west.

fostering of the agricultural enterprises of the nation. Perhaps because agriculture was one of the two concurrent powers set out in the British North America Act, it made sense to associate the department with the other concurrent power – imigration. But, whereas agricultural matters, with the exception of cattle quarantine and control of insect pests (occasioning the appointment of a Dominion Entomologist in 1884), remained marginal until 1886, immigration engaged the full attention of the department until it was transferred to the Department of the Interior in 1892.

It was through its responsibilities for immigrants that the Department of Agriculture acted as the progenitor of the contemporary Department of Health and Welfare, for it briefly supervised the Marine and Immigrant Hospital, until the latter's transfer to Marine and Fisheries in 1872, and was responsible for quarantine and public health generally until 1919.

In addition, three apparently quite extraneous duties – census and statistics, the archives, and patents, copyrights, trademarks, and industrial design – were originally assigned to the Department of Agriculture. All of these fall into the category of central record, registry, and servicing functions previously mentioned. The first and third were brought under the Department of Trade and Commerce in 1913 and 1918 respectively,[13] and the second was assigned to a semi-autonomous agency that became a reporting responsibility of the Secretary of State in 1912. With the emergence of the experimental farms programme in 1886, the Department of Agriculture finally started on a course properly oriented to its title. At the turn of the century it began to acquire regulatory and inspecting powers over many varieties of commodities, along with research and promotional activities that transformed what was once an administrative catch-all into a highly professional department directed towards a large farming clientele.

When we turn from agriculture to the other natural resources of the nation it is necessary once more to traverse a confused path. For example, the exploitation of the mineral resources of Canada was not a problem thought to require its own federal department until 1907. Prior to that time an Office of Superintendent of Mines, created in 1884 and operating as a branch of the Interior Department, was sufficient to look after the inspection and leasing of mining lands, while the Geological Survey undertook the preliminary mapping of mineral areas. The grouping of the survey with the Mines Branch into a Department of Mines in 1907 for some time provided such an insubstantial portfolio that it was readily

13 As previously noted (n. 8 above) the Department of Consumer and Corporate Affairs in 1969 took over patents, copyrights, etc., while the Dominion Bureau of Statistics, created in 1913, reported through Trade and Commerce as a fairly independent entity.

carried by another minister. The centralization of museum activities in 1922, the conferral of inspecting powers under the Explosives Act of 1923, and the gradual development of metallurgical research and testing facilities enlarged the responsibilities of the department. But even so, in 1936, as part of a general consolidation already mentioned in conjunction with land administration, the new Department of Mines and Resources absorbed the former Mines Department as a single branch. In 1949 yet another organizational shuffle took place which resulted in a new Department of Mines and Technical Surveys, very like the original Department of Mines but with a fuller integration of all surveys and mapping and the addition of a Geographical Branch. In 1966 the department was enlarged, as previously noted, to become Energy, Mines and Resources.

The forests were the last of the land-based resources to receive the organizational accolade of a department all to themselves. This development did not occur until 1960 and the resultant Department of Forestry was, in effect, put together out of units extracted from the Departments of Agriculture and of Northern Affairs and National Resources: the Forestry Branch from the latter and the Forest Biology Division of the Research Branch from the former. The two components were primarily research agencies with some promotional and control functions added. The end result was a small, professional department built around the interests associated with one of Canada's most important staple exports. In the organizational shifts of 1966 the department was enlarged to take in rural development, which had been emerging as an adjunct to Agriculture through the Agricultural Rehabilitation and Development Act (ARDA) programme and which promised to be propelled forward by the current enthusiasm for regional development. This merger was adopted in lieu of a counter-proposal to subdivide Agriculture into two departments, one for the west, one for the east. In a more recent organizational shuffle, in 1969, forests were combined with fisheries, the latter having, as we shall see below, achieved departmental status of their own in 1930. Accompanying this reorganization, most of the major area programmes hitherto found in Agriculture, Industry, Energy, Mines and Resources, and concerned either with the Atlantic or prairie provinces, were assembled under the co-ordinating roof of Rural Development, which was subsequently renamed Regional Economic Expansion.[14]

From the land-based resources we turn to those which are water based. In a country 'abounding,' as the tourist guidebooks have it, in rivers and lakes and with oceans on three sides, it is not surprising that water as a resource requiring conservation and development has been so taken for

14 Stats Can. 1969, c.28, part IV.

granted as an eternal gift from the Creator that it has been somewhat overlooked until comparatively recent times. Although the regulation and protection of boundary waters were administered under the auspices of the International Joint Commission from 1909, it was not until the twenties that conservation of water resources gradually gained acceptance. In the main, water resources have been handled as an element of land administration, so that the earliest organizations, such as the hydrographic survey, irrigation, and water power branches, have been incorporated simply as divisions of the department primarily concerned with the administration of land. In 1966–7 this association with land was retained by housing water resource administration in the Department of Energy, Mines and Resources. Three years later the water resource sector was transferred to the new Department of Fisheries and Forestry, while monitoring of water pollution and water surveys were assumed by an even more recent creation of 1970–1, the Department of the Environment.

Just as the land produced agricultural products, forests, and mineral resources that required separate administrative arrangements, so the waters of Canada have produced the annual harvest of the fishermen. The significance of the fisheries in Canadian economic history entailed their recognition in the departmental structure of the new dominion. During most of the period between 1867 and 1930 fisheries were combined with marine services – a juxtaposition which suggests that the protection, conservation, and development of the fisheries were subordinate to the protection and use of Canadian waters for transportation purposes.

The marine transportation aspects of the programme involved aids to navigation such as lighthouses, buoys, piers, and harbours, and control over government vessels and pilotage, including examination and certification of masters, inspection of steamboats, and so on. The fisheries responsibilities were also limited at first to inspection and licensing as well as protection of coastal waters against the intrusion of foreign vessels. Thus, the two sets of functions were not altogether dissimilar and their placement as separate branches in one department was logical. Between 1884 and 1892 the division between the two branches was more fully acknowledged by giving each a departmental status, although the one Minister of Marine and Fisheries continued to preside over both. After 1892 the original arrangement of an integrated department was restored, and it is significant of the apparently close connection between the two branches that the Department of Naval Service, created in 1910, took fisheries under its wing in 1914. After the First World War fisheries were once more reunited with marine, a situation that lasted until 1930 when the fisheries were finally granted a full-blown department of their own and marine services received the same separate recognition until their absorption in 1936 as a branch of the newly created Department of Transport. In 1969, as previously noted, Fisheries was merged with Forestry.

The Department of Trade and Commerce, which must also be regarded as associated with the physical resources of Canada, appeared rather late on the scene. The uncertainty concerning its proper functions was revealed by the five-year delay preceding its final formation in 1892 after the act initially setting it up was approved. The basic function of the department from the outset has been the supervision of a growing force of trade commissioners stationed in countries throughout the world with the objective of promoting the sale of the items whose production it is the purpose of the resource-oriented departments to encourage. This field force is supported at headquarters by a large staff grouped around the industrial and primary products that constitute important elements in Canada's external trade. Much basic and applied economic analysis and research is also centred in the department.

In 1963 a Department of Industry was created, a belated recognition (according to then Prime Minister Lester Pearson) of the importance of the manufacturing industries to the economy of Canada which for so long had been dependent upon natural unprocessed resources; it was to be 'for the manufacturing industry what the Department of Agriculture is for farmers' (to apply the phrase used by Mr Pearson). Clearly this was not the first administrative recognition of the importance of manufacturing in Canada, for both the Departments of Trade and Commerce and of Defence Production had been concerned with many aspects of the secondary industries in Canada. Indeed, in the view of some critics of the new department, the Department of Industry was really redundant and all that was necessary was to rename the long existing Department of Trade and Commerce to make it a Department of Trade and Industry.

It is clear from the debate that arose in connection with the creation of this department that the government expected it to remain a very modest size, concentrating on co-ordinating, informational, and possibly inspirational functions with respect not only to its clients but also to the resource-oriented departments and other departments that might have certain peripheral concern for secondary industry.[15] In 1968 Prime Minister Pierre Trudeau's new cabinet reverted to the original proposal to integrate Trade and Commerce with Industry, thus recognizing the aptness of the criticism directed against the Department of Industry when it was first set up.

Looking back on this tangled organization for conserving, developing, and promoting Canada's wealth in natural resources and manufactured

15 See *Can. H. of C. Debates*, 1963, pp. 802 ff., 1685 ff.

products we can observe one consistent trend: the effort to build departments around a single major resource such as agriculture, minerals, fish,
and forests. However, the logic and organizational neatness in these
arrangements has been consistently frustrated or confused by two factors.
First, a single resource has not always been a viable basis for a department
because the programmes and problems raised in its administration have
not been substantial enough to warrant a whole department to themselves.
This has meant that other and sometimes unrelated functions have had to
be incorporated in the same department. Agriculture, for many years,
typified this situation, as did Mines, Forestry, and even Fisheries. The
other significant factor that caused confusion was that the decision to
organize around one resource created jurisdictional problems. If, for example, organization was to be built around public lands, should this include only the land, the resources on or under the land, or, again, should
it be based on the location of the land with an effort to handle every conceivable programme relating to that location? If organization was to be
built around water, should it be related to the water only as an increasingly
precious commodity or to water as a means of irrigation, a medium of
transportation, a source of energy or of fish? These are problems of
allocating functions which will be examined more fully below, but they
emerge most acutely in this and the following category.

PROTECTION AND DEVELOPMENT OF HUMAN RESOURCES

Throughout the previous description of the evolution of departments
whose programmes relate primarily to conservation and development of
physical resources, passing reference has been made to the fifth general
area of responsibilities– human resources. A glance at the departmental
roster in 1867 is enough to reveal that, for the government, the cultivation
of the nation's physical resources dominated to the point of excluding any
concern for human resources. There were, however, two groups whose
welfare could not be overlooked by the government. First, there were the
Indians who, as virtual wards of the state, imposed inescapable obligations on the central government. In part, as previously noted, the obligation was that of financial trustee or an estate agent for the tribes. But,
in so far as the long-established policy of raising the native population to
the level of its white brethren was given lip-service, with a view ultimately
to bringing them into full citizenship, there were broader social and welfare responsibilities to be implemented. At Confederation the dominion
inherited both the policy and the special administrative machinery which

had been developed in the former Province of Canada.[16] The machinery was clientele-oriented, in that it contained within itself all the financial, accounting, and service functions that had to be performed on behalf of this specially designated group. This arrangement still persists.

However, just as the selection of a single physical resource often proved to be inadequate as a base for a full department, so in the case of the Indians it has nearly always been necessary to give them something less than full departmental status. At the outset Indian Affairs was simply given a branch status within the department most concerned with land administration, for example, the Secretary of State, then the Secretary of State for the Provinces, and from 1874 onward almost always in or associated with the Department of the Interior. While formal departmental status was conferred by statute in 1880, the ministerial head (known as the Superintendent General of Indian Affairs) was always a position held along with another portfolio. This association with physical resources was perpetuated until 1950, for the reorganization of 1936 that brought the Department of Mines and Resources into being continued to harbour Indian Affairs as a mere branch within that department. But in 1950 a further reorganization produced the Department of Citizenship and Immigration in which, for the first time, various categories of people – including the Indians – were brought together. In the 1966 organizational shuffle Indian Affairs was again placed in a physical resource department with a primary focus on the area base of administration, the Department of Indian Affairs and Northern Development.

It is interesting to observe, in concluding this story, that the other group of native peoples – the Inuit (Eskimos) – for whom the federal government has only in comparatively recent times assumed any responsibility, was dealt with by the Department of Northern Affairs and National Resources which, in the 1966 changes, found Indian Affairs substituted for Resources. This is an indication that the physical location of the group has been the guiding principle in associating it with an agency concerned mainly with physical resources in the far north. Indeed, some of the Indian 'clients' of Citizenship and Immigration had already been placed under Northern Affairs and National Resources because of their far northern location – a transfer that was made complete in 1966 when Indian Affairs was removed to the new Department of Indian Affairs and Northern Development.

The other special group for whose welfare, at the very beginning, the federal government assumed major responsibility was the immigrant. The organizational provisions for looking after his health and welfare as well

16 See *Pioneer Public Service*, chap. 13.

as helping him to settle in his new home, in co-operation with the provinces, followed a course very close to that taken by Indian Affairs. The problems did not appear to be sufficient to warrant a separate department; thus, the underworked Department of Agriculture was initially assigned the responsibility. Once again, the close affinity of immigration and land settlement suggested the logic of transferring the former to the Department of the Interior in 1892. This arrangement remained intact until, in 1917, a Department of Immigration and Colonization was set up. However, the historical association with land administration was reasserted in 1936 when immigrant affairs were once again made one of several branches in the new Department of Mines and Resources. Finally, as in the case of Indian Affairs, immigration came to rest in 1950 in the Department of Citizenship and Immigration, an agency built around human rather than physical factors.

The logic of this grouping was superficial, however, for the human clientele were not only located in quite unrelated areas – the Indians on tribal reserves in Canada, the immigrants scattered across Canada – but also had unique problems totally unrelated to one another. Thus, the reorganization of 1966 disassociated the two by placing the immigrants in a new Department of Manpower and Immigration. In terms of the domestic administrative arrangements for absorbing immigrants into the labour force the new organization makes more sense than the previous arrangement, but it may not be as successful in looking after the total broader social or welfare needs of the immigrant.

Another group of Canadian citizens, the ex-servicemen, has managed to convince the government that its needs are so special that it should be singled out for the exclusive attention of a single department. The problems of the veteran came to the fore towards the close of the First World War, but at first were dealt with by several agencies rather than on an integrated clientele basis. Health care of veterans was first assigned, in 1915, to a Military Hospitals and Convalescent Homes Commission. In 1918 a Department of Soldiers' Civil Re-establishment took over the duties of the commission. The related duty of awarding pensions to ex-servicemen was undertaken about the same time by a Board of Pension Commissioners set up in 1916. These two operations were conducted separately, with the Pension Board and its successor in 1933, the Canadian Pension Commission, acting in a quasi-independent capacity in adjudicating on pension awards. In 1928 the health of veterans was merged in a broader Department of Pensions and National Health, but the advent of the Second World War and a new crop of veterans forced the formation in 1944 of a clientele agency, the Department of Veterans

Affairs. The awarding of pensions continues to be performed by a number of semi-autonomous commissions and appellate tribunals. Meanwhile, the rehabilitation of veterans as civilians was undertaken by the Soldiers' Settlement Board from 1917 to 1931, when the board was replaced by a Director of Veterans' Lands. With the formation of an integrated department for providing all the services visualized in the postwar Veterans Charter, this operation was taken under the wing of the Department of Veterans Affairs. The health, rehabilitation, and various educational and welfare grants, including pensions, for this special category of citizens are now sheltered under a single administrative roof.

The foregoing administrative arrangements refer only to those selected categories of Canada's people for whom there were special reasons to undertake the provision of health and welfare services. It is natural, in the absence of any governmental programme for the health and welfare of the general body of citizens, that departments should have grown up specially designed to service specific groups of citizens. There is very little organizational evidence of the national government's interest in assuming responsibility for the well-being of the whole Canadian population until the end of the First World War. Scattered here and there in many departments there were small operations concerned with safeguarding the health of the nation through inspection, licensing, labelling, and so on: a Food and Drug Laboratory was started in the Inland Revenue Department in 1884 to assist in developing standards of safety and purity; the drug traffic was policed under the Opium and Narcotics Act; patent and proprietary medicines, fertilizers, animal feeding stuffs, and so on were also subjected to inspection and regulation. Most of these, along with such ancient functions as the marine hospitals and quarantine services, were assembled under a new Department of Health in 1919.

Much of the pioneer work and agitation that urged the creation of such a department had been undertaken by the short-lived (1909–21) Canadian Conservation Commission. As previously noted, between 1928 and 1944 veterans' health was handled by the Department of Health, but was absorbed after 1944 into the new clientele Department of Veterans Affairs; at the same time a new Department of National Health and Welfare was created. Two clear-cut divisions, each headed by a deputy minister but under a common minister, comprised the major segments of the department. The welfare components were, in fact, slower to emerge than the health side of its activities. In the 1920s child welfare and housing were listed among the preoccupations of the Department of Health; but these matters, along with grants to the blind and the aged (old age pensions began in 1927), were regarded as very much within the ambit of the provinces or voluntary charitable organizations, the federal government simply acting as a channel for distributing these first welfare grants or seeking to improve working relations between governments at all levels and the many voluntary associations which in many provinces bore the brunt of such welfare activities as were then deemed essential. The introduction of Family Allowances in 1944 increased the labours of the welfare branch, though its activities continued to be centred on the supervision of grants rather than direct operation of programmes which remain, by and large, in the hands of local authorities and the provinces.[17] On the health side, in addition to administering numerous grants, the department also implements a regulatory programme and conducts research.

The Department of Labour is also concerned with human resources in a general way. Until the turn of the century one can detect no organizational evidence of the federal government's responsibilities in this important field. Apart from those in the labour force employed by the public service itself or engaged on federal public works, this area was assumed to fall within provincial jurisdiction. Sporadic cases of industrial unrest, towards the close of the nineteenth century and on into the next decade, were met by the creation of *ad hoc* royal commissions of inquiry. Indeed, it was in such work that Mackenzie King came into the prominence that was to make him the first ministerial head of a new Department of Labour in 1909. The new department emerged in close association with the Conciliation Act of 1900, and its modest administrative framework was supervised by the Postmaster General until 1909. Apart from the supervision of arrangements for investigating industrial disputes, the early functions of the department were largely confined to the collection of statistics and publications (still an important element of the Department of Labour's duties). There has since been a steady accretion of functions, including such matters as administration of technical and vocational education grants, and the administration of combines legislation, old age pensions, relief, and unemployment insurance. Many of these activities have involved long court battles with the provinces to determine jurisdiction, constitutional amendments, and, in several important areas, the subsequent transfer of major functions to special administrative agencies such as the Unemployment Insurance Commission and the Restrictive Trade Practices Commission. The Department of Labour, as the first in the field of general human resource administration, has also had to meet the com-

17 An internal departmental survey which is to constitute the basis for a white paper on the government's welfare policies revealed over two hundred separate welfare programmes under the financial aegis of the department.

petition of later entrants such as Health and Welfare and, more recently, Manpower and Immigration as well as Consumer and Corporate Affairs.

This lengthy recital of an administrative evolution covering nearly a century leaves the impression that the founding fathers were remarkably perceptive in selecting departmental portfolios that could survive the test of time and the accumulating burden of responsibilities. The charts at the end of this chapter reveal that seven of the original roster of operating departments have survived intact, at least as to title: Agriculture, Finance, Justice, Post Office, Privy Council Office, Public Works, and Secretary of State. An eighth department, Militia and Defence, was at least an embryonic representative of what was to become the Department of National Defence. Two more, Customs and Inland Revenue, after a long and parallel career were merged in the Department of National Revenue. The Departments of the Interior and Marine and Fisheries over time spawned most of the physical resource departments such as Energy, Mines and Resources, Indian Affairs and Northern Development, Forestry and Fisheries, and Regional Economic Expansion. From the Department of Railways and Canals, born out of Public Works in 1879, and the marine branch of Marine and Fisheries has descended directly – but with many accretions – the modern Department of Transport. In the event only two of the early group of departments proved unnecessary – the Receiver General's Office (which persisted in name as part of the formal title of the Minister of Finance until 1969 when it was carried over to the Minister of Supply and Services) and the Secretary of State for the Provinces. Throughout the remainder of the nineteenth century there were only two net additions to the departmental roster: Indian Affairs in 1880 (though always doubled up with the ministerial head of another department) and Trade and Commerce in 1892.

Up to the First World War only three more significant additions were made to the departmental list – Mines (1907), and Labour and External Affairs (both 1909). Two more genuinely new fields of activity in the human resource area, emerged immediately after the war: Soldiers' Civil Re-establishment (1918) and Health (1919); and from these roots have flowered the contemporary Departments of Veterans Affairs and National Health and Welfare. The period of the thirties witnessed substantial consolidation and transfer of programmes but resulted in no completely new department – unless Fisheries, which was set up on its own in 1930, is considered such. Omitting the special departments that did not survive the war, creations since the Second World War have been Defence Production in 1951, as of 1968 Supply and Services; Forestry in 1960, although the subject matter was embraced as a subdivision of a relevant resource department from nearly the beginning of the century and it has most recently had to share a departmental portfolio with Fisheries; Industry in 1963, as of 1968 merged with Trade and Commerce; Consumer and Corporate Affairs in 1967; and a resuscitated Department of the Solicitor General which occupied a shadowy position vis-à-vis the Department of Justice until 1945 and then in 1966 was given jurisdiction over 'crime and correction'; and, finally, Manpower and Immigration, created in 1966 but in essence incorporating responsibilities for immigrants which had been housed in various departments since well before Confederation. In short, a hundred years has witnessed an apparent growth from fourteen to only twenty-four major operating departments.[18]

Clearly this is a deceptively simple picture which is made much more complex by taking note of three features that are not visible on the surface. The first is the significant impact of federalism which has channelled off many programmes to the provinces, thereby reducing the workload of the federal departmental system. The most obvious example is in the all-important area of human resource development – education. For all provinces educational programmes have become the heaviest consumers of provincial and local revenues, demanding an extensive bureaucracy of their own. Health and Welfare and Transportation – particularly Highways – also make heavy demands on provincial financial resources and contribute to the rapid growth of provincial public services. Were these and other locally administered programmes to be assumed by the central government, the roster of departments would undoubtedly have been much longer than it has in fact become.

The second feature not revealed in a listing of departments is the large number of non-departmental administrative entities – barnacles, so to speak – that cling to or are suspended alongside the departmental ship of state. A separate chapter will be devoted to these phenomena, but it is sufficient to observe here that many of these non-departmental agencies have absorbed the programmes required by an increasingly industrialized and technologically oriented society.

Finally, a mere listing of portfolios fails to reveal the enormous expansion of personnel and of organizational subdivisions that has taken place

18 In 1969 a policy and co-ordinating Department of Communications was created by the Government Organization Act of that year. The portfolio was held initially by the Postmaster General and it is probable that if the Post Office becomes a crown corporation the Department of Communications will become the ministerial co-ordinating centre for a series of such corporate satellites having operating responsibilities in various new areas of communication.

within these relatively stable departmental containers. A tabulation of headquarters personnel for thirteen departments in 1868 gives us a miniscule figure of 255; in 1960, taking roughly equivalent departments, the number is over 18,000[19] The contemporary total is doubled if we add on the departments that have been joining the roster since Confederation. These figures make it obvious without multiplying the contrasts that the original departmental portfolios have swollen nearly a hundredfold, even as their number has nearly doubled. Even so, as will be seen in chapter 7, the departmental system has not been flexible enough to prevent the resort to a host of non-departmental agencies of bewildering variety.

19 See 'First Report of the Civil Service Commission,' *Sessional Papers*, 1869, no 19; and Royal Commission on Government Organization, *Report*, I, *Management of the Public Service* (Ottawa, 1962), report no 3: 'Personnel Management,' pp. 426–7.

CHAPTER SIX

Allocation of programmes: the guiding principles

The previous chapter described the evolution of departmental portfolios to meet the expanding programmes and responsibilities of government. In this chapter the same ground is traversed but with a view to determining what, if any, guiding principles have been employed in an effort to secure a coherent aggregation of work units.

In the traditional literature on organization theory, written in the 1930s, five alternative ways of allocating work to departments were envisaged, each dependent on one unifying or common concept.[1] The work components could be grouped together if they shared: (1) a common purpose, (2) clientele, (3) location, (4) skill or profession, or (5) the use of common facilities or matériel.

Theoretically, this type of analysis appears to be logical and useful; but the effort to apply it to an existing public organization reveals ambiguities in the concepts that make their application to real situations difficult and sometimes unproductive. The uncertainties arise from the interpretations that can be placed on such words as 'purpose,' 'clientele,' or 'process.'[2] For example, is the Department of Agriculture a 'clientele' department servicing farmers or a 'purpose' department concerned with fostering agricultural enterprise; is External Affairs a 'place' department or a 'purpose' department; is Justice a 'process' or a 'purpose' depart-

1 See especially Luther Gulick, 'Notes on the Theory of Organization,' in Institute of Public Administration, *Papers on the Science of Administration*, ed. Luther Gulick and L. Urwick (New York, 1937).
2 For a good criticism along these lines, see C.S. Benson, 'Internal Administrative Organization,' *Public Administration Review* 1 (1941), p. 472 ff.; and R.A. Dahl, 'The Validity of Organization Theories,' *ibid.* 7 (1947), p. 281 ff.

ment; and so on? The inconsistencies arise because, in practice, no one criterion can be applied to the organization of all departments and, in fact, more than one principle of organization will be used not only for the primary aggregation of work units but also for the assemblage of functions at secondary and tertiary levels within a single department.

Given these difficulties and admitting that there is no room for dogmatic assertions about *one best way* of allocating work, these concepts may, nevertheless, be useful as starting points in our efforts to come to grips with the problems of departmentalization. It should be recognized, however, that no matter what principles are applied two inescapable conditions are found to result. First, it cannot be expected (however desirable from the point of view of organizational neatness) that the overall allocation to two dozen departments will result in units roughly equal in size and workload. The range, in terms of personnel, is from a few hundred to nearly fifty thousand; and one would detect the same variation if the amount of money spent by each department were compared. These discrepancies are not necessarily a result of the application of inappropriate criteria for work division. Sheer physical size, in any case, may have little bearing on the relative importance of each department: the complexity, variety, and high policy character of the work assigned to the relatively small Department of External Affairs is as much justification for according departmental status as the need, for example, to assemble more than 40,000 people performing relatively routine, repetitive, and policy-free functions in the Post Office. The real question is not whether the greatest equality in the size of departments has been achieved but whether too heavy and too many unrelated blocks of work have been assigned to a single department.

The second problem which inevitably arises when allocating programmes to departments – no matter what principle is applied – is that there are bound to be conflicts of jurisdiction: the search for a 'water-tight' department, completely self-contained, is bound to be frustrated by the ubiquitous connecting tissue that links a programme in one department to those conducted in other departments. Naturally, it makes sense to bring together under one roof as many as possible of the relevant components, for Luther Gulick's test question[3] 'does it bleed'? is always most relevant when contemplating the wisdom of detaching a portion of one department and placing it elsewhere. In Gulick's graphic expression, we find that if one or more functions or activities organically or sequentially linked to others are cut away from the whole, the total operation may become anaemic. In many practical situations some amount of 'bleeding'

3 'The Limits of Division,' in 'Notes on the Theory of Organization.'

may be inevitable, but obviously the best solution is to opt for the principle of work aggregation which causes the least bleeding. Nor should a reorganizer forget in his anxiety to wield his scalpel that the public service organization can, like the human organism with its tonsils and appendix, carry without any great harm to itself certain apparently 'functionless' adjuncts which need excision only when they become diseased or inflamed. From the taxpayers' point of view their continuation may appear to be inefficient and costly, but their excision may be so disruptive for the total organism that in the long run efficiency is not improved and costs not significantly reduced.

A final precautionary word is relevant in approaching the problem of how best to allocate programmes to departments. The public service organization, as has been argued in chapter 2, is a response to environmental pressures. These pressures are not exerted once and for all time at the stage when the department is created; they play on it continuously and there is a constant interaction between the organization and its environment. The would-be organizer disregards these pressures at his peril, for no department, however coherent and integrated its parts, can afford to operate in a hostile environment. It may be much more important to sacrifice organizational logic for the sake of retaining the good will of those who view the agency as, in a sense, their 'own' department. This observation is especially pertinent in considering the merits of a 'clientele' type of department, for in as much as a clientele arrangement leads to duplication of cadres of expensive specialists, it is far from providing the most effective use of resources.

In the light of these reservations and cautionary notes, we may now revert to the examination of the considerations that have guided the allocation of programmes to Canadian departments. For this purpose it is useful to retain as our frame of reference the categories of government business used in the previous chapter.

PUBLIC SECURITY AND EXTERNAL RELATIONS

The group of departments listed under the first heading raises perhaps the fewest problems. Defence is a department that aggregates all those functions that are already related to a major purpose. But so global is its purpose that it has the potential of standing as an autonomous government in its own right. The major issue is whether, in fact, it is too autonomous in being permitted to meet all its needs with its own resources: constructing its own buildings and military establishments; making its own maps, providing its own communication, transportation, and legal services;

ordering its own supplies and maintaining its own supply depots; repairing its own airplanes, ships, and vehicles; undertaking its own research; and so on. Since there are other departments whose main concern is with matters of this sort, to leave the department free to perform these tasks for itself is but to encourage duplication of effort. Moreover, since the department was divided internally into three relatively autonomous service arms (until integration in 1966), possibilities of duplication within each service were compounded. The major jurisdictional issues arise in respect to construction (where Public Works is vested with the power), procurement (where Supply and Services occupies the field), and research (for which the Defence Research Board holds the prime responsibility).

It is possible the requirements of this one vast department are so large and may be so unique that to make their provision part of the responsibility of other departments would be to strain the capacity of these agencies to perform their central responsibilities for the rest of the civilian departments. Here is a case where a compromise decision appears unavoidable, and the recommendations of the Royal Commission on Government Organization reveal the nature of the compromise.[4] For common office requirements the commission proposed to make the Department of National Defence rely on Public Works, although specialized military construction would remain in Defence. Procurement and supply would continue to be handled by Supply and Services, not so much because of the greater efficiency expected from having specialists deal with the problems, but partly because of the great economies of scale made possible by having one common supply agency controlling depots and inventories, and, even more important, because of the statutory obligation imposed on the central procurement agency to conduct its purchasing in such a way as to strengthen a total industrial base in Canada and to keep it geared to potential wartime mobilization. This broader policy consideration could not be expected to dominate the thinking of a purely departmental supply service intent on getting items to its own specifications as cheaply and as quickly as possible, regardless of the impact which its purchasing policy might have on Canada's industrial development. In the provision of other services, such as transportation and telecommunications, the royal commission was less inclined to dispute the department's claim to meet its own needs within its own four walls. But in view of the costliness of the equipment, a plea was inserted for some external

4 See Royal Commission on Government Organization, *Report*, IV, *Special Areas of Administration* (Ottawa, 1963), report no 20: 'Department of National Defence.'

centre for co-ordinating plans so that civil departments might be able to call on the facilities operated by National Defence to meet their own more limited needs.

The preservation of internal order is broadly speaking a matter for the police and the law courts, both of which are, in the main, in local or provincial hands. General responsibility for the proper and efficient administration of justice throughout Canada, however, is vested in the Minister of Justice. The department proper is the legal adviser to the government and conducts or arranges for the conducting of all cases to which the government may be a party. Clearly, the Department of Justice typifies a 'process' organization employing one professional group almost exclusively. But this is a process and a skill of which other departments have need, and the primary issue here is whether Justice should employ all the legal talent required to service its own programme responsibilities as well as seconding lawyers to all other departments. In theory, such an arrangement would appear to be eminently sensible, not only for the most efficient employment of an expensive skill but also to provide an adequate career service by pooling all lawyers in one department. Against this view, it may be countered that it is more logical to identify certain legal specialists with a related purpose department: for example, that an international lawyer's place is in the Department of External Affairs or that a tax law specialist is best located in National Revenue's taxation division, or that for the special branch of military law the lawyer is better placed in the office of the judge advocate general in the Department of National Defence, or that the veteran's case is best handled by a lawyer in the Department of Veterans Affairs. On the whole, there is a convincing case for making the Justice Department much more of a process organization than it now is by transferring to it the scattered lawyers now attached to other departments, but the special claims on the services of specialized lawyers mentioned above appear to constitute valid exceptions to complete merger, at least until the lawyers elsewhere have been integrated in Justice.[5]

The Department of Justice has been placed in a stronger position to focus on its process orientation by the removal from under its roof of two long-time organizational attachments: the Royal Canadian Mounted Police and the Penitentiaries Branch. Both of these, in 1966, were brought together, along with the National Parole Board, in a new Department of the Solicitor General. The logic of this association can and has been

5 See *ibid.*, II, *Supporting Services for Government* (Ottawa, 1962), report no 11: 'Legal Services,' chap. 4.

disputed, but the general intention is clear: to group together in one department agencies concerned with preserving law and order and providing correctional services. The integration of federal policing activities in one place is another example of a logical application of the process principle, which enables other departments to rely on the RCMP for most of the investigation and enforcement proceedings arising in the course of such regulatory responsibiliites as those associated with narcotics, illegal entry, security risks, and so on. Most of the provinces, too, have recognized the value of meeting their general policing requirements by contracting with the RCMP – a force originally designed to police only the federally owned territories.

Although the Department of External Affairs is only a fraction the size of National Defence, it raises almost precisely the same problems of work allocation. In both instances, though for quite different reasons, there is a strong claim for self-sufficiency which, if fully met, would create within the department a mirror-image of the total public service organization. In the case of National Defence the self-sufficiency argument is sustained by reference to the very large size as well as to the urgency and highly specialized nature of its operations which are allegedly so different from civil departments. The Department of External Affairs finds support for the same claim of self-sufficiency by reference to its unique responsibility for representing Canada in foreign countries. If, for this purpose, embassies have to be constructed, stores purchased, communication links established, local personnel engaged, what more sensible plan than to incorporate all these functions in the one department? On the other hand, a claim for self-sufficiency is bound to produce duplication and to deprive the government of many economies of scale derived from central provision of such common services.

In any event, quite apart from its comparatively modest proportions, the Department of External Affairs has not found it possible to retain a monopoly of its major purpose – the representation of Canada's interests abroad – compared to the Defence Department's uncontested purpose role. Recent years, especially, have witnessed a growth in the external interests of many departments. In addition to the long-established immigration agencies abroad and the trade commissioner service, numerous other departments and agencies have a smaller scattering of foreign outposts. If one were to place the stress on organization according to location, then it would appear to make sense to associate all these external appendages of other operating departments and agencies with the one key department, External Affairs. But, here again, the importance of the 'place' factor may not be as significant as the preservation of organic links between the parent operating department and its scattered outposts abroad: this may be a case where, in considering such transfers, the cutting of organic links may cause a function to 'bleed.'

Admitting this possibility, it is nevertheless equally true that a scattering abroad of small outposts of operating departments whose primary functions are domestic may contribute to a situation where there is very little co-ordination and excessive duplication of staff and facilities. If problems of co-ordination and duplication are to be overcome, their solution must be sought at the centre in Ottawa. Not until agreement has been achieved there will it be possible to establish the proper lines of authority and responsibility between the outposts abroad. Nor is one single solution likely to solve all these issues. For example, it will probably make sense for the Department of Public Works to take over all the major construction and maintenance problems of all agencies that have external outposts, rather than have each competing or conflicting with one another in the same locale. On the other hand, the key role of telecommunications in the work of External Affairs would suggest the merit of leaving this service under its jurisdiction, with other departments meeting their lesser needs for such services by contracting with External Affairs. The dominance of External Affairs in representing Canadian interests abroad suggests, further, that at each foreign location this department be given co-ordinating and supervisory responsibilities, at least as far as strictly administrative matters are involved. It is probable that such administrative co-ordination could be achieved without trespassing on the substantive policy considerations over which each of the parent departments would legitimately wish to preserve its control.[6]

PUBLIC WORKS, COMMUNICATIONS, AND TRANSPORTATION

Historically, the Post Office has always provided the prime example of a purpose department whose jurisdictional boundaries were clear and unequivocal. The only issue of any substance that has arisen is whether the department should be completely self-contained, particularly in meeting its own needs for post office buildings, contracting for services, and the like. The fact that this agency bears most of the marks of an industrial, revenue-producing enterprise has tended to substantiate these claims for

6 See *ibid.*, IV, report no 21: 'Department of External Affairs.' Early in 1971 a study was undertaken of the possibility of integrating, under External Affairs, the work abroad of all relevant major departments, including Trade, Commerce and Industry.

autonomy. In recent years the suggestion that the Post Office be converted into a crown corporation has been gaining favour, but to date the government has not implemented the proposal.[7] Generally the Post Office has been less successful than National Defence, for example, in achieving self-sufficiency and must rely on Public Works to provide most of its office accommodation.

From the relatively clear-cut area of postal operations we move to a much more confusing area which is, in part, concerned with media of communication other than postal services but is more concerned with the means of transport. The fact that the government was at the outset involved not merely as a regulator but more directly as a builder and operator of various transportation services has created a perpetual problem of how best to allocate the heavy workload in this field. We have seen that the first two important transportation media – canals and railways – became so significant that they could no longer be contained in a Department of Public Works and by 1879 claimed a separate department of their own. In the same early period a variety of maintenance and regulatory powers relating to marine navigation was housed in a Department of Marine and Fisheries. Not until 1936, with the formation of the Department of Transport, were these two sets of activities brought together. In the meantime, civil aviation, which had found its home during the 1920s in the Department of National Defence, expanded to the point where it also had to be shifted to Transport. The advent of radio communication, and more recently of telecommunication, both of which are closely linked to traffic control and safety, necessitated further expansion of the department. In fact, there is probably no other single department whose jurisdiction embraces such a variety of functions, covering land, sea, and air.

At first glance the effort to merge in one department all programmes concerned with transportation seems to be a logical application of the purpose basis for allocating functions. But a number of factors conspire to make the arrangement increasingly cumbersome from an administrative point of view. First, transportation now takes place in or on the three basic elements of land, water, and air. Each in turn has built up an impressive servicing structure which has the effect of making Transport the largest centre for engineers, architects, and construction units: airports,

7 A report, 'Blueprint for Change,' compiled by the management consultants who had spent a year examining the Post Office, was released in 1970; it recommended a corporate structure for the department. See Stats Can. 1969, c.28, part II, where the Department of Communications is established, from which it may be inferred that the government's intention is to incorporate the Post Office and make it a reporting satellite of the Department of Communications.

airstrips, air terminals must be built and maintained; ports, harbours, wharves, canals, lighthouses, beacons, ship channels must be constructed and serviced; a fleet of government ships must be built and operated. In so far as these facilities encourage traffic, a host of regulatory and control problems arise: inspection of air worthiness, sea worthiness; licensing of pilots, vessels; traffic control; meteorological reports; and so on.

The Department of Transport is caught up in an almost endless house-that-Jack-built operation in which there is a legitimate and causal chain of sequence springing from an initially relatively modest venture and now extending virtually to infinity. The extent to which the accretion of transportation functions trespasses on the preserves of other departments and agencies, coupled with the fact that sheer size and diversity are rapidly making this department an administrator's nightmare, suggest the need for re-examining the present basis for allocating work to it. Considerable reduction of the workload could be accomplished were the decision taken to fall back on the historical connection which the Department of Public Works once had with construction, maintenance, and real property functions associated with works required for transportation. The recent successful installation of six regional offices for the department would make such a transfer more practicable than it otherwise would have been under its former less coherent regional organization. This rearrangement would then leave the Department of Transport with strictly operating and regulatory services. Operations are perhaps best grouped, as they now are, around the two major elements to which transportation services must be related: land-to-air or shore-to-sea. But this method of allocation may have to be further blended with the locality factor which assumes special importance in administering operations that are scattered across a continent, having to contend with peculiar local conditions. Thus, port administration may have to be devolved to local authorities, while a fleet of government vessels may continue to be operated on a highly integrated basis – provided it is made available contractually to other departments like Fisheries and Northern Development to meet their special requirements of function or place.

Certain operating and regulatory functions associated with transport have been allocated to several other departments and to a large number of special non-departmental agencies: there are, for example, no less than twelve administrative entities involved in various regulatory aspects for the field of transportation. The creation of a Canadian Transportation Commission in 1967 merged three of these major regulatory bodies into one, although each preserves a separate identity as a committee under the commission.[8]

8 Stats Can. 1967, c.69.

It is clear that the primary purpose basis of organization in matters relating to transportation has not overcome jurisdictional battles or contributed to organizational simplicity. Indeed, the present arrangement seems to be getting the worst out of all possible worlds: by stressing major purpose it has created one vast departmental structure that is getting beyond our capacity to administer properly and yet, at the same time, it overlaps with extraneous odds and ends relating to transportation that have been assigned to other departments and agencies. As a result, internal coherence is sacrificed and external co-ordination is notably deficient – though clearly improved as a result of the mergers mentioned above.[9] Even within the department one has the impression of autonomous services almost as rigorously segregated and with just as much *esprit de corps* as was true of the three service arms in National Defence.

Reference has already been made to the Department of Public Works, the other agency concerned with this second segment of the state's programmes. The major problem with which this department has had to contend is that, from the outset, it has been expected to combine two quite different types of function: on the one hand, it has been accorded a central position as the government's construction agency and property manager; on the other, it has been vested with responsibility for operating many of the works it has had a hand in constructing. This duality of function can be explained by reference to its original purpose which, as we have seen, was the construction and maintenance of all major governmental works. But these 'works' were of two kinds, one concerned with the physical means of transportation (canals and railways), the other concerned with the lands and buildings required by all other departments.

The decision to create a special department in 1879 for the first set of functions was a clear acknowledgment that henceforth the Department of Public Works would become a strictly 'process' department for providing the housekeeping needs of all other departments on a common, centralized basis. Logically, this arrangement should have brought together under one roof all the labourers, technicians, engineers, and architects concerned with construction and real property management. In actual fact, two features tended to confuse the subsequent career of the department. First, wherever departments had operating responsibilities which entailed

9 See *Globe and Mail*, Toronto, 18 February 1970, 'Reorganization Aims at Recovery of Transport Costs,' for the minister's announcement of a major reorganization of 'an unstructured conglomerate which over the years has grown like Topsy.' The new 'Ministry' concept was aimed at a total reorganization that would provide separate 'administrations' for air, water, land, and Arctic transportation, a separate meteorological service, and a development agency; a closer linkage of a number of the most important crown corporations to the department's central policy staff was also to be worked out.

the use of major works such as harbours, roads, airstrips, engineering works for irrigation, parks, and the like, such departments sought to retain their own right to construct and maintain these works. Throughout the years this rather natural claim of operating departments tended to drain away the construction and maintenance functions over which Public Works could legitimately claim to have been given jurisdiction. Thus, the Parks Branch of Indian Affairs and Northern Development employs its own staff of engineers and construction people to design and build roads and buildings in the parks; the Department of Transport, equally, has over four thousand employees engaged on such functions as real property management, architecture, design, engineering, and construction. The tendency for construction and operation of works – particularly in the field of transportation – to be viewed as inseparable not only encouraged a 'leakage' of construction responsibilities from Public Works but also had the effect of encouraging that department – wherever it did maintain its hold over construction and maintenance – to assume responsibility for subsequent operation of these works. Thus, when Public Works constructed dredges it naturally assumed responsibility for operating them.[10]

This predicament is common to all departments organized on the basis of 'process': it is always difficult to prevent operating departments from claiming an organic connection between their own peculiar programme and the processes – whether they be architecture, engineering, legal services, or even the recruitment of staff. Similarly, it is equally difficult to preserve the 'purity' of a strict process department, for it tends, following the same line of reasoning, to claim responsibility for the uses to which its work will be applied and thereby gets involved in operations or in seeking control over its clients.

If a process type of work allocation is going to weather these pressures, two essential measures must be taken. First, it must divest itself of any operating responsibilities and act in a strictly service capacity on behalf of other departments. By making this self-denying ordinance the process department is then in a strong position to contest the operating departments' claims to provide these services from their own resources. Second, these services should be costed and charged to the client departments. Not being a charge on the servicing agency's budget, such an agency then is less disposed to delay the service while haggling over standards or what it views as irresponsible requests from the clients. These points can be more easily made than enforced, as the long up-and-down history of the Department of Public Works testifies. Nevertheless,

10 Royal Commission on Government Organization, *Report*, II, report no 5: 'Real Property.'

the effort is worth making because of the economies involved in centralizing common services, the opportunity for pooling scarce and expensive technical or professional resources, and the elimination of substantial duplication.[11]

CO-ORDINATION AND SERVICES FOR THE PUBLIC ORGANIZATION

In this mixed category of government functions we have listed the Secretary of State Department, the Privy Council Office, Finance, National Revenue, and Supply and Services, as well as Justice and Public Works. Apart from the somewhat mechanical and formal tasks of recording and registry the other activities are, in a sense, optional. That is to say, co-ordination and centralized servicing facilities may be minimal and widely dispersed in a relatively autonomous collection of discrete departmental entities. Historically, this tends to be the situation at the initial stages of development in any public service organization. Only as the organization grows in size and as its duties become more elaborate and interrelated does it become imperative to strengthen agencies of co-ordination and service. The decisions concerning the precise allocation of these responsibilities relate to the most sensitive policy issues, where determinations are made as to what agency will be vested with the final authority to settle such important managerial questions as the size of the civil service, its overall deployment, the allocation of resources, the determination of priorities or programmes, and the relationship between programmes. Since money would appear to be the natural and ultimate arbiter in making these decisions, it follows that the department with central responsibilities for revenue raising and expenditure proposals will be accorded primacy of place in exerting control and co-ordinating functions. Thus, the Department of Finance formed the focal point around which these functions tended to build up.

However, the claims of Finance to pre-eminence because of its controlling position with respect to all money matters are countered by two other centres of power. First, as earlier chapters have shown, parliament has a constitutional concern, not only with the raising and spending of money but also with the general effectiveness of the public service organization. In particular this concern found its organizational lodging in the Civil Service Commission, which, in all personnel matters, was viewed as parliament's instrument, set over and against the executive. Since the

11 *Ibid.*, pp. 13–16.

commission was also an inseparable part of the machinery of government, it occupied, as we have seen, an anomalous position in which its statutory powers were substantially watered down by the necessity of having to secure favourable decisions from the central financial control body before implementation was possible.

The other competing source of power is the cabinet. We have already commented on the strength of the political convention that insists on collegial decisions, a convention that differs from the British practice of permitting more decisions by individual ministers. In so far as these decisions relate to the public service organization, the chief instrument traditionally has been the Treasury Board, a committee of cabinet, chaired by the Minister of Finance and staffed by a section of his department. Thus, until recent times, the fact that control and co-ordination of the public service was vested in the Treasury Board, acting for the cabinet, did little to displace the Department of Finance as the major power centre.

With the creation of a President of the Treasury Board in 1963 (as confirmed by the Government Organization Act of 1966) central co-ordination of management policy has been severed from the Department of Finance and assigned to an independent centre for authoritative guidance. There were some who considered the reorganizer's scalpel had caused serious bleeding in thus divorcing management issues from purely financial considerations. On the other hand, such issues should not be settled by reference only to expenditure, for efficient and positive management practices cannot be based narrowly on monetary factors alone.

The emergence of what amounts to a small department of management must be viewed alongside a comparable evolution of the Privy Council Office. As previously noted, this office was elevated above its traditional menial role as a central record keeper when its permanent head was made secretary to the cabinet. Further extension of its functions now makes this office a central co-ordinating and service arm for the cabinet on such emerging policy issues as science, poverty, bilingualism, just as the Office of President of the Treasury Board serves the management committee of the cabinet (Treasury Board) for all major administrative policies and procedures.

The other co-ordinating and service departments listed in this third category raise no fresh issues worthy of comment, for we have already enlarged on the key concern of all specialized servicing or housekeeping agencies: how to preserve their 'purity' against the pressures from operating departments and how to confine them to their servicing functions without attaching their own restrictive conditions to the services.

CONSERVATION, DEVELOPMENT, AND
PROMOTION OF PHYSICAL RESOURCES

As noted in the previous chapter departments most closely concerned with these functions have tended to be organized around one major physical resource or (in the fifth category) one group of human recipients of the services to be provided. At the outset, however, to have organized departments along such specific lines would have been to foster the creation of agencies with insufficient duties to warrant full departmental status. Two measures were taken to counter this difficulty: first, the then limited programmes concerned with human resources were grouped in what seemed the most appropriate physical resource department; second, several physical resources rather than a single resource were used as the basis for departmentalization.

We have previously noted how, after much shuffling of functions, the strictly land-oriented functions were assembled under one roof: the Department of Mines and Technical Surveys (subsequently Energy, Mines and Resources – with a spill-over to Indian Affairs and Northern Development). A late concession to the importance of the forests was made by creating a very small but separate department for this single resource (subsequently adding Rural Development from Agriculture and, ultimately, merging forests with fisheries). But the proper disposition of the programmes associated with land have been perpetually plagued by an alternative and apparently equally logical basis for departmental organization, that is, the location of the land. In its heydey of expansion during the last two decades of the nineteenth century, the Department of the Interior responded to the logic of the 'place' basis of organization by creating within itself a unique Lands Board whose headquarters, as well as its operations, were located in western Canada. The arrangement was abandoned in 1897 and did not reappear until, with the creation of the Department of Northern Affairs and National Resources (now Indian Affairs and Northern Development) a new amalgam of programmes was introduced to concern itself with both physical and human resources of all kinds that were physically located in the northern territories of Canada. An amalgam of a similar order is to be found in the most recent portfolio, Regional Economic Expansion, which is designed to embrace all the special area development programmes, each with a strong 'place' orientation.

The only other natural resource which had been deemed of sufficient importance to warrant departmental status was the fisheries. For most of the time, however, the programmes associated with the fisheries were not substantial enough to warrant the full accolade of a department. Thus fisheries were persistently associated with programmes directed to servicing the navigational needs of the nation on the St Lawrence and the adjoining coastal waters – a marriage of convenience rather than a union of administrative affinities that was only broken off when the marine functions were transferred in 1936 to a more congenial home in the newly created Transport Department. This left no other option, apparently, than to confer full departmental status on the surviving partner – the fisheries. In 1969 this small department was merged with the other small unit of forestry.

The Department of Trade and Commerce previously identified with the group of departments concerned with physical resources is perhaps the most confusing for the administrative analyst to place, largely because it appears to cut across the grain of all the bases used for organizing other departments. Its primary purpose is to promote external trade and encourage domestic commerce and industry. The performance of the first function requires an elaborate network of trade commissioner offices throughout the world, thus immediately setting it up in competition with the key foreign area department, External Affairs. To say that the trade commissioner service is out for business and the foreign service officer is concerned with all sorts of diplomatic and representational matters does not provide a precise way of delimiting the areas jointly occupied by the two. In any event, the essentially economic interests of Trade and Commerce are further sustained at headquarters by a concentration of responsibility for Canada's tariff negotiations and international economic policy. This arrangement, in turn, places it in direct competition with similar activities undertaken by the Department of Finance.

On the domestic promotional side, Trade and Commerce also cuts right across activities which in some measure are already performed by the resource departments like Agriculture, Fisheries and Forestry. These specialist activities of Trade and Commerce are also buttressed by a general concentration of economic analysts, planners, and forecasters at headquarters. Presumably the point of difference is that, while each resource department is concerned with promotion, market analysis, and economic forecasting in its own field, the Trade and Commerce groups are concerned with the Canadian economy in the round. Again, this distinction is not sharp enough to prevent duplication. In particular the creation in 1963 of a separate Department of Industry apparently covering roughly the same jursidtcional field as that occupied by Trade and Commerce, raised doubts about the ability to prevent overlapping and duplication between these two agencies. In the event, a merger was consummated in 1968.

Finally, as an historical accident, Trade and Commerce long retained a concern for regulation of certain elements that enter into the trade in commercial goods, for example, inspection of weighing and measuring devices and the labelling of certain products. From a functional standpoint, work of this type is also undertaken in other departments such as Agriculture and National Health and Welfare.

In 1966 the Government Organization Act initiated the first steps towards a more coherent grouping of such scattered servicing-cum-regulatory functions. A new Department of Registrar General was created to absorb a mixed array of functions relating to combines, mergers and monopolies, patents, copyright and trade marks, bankruptcy and insolvency, corporate affairs, and the office of custodian of enemy property. The bulk of these, including custody of the Great Seal, had historically been housed in the Department of the Secretary of State. In 1967 a new Department of Consumer and Corporate Affairs replaced the Registrar General Department and broadened its scope by drawing from Trade and Commerce, Health and Welfare, and Agriculture an assortment of regulatory, inspecting, and informational functions broadly related to the protection of consumer interests.

Reverting to the Department of Trade and Commerce, it will be seen why it is rather difficult to categorize. In so far as it seeks to promote trade abroad in all Canadian commodities it runs afoul of the Department of External Affairs which occupies many of the same localities; in so far as it builds at headquarters a staff of trade negotiators and international economic experts it trespasses both on External Affairs and the Department of Finance. At the same time the more heavily it becomes involved in analysing Canada's domestic economic situation and in measures to encourage internal economic prosperity, the more it is inclined to intrude on promotional and analytical functions performed by the several resource departments in their own right and also, for a brief time, by the Department of Industry, and, most recently, by the independent Economic Council of Canada. Purpose, place, process, and even clientele – all the possible bases for building an organization – have entered into the allocation of programmes to this department. The result is the prospect that every activity of the department overlaps, competes with, or supplements similar activities performed by most of the other departments.

The department, in short, presents every appearance of being an administrative 'maverick,' superimposed on other departments with a view to providing an essential co-ordinating function in the promotion of domestic and external trade in all products. The fact that no control accompanies the co-ordinating role assigned the department forces it to rely on the acquisition of superior knowledge about the total economic structure of Canada and thereby attain an influence over economic policy-making that none of the more specialized departments could claim to possess. Obviously, it makes sense to have only one department abroad for promoting Canada's economic interests; otherwise every resource department would be much more in the act than it now is. It also makes sense to establish a focal point somewhere in the public service for assembling and analysing the data relating to the whole Canadian economy and equipped to offer advice on measures required to strengthen the weak links. Thus, in line with this philosophy, the merger with the separate Department of Industry makes sense, as does the reassigning of its regulatory and inspecting functions to the Department of Consumer and Corporate Affairs.

Whether the merged Departments of Trade and Industry are performing functions that could be assigned respectively to External Affairs and to the Department of Finance is at least open to debate. Perhaps the basic reason why Trade and Commerce appears to lack a coherent base for the allocation of work assigned to it is that for the promotion of commerce and industry the government has relied on a host of non-departmental agencies concerned with direct operation in these fields or else through providing supporting services or subsidies to or regulating the private sector. In any event, we must leave the Department of Trade and Industry much as it was at the very beginning of its career, with a large question mark over its declared purposes and, as a result, the prime example of the use of conflicting principles of organization cutting athwart all other departments that have achieved a somewhat clearer organizational definition. It is not unlikely that the addition of the Department of the Environment (in 1972 headed by the Minister of Fisheries) will foster a similar situation in which, for example, Energy, Mines and Resources may complain of jurisdictional 'invasion' by this newer co-ordinating department.

PROTECTION AND DEVELOPMENT OF HUMAN RESOURCES

The trend of work allocation to departments concerned with human resource programmes has followed a roughly parallel pattern. Their early conjunction with departments primarily oriented to physical resources was simply a stop-gap arrangement pending the full flowering of federal responsibilities for human resources in this century. In this instance, two types of organization have evolved: one to deal with selected categories of citizens with special claims to government services – the Indians, immigrants, and veterans; the other concerned more generally with the citizen public as a whole.

Strictly clientele-oriented departments emerged to administer the programmes for the special categories: Citizenship and Immigration, Veterans Affairs. But, in the case of the former, the factor of location has entered to complicate the picture, with the result that Indians and Inuit in the north are joined with physical resources to make up the jurisdiction of the Department of Indian Affairs and Northern Development, while immigrants have lost their clientele-based organization with their merger into a Department of Manpower and Immigration.

Two more departments, Labour and National Health and Welfare, share between them the programmes more broadly directed to the citizen body as a whole. Even here, clear-cut jurisdictional lines are confused by the semi-clientele status of the Labour Department in which certain welfare and rehabilitation functions, which might otherwise be in Health and Welfare, have been assigned to the Department of Labour. A recent addition to this group is the Department of Consumer and Corporate Affairs which, as we have seen, combines a mix of registration, informational, and regulatory functions (many of which historically had been located in the Department of the Secretary of State in his other capacity as Registrar General).

In general, these functions and services look to the protection of the individual as consumer or investor. By the same token, the Secretary of State Department has now thrown off its historical registration and recording functions to become a foster parent for a wide assortment of non-departmental agencies broadly devoted to providing cultural amenities for the general public. Thus, in its new role, this department too could be transferred from the third category of governmental services (in which it long fitted) to this fifth category.

AN EXERCISE IN REORGANIZATION

The allocation of programmes concerned with the conservation and development of physical and human resources provides the most striking evidence of the wide range of options open to the would-be organizer of the public service. It would appear that no matter what basis is used for work division jurisdictional conflicts are inevitable, and that with each asset of the present allocation there is a corresponding liability. It is interesting, therefore, to speculate on the prospects of achieving a more coherent departmental framework for these two areas of government activity.

Looking first at the departmental grouping of programmes directed to special categories of the population we observe that, historically, the clientele-based organization has been favoured. Today, the outstanding example is Veterans Affairs. The ex-serviceman constitutes a significant element of the population, is well organized in national interest groups, and politically – in addition to the vote – has been well sponsored in parliament, particularly in the Veterans Affairs Committee.[12] In addition, the veterans have a legitimate moral claim on the whole community for having risked life and limb in its defence. These factors may create a political situation which induces sensitive executive and legislative branches to ensure this influential clientele is well nurtured by a federal agency entirely devoted to this objective. If a reorganization resulting in the demise of this agency were to be undertaken, it should not, in all justice to the ex-serviceman, be done if the package of services and benefits embodied in the so-called Veterans Charter were to be lost.

Given this precautionary note, there are at least three important trends which suggest that the present clientele organization deserves to be reconsidered. First, assuming no further wars, the veteran population is declining in number and as it declines and ages the special services which it once required are also undergoing changes.[13] For example, many of the hospital cases which encouraged the construction of high-class hospitals with the most modern equipment are no longer active treatment centres but are amenable to more modest 'cottage hospital' day care. The second relevant development is the emergence of a full-bodied Department of National Health and Welfare to serve the needs of all citizens. Third, the growth of elaborate and efficient provincial health and welfare services, coupled with various forms of insurance, has been a major feature of postwar developments. These three factors working together suggest that it may now be possible to phase the Department of Veterans Affairs out of the roster of federal departments. The needs of the veterans are not so different from those of any citizen and the services once provided for the veteran group alone are more and more being made available to the whole population through federal and provincial agencies. Under these condi-

---

12 A good illustration is provided in Select Committee on Veterans Affairs, *Minutes of Proceedings* (Ottawa, 1945); and *ibid.*, 1951, p. 186, Mr Gillis: 'The attitude of the government and this Committee over the years toward the legion has been very good. They look upon us as their representatives, not as members of a party ...'
13 Royal Commission on Government Organization, *Report*, III, *Services for the Public* (Ottawa, 1962), report no 15: 'Health Services,' chap. 2.

tions, it becomes more inefficient and uneconomic to retain a clientele-based structure, replete with expensive facilities for which there will be a declining demand and maintaining parallel establishments of doctors, nurses, and technicians.

Two other elements of the Canadian population have also been served over the years by clientele-based agencies, namely, the Indians and the immigrants. Neither of these groups, unlike the ex-servicemen, have been well organized or carried much political weight. Thus, there is likely to be less outcry if reorganization were to lead to the abandonment of the historical clientele arrangements for both groups. Indeed, current indications and recent organizational changes suggest that the phasing-out operation is gradually taking place. From 1950–66 the Department of Citizenship and Immigration sheltered the clientele branches for immigrants and Indians. However, as previously noted, Indians in remote northern locations were being transferred to a 'place-based' organization, the Department of Northern Affairs and National Resources, and the transfer has now been completed by means of the reorganization of 1966 which produced a new Department of Indian Affairs and Northern Development. In the same reorganization, which witnessed the demise of Citizenship and Immigration, the immigrants were assigned to a new Department of Manpower and Immigration.

With respect to the Indians, this regrouping reflects an intention to merge the native population with the general citizenry as perhaps the best way now of implementing a long unfulfilled policy to convert the natives from wards of the state to full-grown citizens. There is a trend now to educate Indians located in the provinces in 'integrated' provincial institutions, just as 'integrated' hospital facilities are becoming increasingly common. In short, health and welfare functions conducted on behalf of the Indians by a special clientele branch would progressively move to the Department of National Health and Welfare and, by arrangement with provincial authorities, would be administered by the provinces. Similarly, education would also devolve on the provinces. In the territories, temporary concentration of these programmes could be retained in Indian Affairs and Northern Development, to take advantage of this area-based department, until such time as the existing Territorial Councils acquired provincial status and were capable of assuming these functions. Administration of Indian trust funds might well be vested in Finance which is already the custodian of a number of special funds.[14]

14 One might also add to the possibilities listed in the text the contemporary desire to promote local self-government on the reserves, precipitated by a general restiveness as 'Red Power' advocates become more articulate and politically conscious.

With regard to the immigrants, once in Canada their merger into the general labour force already seems to be envisaged in their placement in the Department of Manpower and Immigration. However, the services for immigrants are by no means properly covered by this move. There are health services relating mainly to the initial entry of the immigrant which might be absorbed by Health and Welfare, thereby incidentally eliminating duplication of medical examining officers carried on the roster and inducing greater reliance on locally retained doctors in foreign countries to conduct medical examinations. The promotional work now handled by immigration agents abroad might conceivably be taken on by the trade commission offices which are already dispersed in appropriate foreign locations. The registry and certificate-issuing functions of the Citizenship Branch have already passed to the Secretary of State (which itself has evolved as a near equivalent to a Ministry of Culture), while much greater use would have to be made of provincial and voluntary associations to deal with the difficult period of adjustment and possible training preceding their admission to the labour force.

The dispersion of the programmes relating to immigrants away from the clientele base would obviously make life more complicated for the would-be immigrant and it is not nearly so clear in this case as in the case of Indians and ex-servicemen that the reorganization just hypothesized would be effective.

If we look next at the present allocation of programmes concerned with physical resources, are there any promising alternatives that are worth exploring? There are, at present, seven departments sharing the programmes in this field: Agriculture; Fisheries and Forestry; Energy, Mines and Resources; Indian Affairs and Northern Development; Regional Economic Expansion; Industry, Trade and Commerce; and the Department of the Environment. Four of these are built around the programmes associated with promotion and conservation of a single resource, and in this respect are akin to the clientele departments that, as we have just observed, seek to manage all the activities related to a specific group of citizens. Indian Affairs and Northern Development as well as Regional Economic Expansion, relying on an organization based on place, partially cut across the various resource-oriented boundaries, as does Industry, Trade and Commerce. As in the case of clientele departments, organization by single resource encourages the creation in each agency of parallel facilities – in this instance most notably in the common area of research and information.

The search for a better allocation of work reveals that two alternatives are available. Using a strictly functional approach, one could, for example, carve out of each of these departments all the research and ancillary operations and merge them in a single department of research. This would 'orphan' all the remaining activities broadly connected with education, promotion, administration of grants, and development. The grouping of these in yet another department would not provide a particularly satisfactory basis for organization and, more important, would artificially sever the organic connection that should exist between research on the one hand and the dispersal and application of the results of research on the other hand.

The other alternative would be to assemble all the single resource departments in one large holding company – a department of resources. Assuming that the present level of staffing would remain unaffected by these changes, such a department would then comprise a staff of sixteen to eighteen thousand: a large department, but still only about one-third the size of National Defence, considerably smaller than the Post Office, and not much larger than the present Department of Veterans Affairs. But, if the main merit of this exercise is to improve co-ordination in the handling of all resource-oriented programmes, the overall size, coupled with the variety of activities, would probably defeat the purpose.

That there has been much concern over the lack of co-ordination in the physical resource programmes may be demonstrated by the fact that, between 1909 and 1921, a Canadian Conservation Commission existed, ostensibly to fill this need. During its relatively short lifetime the commission's investigative and advisory functions helped to substitute for deficiencies in the scientific and research facilities of existing departments. But, as these deficiencies were made good within each of the resource departments, the Conservation Commission more and more became an extra wheel.

The emergence of the National Research Council (created in 1916) in the twenties as both a promoter of scientific education in the universities and as operator of major research establishments in its own right encouraged a limited consolidation and co-ordination of the government's growing scientific programmes. By the 1960s, however, the proliferation of research activities in many departments as well as in specialized agencies, coupled with the significant outlay of public funds on research, provided strong reasons for introducing more effective central co-ordinating mechanisms. Until 1949 the only instrument available for providing top-level scrutiny of the government's varied research undertakings was the Committee of the Privy Council on Scientific and Industrial Research.

In 1949 an Advisory Panel for Scientific Policy brought together a group of thirteen senior officials who were most concerned with research, but neither this panel nor the Privy Council committee met frequently enough to provide continuous assessment of priorities and co-ordination of programmes.[15]

Following recommendations of the Glassco commission a Science Secretariat was established within the Privy Council Office in 1964 as a co-ordinating and service agency, for departments and other bodies concerned with scientific research and development. In 1966 the Science Council was brought into being to permit a broadly representative body to provide the overview of national science policy and priorities that had failed to emerge under either the National Research Council or the Privy Council committee. In 1970–1, as part of a new approach to cabinet organization, a Minister of State for Science and Technology was appointed, apparently with co-ordination as the prime function.[16]

Thus, it would appear that, since no alternative method of allocating work in the physical resource field is likely to be an improvement on the present arrangements, the necessary co-ordination of the work must be achieved by the new top-level machinery introduced from 1964 on. The solution, then, is not to be found in a drastic reallocation of programmes; it is more likely to be found in the development of co-ordinating mechanisms inserted at a supradepartmental level and specialized to the particular function. Scientific research and development, as has been noted, constitutes the hard core of the resource department's programmes; thus, a central agency for co-ordinating these programmes and establishing priorities by means of budgetary allocation, will be the most practicable approach, not only for providing overall perspective on the research activities of the resource departments but on the research and developmental functions widely scattered in other agencies of the public service. In essence, this would appear to have been the thinking underlying the creation of a Science Secretariat and the Science Council of Canada in 1964 and 1966 respectively; it would also appear to be the major rationale for the recent appointment of a Minister of State for Science and Technology. In a more limited way, also, the creation of a Department of the Environment fits the same co-ordinating objectives.

15 The details of this co-ordinating machinery are critically appraised in Royal Commission on Government Organization, *Report*, IV, report no 23: 'Scientific Research and Development,' p. 219 ff. For an analysis of recent developments, see G. Bruce Doern, *Science and Politics in Canada* (Montreal and London, 1972).
16 This proposal had been prominent before the Senate's Committee on Science Policy. See Doern, *ibid.*, appendix A.

This chapter has dealt with the way in which the many programmes relating to the five main areas of government activities have been allocated to departments. The assumption is that the allocation follows some common denominator, whether it be the similarity of purpose, the identification of programmes related to a selected clientele or a particular area, or a grouping of activities around a particular skill. It is clear that the Canadian departmental system has not been created by applying one particular criterion of organization; it is equally clear that no matter what principles are applied, precise jurisdictional boundaries can never be so satisfactorily established that overlapping, conflict, and duplication can be completely avoided. There are always reasonable alternatives and the selection of one basis of work allocation inevitably creates problems, even as it may solve others. Faced with a range of options, the organizer of a departmental system must make his choice with complete awareness of the benefits he may be sacrificing in discarding the alternative bases for organization.

The balance he has to strike must invariably involve the weighing of many factors. How important is it to achieve co-ordination and standardization of the programmes and services rendered? What is the significance of local or regional variations in physical, economic, and social factors? Is it important to preserve close working relations with selected segments of the Canadian public? What are the comparative advantages of grouping programmes to correspond with a particular profession or technical skill? These are some of the more important practical considerations.

More elusive but equally relevant are the policy implications inherent in work divisions. Does the location of a programme in a particular department subject it to certain biases that are rooted in the responsibilities traditionally associated with a department? Can a programme be submerged and stultified by placing it in an agency whose other functions are much more important or effectively compete with the added programmes? Will the addition of a significant new programme to an existing department distort its activities? The queries could be extended almost indefinitely, but the sample is enough to show the complexity of the problem of work allocation. In particular, the questions should suggest that often more than administrative tidiness or logic is at stake: prominent and inescapable pressures from organized groups, which governments feel obliged to placate in order to retain electoral favour, may necessitate an administratively indefensible method of allocating work. Policy and personal biases among departments and cabinet ministers may dictate an assignment of programmes that, in terms of administrative coherence, is palpably ineffective. Growth or decline of programmes may not be properly reflected or not acknowledged soon enough in the reallocation of work to departments. Nor can one overlook the implications for the cabinet of grouping work units into departments[17]: an overly refined grouping rigorously following one or other criterion of organization may well lead to an unwieldy cabinet; a gross assignment of functions to a few portfolios may solve the problem of an overly large cabinet but leave each minister with an unmanageable portfolio. In short, the labours of the re-organizer can never culminate in the Utopian dream of 'the one best system': he must pragmatically steer as sensible a course as he can between all the shoals that block progress towards the most practicable and effec-tive structure that the totality of these many conflicting forces will permit to exist.

A striking feature of the sixties has been the trend towards repeated and radical sortation of work to existing portfolios. This organizational shifting demonstrates the value of such a flexible act as the Rearrangement and Transfer of Duties Act by which the executive through orders in council can effect such reallocation of duties. At the same time, the organizational instability accompanying such frequent changes must have a deleterious effect on employee morale and departmental loyalties, particularly when it may occur abruptly and with little or no advance warning. Not only is it interesting to speculate on the psychological impact on employees of rapid and radical organizational shuffling, it is equally interesting to ponder the problems for top administrators in seeking – almost overnight – to weld into a new department two or more organizations that have had to develop entirely different organizational responses. One could ask, for example, whether Fisheries and Forestry – each once separate depart-ments – can really be blended or whether they will continue to live separ-ate organizational lives; whether the Immigration Branch will be sub-merged by the broader concern for Manpower; whether a department hitherto highly centralized can adjust to the needs of a highly decentralized agency transferred to it; and so on. What is becoming increasingly clear is that with one new problem after another competing for priority attention by the government, the departmental walls begin to crumble in the face of the demand for combining and then recombining the units concerned with the programmes relevant to the new policies.

An all-out attack on poverty will require one combination of pro-grammes, assembled out of existing departmental portfolios; pollution control or conservation another combination; regional development or

17 On this point, as well as a number of issues raised in this chapter, see the early (but still unique) study by Schuyler C. Wallace, *Federal Departmentalization: A Critique of Theories of Organization* (New York, 1941).

urban renewal yet other combinations. And, if all these vital issues claim equal priority yet require different organizational amalgams to operate their unique programmes, the portents for continued and aggravated organizational uneasiness in the departmental rubric are strikingly clear.[18] The prognosis for organizational simplicity and stability is not improved if we add to the foregoing picture the problem of regional programmes implicit in the work of most federal departments and by no means all brought to a focus in the new Department of Regional Economic Expansion.

While this chapter closes on a note of foreboding it is only fair to say that the sense of organizational uneasiness created by the present state of the conventional departmental system is compounded as we now introduce the welter of organizational non-conformists that, over the years, have grown up as appendages to or quite independent of the departments. These are the subject of the following chapter.

18 See chap. 15 for fuller speculative commentary on this phenomenon.

CHAPTER SEVEN | Structural heretics: the non-departmental forms

Flanking the departmental structure that makes up the 'civil service' proper there exists another, numerically much larger, group of administrative entities whose functions and structures are so varied that they virtually defy classification. Taken in conjunction with the departments they make up what might properly be called, in a global sense, the 'public service of Canada.'[1] This chapter attempts to describe the way in which the programmes allocated to departments have spilled over into this motley collection of non-departmental agencies. In the course of the analysis it will be possible to show why the departmental containers have been unable to absorb the accumulating workload assigned to the state, for in the reasons given for resorting to other types of administrative entities we discover the defects from which departments are claimed to suffer. Some attempt is also made to 'type' and categorize this miscellany, but it should be admitted at the outset that each entity is to some extent *sui generis* and any catalogue is essentially an oversimplification of the infinite variables found among these different containers.

1 The Public Service Staff Relations Act (Stats Can. 1967, c.72) in its definitions, section 2(x), reads: '"Public Service" means the several positions in or under any department or other portion of the public service of Canada specified from time to time in Schedule A.' Part I of Schedule A lists those portions of the public service for which the Treasury Board is the employer; part II has a much smaller list of 'portions of the public service of Canada that are separate employers.' A number of the agencies to which this chapter will refer are not in either part of the schedule, and therefore not in the strictly legal sense part of the 'public service of Canada.' On the other hand, in the context of a comprehensive conspectus of all the non-departmental public organizations, I shall continue to use the term 'public service' in a more global and inclusive sense than the legal definition would admit.

The resort to non-departmental forms of administrative units is rooted in two basic considerations. First, there is the straightforward and simple proposition that as the workload of a conventional department expands a point is reached where the tasks become unmanageable and ways must be sought to lighten the load. The obvious response when this situation arises is to create another department; but, as we have seen, the political conventions surrounding the Canadian cabinet system impose a limit on the number of departments. Thus, a solution had to be found by adopting some administrative variant of the departmental form. The second governing consideration which has grown in importance is that not only do the functions of government expand but, to an increasing extent, they tend to differ so much in kind from the traditional functions that the conventional department is no longer deemed appropriate.

These two considerations provide a convenient frame of reference within which our exploration of these non-departmental entities can be conducted. Since the first consideration dominated in the early stages of growth of the Canadian public service and the second factor has become more influential in recent times, the analysis can follow a reasonably chronological path.

THE 'SPILL-OVER' PROBLEM

Despite the modest dimensions of the early post-Confederation civil service it was not long before the government had to face up to the question of overburdened ministries. The exact nature of the remedy adopted is described in a memorandum prepared for Sir John A. Macdonald in 1883 for presentation to council; it deals with the proper disposition of the Mounted Police and Geological Survey:[2]

Though a quasi-military organization, the Mounted Police Force being, as its name implies, one with the maintenance of law and order in the Territories in which it is placed, it might from a certain point of view be supposed to come properly under the supervision of the Department of Justice, but as, for other reasons, Government has decided that the force should be under the control of the Minister of the Interior, there exists the apparent anomaly of the management of such force through a Department that is, otherwise, to a great extent, if not exclusively, a land department.

It is therefore suggested that the Comptroller of the Mounted Police Branch should be given the rank of a Deputy Head, and the branch be constituted another Department of the service under the Minister of the Interior.

The operations of the Geological and Natural History Survey are so largely

2 PC 2122, 17 Oct. 1883.

professional in their nature, and so entirely dependent on their effective prosecution upon the skill and judgment of its director that he should be immediately responsible to the Head of the Department.

It is therefore suggested that he also should have the rank of a deputy head and that the business of his branch should become that of a separate department under the Minister of the Interior.

In essence, the solution, as advocated in this memorandum and adopted by the cabinet, was to relieve an overloaded department by singling out a large, distinctive function that had no organic connection with the other activities for which the department was responsible and then to give its permanent managerial head the same status as a deputy minister. The normal constitutional chain of command and control was retained by having the statutory head report directly to the minister. The fact that such segregated, self-contained functions were sometimes statutorily defined as 'departments' confuses the nomenclature, as we have already seen, and for our purposes they are best viewed as 'junior' departments which, even though answerable to a minister, lack direct ministerial representation in the cabinet. In Britain, typically, these might well have been given a junior minister of their own but without a place on the cabinet; however, in Canada the idea of junior ministers never really gained acceptance.

These two organizational expedients established a precedent for similar reassignment of workloads in situations where a function was large enough, sufficiently complete within itself, and, on the whole, somewhat remote from the normal operation of a regular line department. In addition to the Royal Canadian Mounted Police and the Geological Survey other specimens of this genre include the following: the Public Archives, the Department of Public Printing and Stationery, the commissioner of penitentiaries, the Department of Insurance, the inspector general of banks, the master of the Mint (in 1969, transformed into a corporation), the chief electoral officer, the custodian of enemy property, the dominion statistician, the national librarian, the commissioner of the Yukon, the director of the Prairie Farm Rehabilitation Administration, the government film commissioner, and the director of the Veterans Land Act. All of these were set up in the same general form in pursuit of the same objective of devolving the workload. The only feature shared by this wide range of dependent departmental entities is that they are each concerned with a function that can be severed sharply from the normal department with a minimum of 'bleeding.' They also share the same direct relationship to a minister, rather than reporting as part of the regular departmental hierarchy through the deputy head to the minister. In the main, these junior appendages are required to report to a minister whose main port-folio is not totally unrelated to the special, separate function they perform.

One must assume, if the purpose of this junior departmental organiza-tion is to drain off some of the workload of a department and lighten the minister's supervisory responsibilities, that they will receive less active attention from the minister (or his deputy) than is given to the function of the department proper. Indeed, a feature common to most of these entities is that they function in areas where policy issues do not arise (for example, the Mint or the Archives) or where policy can be laid down so clearly that no important discretionary powers are involved (for example, chief electoral officer, custodian of enemy property, etc.). Thus, it is possible to visualize a single minister capable of answering for several of these junior appendages as an almost routine operation, with no great addition to his regular departmental duties and no undue stretching of his effective span of control.

In short, the creation by statute of these quasi-departmental appendages does the least violence to the constituted system of ministerial responsi-bility, even as it provides a means of removing selected, self-contained functions from overburdened major departments.

In recent times a variation on the 'junior' department approach to overloading has been introduced; this is the so-called 'departmental cor-poration.' Once again, as with the junior departments, a particular, self-contained function has been singled out from the normal work of a department and a special legal status of a 'corporation' has been conferred on the agencies set up to perform the function. We shall have occasion in the next section of this chapter to consider the use of the corporate form of administrative entity for activities that are similar to those performed by private industrial and commercial concerns. This is not the type of function, however, for which the departmental corporations have been brought into existence: they are, to quote the definition provided by the Financial Administration Act, section 76(3)(a), 'responsible for ad-ministrative, supervisory, or regulatory services of a governmental nature.' In short, they are performing functions which a branch of any department might well be expected to perform, but their relationship both to the regular department and to the central financial and personnel agencies of the government is by no means uniform. The only common feature to be found among these agencies is that each is managed by a board rather than by a single head, and one must assume that collegial management (and hence the corporate status) is deemed more appropriate for the particular functions than is the conventional one-man direction provided through the departmental hierarchy.

If the board form of organization is, indeed, at the base of this type of structure, one may well ask why for one set of functions such as those carried out by the National Research Council it is essential to give independent corporate status, while for other and apparently similar functions (for example, in Agriculture or Energy Mines and Resources) no such corporate board form has been instituted. Moreover, why should some of the agencies in this group be quite free from the central personnel control imposed on the normal department (for example, the NRC) while in other cases they are treated by the Public Service Commission and the Treasury Board like the staff of a department (for example, the Unemployment Insurance Commission)? In some cases, such as the Agriculture Stabilization Board, the Fisheries Prices Support Board, the Canadian Maritime Commission, and the Dominion Coal Board, the board members are all drawn from the permanent staff of the parent department. In other cases, such as the National Research Council, the National Gallery, and the Unemployment Insurance Commission, the boards are separate and distinct from any departments. The Atomic Energy Control Board, on the other hand, is a composite agency – essentially a device for bringing together the heads of the bodies that have operating and research responsibilities in the field of atomic energy. Nor is there any consistency in the method by which these agencies are associated with the formal structure of ministerial command and responsibility that is a feature of the regular departmental system. Several of the agencies appear to be precisely in the same position vis-à-vis the minister as are any of the conventional branches of the same department; others are subject only to such directives as the minister cares to issue.

No useful purpose is served by expanding on these contradictions and inconsistencies found among this particular group of agencies. Our primary concern is with discovering a rationale for the particular mode of work division selected and, in this instance, the clue is the board form of organization. Obviously, the ordinary hierarchical pattern within a department is not adapted to vesting responsibilities in a collegial body, hence we must see what justifications there are for adopting a board form of organization that forces the entity out of the conventional departmental structure.

Broadly speaking, there appear to be two justifications for a board in this particular context. First, the nature of the work assigned is such that it is desirable to provide a means of representing various expert or interested opinions – an objective which only a collegial arrangement could meet. Thus, the National Gallery, the National Research Council, and the Unemployment Insurance Commission all specifically provide in their statutes for the representation of outside interests whose opinions are regarded as essential for policy making, regulating, or operations. If this be so, then we have every reason to add to this group – even though they may not share the same corporate legal status – such bodies as the Fisheries Research Board, the National Film Board, the Canada Council, and the Economic Council and the Science Council.

A board may also be essential – on the premise that several heads are better than one – in the handling of special funds. This would appear to explain the Agriculture Stabilization Board, the Fisheries Prices Support Board, the Maritime Commission, and the Coal Board, as well as the long-lingering Halifax Relief Commission. In all these cases, however, the board is much more a part of the regular departmental structure than is the case with the other boards mentioned immediately above. The necessity for such formal arrangements to provide what is, in essence, an intra-departmental committee for conducting a particular operation is not nearly so apparent and one may well query the solution adopted in these cases since many special funds are administered elsewhere in the public service by conventional branches of a particular department.

In summary, the organizational response to what we have termed the problem of 'spill-over' in the workload assigned to departments has been the creation of a veritable jungle of quasi-departmental agencies. Many of these are virtually junior departments – in some instances even bearing the statutory label of 'department'; an equally large number are under collegial management, in some instances carrying the legal status of a 'corporation' but with few, if any, similarities so far as their relation to a minister, department, and central financial or personnel control agencies is concerned. The mutual inconsistencies and contradictions reflect the pragmatic nature of the response to the growing burdens of government. In consequence, the conventional channels of ministerial responsibility and control are clogged up or obscured, while parliamentary supervision and public comprehension are correspondingly diminished.

THE CHANGING CHARACTER OF STATE FUNCTIONS

It is when we come to the second consideration, the change in the character of government functions, that a whole new complex of non-departmental administrative forms is brought into view. The first important demonstration of the potency of this factor is to be found in the creation of the original Board of Railway Commissioners. Such a board was envisaged in the report of a royal commission on transportation in 1886–

7.[3] Its recommendations were clearly influenced by the evolution of regulatory machinery in the United States that culminated in 1887 with the setting up of the Inter-State Commerce Commission. A new term and a new organizational concept entered the administrator's vocabulary at this time: the word was 'independent' and the concept was an autonomous board or commission. Since both the legislature and the judiciary, as a result of the many years' experience with railway regulation, were deemed to be incapable of handling, on a day-to-day basis, the complex tasks to be faced in this area, the executive branch had to assume the burden. But, in the process, the executive was being asked to undertake functions which called for both adjudicative and law-making operations that were substantially different from those traditionally associated with conventional departmental operations. It followed, therefore, that a new type of administrative entity was required that could take on the impartial and independent stamp of the judiciary and could be entrusted with subordinate law-making functions that would have to be delegated to it.

In some such terms as these the case for allocating work to a nondepartmental agency was framed. The primary consideration, as distinct from the purely practical question of how to relieve an overburdened department, was, in this instance, the allegedly unique character of the function which in turn necessitated a departure from the administrative entity through which conventional governmental activities had traditionally been performed.

The first significant organizational response to this line of reasoning was, as noted, the Board of Railway Commissioners, which came into being in 1903, was enlarged and strengthened as the Board of Transport Commissioners in 1938, and in 1967, with the merging of two other regulatory bodies, became a part of the Canadian Transport Commission. The precedent established by this first organization was shortly followed up, this time as a device for collaborating on a governmental basis with the United States, by the creation of the International Joint Commission in 1909, followed by an International Boundary Commission in 1925.[4] After

3 A concise résumé of the rise and development of the Board of Railway Commissioners is to be found in Arthur R. Wright, 'An Examination of the Role of the Board of Transport Commissioners for Canada as a Regulatory Tribunal,' *Canadian Public Administration* 6 (Dec. 1963), pp. 349–85, and extensive references contained in footnotes.
4 The International Boundary Commission, in 1960 (Stats Can. 1960, c.31) had its original functions of inspection, repair maintenance, and arbitration of disputes extended to include the regulation of all works or construction within ten feet of the international boundary. The International Joint Commission is concerned with the use, obstruction, and diversion of boundary waters and rivers crossing between Canada and the United States.

a wartime interregnum a renewed spate of similar bodies appeared, each vested with the broad power to legislate through the issuance of rules and orders and to adjudicate all controversial questions arising from the application of the legislation. The Board of Grain Commissioners, the Tariff Board,[5] the Air Transport Board, the Restrictive Trades Practices Commission, the Board of Broadcast Governors (as of 1968 the Canadian Radio-Television Commission), the Atomic Energy Control Board, the Copyright Appeal Board, and the National Energy Board were the major representatives in this new category of semi-independent, 'quasi-judicial,' administrative agencies.

It is interesting to observe that practically all of these non-departmental agencies function in sectors of the economy which, as a reference to the previous chapter will show, had not been included as part of the jurisdiction of the conventional departments. But the impact of the changing character of governmental activities extended beyond those areas of the economy that increasingly required regulation. In addition, the mounting momentum of the welfare state began to reveal itself in an increasing number of benefits and services directed to selected categories of citizens. At once the question arose: who should be entitled to qualify for the benefits which parliament had declared should be made available? Traditionally, the law courts have been assigned the tasks of adjudicating questions involving individual rights. But as we have pointed out elsewhere the typical *modus operandi* of the courts was 'compensatory and punitive.'[6] They have been geared to a leisurely pace dictated by the historical interest in showing that justice manifestly be done – an interest safeguarded by cumbersome and expensive procedures along with a hierarchy of appeals. With these new benefits to be allocated, the number of individual cases would have swamped the regular judicial machinery which, in any event, was unsatisfactory because of its cost and deliberateness. Again, the judicial character of the work suggested the value of assigning it to a non-departmental entity. These considerations were operative, for example, when numerous benefits were conferred on the returning soldiers: the Canadian Pension Commission and the War Veterans Allowance Board were, therefore, created to adjudicate the individual claims of the veterans. The Merchant Seamen's Compensation Board plays a similar role with respect to a much more limited group of claimants. The largest

5 The Tariff Board operates in a judicial fashion in making inquiries and tendering reports to the government; it also acts in an appellate fashion in rulings from the Customs and Excise division of the Department of National Revenue. The board therefore occupies both an advisory and adjudicative position.
6 J.A. Corry and J.E. Hodgetts, *Democratic Government and Politics* (3rd ed., Toronto, 1959), pp. 415, 528.

and most important of the agencies in this category is the Unemployment Insurance Commission.

Two other important agencies in this category are concerned with appeals against decisions made by government departments rather than with specific claims to benefits. These are the Tax Appeal Board (1958), first created in 1946 as the Income Tax Appeal Board, and the Immigration Appeal Board (1967). Before these bodies were brought into being appeal on decisions was strictly internal, ending with the minister or the cabinet. Finally, we might place in this group the Canada Labour Relations Board (1949) and its counterpart for government employees, the Civil Service Staff Relations Board (1967). It should be noted that the number of bodies empowered to adjudicate individual or group claims is much larger in the provinces than at the federal level because so many benefits and rights are conferred under provincial programmes.[7]

There has been an inconsistent organizational response to the judicial qualities of the type of work embraced by the foregoing agencies. In the cases just noted the argument for a special extradepartmental agency has been acknowledged; but in many other instances functions of an adjudicative nature have been left within the department. This was true until quite recently for immigration appeals and tax assessments and still holds true for such matters as claims for patents, courts martial, and regulation under the food and drug acts.

The interests and rights of individuals and firms are intimately affected by the action and decision taken by regulatory boards or agencies adjudicating claims, as well as by a number of departmental divisions that have somewhat similar authority. The possibility that injustices may be perpetrated by these administrative courts of the first instance – whether outside a department or as part of it – has been recognized in the creation of yet another tier of non-departmental agencies – this time primarily appellate bodies, though still part of the administrative organization rather than the judiciary. Thus, the Copyright Appeal Board exists, in part, to hear appeals from the commissioner of patents. Or again, decisions rendered by such non-departmental agencies as the Pension Commission and the Board of Grain Commissioners can be reviewed, respectively, by pension appeal boards or grain appeal tribunals; while the decision of administrators within the Prairie Farm Rehabilitation Administration and the Veterans Land Administration are equally subject to review by special boards.

7 For the province of Ontario, see (Gordon) Committee on the Organization of Government in Ontario, *Report* (Toronto, 1959); for a critical analysis of this development, see Peter Silcox, 'The Proliferation of Boards and Commissions,' in *Agenda 1970: Proposals for a Creative Politics*, ed. Trevor Lloyd and Jack McLeod (Toronto, 1968), pp. 115–34.

It is important to observe that in most instances these appellate bodies are creations of (if not the creatures of) the agency whose decisions are being contested. Thus, grain inquiries tribunals – *ad hoc* creations of the Board of Grain Commissioners – usually have at least one member of the board's inspection staff represented on them. In a few important cases there is an opportunity for transferring the appeal process from this administrative setting to the conventional judicial setting of the law courts (as, for example, in income tax or labour relations cases) but the limitations on this transaction and the disposition to give the administrative tribunals the last word raise fundamental questions about the accountability of the public service that cannot be further explored here.[8]

Yet another distinctive type of non-departmental administrative entity has emerged in response to the factors which have contributed to the rise of regulatory and adjudicative organs. This extremely large group may be characterized as advisory bodies, and it is no accident that their appearance coincides with the multiplication of the other types of agencies already described. In the performance of their regulatory functions, departments and agencies are required to impose standards, inspect, license, and make orders of both a specific or general nature. It is therefore desirable that the vital interests affected by the regulations can be induced to co-operate by being given an opportunity to influence the administrator's decision. Perhaps the increasing resort to advisory bodies implies a failure of our conventional party and legislative machinery to provide the necessary liaison and 'in-puts' into the political system. In this sense, public administrators are seeking ways of devising their own 'constituencies' with which they can maintain a direct relationship. Possibly a restructuring of the committee system of the legislature, paralleling the structure in the United States Congress, would reduce the need for such extraparliamentary institutions and improve the capacity of parliament to channel the interested public's views to the bureaucracy.

The chief value of advisory bodies lies in their ability to give the affected interests the opportunity to forestall complaints and criticisms that would ultimately plague the adjudicative and appellate bodies described above. They are also an obvious alternative to placing such interests directly on the regulatory bodies. Some of the typical advisory bodies falling in this category are: the Feeding Stuffs Advisory Board, Fertilizer Act Advisory Board, Livestock Products Advisory Committee, Pest Control Products Advisory Board, Proprietary or Patent Medicine

8 There is an extensive literature on this topic, but for a useful, concise treatment of the problems as they affect labour relations, see Canada, Department of Labour, *Judicial Review of Decisions of Labour Relations Boards in Canada* (Ottawa, 1969).

Act Advisory Board, Salt Fish Marketing Advisory Committee. At a much more general and sophisticated level the Science Council of Canada, the Economic Council, and, most recently, the Prices and Incomes Commission play the role of advisers to the cabinet, as in part does the Tariff Board. In a special advisory relation to parliament itself is the Office of Representation Commission,[9] while, since 1969, the Commissioner of Official Languages has been accorded a status akin to that of the Auditor General in performing his 'ombudsman' functions.

Among the advisory bodies associated with agencies responsible for distributing welfare and social benefits the following may be listed: Blind Pensions Advisory Board, Canadian Fishermen's Local Loan Advisory Board, Maritime Marshland Rehabilitation Advisory Committee, Old Age Assistance Advisory Board, Unemployment Insurance Advisory Committee, Veterans Land Act Advisory Committee, Vocational Training Advisory Committee, Prairie Farm Rehabilitation Administration Advisory Committee, National Employment Committee, the Labour Management Co-operation Service Advisory Committee.

This list does not even begin to touch the much larger number of advisory bodies (referred to in chapter 3) that exist primarily for dealing with problems of co-ordinating administrative services in which both the federal and the provincial governments have an interest. A recent compilation reveals that in a period of about a decade the number of these bodies has doubled from 65 to 125; this list does not include *ad hoc* advisory agencies set up for specific purposes.[10]

Advisory bodies must be considered an indispensable part of the Canadian public service organization – although they stand at the margin of the public service proper. They are an obvious response to changing functions of government that bring the public service into close contact with the public, either through its regulatory powers or its relatively new role as a dispenser of benefits. They may also be identified with the increasing technical complexity of the matters now coming within the purview of the state and the corresponding need of the state to avail itself of every possible source of skilled advice, not only in policy-formation but in

9 Public organizations such as the Science Council and the Economic Council represent an 'institutionalization' of the advisory functions performed by temporary, *ad hoc*, advisory teams such as are found in task forces and royal commissions. The Economic Council, for example, may be said to have been fostered as a device for continuing on a permanent, on-going basis, the kind of analyses developed by the Royal (Gordon) Commission on Canada's Economic Prospects. However, the Government Reorganization Act of 1969 transformed the Science Council into a public corporation, signifying a change in its purely advisory role.

10 See above, chap. 3, n. 2.

the execution of programmes. As noted above, for such agencies as the National Research Council or the Film Board, one way by which the government can avail itself of such assistance is by representing various groups on the directing board itself; advisory committees offer an alternative or, at times, supplementary means of bringing such views to bear on policy and administration.[11]

The changing character of state functions is attributable not only to growing responsibilities for regulating the economy and dispensing a variety of benefits, it is also related to the appearance of the state as an entrepreneur – the owner and operator of concerns destined to provide goods and services to the Canadian public. This is not altogether a novel role for the Canadian public service despite notions concerning the essentially laissez-faire nature of Canadian economic growth that erroneously depend on a rather romantic view of a 'pioneer' world in which the sturdy 'Canuck' is observed to shoulder his axe and independently carve out his own destiny from the bush. The fact is that the sturdy pioneer has always leaned heavily on the government, whether for land grants, roads, canals, or railways. The price of cementing and expanding the Canadian union has constantly necessitated a state involvement in settlement, transportation, and communication. Nevertheless, all these activities in early days were contained within the regular departmental system until their growing size and expanding responsibilities, fostered by the philosophical trend that supported positive state intervention in the economy, burst the walls of the old departments.[12] The First World War, rapid changes in technology affecting transportation, communication, and the exploitation of resources, and then the Second World War, all hastened the trend towards state operation and ownership – and the pace, if anything, is accelerating.

The organizational response to these trends has been the allocation of entrepreneurial functions to government corporate entities obviously modelled on the structures that have proven successful in private industry and commerce.[13] The corporate form has not been used solely for such

11 An interesting strategic problem for organized interest groups seeking 'access' to government is whether it is preferable to secure a place by direct representation on a deciding tribunal or to maintain a more independent arm's length relationship by seeking representation on an advisory body. Given this choice by the government when the Agricultural Prices Support Board was being created in 1944, organized agriculture opted for representation on the powerful Agricultural Advisory Committee. See *Can. H. of C. Debates*, 1944, p. 5377 ff.

12 The Board of Works for the Province of Canada in pre-Confederation times would be viewed today as a forerunner of the crown corporation. See my *Pioneer Public Service* (Toronto, 1955), pp. 176, 180, 190.

13 For more detailed discussion, see my 'The Public Corporation in Canada,' in *Government Enterprise: A Comparative Study*, ed. W. Friedmann and J.F. Garner (London, 1970), chap. 12.

new functions because, as noted above, it has also been employed as a means of injecting the board form of organization into the departmental structure. At this point, however, we shall concentrate on its use for activities of a commercial or industrial nature that have close parallels in private sectors. It should also be added that the corporate form has not been employed for certain traditional functions which would appear to fit all the reasons given by its protagonists; for example, the Post Office, Public Printing and Stationery, and the Mint are essentially business operations that might easily be regarded as suitable candidates for the corporate form of organization.[14] On the contrary, there are any number of agencies that have been accorded corporate status even though their functions afford no ready clue as to the necessity of distinguishing them in this fashion from ordinary departments.

The procession of corporate entities engaged in the provision of goods and services is headed by the Canadian National Railways which was set up in 1919 and is still, by far, the largest governmental enterprise. With its subsidiary, Canadian National (West Indies) Steamship Limited, set up in 1927, this corporate entity occupied for over a decade the position of sole representative of the strictly business-type government enterprise. The second experiment with this particular form of administrative entity came in 1927 with the creation of the Federal Farm Loan Board – subsequently renamed the Canadian Farm Loan Board in 1935 and reconstituted again in 1959 as the Farm Credit Corporation. In the 1930s the corporate device came into full bloom: in 1932 the Canadian Radio Broadcasting Commission – the forerunner of the Canadian Broadcasting Corporation of 1936; in 1932, again, the first experiment with a central bank designated by Prime Minister R.B. Bennett as 'a privately owned public trust' was fully converted through successive stages into the present Bank of Canada by 1938; the Canadian Wheat Board appeared in 1935; in 1936 the National Harbours Board was added to the list; and two years later Trans-Canada Airlines (Air Canada) made its appearance as a sub-

14 In 1972 the government had still to produce its long-promised white paper, recommending the reconstitution of the Post Office as a public corporation; under the Government Organization Act of 1969 the Royal Canadian Mint, for thirty-eight years reporting to the Department of Finance, was scheduled for conversion to a public corporation. In March 1964 the technical side of the Department of Public Printing and Stationery was transferred to the Department of Supply and Services, leaving the former as a centralized servicing agency. The Canadian Government Printing Bureau reports through its general manager to the deputy minister of its new foster parent, and to this extent remains in the traditional line of command rather than occupying the more autonomous role conferred on statutory executives that report directly to the minister (for example, Statistics Canada, formerly the Dominion Bureau of Statistics).

sidiary to the CNR. But it was in the decade of the forties that the heaviest additions were made to the roster. Several important corporations were set up to engage in lending and guaranteeing transactions, including the Industrial Development Bank, 1944 (a subsidiary of the Bank of Canada); Export Credits Insurance Corporation, 1944; and Central Mortgage and Housing Corporation, 1945. Another category of corporation emerged to carry on commodity trading and procurement functions, some of which were absorbed or abandoned after the war: Commodity Prices Stabilization Corporation Limited, 1941 (now defunct); War Assets Corporation (which became Crown Assets Disposal Corporation in 1950); two price support boards for agriculture and fisheries products in 1944; Canadian Commercial Corporation, 1946; Canadian Sugar Stabilization Corporation the following year; and Defence Construction, 1944 (which in 1951 assumed the charter of Wartime Housing Limited). Corporate agencies concerned with industrial and commercial enterprises included Polymer Corporation Limited, 1942; Eldorado Mining and Refining Limited, 1944; Northern Transportation Company Limited, 1947 (a subsidiary of Eldorado); Canadian Arsenals Limited, 1945; Northwest Territories Power Commission, 1948 (as of 1956 Northern Canada Power Commission); and Canadian Overseas Telecommunication Corporation, 1949. In the 1950s the crop was smaller but included such important newcomers as Atomic Energy of Canada Limited, 1952; the St Lawrence Seaway Authority, 1952; and Northern Ontario Pipe Line Crown Corporation, 1956. The 1960s witnessed an acceleration of the trend, beginning with the Atlantic Development Board in 1962 (but transformed from corporation to advisory body in 1969 and renamed Atlantic Development Council); the National Arts Centre Corporation, 1966; the Cape Breton Development Corporation, 1967; and the National Museums of Canada, 1968, that swept into a species of cultural holding corporation the National Gallery and the three museums of Human History, Natural History, and Science and Technology. Closing out the decade with a flourish, the Government Reorganization Act of 1969 conferred corporate status on the Mint, the Science Council, and the Medical Research Council, even as a separate act created the Canadian Film Development Corporation. The decade of the seventies opened auspiciously with the launching of the Canada Development Corporation (1971), even as long-deferred proposals for converting the Post Office and the Department of Public Works into crown corporations were still waiting in the wings.

The Financial Administration Act categorizes the various agencies listed above as either 'proprietary' or 'agency' corporations. The former category includes the corporations that most closely resemble their counterparts in the private businessworld: they provide goods and/or services for a fee or set price; they enjoy substantial freedom in the realm of policy, finance, and personnel; their organization is modelled closely on the board-management structure of the private corporation. The agency corporations include those that are engaged in governmental trading, lending, and procurement functions, as distinct from the sale of commodities or services at a price designed to make their operations self-sufficient. These agencies are all closely tied in with the system of central control to which regular departments must submit, but at the same time enjoy a measure of financial autonomy usually provided by means of revolving funds which relieve them of the annual necessity of seeking parliamentary appropriations to undertake their transactions.

Included in the list of agencies presented above is a group of variants known as 'crown companies,' immediately distinguishable from the others by virtue of the word 'Ltd.' which is appended to their title. Many of these administrative entities were born in the war – some three dozen crown companies having been on the list at the peak period of their use. Some of them have been continued as permanent additions to the nondepartmental roster. They differ from the public corporations proper in a number of ways. While the latter obtain their authority from specific acts of parliament, crown companies receive their powers in a more complicated, indirect fashion. The right to recommend, for cabinet approval, creation of a crown company is vested by separate statutes in four agencies: the Minister of Defence Production, the Atomic Energy Control Board, the National Research Council, and the St Lawrence Seaway Authority.[15] Issuance of an order in council provides authority for the next step in the creation of the crown company, namely an application to the Secretary of State under the terms of the Companies Act[16] for a charter of incorporation as a 'private' company. In 1965, the Companies Act became the Canada Corporation Act[17] (c. 52, 1964–5) and in 1970 the Minister of Consumer and Corporate Affairs took over the Secretary of State's functions. In addition to complying with the obligations outlined in the Canada Corporation Act an additional document, an 'Agreement' between the crown company and the sponsoring minister or agency, sets out in more explicit terms the structure, financing, and powers of the company.

When the wartime boom in incorporation was over, the government sought to rationalize and standardize the arrangements for the crown

15 Stats Can. 1951, c.4, s.7; Stats Can. 1946, c.37, s.10; Stats Can. 1946, c.31, s.9; Stats Can. 1956, c11, s.24A, respectively.
16 RSC 1952, c.53.
17 1964–5, c.52.

companies that still remained. In 1946 the Government Companies Operation Act[18] was passed with a view to unifying the legal and fiscal position of these companies. This measure was largely supplanted in 1951–2 by the Financial Administration Act in which the crown company was thoroughly mixed in with the regular statutory corporations by including it in either Schedule c (agency corporations) or Schedule d (proprietary corporations). A classification legitimately concerned with grouping agencies in relation to their degrees of fiscal independence and specific function tends, however, to conceal the very real differences between the legal bases of the crown companies and of the public corporations.

Even this sketchy survey of the use of the corporate form of administrative organization is enough to reveal that the resort to this practice has been extremely unsystematic and haphazard. Included in the schedule to the Financial Administration Act are many agencies that are there simply because they are in law 'bodies politic and corporate,' in no way concerned with functions akin to the industrial or commercial activities which gave rise to the corporate form in the private sector. Moreover, even if we separate out the corporate entities whose functions are not of a commercial or industrial nature, we are still left with a collection of public agencies characterized by almost infinite organizational variations, paradoxical relations with the conventional chain of ministerial command, viewed by the law courts in contradictory decisions, and possessing little in common so far as their alleged autonomy is concerned. While the indirect means of bringing crown companies into being was appropriate to a wartime situation where secrecy and speed were essential, the permission accorded the executive by several statutes to continue this procedure in peacetime seems to reduce unnecessarily the already meagre opportunities afforded to parliament to discuss the creation and subsequent operations of such agencies. Agreeing that part of the charm of the public corporation is its flexibility and adaptability to the peculiar circumstances surrounding the performance of a special function, this variability and inconsistency can only add to the confusion of parliament and the public as they contemplate the public service organization.[19]

The allocation of the government's workload, over the years, has resulted in the creation of a bewildering variety of organizational containers. The pragmatic and haphazard approach to the problem of work allocation

18 Stats Can. 1946, c.24.
19 For analysis and critique by the Royal Commission on Government Organization, see *Report*, v, *The Organization of the Government of Canada* (Ottawa, 1963), report no 24: 'The Organization of the Government of Canada,' p. 58ff.

makes the effort to order this universe a rather forced and artificial exercise. Nevertheless, some design must be superimposed on this disorderly structure if we are to gain even an impressionistic conspectus of the public service organization. The primary division has been made between the major operating departments and the myriad of non-departmental administrative entities. The first group is relatively small – only twenty-six active departments with ministerial heads in the cabinet having been identified.[20] There has, in fact, been astonishingly little increase in the number of departments with which we began one hundred years ago. Within the four walls of each of the major departments, however, there has been an expansion of staff and activities that makes today's departments quite unrecognizable in terms of the original. It is this internal growth that generates the problems of subdivision of labour with which the next two chapters are concerned.

The non-departmental organizations are so varied and have arisen in response to so many special problems of work allocation that they present a forbidding problem for the classifier. The closest equivalent to the departments proper are those agencies which we have characterized as junior or quasi-departments. All of these are statutory creations, each has a permanent head, reports to a relevant minister, but none can be said, for this reason, to have the status of a major department. These are the agencies which, by and large, have absorbed what we have called the 'spill-over' of functions from the conventional departments. They will invariably be found administering a specific programme which can be severed from the regular departmental hierarchy because it is not organically related to the main purposes of a department and because it is a complete unit in itself. Something of the order of sixteen such agencies can be fitted into this group.

A variant on the quasi-department is the agency that is set up under collegial supervision. Many of these have been vested with corporate status by their sponsoring statutes – a practice that has led to their confusion with another array of corporate governmental agencies that are engaged in commercial or business transactions. The board form has been adopted primarily as a method of giving representation to 'outside' in-

20 In the current (March 1972) roster of the 'Ministry' the prime minister, the leader of the government in the Senate, two ministers of state for designated purposes – urban affairs and science and technology, and one minister of state, along with twenty-seven parliamentary secretaries, are listed, for a total of fifty-seven. Although there are twenty-six separate departments of the conventional type, two of these – Fisheries and Forestry and Environment – are held by one minister. Assuming that all ministers of state are in the cabinet, it numbers thirty persons as of 1972.

terests (or the interests of several departments) in the management and execution of a particular programme – the programme itself, as in the case of the quasi-departments, comprising a self-contained activity that may have little organic connection with what goes on in a regular department. Roughly a dozen such entities fit into this category.

The remaining non-departmental units have, in the main, emerged in response to two basic changes in the conventional functions assigned to departments, quasi-departments, and operating boards. The first change is associated with the state's increasing responsibilities for regulating various sectors of the economy and dispensing a number of individual benefits. In the course of these transactions functions of a judicial and legislative nature had to be assumed by the public service. While it is true that some of these were, in fact, absorbed within the regular departmental apparatus, to an increasing extent they have been assigned to special deciding tribunals, separated off from the departments so as to emphasize their independence – an independence which was deemed essential if they were to arbitrate among conflicting interests that had to be regulated or to settle the claims of individuals for various benefits. This line of reasoning has led to the creation of more than a dozen regulatory or deciding tribunals whose functions are akin either to the law courts or to the legislature itself but who are part of the executive machinery of government.

Supplementing these bodies, yet another group of non-departmental agencies have evolved to act as appellate tribunals sitting in judgment on the decisions rendered by administrative courts of first resort. Some five or six of these can be identified.

The need to bring the outside point of view to bear on the programmes administered by the public service has encouraged the growth of boards on which such interests could be directly represented; it also encouraged the resort to advisory committees which, so to speak, stand at the margin of the public service organization acting as two-way channels of communication between outside interests and the civil servants responsible for implementing programmes. The profusion of these advisory committees makes difficult even a crude count of their number, but the reasons for their appearance are clear. The regulatory and dispensing functions of government necessitate the creation of close links with various sections of the public; moreover, the increasing complexity of decision-making and execution in highly technical fields forces heavy reliance on such devices to bring the best available expert knowledge to bear on such problems.

The second major change in the character of government functions has been occasioned by the advances of the government into various commercial and industrial undertakings, infrequently as a monopolist and more often to supplement facilities and services provided by private enterprise. It has been argued that whenever such entrepreneurial activities are undertaken they ought to be assigned to organizations that are moulded to the pattern of private enterprise. Thus, the public or crown corporation has come into existence, endowed with special autonomy in financial and staffing matters, and removed from the direct play of politics so that policies can be evolved independently of the normal 'line' operations of departments, and day-to-day administration can be conducted on 'sound business' lines. A mode of reasoning that is strictly relevant to the direct business undertakings of government has, as we have seen, been extended to embrace a significant number of other non-departmental agencies whose functions do not really fit this pattern. The result has been an undue extension of corporate status to agencies that have nothing to gain by it and yet whose inclusion with the crown corporations has simply added confusion to an already complex organizational structure. One can single out some two dozen crown corporations and crown companies that genuinely represent these new entrepreneurial functions of government for which the claims of autonomy may legitimately be made.

CHAPTER EIGHT

Internal division of labour: devolution and the hierarchy

The three preceding chapters describe how the government's workload has been broadly allocated to departments and agencies. In this and succeeding chapters attention is focused on the more technical aspect of subdividing labour *within* the departments and agencies of government. The initial allocation of jurisdictions is largely left to the political executive and requires parliamentary approval. The more detailed, refined breakdown of tasks is legally assigned to the ministerial or agency heads, operating within the limits of money and staff placed at their disposal by annual parliamentary action.

In the Canadian context there are three major factors that circumscribe the minister's task of internal work division. First, the doctrine of ministerial responsibility must be preserved, even in the face of greatly expanded staff and a growing variety of functions. Second, the political conventions which set limits on the number of departmental portfolios often necessitate the combining of major activities that may not be particularly closely related; the task of subdividing work within such multi-purpose departments is, accordingly, much more complicated. Finally, because of the geographic spread of the public service, internal division of labour within many departments must insure both a functional and a geographical allocation of tasks, together with the means of relating the work done in the field to the work done at headquarters.

As to the doctrine of ministerial responsibility, it is clear that at the time of Confederation, when the headquarters' staff of a typical department numbered two or three dozen persons, the ministerial head could deal quite comfortably with the problems of internal work division.

Indeed, the first royal commission on the civil service was able to offer in 1868 a 'theoretical organization' according to which every departmental employee was assigned by name his appropriate status and function within the primitive hierarchy.[1] Even as late as 1881 another royal commission recommended a similar theoretical organization for an entire headquarters' staff (the so-called 'inside service') which totalled 551 employees – no more and no less![2] On such occasions the records of the Privy Council Office show that the cabinet itself was able to devote detailed attention to the measures by which the several departments proposed to allocate work in conformity with the framework laid down by the royal commission.[3]

In short, a minister in these comparatively simple conditions could quite readily maintain full responsibility for the division of work and the performance of his small staff, even as the cabinet realistically assumed collective responsibility for what was done and was fully apprised of the details of administrative organization.

Today, the constitutional position of the minister and the cabinet remains as it was in 1867, but it is obvious that the conditions under which this individual and collective responsibility has to be exercised have altered drastically. A minister may now expect to deal with a staff numbering in thousands, while the number and variety of tasks which have to be subdivided among them have grown in the same proportions. Faced with these conditions the minister must seek to preserve a precarious balance in effecting the internal distribution of labour. Practical necessity, on the one hand, dictates an extensive devolution of the workload; constitutional requirements, on the other hand, still insist that he be held solely responsible for the way in which the work is performed.

The dilemma inherent in meeting these valid but conflicting requirements is reflected in each department's organizational structure. Although many volumes would be required to detail this organizational response in every department, there is sufficient uniformity in the overall pattern to permit a generalized assessment. The challenge to ministerial responsibility posed by the growth and change of functions within the departments has precipitated three organizational responses. First, the structure of the department has assumed a pyramidal or hierarchical shape that is designed to devolve the workload down the 'line' to various subordinate

1 See 'First Report of the Civil Service Commission,' *Sessional Papers*, 1869, no 19.
2 See 'Second Report of the Civil Service Commission,' *ibid.*, 1882, no 32.
3 As an illustration of the cabinet's concern for detail, see Public Archives of Canada, Records Group D4, vol. 2, Departmental Reorganization 1868, 1869; also reference to a cabinet committee for continuous supervision of the civil service in early post-Confederation years, PC 878, 8 July, 1873.

levels and, at the same time, preserve a flow of responsibility back to the ministerial head. Second, as departments have increased in size and complexity, specialized offices have been created to provide housekeeping or auxiliary services in support of the operations of the so-called 'line' administrators. Third, just as the military commander has been given a general staff, so the heads of large civil departments have been induced to pull out of the line certain personnel to act as their *alter ego*, sifting and supplying the information and advice the ministers need if they are to carry their constitutional responsibilities for the efficient performance of the total operation under their total command.

The concepts of hierarchy, line, auxiliary, and staff functions are featured in the classical literature dealing with work allocation in both private and public organizations.[4] They are an obvious response to the incredible growth in the size of bureaucratic structures, be they in the public or the private sectors. They have a special significance for public administration because of the peculiar necessity of preserving ministerial responsibility at the top and at the same time permitting an effective distribution of work within a limited number of departments, many of which have to face the further problem of dispersing their work force across a continental domain.

The remainder of this chapter will explore the problems of establishing the hierarchical pattern in Canadian government departments. Succeeding chapters will examine the auxiliary and staff aspects of work division and the special problems of dividing work between headquarters and field establishments.

THE HIERARCHY

The devolution of functions and authorities down the organizational ladder or 'scaler chain' – as it is often called – creates the typical hierarchy in any large organization. As Max Weber argued, in his account of bureaucracy,[5] hierarchy is the organizational consequence of the lengthy historical process by which man has sought to eliminate personal rule and substitute objective rationality for the conduct of his affairs. Hierarchy is intended to create a logical arrangement of offices, not of people; it is supposed to provide a coherent, stable framework within which authority and functions are arranged in descending order of magnitude. By means

4 See John D. Millett, 'Working Concepts of Organization,' in *Elements of Public Administration*, ed. F.M. Marx, (New York, 1946), chap. 7.
5 Weber's views on bureaucracy are conveniently found in translation in *From Max Weber: Essays in Sociology*, trans. and ed. H.H. Gerth and C.W. Mills (New York, 1946).

of successive formal devolution the top command should theoretically be able to concentrate on only the most important matters, as each level, in turn, processes the issues within its jurisdiction and sifts out those that must be referred up the line for decision. The typical large bureaucracy, then, takes on the form of army organization, with a broad base made up of 'privates,' a general at the top, and a progressively smaller number of officers the higher one moves from the base of the pyramid. In this fashion, no matter how large the structure, formal unity of command is preserved at the top, thereby sustaining the doctrine of ministerial responsibility.

It also follows that the clear-cut assignment of authorities and functions provides a description of the kinds of technical competence required by those officials who occupy the successive levels in the hierarchy. Consequently, the hierarchy ideally provides an objective guide to those vested with responsibility for recruiting suitable personnel. Again, this means that judgments made on the basis of personal favouritism can be replaced by objective tests designed to secure those with knowledge and skills appropriate to each legally defined position in the hierarchy. The advantages for a positive, objective recruitment programme are matched by related advantages in designing and maintaining a comprehensive plan of classification for the entire public organization. A systematic classification scheme, in turn, is a prerequisite for an equitable compensation system as well as an essential tool for developing a sensible pattern of promotion. In short, the hierarchical form of organization not only provides the stable structuring of authority and responsibility but it also serves as a foundation for effective classification plans, objective recruitment and placement, and equitable pay and promotion schemes.[6]

These merits notwithstanding, it should be observed that the hierarchical approach to the division of labour has certain drawbacks. Hierarchy, with commands emanating from the top and responsibilities seeping up from the bottom, is a hallmark of an authoritarian régime. Thus, one of the great differences between the public service organization and other elements of the machinery of government in the democratic state is that internally the structure of the public service has an authoritarian ethos which is less noticeable in the more dispersed, less coherently structured, power pattern in parties or parliaments.

The authoritarian implications of the hierarchy have not passed unnoticed. In the effort to objectify and rationalize the distribution of labour, the personal factor must be deliberately toned down. It will become ap-

6 Luther Gulick, Notes on the Theory of Organization in *Papers on the Science of Administration*, ed. L. Gulick and L. Urwick (New York, 1937).

parent, for example, in a later chapter dealing with problems of staff participation in management decisions, that the depersonalizing impact of the hierarchy has plagued most efforts to achieve a balanced programme that seems equitable to the staff associations and yet does no serious damage to the constitutional doctrine of ministerial responsibility and parliamentary supremacy. Since the mid-thirties there has been a growing body of literature concerned with the need to leaven the authoritarian lump of the hierarchy with a more substantial recognition of the rights of the worker as a human being.[7] Moreover, in more recent times, a prolific school of experts, drawing on the disciplines of social psychology and sociology, has been pointing to the significant strain on the human psyche that is created for those who increasingly live out their working lives in large, depersonalized bureaucracies.[8]

Finally, the appearance of a growing number of scientists and professionals in the public service is throwing a fresh strain on the traditional hierarchical distribution of labour. The hierarchical pattern is based on a vertical devolution of legally defined jurisdictions; the newer trend cuts across a hierarchy based on status defined in terms of legal authority by stressing the authority of knowledge or technical competence that is attached to the person. The significance of this trend is that the man vested by his place in the hierarchy with the authority to decide may not in fact be capable of making a decision.[9] Indeed, for many of the complex issues now confronting bureaucracies, there may not be a single position in the hierarchy capable of rendering a decision; it must, in fact, be a team product. The 'decision' that formally still issues from the legally authorized official in the hierarchy may be nothing more than an official stamp of approval for an amalgam of compelling technical factors which leave little room for the application of creative intelligence by the official at the top of the pyramid. His role becomes more and more that of a skilled compiler and co-ordinator of all the information that is relevant to the decision. The test of the effectiveness of an organization then rests on its capacity to draw forth, distil, and correlate the 'group wisdom' of the participants in the organization. It is possible that the advent of the computer will facilitate and speed up this process but clearly it is incapable

---

7 For a short review of this development and citation of references, see John M. Pfiffner and Robert V. Presthus, *Public Administration* (4th ed., *New York,* 1960), p. 7 ff.; also Avery Leiserson, 'The Study of Public Administration,' in Marx, *Elements of Public Administration,* chap. 2.

8 W.H. Whyte, Jr., *The Organization Man* (New York, 1956), is perhaps one of the most influential early expositions of this feature of bureaucracies.

9 Victor A. Thompson's *Modern Organization* (New York, 1961) provides an excellent and rewarding analysis of this feature of hierarchy.

of providing the final ingredient of judgment required whenever the possibility of choice is present. In the making of these critical choices the top command, as noted previously, will increasingly have to rely on the advice of specialized 'staff' agencies.

These somewhat speculative comments on the nature and implications of the hierarchical pattern of work division within departments raise issues that are beyond the present focus of this chapter. Returning to a more mundane level of analysis we find that work division *within* the departments raises problems parallel to those already encountered in chapter 6 dealing with the allocation of work *between* departments. In the latter situation it was noted that excessive subdivision would create so many departments that collegial action in the cabinet would be jeopardized. A similar restraint comes into play when seeking to divide up the labours within a department. In this case, if the initial subdivision is too refined there will be far too many officials reporting to the permanent head of the agency. If this official's span of control is excessive he is in no position to preserve command and his minister is ill-equipped to meet the constitutional necessity of accepting responsibility for operations and decisions.

Unfortunately, the traditional theories of organization provide little positive guidance on this point: the ideal limits to the span of control are set within a rather wide range, usually from six to twenty. There is agreement now that the manageable span of control will depend on a number of variables, such as the nature of the activities (routine or complex), their variety, geographic dispersion, and the quality of assistance provided for the top command in exercising its supervisory functions.[10]

Despite these discrepancies in the estimates of the appropriate number of reporting officers, the concept 'span of control' cannot be discarded for it has practical implications for the entire hierarchy. If, for example, a decision is made to keep the top command's span of control very small by an initial allocation of work to a few units, there will have to be a correspondingly larger number of subdivisions at the next level down. That is, the effort to keep the span of control reduced to a minimum at the very top level simply pushes the problem further down the chain of command; and the fewer the number of subdivisions at each level the more levels will have to be inserted into the total structure. The final outcome is that with every increase in the number of levels the minister at the top is progressively removed farther and farther from the front line where actions and decisions occur – actions and decisions for which, it should be recalled, he alone is ultimately responsible. Thus, two conflicting pressures

10 See John D. Millett, *Organization for the Public Service* (Princeton, 1966), pp. 85–6.

must be reconciled in effecting internal work division: on the one hand, subdivision cannot be so minute as to create an impossible span of control for superior officers; on the other hand, the effort to reduce the span of control should not produce an unnecessarily large number of reporting levels that stretch out the hierarchy and leave the head in an impossibly remote stance in relation to the action points.

One other parallel between work division within departments and among departments is worth noting. We have already observed that the allocation of work to departments should ideally follow some unifying principle such as a common purpose, a physical locale, a specific clientele, or a special process or skill. These same considerations have to be invoked in contemplating the distribution of the workload within a particular department. Again, it is impossible to adopt a dogmatic approach in the expectation of finding 'one best way' to allocate work; in most departments, even at one level, more than one of these organizational criteria will be found and, as one progresses down the hierarchy, different methods of aggregating the work units will be discovered.

CURRENT PATTERNS OF WORK DIVISION

The relevance of these general observations needs to be illustrated by reference to current departmental practices. It will be appropriate to use the deputy head of the department as our starting point since we are here concerned with the elements of organization that stress permanence and stability. For the moment we may set aside the complex relationship between the deputy and his ministerial head which, in essence, represents the crucial dividing line between the managerial realm, with its stress on continuity and regulated relationships, and the political realm, with its more flexible, personal relationship and its openness to the forces of change.[11]

Beneath the deputy minister, then, we find a fairly uniform pattern of organizational subdivisions – although the terminology is by no means consistent. The first allocation of work is made through units, commonly designated 'branches,' though often 'services' is the preferred term; branches in turn are broken down into 'divisions'; within the division the subordinate units are generally called 'sections.'[12] Inconsistency of nomenclature makes it preferable to refer in the ensuing analysis to allocations made at the primary, secondary, and tertiary levels.

11 See below, chap. 9.
12 In the late 1960s the new term 'group' established the vogue for describing the first major subdivision within a department: for example, the four Groups in the Department of Energy, Mines and Resources.

The existing roster of federal departments can be conveniently grouped into four categories in developing the analysis of internal work division.

1 Departments with one primary purpose or function which can best be performed by a centralized headquarters' staff:

1 Privy Council Office
2 Finance
3 Justice
4 Treasury Board
5 Labour
6 Defence Production (in 1969 enlarged to Supply and Services, moving to category 4)
7 Regional Economic Expansion
8 Solicitor General
9 Communications
10 Environment

2 Departments with more than one major function for which a centralized organization is also required:

11 Secretary of State
12 Mines and Technical Surveys (merged in 1966 with Energy, Mines and Resources, thereby moving to category 4)

3 Departments with one primary function that is best performed by means of a dispersed staff and organization:

13 Fisheries and Forestry (merged in 1968, thereby moving to category 4)
14 Post Office
15 Veterans Affairs
16 Public Works
17 External Affairs
18 Industry, Trade and Commerce (after merger in 1968, moving to category 4)
19 National Defence (before integration in 1964, properly in category 4)
20 Transport

4 Departments with more than one major function in which dispersed operations are essential:

21 National Revenue

22 National Health and Welfare
23 Manpower and Immigration (partly out of Citizenship and Immigration in 1966)
24 Indian Affairs and Northern Development (after 1966, partly out of Citizenship and Imigration, and from Northern Affairs and National Resources)
25 Consumer and Corporate Affairs (in large part out of Secretary of State, but with accretions from other departments)
26 Solicitor General

Reorganizations have brought departments 6, 12, 13, and 18 into this category.

Single purpose centralized departments

In this category can be placed the three long-standing control or policy departments: Privy Council Office, Finance, and Justice. We should add to these three departments created in the latter half of the 1960s: Treasury Board, Regional Economic Expansion, and Communications, each of which is concerned largely with policy, co-ordination, and assistance. The Departments of Labour and of Defence Production also fit this category, although both have a limited geographic dispersal problem to contend with, and Defence Production, expanded into Supply and Services in 1968–9, is now more suitably included in category 4. The Department of Communications, originally held by the Postmaster General, would appear to comprise a small, centralized policy group at this stage. The Solicitor General's Department is also a small policy co-ordinating agency for crime (RCMP) and correction (Penitentiary Service).[13]

These departments are not only among the smallest in terms of the staff employed but are also confronted with fewer organizational problems than departments in the other categories.

The Privy Council Office (combined with the Prime Minister's Office) employs fewer than three hundred persons, yet beneath the clerk of the Privy Council (equivalent to deputy minister) there are six 'chiefs.' Three of these are concerned with the cabinet secretariat functions, two with

13 This chapter has been especially plagued by the series of drastic reorganizations of departmental portfolios between 1966 and 1970. Several of the author's 'best' examples of 'bad' work division have now disappeared with progressive rationalization of work division within departments. Some of these references to past patterns have been retained in order to demonstrate certain features of the hierarchy. One may speculate that the recent rapid rationalization of work division may be accounted for by the struggle to introduce programme budgeting: the identification of programmes then leads to a more logical regrouping of the work relating to each programme.

specialized co-ordination services (federal-provincial relations and science), one with custodial, registry, and internal administrative services. The hierarchical pyramid is flattened and very squat because work division has been so refined at the senior level.

The organization of the Treasury Board, following implementation of the Glassco commission's recommendations in the early 1960s, has three assistant secretaries (assistant deputy ministers) under the secretary and leaves the specialized refinements to the tertiary level. For example, the assistant secretary (programme branch) in November 1966 had six divisions reporting to him, five of these based on the broad purposes of the programmes (for example, defence, transportation, works and telecommunications, natural resources, and scientific research, etc.), and a sixth based on process (estimates and supply procedures). The hierarchical pattern in this case shows a slightly more elongated pyramid consequent on the postponement of more refined subdivision of tasks until the tertiary stage of the structure is reached.

In the case of the Department of Justice the small size and homogeneity of the staff based on a single profession enable the work to be subdivided on a rather flexible basis relating it closely to personal qualifications and not subjecting it to the rigid patterns required by larger, less cohesive agencies.[14] Thus, the primary subdivision of labour in the Justice Department is geared to the type of legal work that has to be performed, that is, criminal law, civil litigation under common law, civil law, legal reference work, legislative drafting. In this fashion Justice illustrates the point made above, namely the tendency for professional skill or a special knowledge to cut across the traditional hierarchy based on differences in legally conferred authority and status. The end result, once again, is a broad foreshortened pyramid, with a minimum of reporting levels.

The Department of Defence Production was rather like Justice in having to rely on staff sharing common skills required for its procurement tasks – skills in contracting, purchasing, and, to a lesser degree, sales promotion. On the other hand, the primary subdivision of responsibilities showed a mixture of organizing criteria: by process – six branches for legal, economics and statistics, finance, etc.; by materiel – six branches for aircraft, ammunition, electronics, guns, etc.; and by place – one general purchasing branch in charge of fourteen district offices and offices in Washington and London.

14 For details on the Department of Justice see Royal Commission on Government Organization, *Report* II, *Supporting Services for Government* (Ottawa, 1962), report no 11: 'Legal Services.' The reassignment of police and corrective institutions from Justice to Solicitor General leaves Justice much more clearly as a servicing, 'process' department.

It is clear that this method of work division tends to violate the concept of a limited span of control, for under this arrangement no less than sixteen officials reported to the deputy minister. This defect was offset by an elaboration of the supervisory apparatus reproduced by a number of other departments, namely, the insertion of assistant deputy ministers in the structure. In this instance, although the two assistant deputies had no formally assigned responsibilities, in practice they relieved the deputy by assuming direction of a number of branches for all matters except new purchasing programmes.

The Department of Labour afforded until 1967 a parallel illustration of a primary work division that followed no single criterion of aggregating work units and, as a result, produced an excessively top heavy superstructure consisting of thirteen separate branches reporting to the deputy minister. In fact, each separate activity as it was assigned to the department was given its own branch and director. The results were readily apparent: there were extraordinary variations in the size of each of the major subdivisions. The smallest (international labour) had only three employees, the largest (annuities) had 170; the others ranged in size from eight to twenty-two employees. A second consequence was that over-refinement of work division at the primary level necessitated very little subdivision at the secondary level. In short, the hierarchy displayed a 'flattened' shape that immediately revealed the existence of an excessive span of control for the permanent head. As with the Department of Defence Production, this problem was offset by providing the deputy with two assistant deputies, one of whom assumed responsibility for the Industrial Relations Branch – the only branch that had a significant regional distribution of staff. The revised chart for the department in 1968 shows a more conventional hierarchy, with the operating (purpose) units grouped at the tertiary level under two assistant deputy ministers, along with a director general in charge of research and development (process).

In general, it may be said of nearly all the departments in this first category that small size and single purpose or process encouraged the growth of structures that tended to have a disproportionately large number of 'chiefs' in relation to the 'braves' employed below them. Over-refinement of the work units at the primary level not only necessitated directing heads for each but the addition of assistants to the deputy so that he could cope with the consequent problems of excessive span of control.

The simplified diagrams in Figure 1 summarize the main features of work division in this first category. The natural progression is from a flat pyramid with an excessive span of control for the deputy minister and little, if any, subdivisions to the insertion of a second tier of assistant

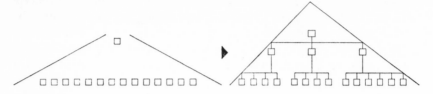

Figure 1

deputy ministers, a corresponding reduction in the span of control at the top, and an elongation of the pyramid as the number of reporting stages is increased.

Multiple purpose centralized departments

This second category contains only two examples, the Department of the Secretary of State and Registrar General of Canada (to give the full ancient title) and the Department of Mines and Technical Surveys. By the Organization Act of 1966 both these departments underwent substantial changes: the former had the Registrar General Office removed from it to become a separate portfolio (subsequently enlarged in 1967 to become the Department of Consumer and Corporate Affairs) and at the same time the Secretary of State began to assume reporting responsibility for such agencies as the National Gallery, the National Library, and the Canadian Broadcasting Corporation which may now entitle it to a more resounding title as Canada's Department of Culture; the Departments of Mines and Technical Surveys has been merged in a new Department of Energy, Mines and Resources. The brief analysis of the division of labour within these two agencies that follows is based on their former arrangements, but nevertheless still contains pertinent lessons for their current operations.

The Department of Secretary of State contained six main branches, with the same disparities in size as those we noted in Labour, ranging from six in the Special Division (protocol, etc.) to three hundred in the Bureau of Translations and 317 in the Patents Branch. These branches were virtually water-tight containers, quite unrelated to one another, each working within policy lines more than usually clearly defined in their respective statutes. There was little here for the minister or his deputy to co-ordinate. The Secretary of State was obliged to table their reports, present or defend their estimates, but was otherwise left with a much lighter burden of administrative oversight than any of his colleagues; consequently there has been no need, until recent changes, to back up the deputy minister with extra assistant deputies as in the departments previously mentioned. The contemporary structure of the department still retains overtones of an agency required to assume a catch-all function: as a result the pyramid is flat, the major subdivisions carry on quite unrelated functions – citizenship, education support, translation bureau, and assorted non-departmental agencies semi-detached from the department, such as museums, archives, CBC, chief electoral office, etc.

The Department of Mines and Technical Surveys enclosed a more coherent group of related functions than did the Secretary of State Department. One might ordinarily anticipate that this department would need to be highly dispersed but in practice most of the work done in the field has been performed by seasonal employees or by headquarters' personnel who returned to home base in the off-season. Four of the six main branches at the primary level of organization clearly reflected a breakdown by functional specialization: surveys and mapping, mines, geography, Geological Survey. Each functional branch was further subdivided by refining the main function into its specialist components and carrying the process to even more minute subdivision at the tertiary level. Thus, the Mines Branch separated out into five divisions: physical metallurgy, fuels and mining practices, extraction metallurgy, mineral science, and mineral processing. The heads of the first two divisions in turn had to contend with no less than seventeen and fourteen reporting units respectively. Thus, rather like the proliferation of subject matter in scientific courses at a university, this department had an ultra-refined allocation of work in accordance with special technical skills. The organizational consequences were that at the tertiary level the division heads had a rather large span of control and each operating unit tended to be isolated in extremely small compartments. These organizational defects may explain the incorporation of a unique feature into this department, a Directorate of Scientific Services, which existed for the purpose of pulling together the disparate research and scientific units, particularly for work in such integrated team efforts as the Polar Shelf project and the related interdisciplinary field of oceanography. After reorganization in Energy, Mines and Resources in 1966, the various programmes were regrouped under four assistant deputies – research, mineral development, water, and energy development. The new structure at the top level is much more coherent but it is probable that the span of control problem has, thereby, only been shunted down the hierarchy to lower directing levels to accommodate to what in effect is an expansion to a multiple purpose department (see Figure 2).

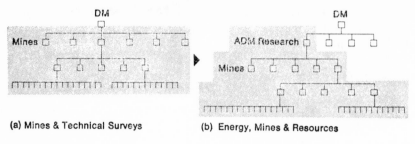

(a) Mines & Technical Surveys   (b) Energy, Mines & Resources

Figure 2

Single purpose dispersed departments

In this third category of departments is included about half of the total federal portfolios. These departments, faced with the necessity of dispersing their operations across the continent, must not only develop effective work division at headquarters but undertake the task of organizing, co-ordinating, and controlling a field service that may be several times the size of the central staff. A later chapter examines the specific problems of headquarters-to-field relationships; at this point it will be sufficient to deal in general terms with the ways in which departments have accommodated their organizations to meet the problem of place administration.

Three of the departments in this category were organized (until the merger of the first two in 1968) around a single resource: Forestry, Fisheries, and Agriculture. The combination of Forestry and Fisheries places this department in the fourth category examined below. However, a few observations on their structure as separate entities is in order, if for no other purpose than to show how a merger of convenience may not result in genuine integration, as the two components are organizationally not compatible. Forestry is a relative newcomer, quite small, and its organization still comparatively simple. These circumstances permit it to make a primary allocation of work by special function that affords a grouping of particular technical skills related to the department's responsibility for conserving and developing a single resource. The relatively simple primary division eases the span of control problem for the deputy minister but, by the same token, shifts that problem to the branch heads. Since the operations are geographically dispersed, each branch head faces not only his own headquarters' divisional chiefs but also a number of district officers. Thus, the director of the Forest Research Branch, in addition to five headquarters' divisions, has seven district officers and one experimental station all reporting to him; his counterpart in the Entomology and Pathology Branch has no less than eleven officials reporting to him.

The influence of the 'place' factor is more prominently displayed in the Department of Fisheries and its organizational response establishes in perhaps the clearest form a pattern that is followed in broad outline by several other departments. First, it is important to note that the research element associated with this resource has been isolated from the department proper and assigned to a special Fisheries Research Board. Thus, research that constituted the largest component of the tasks of the Forestry Department is in this case not a direct responsibility of the Department of Fisheries. The deparment is left, then, with protection, promotion, and development aspects of the fisheries programme. Most of these functions can best be performed on the spot in the relevant localities, with the result that Fisheries is the most geographically dispersed of all the federal departments – over 90 per cent of its staff being employed outside headquarters.

The pattern of organization that has evolved in response to this geographic challenge might best be called a functionally dispersed, mirror-image structure. It is functionally dispersed because at the primary level there are nine headquarters' services each responsible for one function, such as protection, conservation and development, consumers' services, and the like. It is a mirror-image structure because under the area directors in each of the five areas are smaller versions of the headquarters' units divided in virtually the same functional way. The end result is five miniature Departments of Fisheries organized within each area in such a way as to mirror the functional organization of the headquarters' staff. To reduce the burden on a deputy minister who has to contend with the heads of nine headquarters' services, the familiar technique is employed of injecting an assistant deputy minister into the top level, to whom the area directors report. There is a second assistant deputy minister in charge of international and jurisdictional affairs, a legal and policy division at headquarters that has no corresponding regional components.

The Department of Fisheries represents possibly the most straightforward example of an organizational pattern that has its counterparts in other highly dispersed departments like the Post Office, Veterans Affairs, and, more recently, Public Works.

Although the Post Office is the second largest federal department its programme is neither as varied nor as policy-ridden as is the case for several smaller departments. On the other hand, it is almost as highly dispersed as the Department of Fisheries and the need to provide uniformity and consistency in its services and charges, as well as quick dispatch of an enormous workload, entails a careful integration of the hierarchy proceeding in several stages out from headquarters. The primary work division is on a functional basis, giving rise to twelve branch heads reporting through two assistant deputy ministers and a comptroller to the deputy minister. The major administrative structures in the field are the fourteen district offices. A typical district office contains, in smaller compass, roughly the same functional components that make up the headquarters' branches. In this respect the Post Office is simply a more complicated version of the organizational pattern described for Fisheries. The additional feature is the insertion of subdistrict units to bring operations closer to the people served. Each district has between four to seven areas or large post offices with the same status; each of these in turn accounts for the so-called 'staff' and 'revenue' post offices that make up the lowest tier in this organizational complex and constitute nearly seven thousand of the total of over eleven thousand post offices scattered throughout Canada.

The Department of Veterans Affairs with special responsibilities for a scattered clientele has adopted much of the same general pattern. Within five regions there are district and subdistrict offices, each of which mirrors in its own functional units the main branches of the headquarters' establishment. Over against the main headquarters' branches for treatment services, pensions, and welfare, the district office has such closely related refinements of the major functions as prosthetic services, hospitals, clinics, and veterans homes.

The Department of Public Works has been gradually moving towards the same organizational pattern. Its major headquarters' branches have been built around the common technical skills required for the provision of the government's housekeeping needs, that is, design, programme planning, programme evaluation, and operations – the latter branch being headed by the senior assistant deputy minister to whom the regional directors report. Until quite recently the several headquarters' branches each pursued their own independent ways to adjust to the operating and management needs associated with widely scattered real estate holdings and a variety of public works. A relatively new master plan called for the creation of six regions, each region grouping under a regional director the same functional units that are found at headquarters. With its now completed reorganization, the Department of Public Works will parallel the pattern established in Fisheries, with each region constituting a minor mirror-image of the headquarters' establishment and each in charge of a varying number of district offices (see Figure 3).

The efforts of the Department of Agriculture to grapple with the

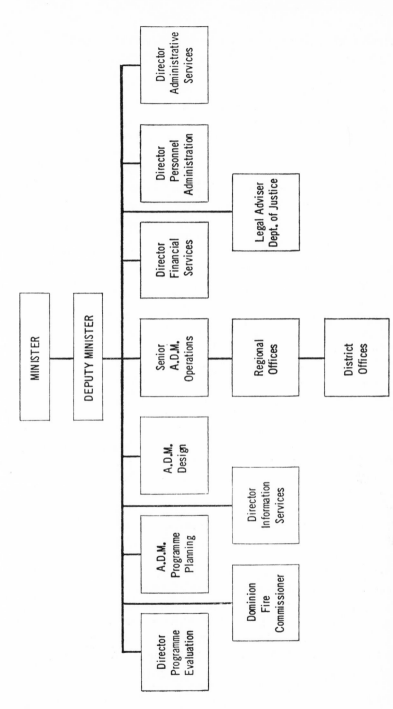

Figure 3 Department of Public Works

problem of work allocation within a highly decentralized context afford an interesting contrast to the mirror-image pattern exemplified in varying degrees by the foregoing departments. From the 1880s on, the Department of Agriculture adopted the simplest organizational technique: with the accretion of each new function associated with the development and regulation of agricultural resources, it simply added a fresh branch. By 1928 the department was an exaggerated version of the broad, flat pyramid which was observed in a department like Labour until its recent reorganization. Unlike the Department of Labour, however, Agriculture had to contend with a widely dispersed field force, and, again, the readiest answer seemed to be a piecemeal, *ad hoc*, geographic extension of each of the many product-oriented headquarters' branches. From 1928 onwards the Department of Agriculture progressively integrated its headquarters' branches in an effort, as it reported in 1937–8, to carry out 'the principle of bringing under one administrative head activities similar in character and purpose in the broad fields of work with respect to the marketing of agricultural products, their production from a national point, and the experimental and scientific investigation in connection therewith.' In pursuit of this reorganizing theme, the department has now consolidated its headquarters' work into three major functional services: marketing and health of animals, research, and economics; the various housekeeping services for the department report to the deputy minister.

The price paid for the achievement of this apparent logical simplicity at the very top levels of the organization is that the span of control problem has been pushed further down the hierarchy and has multiplied the number of reporting stages that intervene between the points of action and the responsible minister. That this defect is not just a theoretical possibility was forcibly demonstrated, to the discomfiture of the department in 1951, on the occasion of the disastrous outbreak of the foot-and-mouth epidemic. In the imbroglio that followed, the testimony presented to a parliamentary committee by a long procession of departmental officials reinforced the opinion that the internal chain of command and communication had broken down at several points.[15] The breakdowns were attributable to the number of reporting stages separating the field force from the minister at headquarters.

Reference to the current organization of the department provides ample evidence to support the generalization that the number of levels in the hierarchy is increased when a highly consolidated work allocation is adopted at the primary level. Each of the three programme branches under

15 For a summary of the evidence, see J.E. Hodgetts and D.C. Corbett, eds., *Canadian Public Administration* (Toronto, 1960), p. 165 ff.

the deputy minister has been assigned an assistant deputy minister; two of these have each been provided with a director general, and one has an associate with two assistant directors general. This arrangement already carries us three reporting levels down from the minister. Having, so to speak, thus thoroughly braced itself at the top levels to take on the host of special functions assigned the department, the actual subdivision of these functions in terms of operating programmes is consigned to a large number of divisions grouped, as in the old days, on the basis of individual products (for example, dairy, livestock, plant protection, fruit and vegetables, plant products, poultry, etc.) or on the basis of specific research programmes (animal, plant, entomological, soils research, etc.). In turn, each division is carved up into a varying number of subordinate units based on a detailed refinement of the function or the research subject.

Nor is this the end of the complications for as yet nothing has been said about the need to extend the tentacles of this elaborate headquarters' organization into the field. Two quite separate organizational solutions to this problem have been incorporated into the department. First, several distinct activities have been segregated from the regular hierarchy and organized on a virtually autonomous 'place' basis. The agencies in question are the Prairie Farm Rehabilitation Administration, the Prairie Farm Assistance Administration (both centred in Regina), the Maritime Marshland Rehabilitation Administration (with headquarters in Amherst, Nova Scotia), and the more recent Agricultural Rehabilitation and Development Act (ARDA) programme. The directors of these area organizations operate separate and self-contained programmes, and, when added to the three assistant deputy ministers, the deputy minister's span of control was extended to more than six reporting officers. Most of these regionally based programmes were transferred to an enlarged Department of Forestry and Rural Development in 1964 and 1966, and subsequently to a new Department of Regional Economic Expansion in 1968.

The second solution to the geographic dispersion of workloads has been developed within the three functional branches of the departments, but in no instance do we find the pattern of co-ordinating regions that produces the mirror-image type of arrangement already described. In effect, each of the many functional subdivisions within the three branches has been permitted to develop in its own way such external ganglia as it deems necessary for the performance of its respective tasks in the field. Thus instead of a single inspectorate there are district inspection offices for the Health of Animals Division, and the livestock, dairy products, plant protection, fruit and vegetables, poultry, and other divisions that are organized by particular products. The proliferation of regional units organized as appendages to divisions that are themselves based on a highly refined breakdown of subject matter led to the situation described in the report of the Royal Commission on Government Organization:[16] in Winnipeg, for example, there were 282 officials employed in no less than twelve distinctive regional outposts of headquarters' divisions concerned with inspection and research. Most of these occupied separate offices, serviced their own needs, and provided specific services with little or no reference to one another.

There was one final complication that had as its only counterpart a situation that existed until quite recently in the Customs Branch of the Department of National Revenue. There are more than sixty separate experimental farms and research laboratories or stations scattered across Canada. All of these were portrayed as reporting to the director general of the Research Branch. If one also takes account of two statutory boards – the Agricultural Products and the Agricultural Stabilization Boards – which are primarily composed of senior departmental officials, the reasons for the several top tiers of officials, comprising a deputy, assistant deputies, directors general, and their assistants can be readily appreciated.

Among the departments analysed to this point, the Department of Agriculture stands out as a genuine departure from the organizational patterns established by other departments confronted by the same problems. Agriculture had taken great pains to consolidate its top branch structure but had done so at the expense of an elongated hierarchy of multiple reporting stages. Moreover, instead of consolidating its field forces into regions it had elected to permit each of its many divisions to develop its own diverse and wholly unco-ordinated place organizations. In 1967, while maintaining a highly co-ordinated top structure with several tiers of senior officials, the department moved to integrate the sprawling ganglia of its field forces. The separate research stations, experimental farms, and research laboratories were grouped into western and eastern divisions, each under an assistant director general; an assistant director general was also placed in charge of the various specialized institutes (see Figure 4).

There remain four important departments that can be grouped in the third category under consideration: Trade and Commerce, External Affairs, National Defence, and Transport. Two of these, Trade and Commerce and External Affairs, have certain parallel problems since their operating front lines are widely dispersed beyond Canada's boundaries and a large proportion of their headquarters' establishment acts either in a supporting capacity for the operations abroad or as a recipient and 'processor' of the information channelled to them from their outposts.

16 *Report* v, *The Organization of the Government of Canada* (Ottawa, 1963), p. 88.

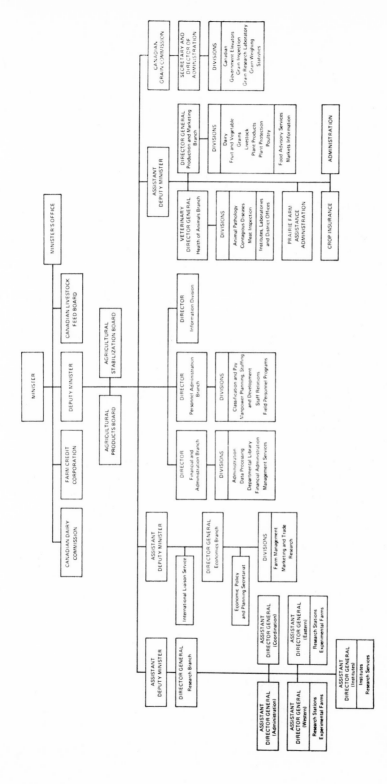

Figure 4 Department of Agriculture

Looking first at the Department of Trade and Commerce (before it merged with the Department of Industry), we find a primary subdivision of labour under the deputy minister that produces a heavier super-structure of assistant deputies than is to be found in any other department of comparable size (about fifteen hundred). There are, in fact, no less than four assistant deputy ministers (recently reduced to three). Their specific assignments indicate that the initial subdivision of work has been based on an elaborate refinement of the department's major purpose, that is, fostering Canada's foreign trade. The effective performance of this task requires the department to keep a central organizational anchor in Canada for the numerous groups located throughout the world. That portion of the service that is provided abroad is integrated under a single assistant deputy minister (external trade promotion) who is placed in charge of the Trade Commissioner Service. Thus, the hard core of the area-based organization is represented by over sixty trade commissioner offices scattered abroad and held together at home by one assistant deputy.

It is when we come to the domestic adjuncts to this corps of trade promoters that we encounter the detailed refinement of programmes that has necessitated adding three (now two) more assistant deputy ministers to the top command. The basic purposes of the headquarters' branches clustered around the deputy and these assistants are presumably to receive information from the external trade commissions and to feed information to them on the strength of data compiled and analysed from domestic sources. Compilation of data and research on or analysis of these data are done on the basis of particular products, both industrial and natural (assistant deputy minister – commodities and industries). But, within the International Trade Relations Branch (now Trade Policy), trade policy based on these analyses is formulated in divisions organized by geographic area, such as Comonwealth, United States, Latin America, Europe, etc.

We have already had occasion to observe the way in which the responsibilities assigned to this department tend to trespass on the preserves of such resource-oriented departments as Agriculture and Fisheries and Forestry, particularly for such matters as marketing and economic analysis. Similarly, we have seen that in its trade policy functions it tends to overlap the areas assigned to the Departments of Finance and External Affairs.[17] The creation of yet another department – the Department of Industry – brought another contender into the same orbit, and its merger with Trade

17 The Secretary of State for External Affairs, Mitchell Sharp, announced on 13 April 1970 the results of a task force study which proposed 'a movement toward integration' of trade commissioners and foreign service officers of the two departments of Industry, Trade and Commerce and External Affairs. See *Globe and Mail*, Toronto, 13 April 1970.

and Commerce in 1968 was to be anticipated. It would appear that the excessive refinement of divisions within Trade and Commerce responsible for collecting and analysing data and making policy recommendations is both a response to and an aggravation of a situation in which a number of departments vie with one another in the performance of overlapping and often duplicated tasks.

The Department of External Affairs faces a comparable organizational problem.[18] The large force of foreign service officers is required to carry the central representational functions for the federal government abroad. Like Trade and Commerce, this department must also make provision at headquarters for supplying its representatives abroad with common services, information, and advice required for the effective performance of their tasks. Headquarters, too, must be equipped as the other end of the transmission line, to analyse the flow of information from abroad and to devise the appropriate policy responses.

In view of the apparent similarity of needs, it is interesting to observe that External Affairs, quite unlike Trade and Commerce, has erred on the side of understaffing its top command. In part this may be explained by the fact that, in legal form at least, all of the sixty-five-odd missions abroad report directly to the Secretary of State for External Affairs rather than through a single assistant deputy (as in Trade and Commerce). Of course, in practical day-to-day terms, the dialogue between missions and headquarters is conducted at a much lower level, and it is to cope with this reality that the present allocation of work has evolved in Ottawa headquarters.

The problem of work division facing External Affairs is perhaps best appreciated by thinking of the department, ideally, as a miniature replica of the government as a whole. That is, the policy issues it confronts may contain legal, economic, strategic, cultural, or scientific elements, the proper resolution of which would require the department to be fully equipped with experts in all these fields. Moreover, in performing its task, External Affairs has need of special communications facilities, property management specialists, librarians and record keepers, information officers, and the like. In short, the comprehensive responsibilities of the department for representing Canada abroad could readily encourage the growth of a smaller, self-contained version of the entire public service. Naturally, this logic has to be resisted but the inherent pressures towards

18 For a detailed description and critique of this department's internal work division, see Royal Commission on Government Organization, *Report, IV, Special Areas of Administration* (Ottawa, 1963), report no 21: 'Department of External Affairs.'

self-sufficiency give rise to a remarkable complex of subordinate units which have to bridge such a wide spectrum of activities that it is difficult to identify the most appropriate basis for putting them together. A further complication is the tendency for the department's workload to vary in response to external circumstances over which it has no control and which often cannot be anticipated sufficiently far in advance to plan an appropriate organizational response. Finally, the need to create an organization that can be quickly adapted to changing and uneven workloads, together with the pressures towards self-sufficiency, have induced the department, as a matter of policy, to rotate its officers from division to division at headquarters and from headquarters to posts abroad. All these special features combine to lend an unusual element of organizational 'uneasiness' to the entire structure and to the allocation of work within the structure.

Given these special considerations, it is not surprising to find that the primary distribution of functions within the headquarters' framework of the department extends over a wide spectrum, covered by no less than twenty-eight separate divisions. Each division is headed by a director, and the operational front lines are manned by a varying number of so-called 'desk officers.' It is at the desk level that the daily pack of telegrams and memoranda from abroad is processed and passed up the line for decision and action.

Allocation of work to these numerous divisions is not in accordance with a single criterion: thirteen are geared to particular functions – legal, historical, economic, consular, information, etc.; six are based on geography – Far Eastern, European, Latin American; the remaining divisions are concerned with strictly housekeeping activities – supplies and properties, personnel, finance, communications, etc. The combining of these divisions under assistant under-secretaries until quite recently showed the same admixture of organizational criteria; that is, not all the area-based divisions came together under one assistant under-secretary, nor did all the functional divisions report to the same deputy under-secretary. The organization chart for January 1968 (Figure 5) indicated a realignment under four assistant under-secretaries that brings together regional, functional, and housekeeping activities.

Even more clearly than in Trade and Commerce, the work of External Affairs would appear to divide into policy-making or political divisions and the divisions responsible for providing services in support of these line activities. The technical skills required of the staff in the latter divisions are obviously different from those required at home or abroad in the policy divisions. Thus, it would appear logical, following the recommendations of the Royal Commission on Government Organization, to

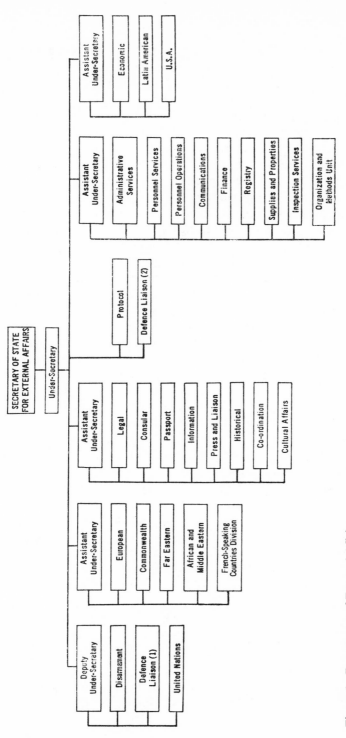

Figure 5 Department of External Affairs

base the primary subdivision of work on these distinctions, putting separate assistant under-secretaries in charge, respectively, of the technical and servicing divisions on the one hand and of the functional, geographic political divisions on the other hand. While it is possible that the use of both area and function as a basis for allocating work to the political divisions is unavoidable, the more coherent grouping of related divisions recently effected should bring improvement. It is equally clear that changing demands on the department will frustrate any attempt to produce an organizational prescription suitable for all circumstances. Efforts should be focused on achieving the most flexible and adaptable subdivision of work and this implies continued reliance on the 'generalist' tradition explicitly recognized in the practice of rotation between the political divisions and between headquarters and the field.

The Department of National Defence might well have been included in the final category of multi-purpose departments were it not for the major reorganization beginning in 1967 designed to integrate the separate service arms.[19] Historically, the organization of this department adhered to a pattern common throughout the world, namely, organization in accordance with the element in which one does battle – land, sea, or air. Indeed, each service tended to build up its own separate department, ultimately held together under one ministerial roof in a sort of loose confederacy. Compounding the disintegrating impact of this primary subdivision, each service in turn sought self-sufficiency by having its own segregated specialist services, whether they were padres, doctors, dentists, musicians, historians, accountants, or engineers. Within the army the subdivision went further because of the corps system built around specialized skills or matériel. Even the advent of new techniques of warfare and defence which relied for their effectiveness on a close combination of all three services, whether on land, sea, or air, failed to break down the self-contained compartments. Co-operation and co-ordination had to be achieved through cumbersome and time-consuming techniques of inter-service committees at all levels. Now, the logic of combined operations for the various missions of our defence forces has induced the government to embark on the long drawn-out but obviously essential process of integrating this complex, cumbersome structure.

Integration of the three services has significant consequences for the organization of the civilian side of the Defence Department. Over against the uniformed personnel one must place the enormous civilian 'tail' whose

19 A good description of internal work division in National Defence prior to integration is to be found in *ibid.*, report no 20: 'Department of National Defence.' See, also, Stats Can. 1966–7, c.96.

organization has to mirror that of the military groups it exists to support. One should not visualize the civilian components as units under the deputy minister, segregated from the uniformed personnel in the service arms, for most of the civilians work for one of the services. Indeed, in many instances uniformed personnel and civilians work side by side on similar desk jobs or trades. Thus, there are many who believe the 'civilianization' of the services has not gone as far as it could. But even as matters now stand one can see the remarkable interpenetration of civilian and military personnel. The civilians, nearly fifty thousand strong, come under the deputy minister, and until the recent reorganization tended to be organized in parallel to the services. That is, four assistant deputy ministers, respectively in charge of administration and personnel, construction engineering and properties, requirements, and finance, had their branches divided immediately into replicas of the corresponding services. Thus, the superintendent of civilian personnel had directorates of civilian personnel for navy, army, and air – a pattern that was repeated for each of the other branches. Integration of the service arms has resulted in a corresponding integration of the civilian side of the department: three assistant deputy ministers are now respectively in charge of personnel, logistics, and finance, while the deputy minister assumes responsibility for information and the judge advocate general's division.

The Department of Transport has some of the same features as the Defence Department, having been built up from separate departments that were amalgamated in whole or in part in 1936. Unlike Defence, however, the Department of Transport has not had to contend with the problem of mixed civilian and military personnel. Rather like Defence, on the other hand, this department has geared its primary organization to the element in which the transportation activity is carried out. That is, its two major operating divisions are Air and Marine Services, and these might be likened to separate armed services in Defence. And there are four smaller functional services for transportation policy and research, personnel, finance, and property and legal services which might be equated with the 'civilian' groups under the deputy minister of National Defence. The administration services, until 1967 for example, were even divided by air, marine, and canal personnel – very much like the former structure in Defence.

This particular arrangement provides an apparently simple structure at the top levels, considering the fact that the department is responsible for administering no less than forty-two separate statutes. Not only is the deputy's span of control kept to manageable proportions, but the same is true for his assistants. What should be noted, however, is that the Minister of Transport has not secured the same relief, for he presides at the centre of a remarkable network of non-departmental agencies with regulatory or operating responsibilities for harbours, railways, air lines, and so on, numbering at one time no less than thirty-seven separate reporting entities! Through amalgamations, such as the combining of several separate regulating agencies in the Canadian Transport Commission, this number has been drastically reduced to seven.

It is equally important to point to the price that has to be paid for keeping such a tight rein on the top management's span of control. The progressive refinement of the work division carries down a chain of command that has had to be enormously extended because of the need to insert an unusually large number of levels in the hierarchy. Thus, for example, the deputy minister is quite remote from a decision taken in the regulations and licensing section which is under the controller, civil air operations and regulations division, who in turn reports to the director, civil aviation branch, and thus to the assistant deputy minister Air Services who reports to the deputy minister. Not only is the chain of command extended, but the consequence of starting with the simplest form of work allocation – transport by air and water – is that parallel groups, such as engineers and construction services, have to be set up for each service – rather like the situation that existed in the unreorganized Department of Defence.

The final complication that must be mentioned relates to the fact that Transport conducts its operations on an extremely dispersed basis, with nearly 90 per cent of its staff in the field. The Meteorological Branch, a clearly distinguishable operation, is in fact based on Toronto with liaison offices for Ottawa headquarters and the Department of Defence. Air Services is organized on a 'mirror-image' pattern typified by the Department of Fisheries, each of the six regional directorates having subdivisions corresponding to headquarters' divisions in Air Services. Marine Services, on the other hand, is much less clearly co-ordinated for, apart from eleven district marine agents reporting to the assistant deputy minister Marine Services, there are distinct and different regional outposts for each of the headquarters' directorates.

In short, the semblance of a simple top organization gives way on closer inspection to a picture of a multi-tiered structure in two parallel columns of operating units served by administrative arms which tend to be subdivided to correspond to the operating units. The progressive dispersion of the operating units across a continent adds to the sense of sprawl, while at headquarters the minister himself is still overwhelmed by a galaxy of non-departmental satellites that report to him (see Figure 6). The re-

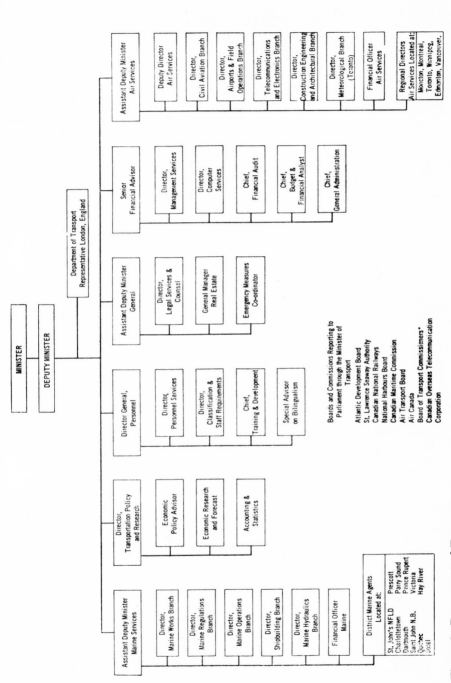

Figure 6 Department of Transport

organization in 1970 that created a Ministry of Transport was aimed at resolving the problems mentioned above.

Multiple purpose dispersed departments

Two departments that have consistently occupied this category are National Revenue and National Health and Welfare. The former Departments of Citizenship and Immigration and of Northern Affairs and National Resources also fell into this grouping, and with the surgery and grafting performed on them in 1966 continue to qualify as multi-purpose, dispersed departments. Immigration was merged with a new Department of Manpower. National Resources was joined to the former Department of Mines and Technical Surveys to become the Department of Energy, Mines and Resources; Indian Affairs, once part of Citizenship and Immigration, has been united with Northern Affairs to become a joint department. Merger of two sets of single purpose departments has brought Forestry and Fisheries together, as well as Industry and Trade and Commerce. Finally, the enlargement of the former Department of Defence Production to become Supply and Services has produced another candidate for this category. The rationale behind these organizational changes can be clarified by the following brief analysis of the problems of internal work division in multi-purpose departments. We begin with the two departments, National Revenue and Health and Welfare, that have been left intact by the administrative changes completed since 1966.

National Revenue from its title does not suggest its double-barrelled nature, but this department has never broken free from its initial separation into two entirely separate departments of Customs and of Inland Revenue. The two divisions have a common purpose – revenue collection – and a single minister. But beyond that the two operations are organized in two quite distinctive structures, each with its own deputy minister. There is not even a token acknowledgment of an organic unity for no attempt has been made to share common housekeeping, accounting, legal, or other services. We confront a marriage of convenience, at the ministerial level only, with the apparent objective of keeping down the number of departments to be represented in cabinet. The only way to examine the internal work division is to treat Customs and Excise and Taxation as if they were two separate departments – as indeed they are treated in the distinctive organizations under the single ministerial head.

Customs and Excise, under its own deputy, makes its initial division on the basis of the two special taxes collected and adds a third division for common administrative services. Each of these divisions, with its own assistant deputy ministers, faces a problem of physical dispersal of the work force, and, rather like the Department of Agriculture, has separate and quite unrelated local ganglia appended to each of the branches attached to the headquarters' divisions. Thus, two of the three branches – customs drawback and customs appraisal – under the assistant deputy minister of Customs have their own separate local offices; while three of the six branches under the assistant deputy of Excise have their own separate local units. Moreover, the deputy minister (customs) – until the recent addition of an assistant deputy minister (operations) to undertake this task – faced the extraordinary burden of having the customs collectors at no less than 281 ports of entry across Canada reporting directly to him. He appears to be responsible as well for Financial and Management Services, Personnel and Inspection Services – some of these also equipped with their own distinctive regional offices.

Under the deputy minister of Taxation the division of work is less complicated but nevertheless still imposes a heavy burden on the deputy. The seven headquarters' branches are divided on functional lines – assessments, legal, inspection, etc. – but there are another twenty-seven district heads who also report to the deputy minister. Each district office is organized on the basis of refined subdivisions of the functions represented in the headquarters' branches. It is clear that Taxation has achieved a more streamlined organizational response to the problems of area administration, but has nevertheless left the permanent head with a formidable span of control. Recent organizational changes reflect a recognition of this fact and, again, the response has been to insert three assistant deputy ministers into the structure (see Figure 7, and note that the Government Manual quite frankly acknowledges the presence of two separate entities by presenting the charts for each on separate pages).

National Health and Welfare, like National Revenue, gives organizational expression to its dual purpose in having two deputy ministers under a single minister. In this instance, however, a deliberate effort has been made to preserve closer organizational ties than in National Revenue by sharing a group of common administrative services that are 'looked after' by the deputy minister of Welfare (see Figure 8). The intent is laudable but does not appear to have prevented the duplication of such services farther down the two parallel structures of this double-barrelled department.

On the Health side of the department primary subdivision follows a functional approach, a Directorate of Food and Drugs and three separate units (narcotics control, quarantine, civil aviation medicine) handling regulatory functions; services to the general public in a Directorate of

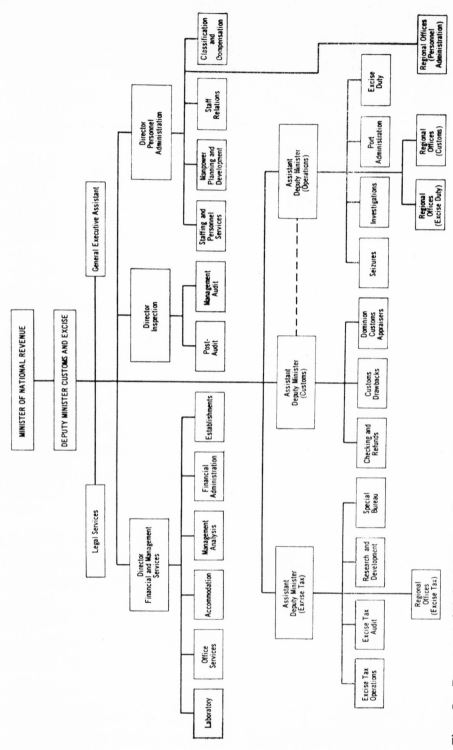

Figure 7a   Department of National Revenue – Customs and Excise

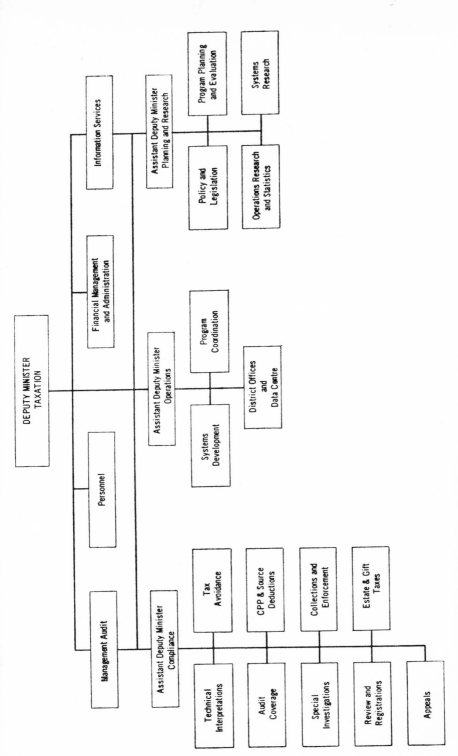

Figure 7b Department of National Revenue – Taxation

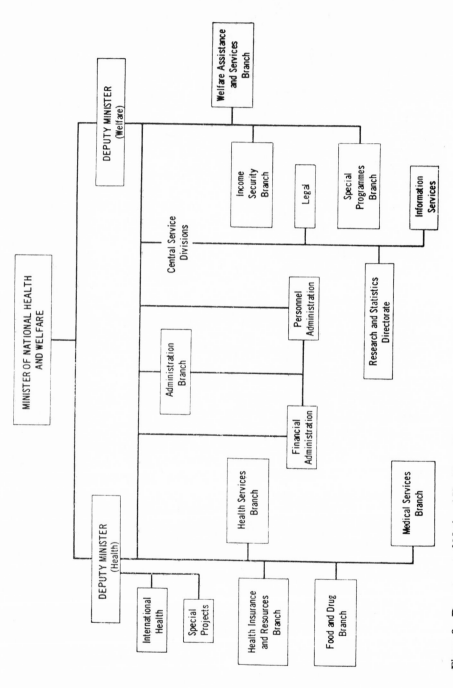

Figure 8　Department of National Health and Welfare

Health Services; and services to special groups in a Directorate of Indian and Northern Health Services and a Civil Service Health Unit. A breakdown below this point tends to follow a typical refinement of particular service (for example, child and maternal health, blindness, dental, hygiene, mental, etc.) and/or place – with each unit selecting its own diversified area base.

On the Welfare side there are a variety of recipient groups for each programme, but in functional terms the prime responsibilities are for the disbursement of grants and an audit of their expenditure. The primary breakdown by programmes would appear to create an overly elaborate headquarters' structure for a small staff of slightly over sixty. But it is reasonable to suppose that this structure is dictated by the need to deal with counterpart organizations at the provincial level, just as the large field force of one thousand may be viewed as a reflection of the federal government's suspicion of the capacity of provincial services to perform without a good deal of central supervision.

It is possible that the double-barrelled nature of this department has fostered a tendency to multiply individual programmes in order to give an impressive picture of size and commitment, and that, in turn, the existence of such units has encouraged a proliferation of research and publication which is a somewhat self-conscious response of federal agencies to an uncertain constitutional situation in which the provinces have an increasingly large stake.

The former Department of Citizenship and Immigration may be commented on only in so far as its deficiencies point to the logic of the reorganization recently effected. This department was, in fact, a triple purposed department, carrying a responsibility for Indians, immigrants, and citizenship. The other multi-purpose departments openly acknowledge the uniqueness of each function by setting up separate deputy ministers but, curiously, there was only one deputy for this department. The primary subdivision of work followed the three main purposes and then added separate branches providing such functions as economic and social research, information, legal, inspection services, personnel – for a total of no less than ten officials reporting to the lone deputy minister. At first glance this arrangement suggests a sensible attempt to seek economies of scale by joint handling of staff and servicing needs for all of the separate programme-oriented branches. In fact, however, each branch created its own replicas of personnel offices, purchasing and supply, finance, etc.

The organization of services built around human resources has a superficial logic but in fact the only thing these three branches had in common was a need to organize on an area base. But even here there were slight prospects of dovetailing, for example, work on Indian reservations with the work of district offices for immigrants or regions of the Citizenship Branch. In short, there was very little in common among the several purposes embraced within this department for a single deputy minister to co-ordinate; and the prospect of achieving administrative economies through amalgamated common services or common regions were not realized because services were duplicated in each branch and regions were not at all compatible. Again, we face a marriage of convenience presumably designed to keep the number of departments reduced, for one could visualize a much more viable arrangement that would split the operations into three separate departments, leaving each fully equipped to carry on by itself if each were given its own permanent head. The reorganization of 1966 has created new double-barrelled departments that will at least have the merit of bringing together more closely related purpose units with much more comparable administrative areas.

The multi-purpose Department of Northern Affairs and National Resources has, like Citizenship and Immigration, undergone a significant change after the reorganization of 1966, some explanation for which may be provided by examining the department in its unrevised form. The title of the department suggests an allocation of work based on place and purpose. Despite this implied duality, a single deputy minister presided over the two sections, each headed by an assistant deputy minister. The department, rather like Trade and Commerce, suffered from the combination of 'place' and 'purpose' in its primary organization and was even more embarrassed by the fact that its resource purpose was already in the hands of specifically resource-oriented departments, like Agriculture, Fisheries, Mines, and Forestry. This situation left the department with special land (parks and historic sites) and water resource conservation (basically hydrometric surveys and administration of federal water power regulations). In similar fashion the 'place' aspect of its organization (northern affairs) was shared with other departments already in the place and was further complicated by the fact that the Territories in which or for which the functions have to be performed are themselves evolving their own local forms of administration.

On the resources side the National Parks Branch made up over half the total staff of the department and reported directly to the deputy minister. The Historic Sites Division and the Canadian Wildlife Division, although both in the Parks Branch, reported to the assistant deputy (resources). These entities, along with the Water Resources Branch, are all highly dispersed, using a place basis for organization.

Under the assistant deputy minister (northern affairs) the key agency is the Directorate of Northern Administration in which the full weight of the place organization finds ample expression. The headquarters' division under the directorate reflect the intention to provide all services required in the north: industrial, resources, engineering, education, and welfare. These have their area counterparts in the units under the administrator of the Mackenzie District, covering the full range of parks, forests, resources, game, industries, schools, property, buildings and equipment, etc., and in the regional offices at Churchill and Frobisher Bay. Because the Yukon is closer to provincial status than the Northwest Territories the area's governing machinery is more elaborate – a council of its own and an embryonic public service partly made up of federal civil servants under the controller of the Yukon who also reports to the director of northern administration in Ottawa.

Obviously, the attempt to bring a full, co-ordinated range of administrative services to the locality has necessitated the provision of a miniature version of the federal public service, with all the possibilities of friction and duplication with resource and service departments operating their own regional outposts in the north.

The reorganization of 1966 removed the resource (purpose) functions to a new Department of Energy, Mines and Resources being erected within the framework of the old Department of Mines and Technical Surveys. This change compelled Mines and Technical Surveys (now Energy, Mines and Resources) to adjust its structure to the important place basis of administration that is such a striking feature of the resource side now extracted from the old Department of Northern Affairs and National Resources. In effect, while leaving a single deputy minister at the head of this multi-purpose agency, four assistant deputies were introduced, each to preside over the old Mines and Technical Surveys (research group and mineral development group) and the component from the old Department of Northern Affairs and National Resources concerned with water (water group) and a newly constituted energy development group. The attachment of Indian Affairs to Northern Affairs, which completes the organizational shuffle, should provide a happier combination of clientele-cum-place organizations designed to provide a full range of services to clients that will increasingly be localized in the north (assuming the provinces will absorb health and education services for Indians within their boundaries).

Two of the three additional mergers consummated after 1966 provide notable examples of marriages of convenience. The Department of Fisheries and Forestry reduces the number of ministerial heads from two to one (an important consideration in keeping the cabinet to a workable size), but it retains separate deputy heads and two separate operating infrastructures that hold out no prospect of genuine integration, either of functions or of regions. There may be a slightly better prospect of achieving organizational integration of the components of Trade and Commerce and Industry. Finally, the Department of Supply and Services has frankly recognized the duality produced by combining the former Department of Defence Production (supply) with service components extracted from the former Office of Comptroller of the Treasury and other central services removed from the Treasury Board and the Public Service Commission: the department has one minister but two deputy ministers, although it is proceeding on the model of Health and Welfare to develop a co-ordinated set of internal services for the two branches.

Looking back over this complicated story of work division within departments, several points may be singled out for emphasis. Those departments that have a single major purpose or function and are highly centralized face the least number of organizational problems. They display one or more of at least three prominent features: (1) a tendency, as in Justice, to create a disproportionate number of 'chiefs' in relation to the number of the 'braves' whom they supervise; (2) a tendency, as in Labour, to develop a broad flat pyramid, with a minimum of reporting levels and a correspondingly broadened span of control for the deputy and his minister; and (3) a tendency, attributable to both the foregoing characteristics, to provide a relatively large number of assistant deputies as a means of relieving the burden on the deputy.

There are few departments that embrace more than one major purpose and concentrate their staff at headquarters: the Secretary of State Department is now the major example since Mines and Technical Surveys has absorbed Resources and has thereby inherited from Northern Affairs and National Resources a major problem of field organization. The key feature of the Secretary of State Department has been the broad flat pyramid deriving from a mix of functions on the whole so unrelated in their purposes that there is little for the deputy to co-ordinate. Even under the recent dispensation whereby the department carries reporting responsibility for most of the 'cultural' agencies of government, there would appear to be little such a department could do without infringing on the autonomy with which so many of these agencies have been vested.

In the largest category of departments, those with a single purpose and highly dispersed, the most significant feature is the organizational response which each has made to the problem of allocating work out of headquarters to the operational level in the field. One or two alternatives, with some variations on each, has been selected. The most straightforward response has been to create what we referred to above as a mirror-image of the headquarters' subdivisions, that is, the replication in the region of a miniature version of the headquarters' division of work. At the other extreme is a loose-jointed structure in which each headquarters' branch disperses its workload to the field, employing completely different concepts of area or locality for the field organizations. The first pattern of work division reflects a deliberate effort to disperse the work in systematic stages, from headquarters, to region, to local office, with co-ordination of all related functions at each successive level. The second pattern suggests the line of least resistance has been followed simply by letting each separate function or programme find its own appropriate operating level in the place where the tasks have to be performed.

When we consider the last group of departments with multiple major programmes we find the merger is based either on genuine affinity of programmes or simple expediency. However, even where genuine affinity exists, as in revenue collection or health and welfare, work division down the line is based on differing applications of functional and place criteria for organization. Nor does the merger effectively simplify the supporting service apparatus but on the contrary tends to create as much elaboration of this apparatus as if the programmes were mounted in separate departments. Where merger has occurred because of administrative necessity (that is, the programme is not large enough to warrant a whole department to itself) the lack of relationship between programmes, the incompatability of their respective regions, or the differences in clientele served have accentuated the tendency to divide work differently and to set up separate common service units for each programme. There would appear to be neither economies to be achieved by such mergers nor more effective service, since unlike things (even within such a related programme as revenue collection) are not amenable to co-ordination. In short, the pressure to preserve multi-programme departments does not derive from internal economies or the prospect of more effective service; it must come from those conventions relating to cabinet-building that have imposed restrictions on the size of the cabinet.

CHAPTER NINE

Buttresses for the hierarchy: auxiliary and staff functions

The previous chapter has described how the hierarchical pattern has evolved in response to the problems of allocating the workload of departments. As the size and complexity of departmental operations increase, the hierarchy inevitably broadens and is elongated, thereby adding to the supervisory burdens on senior line officers. Unless measures are taken to relieve these senior administrators, the organizational mass threatens to become 'critical.' The common method of providing relief (the 'care and feeding of the line') is to reassign the responsibility for purely housekeep activities to auxiliary agencies. As the terminology implies, such activities can be separated from the substantive work of a department and when efficiently handled can contribute to the capacity of the line operators to implement the major purposes of the department free from such distractions. The supplementary benefits are that the skills required for the performance of such housekeeping tasks as accounting, supplies, and property management can be pooled and that such duties, which might otherwise receive only sporadic attention from overworked line officials, become the full-time responsibility of experts.

THE AUXILIARY FUNCTION

Few will dispute the need to set aside parts of the public service structure to grapple with the mounting problems of keeping the administrative machine in full operating trim; nor can anyone deny the obvious benefits to the line operators when such specialized provision for common service requirements is made. What remains less clear is at what stage of development and at what level in the hierarchy these specialized needs should be recognized.

The size and complexity of most major departments have undoubtedly settled the first question: the day has long since passed when the minister or his deputy could be expected to attend personally to the department's housekeeping needs. But the key issue still remains: at what level in the hierarchy should these auxiliary services be hived off to separate officials or units?

Three alternative methods of resolving this issue are available. It is conceivable that all the common service needs of the line departments could be merged in one super-auxiliary agency with departmental status of its own. With some qualifications this is, in fact, the solution adopted in the United States where, following recommendations of the Hoover commission, a General Services Administration was created.[1] A second and less comprehensive solution is to assign particular service functions to a number of supradepartmental or departmental agencies. In part, this approach has been adopted by the Canadian public service: for example, personnel and accounting services have traditionally been centralized respectively in the Public Service Commission and the Comptroller of the Treasury, office accommodation and equipment in Public Works, print requirements in the Department of Public Printing and Stationery, procurement in the Department of Defence Production, legal services in Justice, and translation services in the Bureau of Translation. The third alternative is to leave each department to fend for itself and make its own internal arrangements for its housekeeping needs.

The Royal Commission on Government Organization accepted in principle the dispersion of these auxiliary services to appropriate agencies, rather than recommending their amalgamation into a Canadian equivalent of the us General Services Administration.[2] At the same time the commission was critical of existing arrangements on what appear, at first glance, to be two contradictory grounds. In the case of the Public Service Commission and Comptroller of the Treasury, for example, the commission considered the process of consolidation had gone too far; whereas, in the provision of accommodation and construction needs as well as in the handling of procurement, telecommunication, and legal services, much more consolidation in the appropriate specialized agencies was favoured.

1 The General Services Administration in the United States was introduced in 1949 following a recommendation from the first Hoover commission. The Glassco commission commented briefly on this structure: see Royal Commission on Government Organization *Report*, ii, *Supporting Services for Government* (Ottawa, 1962), 'General Introduction,' pp. 14–15.
2 *Ibid.*, pp. 15–16.

The apparent inconsistency of these conclusions may be defended on the score that some of the common requirements of departments are such integral parts of the total objectives of the line operators that they should not be severed from the individual departments. While this conclusion holds true for personnel or finance, it is not so clear that the provision of other common requirements by centralized housekeeping agencies would in any way impair each department's capacity to get on with its job. As long as centralized auxiliary agencies keep uppermost in their minds the fact that they exist to serve the client departments and not to control their requests, the full economies of scale implicit in centralization can be achieved without necessarily trespassing on the line operator's main concerns.

There is, however, a limit to the number of departmental portfolios that should be reserved for departments providing these common services. In the context of the analysis in the previous chapter, departmentation would be achieved by aggregating work on the basis of common process. Obviously, it is inconceivable that all government departments could be organized in accordance with this criterion; this would be to set process above purpose, with the stress on the manner of the doing rather than on what in fact had to be done. A cabinet composed of ministers heading 'process departments' would be equally unsatisfactory if, indeed, it is supposed to act as the policy-programming board for the entire executive branch. That there is room for two or three essentially process departments would, however, appear to be a logical response to the common requirements of a large organization and quite a practicable arrangement within the confines of the cabinet system.[3]

However, if past experience with process departments is any guide to the future, one may confidently predict that the aggregation of work units on this basis will be relatively unstable.[4] The pressures are all centrifugal, tending to drag housekeeping functions away from the centre and back into the separate departments from which they first sprung. It is safe to say that Canadian citizens are not alone in being caught up in the 'do-it-yourself craze': departments, too, whatever the extra cost or additional burden, are prone to argue in favour of retaining their own housekeeping services.

A centralized common service agency must constantly carry the burden of proof for its separate existence. Unless it can show itself more econo-

3 On the impact of aggregating work on the basis of process, see the excellent pioneer study by Schuyler C. Wallace, *Federal Departmentalization: A critique of Theories of Organization* (New York, 1941).

4 See my *Pioneer Public Service* (Toronto, 1955), chap. 11, 'Public Works: Department of Transport and Housekeeper Extraordinary,' especially pp. 183–4.

mical and more efficient and equally prompt in the provision of common services, each dissatisfied client department will find ways to circumvent the formal arrangements. It would appear that the only sensible solution to the problem of centralized common service agencies is to let the customer departments be the judge of their own requirements rather than permitting the central agencies to trim and pare their requisitions before supplying the goods or services. In turn, departmental requests can be kept within reasonable bounds only by making departmental budgets bear the full costs: if, in its wisdom, a department orders silver-plated paper clips it must be prepared to pay for them and thereby knowingly forego some other expenditure. The persistence of a 'silver-plated paper clip' mentality in a department should be a ready index to that department's managerial talents and a sure invitation to take remedial action.

But, whether the decision is to consolidate certain common services in an agency outside the line departments or to leave them to each department, internal organizational arrangements must be made to cope with these functions. Each department needs its own auxiliary service units either to act in liaison with the corresponding central agencies or, in their absence, to perform the entire function within the four walls of the department. In Canada it can be said that nearly all the essential housekeeping functions were brought together initially outside the line departments, well before the departments themselves had built up elaborate units of their own. Indeed, it was precisely because departments neglected these housekeeping chores or displayed a casual and sporadic interest in their efficient performance that the centralized servicing agencies were brought into existence. Because neglect or inefficient management of these functions as costly, these central agencies were given elaborate powers to control the manner and mode of provisioning the departments.

The Royal Commission on Government Organization began its inquiries at about this stage in the evolution of the public service. It found that the individual departments, whatever justification their early neglect of these services had provided for the erection of centralized control-cum-service agencies, had now outgrown the system. Within each department the commission found universal frustration with the irksome system of control that stultified the initiative of departmental managers. Similarly, it found most departments had in recent years been strengthening their internal machinery for attending to their own domestic requirements. In a few instances an informal devolution of authority to the departments was made in recognition of this progress but, by and large, the control orientation rather than the servicing motive of the central agencies brought them into constant conflict with the deparments' own housekeeping units. A situation which should have been characterized by co-operation offered instead the picture of guerilla warfare in which the time and attention of many people on both sides were taken up with prolonged bickering over details. The central agencies suffered by being unable to direct their full energies to establishing the general standards of performance or providing expert assistance where required; the departments suffered because they lacked the authority to secure those services that were crucial to the effective fulfilment of their objectives.[5]

The foregoing paraphrase of the royal commission's findings is sufficient to establish the important point that the consolidation of common services outside the departments has given rise, in the Canadian context, to an accompanying system of controls. As each department, responding to its own internal growth, has begun to pay more attention to the provision of its own needs, there has been an inevitable conflict with the central agencies. The resolution of the conflict is not easy nor is it susceptible to one pat organizational answer.

On the one hand the growing size and complexity of each department indicate the need for much greater devolution of control over such vital matters as personnel and finance away from the long-standing central agencies to the departments. On the other hand the ever-increasing operating burdens of the departments suggest that, wherever housekeeping functions are not organically connected with departmental programmes, they should be handed over to specialized bodies equipped to service their needs. These somewhat contradictory considerations lie at the heart of the recommendations of the Royal Commission on Government Organization and help to explain why it proposed that certain functions be devolved much more on departments than they now are, while others should be more thoroughly consolidated in agencies with a stronger service (rather than control) orientation.

Whatever the outcome of these proposals, as has been observed, each department will have to be properly equipped internally to grapple with the auxiliary functions. It will, therefore, be useful now to examine briefly those parts of the departmental structure that were passed over in the previous chapter where attention was focused on the line organization. For present purposes it will be sufficient to confine the analysis to selected samples.

It is at once apparent that even the smallest department has no option in deciding whether or not it is necessary to create specialized house-keeping units: time and growth have answered that question in the affirmative. What still remains to be decided is: should all the auxiliary services

5 Royal Commission on Government Organization, *Report*, i and ii, passim.

be combined in one unit and at what level in the internal hierarchy should the segregation from the line take place?

No two departments have produced precisely the same organizational answers to these questions. Substantial differences in their size, the variety and complexity of their tasks, and their geographic dispersion are bound to influence the particular pattern that is evolved. Nor is it always possible to catalogue precisely the functions that are clearly of a housekeeping or supporting service nature. Generally speaking, the activities associated with records, files, registries, stenographic pools, machine rooms, and office supplies are readily placed and categorized. Units concerned with property, building, equipment and stores, purchasing or procurement, transportation and communication are also part of the supporting services. Most important are the offices concerned with personnel, organization and systems, finance and accounting. There is less certainty about the inclusion of legal, public information, and research and statistical services for in many cases they are inseparable from the 'line' functions of the department rather than providing services to the line. In any case, these services are usually grouped in separate units distinct from those that are more clearly of an auxiliary nature.

An examination of departmental organization charts reveals that all but the very smallest departments have withdrawn several or all of the foregoing auxiliary services from the line operations and set them up in separate units.[6] The Privy Council Office has only recently found it necessary to develop auxiliary units, and both the Department of Justice and the Secretary of State Department have correspondingly simple arrangements to handle their domestic servicing requirements. For all other departments the pattern of specialization is much more complex – although it tends to follow two alternative arrangements. In one, all the auxiliary units are grouped at a high level in the hierarchy and are expected to serve all the common housekeeping requirements of the operating branches. The alternative to this integrated system is a dispersal of

6 Extensive use was made of separate organizational studies prepared largely as internal working papers for the Royal Commission on Government Organization. Most of these, when compared with the updated revisions contained in the loose-leaf manual, *Organization of the Government of Canada*, have been much altered by the spate of reorganizations during the 1960s. For this reason, though every effort has been made to keep the factual references accurate, some of them will inevitably have been overtaken by yet further changes. Several departments whose organizations in 1960 offered excellent targets for critical comment have so altered their structures that they no longer offer the contrasts the organizational analyst requires to make his point. In some instances this has necessitated a reference back to the unrevised structure in order to demonstrate the merits of the newer trends.

auxiliary units to each of the subordinate operating branches, divisions, or sections. In several departments both the integrated and the dispersed pattern is found.

The Department of Transport provides one of the most clear-cut illustrations of a highly integrated auxiliary service arrangement. None of the major operating or functional branches has special housekeeping units; these are all to be found at a superior level in the hierarchy with Legal and Real Estate Divisions reporting directly to an assistant deputy minister and various financial services grouped under a senior financial adviser, reporting to the deputy minister, and all major personnel services placed under a director general, personnel, also reporting to the deputy minister.

The Department of Trade and Commerce, with Administrative Services reporting directly to the deputy minister, displays a comparable integrated pattern, as did the Department of Defence Production with a Secretary's Branch, and an Administrative Branch sharing the auxiliary services and reporting to the deputy minister. The Department of Labour has its four major auxiliary services grouped around the deputy minister (financial and management services, legal services, personnel, and press and information services). The Departments of Finance and of External Affairs, the Customs and Excise Division of National Revenue, also show the same integrated arrangements. Similarly, the Department of Veterans Affairs has an assistant deputy in charge of such auxiliary services as legal, architecture and designing, management, and information services. The director of personnel administration and financial management reports directly to the deputy minister. The extensive dispersal of this department's work has necessitated a corresponding dispersal to each district office of regional auxiliary units parallel to the headquarters' assemblage. The Department of Fisheries, faced with the same problems of place organization, has also created area counterparts of the auxiliary services concentrated at headquarters and reporting to the deputy minister. Finally, the Department of National Defence – a very special case – can perhaps be grouped with the foregoing departments. In this instance, virtually the whole of the civil side under the deputy minister occupies the position of a single integrated auxiliary service agency, dedicated to providing the armed services with all their needs. However, within each of the military branches there were comparable auxiliary functions associated with personnel, finance, supply, properties, and information – a duplication which integration of the three services was expected to eliminate.

The remaining departments display a more confusing picture in which dispersed auxiliary units proliferate through the separate branches and divisions and in most instances are duplicated in an integrated set of servicing agencies at a senior level. These departments appear to have been unable to decide whether to integrate auxiliary services at a senior level or to segregate these servicing functions farther down the line at the branch or divisional level. In practice they have done both, with what would appear to be inevitable duplication.

In the Department of National Health and Welfare the motives for creating the present pattern are apparent and laudable: faced with a double-barrelled top structure, auxiliary services required by both Health and Welfare were moulded into a joint unit providing common legal services, information, research, and statistics. Similarly, a common Administration Branch handles financial and personnel problems. Perhaps because the deputy minister (welfare) is responsible for these auxiliary units, no further attempt is made on the Welfare side to duplicate them. On the Health side, however, each of the operating units has created its own auxiliary services. Northern Affairs and National Resources, before its functions were shuffled in 1966, showed even clearer signs of the same duplicate auxiliary mechanisms: each of the operating divisions had its own panoply of housekeeping organizations, but in addition, at the senior level, a personnel and organization division as well as a chief administrative officer had been created, presumably to service the whole department. This dual arrangement was even more noticeable in what was the Department of Citizenship and Immigration where the two main branches of immigration and Indian affairs each had their own housekeeping units and yet in addition there were directors of administration, of information, and of personnel, as well as a legal adviser all reporting to the deputy minister. The restructuring that brought Indian Affairs and Northern Development together has resulted in an attempt to mould common services for both sides of the department, comparable to what has been done for Health and Welfare. The newer double-barrelled Department of Supply and Services has also invoked the pattern of joint auxiliary services for both arms of the department.

The Department of Agriculture until well on in the sixties was prodigal in its housekeeping arrangements. In addition to a director general of an Administrative Branch reporting to the deputy minister, it also had central directorates for property and finance, for organization and personnel, and for certain machine operations. These elaborate arrangements were supplemented by separate auxiliary services attached to most of the numerous divisions into which the department's work was divided at the secondary level. As a reference to Figure 4 in chapter 8 will reveal, recent changes have produced a set of integrated auxiliary services reporting directly to the deputy minister.

The Department of Public Works is itself a centralized common service agency meeting other departments' requirements for accommodation, engineering, construction, and architecture. Within the department, however, there are several clearly distinguishable units that provide such internal auxiliary services as personnel, financial, and administrative services. Each of these is in a separate branch reporting directly to the deputy minister.

Finally, the Post Office, with the second largest number of employees and a widespread operating network of post offices, obviously has reason to create highly developed auxiliary agencies. In view of the large staff and the continuing problems with collective bargaining, personnel administration is obviously the most vital housekeeping function and its importance has been recognized since 1966 by placing an assistant deputy minister in charge of this function, with counterpart personnel officers in the district offices. The comptroller, with such branches as systems and procedures, is at least partly auxiliary.

Several generalizations are suggested by the foregoing description of departmental arrangements for handling their domestic servicing needs. First, the high status of the auxiliary agencies seems to be firmly established by the most common practice of placing them well up in the hierarchy immediately under the deputy minister or an assistant deputy. But there is a real danger that this arrangement may unduly extend the senior officials' spans of control, particularly if the auxiliary functions are each given separate recognition as divisions. If care is not taken to keep their number reduced the senior officials may find their time too much taken up with supervising the 'care and feeding' of the machine rather than ensuring that the line operators are dealing properly with substantive issues. This danger has been alleviated in several departments by making an assistant deputy minister responsible for the integrated auxiliary services.

Second, some of the departments reveal that they may have gone too far in multiplying the number of servicing units attached to subordinate line divisions and sections. Having thoroughly organized the auxiliary functions at the senior level, several departments have gone on to create another series of servicing units for the separate operating branches, and the divisions within each branch may in turn have done the same thing. This situation may be only transitional: auxiliary units that probably first emerge as attachments to subordinate line operations have in more recent times been supplemented by the department-wide arrangements previously noted. It would be logical to suppose that in proportion as the integrated auxiliary agencies for the whole department prove their worth, the subordinate servicing units should atrophy. On the other hand, the present multiplicity of these subordinate units may be attributable to illogical distribution of the workload to the several line divisions. If each of these, as has been shown to be true of several departments, is permitted to operate as virtually autonomous branches performing tasks unrelated to the other branches with which they have been grouped, there would appear to be no justification for an integrated set of common services for the whole department.

A third consideration is that overcentralization of the housekeeping functions at a very senior level – however neat and logical it looks on a chart – may in fact make the auxiliary agencies too remote from the line operators they are expected to serve. This possibility is accentuated where, as is true for most Canadian departments, the line operators are mainly in the field, well removed from headquarters. From a practical standpoint, auxiliary units can provide the most effective service when they are located in close proximity to their 'client' line operators. This suggests the need for a substantial devolution of common service activities to the field. But there is a very real limitation on this arrangement: the size of the operating units in the field has to be substantial enough to warrant a segregation of auxiliary functions from the line – after all, a personnel office for a staff of ten simply does not make administrative sense. While the next chapter will take up the problems of field organization in detail, enough has already been said to indicate that field units have proliferated, often in an unplanned fashion, from headquarters. Failure to consolidate and co-ordinate these multiple local entities means that in many cases they are too small to warrant attaching local auxiliary units to them. Accordingly, all such housekeeping matters have to be referred back to remote servicing agencies at headquarters. Moreover, because many important auxiliary functions have to be centralized in service-cum-control agencies outside the operating departments, the desirable devolution of such services to match the decentralization of operating functions has been frustrated. One must conclude, therefore, that the most effective organizational arrangement for providing departmental supporting services cannot be achieved independently of the decisions taken on such matters as the internal allocation of work to operating units and the manner in which the problems of field organization are resolved; nor can it disregard the pattern of extradepartmental centralized housekeeping arrangements that has been a special feature of the Canadian public service.

THE STAFF FUNCTION

The literature of public administration has not settled on a standard terminology for defining what has been somewhat arbitrarily described in the previous section as the 'auxiliary' functions. Some authorities speak only of 'line' and 'staff' – including in the latter what has here been called the auxiliary functions and adding to this list planning, co-ordination, and research. Others prefer a threefold distinction between line, auxiliary, and staff, a distinction employed in this analysis.[7]

Recognizing the difficulty of distinguishing 'staff' in this narrower sense, as employed here it is intended to refer to a set of functions which, unlike the auxiliary functions, are not concerned with the housekeeping needs of a department. Rather, 'staff' refers to the assistance that can be provided to a minister and his deputy in sifting data, giving long preliminary thought to where the organization is or should be going, developing the implications of new or projected programmes, and checking on the performance of the line operators. This is to describe a task that is a compound of research, more than a dash of public relations, with time to think and compose one's thoughts, and all stirred well by the capacity to present facts skilfully and arguments tactfully: in short, the administrative planning and co-ordinating function.

This description is so idealized that one would find few paragons in the public service meeting all the requirements; nevertheless, it includes the tasks and virtues that most senior public servants find themselves deploying on their daily round. They would be the first to admit that even in the long hours they spend in the office there is never enough time to perform even one of these tasks properly and seldom that quiet hour for composed thought that lifts the mind above the contents of the in-basket. Yet, if the minister is to assume responsibility for his department he must have the assurance that it is being efficiently managed, that the various elements are not working at cross purposes, and, at the same time, be in a position to initiate and defend new programmes or changes in on-going programmes. For this assurance and these tasks the minister needs special assistance – that is, the staff function now under consideration. In view of the close identification of the deputy minister with the minister in the performance of these creative and integrative functions, he, too, must be similarly equipped with staff assistance.

It is clear that the activities embraced by the staff function all take place at a very senior level in the hierarchy. It may be that the sources of information on which the staff officials rely for exercising their co-ordinating

7 I have relied on the distinctions employed by Leonard D. White in what was one of the first classic textbooks, *Introduction to the Study of Public Administration* (4th ed., New York, 1948), p. 31 ff. John Pfiffner's comparable text *Public Administration* (rev. ed., New York, 1946), chap. 6, prefers the simpler dichotomy of staff and line, relying heavily for analysis on military and industrial organizational concepts of the period.

role and preparing policy recommendations are located well down in the hierarchy; in a sense the whole structure from top to bottom is one long communication link for receiving and transmitting vital facts and opinions to the policy-makers at the top. But, in addition, each department operates in a public milieu from which again there is a constant flow of citizen reactions – both organized and unorganized – moving into the main communication circuits of the organization and all relevant to the decision-taking process. Whether the 'intelligence' comes from outside the department or is inspired by the work of researchers, programmers, lawyers, and information experts inside the organization, in the final analysis it must flow to the top where the responsible policy-makers and co-ordinators preside. Thus, the inchoate nature of the staff function can best be pinned down by confining attention to the arrangements made at the very top of the structure for receiving and using the data derived from these various sources.

In the final analysis the minister of a department presides over an organization which exists not only to execute programmes but to formulate plans for revising old or initiating new programmes. Not only does the minister preside as policy supervisor and policy former: he is also a member of parliament with a constituency to cultivate if he is to remain in public life; he is a member of an executive team, the cabinet, sharing a joint responsibility for government policies; and he is his own department's most important public relations officer both in parliament and outside among the general public. Even if a minister could escape these varied tasks, his statutory obligation to manage and have control over his department would be more than enough to keep a conscientious person fully employed. Thus, sharing many of these responsibilities is the deputy minister who by statute is empowered to act on behalf of or in the place of his minister. Although the statutes nowhere make the point explicit, it stands to reason that sharing the minister's powers and authority with the deputy cannot be total and complete. If this were, indeed, the case then one would expect deputies to act in place of their ministers in cabinet or to take major policy decisions on their own. Such situations could not arise because, whatever the law says about deputies acting for their ministers, only ministers can be held politically accountable.[8]

The amorphous and somewhat ambiguous relationship that does, in fact, exist between a minister and his deputy was well described by a deputy minister in testimony he presented to a royal commission in 1892: 'The fact would appear to be that at present the deputy head of a depart-

8 On this point, see the illuminating article by D.R. Yeomans 'Decentralization of Authority,' *Canadian Public Administration* 12 (Spring 1969), p. 13.

ment has to bear all the responsibilities but has no distinctive power whatever except such as his minister may choose to give him.'[9] This statement holds true today, in so far as the larger policies and programmes of a department are by statute confided to the minister; however, as of 1967, deputy ministers may receive (and in practice have received) by delegation from the Treasury Board or the Public Service Commission managerial authority of specific kinds. In the sense that this authority does not flow from or depend upon the minister, but may be devolved directly on the deputy by the two central management agencies, an important formal alteration in the conventional minister-to-deputy minister relationship has occurred.[10]

The deputy minister, then, is seen to occupy a curious half-way house: for all practical purposes a part of the permanent hierarchy of the public service, but in a constitutional and legal sense the *alter ego* of the ministerial head who enters or leaves the department with the ebb and flow of his political party's fortunes. This half-in, half-out status is confirmed by the fact that the deputy is a political appointee, deliberately excluded from

9 'Report of the Royal Commission Appointed to Enquire into Certain Matters Relating to the Civil Service of Canada,' *Sessional Papers*, 1892, no 16c, evidence, Q. 523.

10 Section 6, 'Delegation of Authority' of the Public Service Employment Act, Stats Can. 1966–7, c.71, states: 'The [Public Service] Commission may authorize a deputy head to exercise and perform, in such manner and subject to such terms and conditions as the Commission directs, any of the powers, functions and duties of the Commission under this Act, other than the powers, functions and duties of the Commission in relation to appeals under sections 21 and 31 and inquiries under section 32.' Likewise, the amended section 7(2) of the Financial Administration Act, Stats Can. (1966–7), c.74, states: 'The Treasury Board may authorize the deputy head of a department or the chief executive officer of any portion of the public service to exercise and perform ... any of the powers and functions of the Treasury Board in relation to personnel management in the public service and may, from time to time as it sees fit, revise or rescind, and re-instate the authority so granted.'
These clauses should be compared, however, with earlier formulations in the Civil Service Act; section 7 of Stats Can. 1918, c. 48, reads: 'The deputy head of a department shall, subject to the directions of the head of the department oversee and direct the officers, clerks and employees of the department, have general control of the business thereof, and perform such other duties as are assigned to him by the Governor in Council,' The revised Civil Service Act, Stats Can. 1961, c.57, section 39, reads: 'The Commission may authorize a deputy head to exercise and perform any of the powers or functions of the Commission under this Act in relation to the selection of candidates for a position.'
From these citations it will appear that direct delegation to the deputy minister, without reference to the minister, has been possible in the past; the legislation of 1967 is more explicit and, in the context of freeing departmental management, more extensive in application.

the provisions of the Civil Service Act.[11] Hovering on the fine margin that divides the permanent civil service from its political super-structure of ministers and cabinet, the deputy has, none the less, steadily enjoyed the same permanency as that conferred by law on his departmental subordinates. His permanency has developed strictly as a matter of conventional usage – a practice that was well described for a select committee of the House of Commons in 1877 by Deputy Minister Brunel of the Inland Revenue Department. When a member of the committee put it to him that 'it is sometimes supposed that political Heads of Deparments do not always treat the permanent deputy heads well when the latter are appointed by political opponents,' he replied: 'I was appointed under the administration of Mr. Sandfield Macdonald, and I have been treated well by both political parties. It is a matter of perfect indifference to me which is in power.'[12]

The usage has been supported by that most powerful of forces, practical expedience – a conclusion which yet another royal commission reached in 1881 when it reported: 'Ministers will, for their own comfort, choose the best man available, and in that way it will, as a rule, happen that if there is a competent man already in the Service, he will be selected. Apart from this, it is obvious that for appointments of such importance the responsibility of the Ministers to Parliament will be a sufficient guarantee against bad selection.'[13] In practice, since 1922, an order in council has regularized the procedure for appointing deputy ministers by conferring this special prerogative on the prime minister to recommend the candidate for approval of council after consulting the relevant minister.[14] All such orders in council appointments must be tabled in the House of Commons as well; correspondingly, the discharge of a deputy minister requires the same executive action and must be reported to the House.

This elaboration of the status of deputy minister is pertinent to our

11 The formal status of the deputy head was firmly spelled out in the original Civil Service Act, Stats Can. 1918 c. 48, s. 6 (1)(2)(3); section 6(3) reads: 'Where a deputy head is removed from his office a statement thereof shall be laid on the table of both Houses of Parliament within the first fifteen days of the next following session.' While the revisions of 1961 and 1967 do not include this detail, the deputy head is treated throughout as an official apart from other officers, clerks, and employees.

12 'Report of the Select Committee Appointed to Inquire into the Present Condition of the Civil Service,' *Can. H. of C. Journals*, 1877, appendix 7, evidence, p. 90.

13 'First Report of the Civil Service Commission', *Sessional Papers*, 1881, no 113, p. 26.

14 The order in council, PC 1639, 19 July 1920, is reproduced in R. MacGregor Dawson, *Constitutional Issues in Canada* (Oxford, 1933), pp. 125–6.

present concern for the way in which the top command is geared to deal with the staff function. Clearly, the relationship between the minister and his deputy must be a highly personal one in which mutual confidence and trust dictate the completely informal arrangements according to which these two top officials co-operate in the execution of their statutory duties. In such circumstances, differing personal preferences and particular skills will lead to the development of relationships and an allocation of duties that will vary from department to department and even within one department at different times. One minister may have a strong bent for management and devote much time to detailed supervision; another may have no patience with or inclination for that part of his duties and will direct most of his attention to policy-making or cultivating public relations. Similarly, the deputy minister may be almost totally preoccupied with policy issues either because of personal predisposition for such matters or because his minister is otherwise engaged; or, on the other hand, he may assume a more reticent position and concentrate on managing the department efficiently. By and large, the royal commissioners who investigated the civil service in 1880–1 were probably expressing the most widely accepted view of the appropriate division of labour when they remarked: 'We think, as far as possible, the duties of the Deputy Head should be limited to control and supervision.'[15] But no amount of wishful thinking – short of a formal detailed statutory allocation between the minister and his deputy – will be successful in marking out the jurisdictional lines in an area which is governed so much by personal factors. Unpalatable as the conclusion may be, the present dimensions and burdens of the duties assigned to a department are such that the deputy minister is likely to be more rather than less involved in helping the minister shape overall policies. By the same token, the deputy is forced to rely increasingly on subordinate staff to help ease his labours as general manager of a concern whose staff is numbered in thousands and whose annual expenditures may run into many millions of dollars.[16] The strong preference shown in recent Liberal cabinets for appointing erstwhile deputy ministers to ministerial portfolios may be an indication of the increasing disposition of such officials to cross over the traditional but always hazy boundary that separates the

15 'Second Report of the Civil Service Commission,' *Sessional Papers*, 1882, no 32, p. 2.
16 See the statutory recognition of this managerial fact of life in the provision for delegation of deputy's authority to 'any person employed in his department to exercise any of the powers, functions or duties of the deputy head under this Act.' Stats Can. 1960–1, c.57, s.3(2). A similar provision, in more detail, is in 1966–7, c.71, s.6(5).

partisan policy-former from the politically neutral administrator.[17] In any event, the minister can no longer rely exclusively on his deputy to play the role of staff adviser; both are now sharing such a range of choices relating to managerial and policy issues that each requires staff assistance.

The organization charts are not particularly helpful when one comes to assess the staff function at the top, but they give a general indication of the increasing attention that has had to be devoted to easing the burdens of ministers and deputies. Beginning with the minister we at once observe that a two-pronged approach has been followed in an effort to overcome the problems of congestion and overwork to which Sir George Murray called attention in his report of 1912. On the one hand the purely political and parliamentary duties of the minister have in comparatively recent times been eased somewhat by the creation of parliamentary assistants, or parliamentary secretaries as they have been renamed. The provision of this additional help on the parliamentary side was bruited for many years befor the office was widely adopted. At the outset their legal status rested uneasily on an unorthodox base – an item in the annual Estimates providing for a salary in addition to the regular stipend of a member of parliament. But, in 1959, a statute was passed to give formal parliamentary sanction for their appointment.[18] It is significent of the highly personal nature of the relationship between the minister and his assistant that the statute made no effort to spell out the duties of the office. Like the deputy minister whose role, as we have seen, depends very much on a personal *modus vivendi* with his minister, the parliamentary secretary's activities are expected to vary at the discretion of his chief. Generally, these duties have been confined, as the title implies, to helping the minister carry out his parliamentary responsibilities, but it is probable that some assistants participate from time to time in the minister's administrative duties as well; however, their authority ends where the minister's sole responsibility to parliament for all departmental measures begins.[19]

The parliamentary secretary is a relative newcomer, but the minister's personal secretary is a long-established office.[20] The corresponding office

17 For the broader implications of this hazy distinction between politician and bureaucrat, see my 'The Liberal and the Bureaucrat,' in *Queen's Quarterly* 62 (Summer 1955), pp. 176–83.
18 Stats Can. 1959, c.15; see also *Can. H. of C. Debates*, 1959, p. 2353 ff., for a description of the evolution of the position of parliamentary secretary.
19 *Ibid.*, s.3: 'The Parliamentary Secretary or Secretaries to a Minister shall assist the Minister in such manner as the Minister directs.'
20 Provision for a minister's private secretary goes back to early civil service acts and similar provisions were brought forward to the major act of 1918 (s.49 of c.12). The latest version appears in RSC 1970, c.P-32, s.37.

in Britain has invariably been filled by a civil servant seconded from the administrative class and returned to his desk after a short period of service.[21] In Canada, on the contrary, the appointment has invariably been made by the minister from outside the civil service. Once appointed, however, there is statutory authority which grants the private secretary the right to a position in the permanent civil service (if he so desires) when his ministerial patron leaves the department. In days not long gone by it was not uncommon for private secretaries who thus remained in the civil service to rise quite abruptly to positions as exalted as that of deputy minister.[22]

For many years the private secretary was the only personal assistant retained by a minister, his functions being confined almost exclusively to helping his chief deal with the public and more particularly his electoral following in his own constituency. Today, the minister's office for many departments consists of a much more impressive array of staff.[23] Among this personal coterie the most important newcomer is the executive or special assistant. The executive assistant, like the private secretary, has also been accorded the privilege of obtaining a berth in the permanent public service (assuming he has held the appointment for more than three years) once his political master has departed office. We have scattered information about the specific tasks assigned to these assistants, but it is clear that they vary greatly depending on the whims and needs of the minister. Some executive assistants appear to devote much of their time to the public relations aspects of the ministers' duties – a number of them have been drawn from journalism with this objective in mind. They may also be used as parliamentary liaison men, not on the floor of the House from which they are excluded but in the lobbies and members' offices. In addition, a few assistants perform what are quite clearly staff functions on behalf of their ministers in relation to the permanent administrative branches. Potentially, in this role executive assistants could constitute a threat to the authority of the senior line official, the deputy minister, though their lack of experience and limited contact with the administrative

21 See W.J.M. MacKenzie and J.W. Grove, *Central Administration in Britain* (London, 1957), pp. 191–4.
22 Mr Watson Sellar, who rose from private secretary to become auditor general of Canada, liked to describe himself as a 'patronage appointment' and invariably listed half a dozen contemporary deputy ministers who had come up by the same route in the 1920s and 1930s.
23 The Civil Service Act of 1961 (s.71) was the first formal acknowledgment of the appearance of a ministerial office staff, extending beyond the traditional private secretary. On 2 May 1963 the Treasury Board confirmed the normal establishment for a minister's office at ten persons.

side of a department's life are hardly likely to qualify them as grey eminences of the minister.[24]

The organizational arrangements for a minister's office are prescribed by a Treasury Board Minute of 29 June 1960 as amended. In effect, this executive decree lays down a total salary budget (as of 1966, $78,000 per annum) to be allocated to 'exempt staff' (that is, exempt from the provisions of the Public Service Employment Act) and provides for an establishment of up to ten – including the private secretary. These are subject to appointment by the Governor in Council on the recommendation of the minister.

Among this 'administrative support staff' – largely clerical – there is no clear evidence of a ministerial planning or co-ordinating group akin, for example, to the secretariat or *cabinet* of a French minister. The present Canadian system, by stressing the political and public relations functions of the officials in the minister's office, imposes a buffer between the permanent deputy and the political arena and at the same time minimizes the chance of a personal ministerial coterie trespassing on the preserves of the career administrator. It is still conceivable that under this arrangement the permanent civil servant can be caught by surprise or embarrassed, because he was not consulted prior to a policy pronouncement issued from the purely political enclave of the minister's office. But this is a perennial hazard to which career administrators must learn to adjust and, from their standpoint, a risk worth accepting if the separation between the two groups means that the minister's office seldom if ever will be caught intervening in the administrators' affairs.

If, as seems likely, the minister's office plays a staff role limited to dealing with parliament, public, and constituents, where does the long-range planning and co-ordination within a department take place? One would expect the answer to be, in and around the office of the deputy minister. In fact, until the mid-1960s there was only scattered evidence that staff functions had been segregated and institutionalized. A few deputies, like their ministers, had (and still have) their own executive assistants drawn from the public service, and these presumably constitute staff arms for the deputy.

24 See J.R. Mallory, 'The Minister's Office Staff: An Unreformed Part of the Public Service,' *Canadian Public Administration* 10 (March 1967), pp. 25–34, for a general description as well as a specific case study of the 'Rivard affair' which involved a minister's executive assistant. The affair was subjected to a special public inquiry in which much information about the functions of executive assistants was presented. See *Special Public Inquiry: Report of the Commissioner* (Ottawa, June 1965).

In the main, such planning and co-ordination within a department tended to be matters for informal discussions between small groups of senior administrators. For many years, the Department of Finance formalized these sessions by having weekly 'cabinet meetings,' a procedure that has apparently caught on in other departments as well. This development would appear to be a natural evolution of the collegial consideration devoted to complex problems which has for so long characterized the political heads' mode of conducting business in cabinet.

In the 1950s and early 1960s a few departments evidenced modest attempts to organize the staff function. In the Department of National Health and Welfare, a Health Service Directorate featured several divisions headed by principal medical officers who appeared to act in a consultative capacity to the director. The Department of Mines and Technical Surveys provided for a director general of scientific services, one of whose functions was to co-ordinate common services and the scientific specialities that enter into certain joint programmes such as the Polar Continental Shelf Project. Before integration, the Department of National Defence displayed the most advanced organization of the staff function in its Chiefs of Staff Committee and in its Vice-Chiefs of Staff with divisions for plans and intelligence or plans and operations. The Defence Council is now presumably the top staff agency in the integrated Department of Defence. For a time the deputy postmaster general had two senior staff assistants and there were also four regional directors who were essentially personal representatives of the deputy in the field providing advice to line officers in their regions and reporting their observations to the deputy.

In the mid-1960s the organizations of nearly all departments began to recognize the staff function, with the creation of divisions variously titled programme development, planning and research, programme management evaluation, and so on. Practically all of these divisions were made the direct responsibility of an assistant deputy minister. In a few instances an advisory group to the deputy minister was created.

There is little doubt that the abrupt organizational recognition of the staff function in departments was a response to the recommendaions of the Royal Commission on Government Organization. The emphasis it placed on programme budgeting and evaluation of programmes resulted first in a reorganization of the Treasury Board and then in a corresponding organizational response within the departments.

Until the mid-1960s, when the impact of the Glassco commission's reports began to be felt in the public service, most departmental and even service-wide planning had to be wedged into the life of overworked line administrators. Much of this was done through the ubiquitous committee system. But committees, we are told, are addicted to saving minutes and wasting hours and the failure to institutionalize the staff function in departments contributed to the endless cycle of committee meeings.

The one dominating motive for planning was the annual necessity of drawing up the estimates for the coming year. Until the mid-1960s the considerations entering into the preparation of the estimates by and large encouraged a sporadic, somewhat *ad hoc*, response to short-term pressures. Departments needed to look only one year ahead and take one year at a time: sufficient unto the year are the current estimates thereof. The importance of budget-making in inducing departments to take a long look at current programmes and priorities as well as casting a longer look forward cannot be overestimated; but past procedures provided little incentive to the forward planners. The new emphasis on programme budgeting which has only in recent times been reflected in revised estimates as well as the extended use of five-year expenditure forecasts has undoubtedly contributed to the more elaborate and institutionalized arrangements for dealing with the 'staff' function.

In summary, the search for specialized staff agencies within major departments reveals that this function has come into its own only in quite recent years. To the deputy minister and private secretary the minister has now added a parliamentary secretary, an executive or special assistant, and a corps of relatively low-level office staff numbering less than a dozen. This is a far cry from an institutionalized research and planning body attached to the minister's office but represents none the less a substantial strengthening of the 'staff arm' of the minister. Within many departments the growing practice of holding 'cabinet meetings' of senior officials to take soundings on policy stands or to develop a departmental response to immediate issues has, in recent years, provided perhaps the best approximation to the staff function. This practice realistically meets one of the major problems faced by staff agencies: if they are too 'pure,' that is, too divorced from the line, too uncommitted, they invariably wither on the organizational vine. The departmental 'cabinet meeting' provides a happy blend of collegial advice informed by the responsible realism of officials carrying line authority.

The belated development of modest staff adjuncts and staff functions within departments which has so recently occurred has been matched at the supradepartmental level by a gradual transformation of the cabinet into a genuine planning body for the nation. The most significant indication of an organizational adjustment along these lines was the creation, during the Second World War, of a cabinet secretariat within the Privy Council Office to serve the cabinet, its policy committees, and the counterpart senior officials committees. Recent accretions of special planning activities in the Privy Council Office have provided further confirmation of the trend.[25] Parallel to and associated with this development, Treasury Board has emerged with a minister of its own and a new mission which stresses central staff services and co-ordinating functions, separated but not isolated from the older connection with short-range planning that has been associated with budget preparation in the Department of Finance. Finally, the more recent addition of the Economic Council of Canada and the Science Council of Canada provides further support for the view that, at the supradepartmental level, Canada is gradually accepting planning as a politically acceptable concept and as an administratively necessary tool of government if it is to keep on top of the forces of economic and technological change.

Accompanying these significant modifications of central governmental organs performing staff functions there has been a continuing reliance on quasi-governmental fact-finding and research functions performed by *ad hoc* royal commissions. Parliamentary committees that might well have performed these functions – and in some isolated instances have done so – have not, to this point, been equipped with the sophisticated research staff now required for such inquiries. The Senate has occasionally broken its lethargy by mounting excellent far-ranging inquiries into long-term policy questions – even managing to employ a small number of experts. The budget for the legislature does not, as in the United States, provide for a legislative reference service or staff assistants for individual members of parliament. However, the adoption of a plan of parliamentary internship for 1970, on the model of congressional internships in the United States, marks a new and healthy departure. Similarly, the government's provision, though still quite modest, for research funds for the opposition and for

25 The standard reference for these developments is A.D.P. Heeney's article 'Cabinet Government in Canada: Some Recent Developments in the Machinery of the Central Executive,' *Canadian Journal of Economics and Political Science* 12 (Aug. 1946), pp. 282–301. An interesting description of expansion of the Privy Council Office to provide staff support for the prime minister is to be found in Fred Schindeler and C. Michael Lanphier, 'Social Science Research and Participatory Democracy in Canada,' *Canadian Public Administration* 12 (Winter 1969), pp. 481–98. It is worth noting that the attempts by Mr Trudeau to strengthen the staff arm of the Prime Minister's Office, independently of the staff support given to the cabinet, has created much adverse public commentary, and yet one is reminded of the comments of one of his predecessors in the 1930s: 'I think there is need [said Mr King in 1935] in connection with the Prime Minister's Office of provision for more effective advisory assistance to whoever may be holding the office ... What I think is not generally realized ... is that it is the only office in which a Minister of the Crown finds himself isolated without assistance such as is to be found in other departments of government.' *Can. H. of C. Debates*, 1935, pp. 1797–8.

backbenchers is another recognition of the need to provide some counter-balance of knowledge and information to the vast pool of talent in the public service that is at the command of the executive. On the other hand, the major parties, unlike their British counterparts, continue to be relatively quiescent in initiating independent research on major policy issues.

Thus, even with these modest additions to the resources of parliament, royal commissions appear to remain the chief source of 'outside' inspiration for longer term programme development. No longer are they judicialized scouting trips, gathering information across the land, like a circuit court, by hearing testimony from all and sundry; increasingly, they become temporary research institutes, assembling the best available outside talent to carry on the sophisticated analyses of complex social and economic problems.[26] Despite their invaluable services in filling lacunae created by inadequate staff services within government, royal commissions suffer from their temporary status. When they tender their reports to the executive they cease to exist; there is no on-going instrument for ensuring implementation of their recommendations. In short, they suffer from the defects of the 'pure' staff agency, totally divorced from the line. And perhaps this explains the rising popularity of 'mini-commissions' – the task forces – with more specific terms of reference, working to tighter time-schedules and in closer conjunction with the line operators in government.

Royal commissions and task forces, as outside staff agencies, provide the resources required to assemble scattered and sometimes isolated experts so that a genuine team research can be undertaken. But there is usually an unproductive 'breaking-in' period, an insistently mounting pressure to produce a report within a time-span that may seem long to the tax-paying public but is all-too-short for the digestion period required by those seeking to bring order and comprehension to intractable social data. And there is always a danger that free inquiry and deepening theoretical insight may be stultified by what amounts to a form of contract research into practical policy issues for which the government is seeking immediate remedies and practicable programmes of action. Added to these problems is the discontinuity of research on what have now become the perennial policy issues of our generation which is an inescapable element of the 'crash' inquiry techniques of royal commissions.

The staff function of which we have been speaking is thus seen to raise

26 For expansion of this theme, see my 'Should Canada Be De-commissioned?' *Queen's Quarterly* 70 (Winter 1964), pp. 475–90; and also articles by A.M. Willms, 'The Administration of Research on Administration in the Government of Canada,' and by G. Bruce Doern, 'The Role of Royal Commissions in the General Policy Process and in Federal-Provincial Relations,' both in *Canadian Public Administration* 10 (Dec. 1967), p. 405 ff.

much broader issues than the technical concern with internal division of labour to which this chapter has been primarily devoted. In effect, consideration of the ways and means of organizing the staff function for government leads on to one of the basic issues confronting society: how do we bring knowledge to the service of public organizations and yet still preserve the objectivity and autonomy of the sources of knowledge?[27] Obviously, pursuit of the answers to this question would carry us beyond the immediate issues considered in this chapter that have revolved around the task of work division and work specialization within departments. One further, important aspect of work distribution awaits attention in the next chapter: the problem of assigning work to the scattered forces of the public service in the field.

27 The article by Schindeler and Lanphier (n. 25) has some useful commentary on the broader issues, as does a brief piece by Lloyd Stanford, 'Ivory to Replace Brass?' also in *Canadian Public Administration* 12 (Winter 1969), pp. 566–71. Stanford's article is, in part, a critique of my contribution to *Agenda 1970: Proposals for a Creative Politics*, ed. Trevor Lloyd and Jack McLeod (Toronto, 1968), 'Public Power and Ivory Power,' pp. 256–80.

CHAPTER TEN

The geographical
dispersal of work

The preceding chapters have described the allocation of programmes to departments and their non-conformist brethren and have pursued the problem of division of labour through the hierarchy and into the auxiliary and staff agencies. There has been frequent reference to the special problems of assigning programmes and dividing work in the context of continental administration. We must bring these problems into sharper focus and observe the organizational response to this special feature of the Canadian environment.

Under Canadian conditions a public service with all its staff concentrated at headquarters would be much like a baseball team trying to play without its outfielders. The physical dispersal of the vital centres at which administrators must perform their tasks means that nearly all departments have had to give special attention to the arrangement of their units in the field and to the maintenance of effective working relations between these units and their respective headquarters.

It has already been observed that the allocation of work within a department is very much a matter to be determined by the minister and his advisers. Similarly, parliament has wisely disclaimed any intention to guide or restrict the executive in the geographic dispersal of the workload. On the other hand, the installation of a field unit in a particular location tends to build up local pressures that readily make themselves felt, should the department seek to alter its field organization, through such channels as the local member of parliament. As a result, although there are no legal restrictions on the executive's capacity to rearrange the pattern of work

TABLE I

Distribution of employees in departments within the National Capital Region
and outside the National Capital Region, as of September 1971*

Department	Within	Outside	Total	Percentage outside
Agriculture	2322	6804	9126	74
Communications	864	447	1311	34
Consumer and Corporate Affairs	1029	602	1631	37
Environment	1799	7488	9287	80
Energy, Mines and Resources	2540	637	3177	20
External Affairs	1503	979	2482	39
Finance	416	8	424	2
Indian Affairs and Northern Development	1319	6846	8165	83
Industry, Trade and Commerce	1680	348	2028	17
Justice	442	170	612	27
Labour	515	151	666	23
Manpower and Immigration	1317	7221	8538	84
National Defence	5742	27,313	33,055	82
National Health and Welfare	2236	4412	6648	66
National Revenue	2424	14,558	16,982	83
Post Office	2623	38,283	40,906	93
Privy Council Office	233	92	325	28
Public Works	2276	4961	7237	68
Regional Economic Expansion	613	1037	1650	62
Secretary of State	1167	281	1448	19
Solicitor General	77	3	80	4
Supply and Services	5809	2572	8381	30
Transport	2678	12,337	15,015	82
Treasury Board	513	0	513	0
Veterans Affairs	991	9080	10,071	90
Total	43,128	146,630	189,758	77

*Figures provided by Public Service Commission.

dispersal to the field, informal political pressures constitute a conservative force that departmental administrators cannot afford to overlook.

The geographical distribution of full-time departmental civil servants is shown in Table I. It should be emphasized, however, that the extensive dispersal of staff revealed in the table should not necessarily be equated with decentralization. The staff may be physically dispersed but without authority to act independently of the headquarters' officials. The real criteria for decentralization cannot be found in statistics alone but in the mode and manner of devolution of effective authority to the field.

Table I reveals that only four departments, Finance, Treasury Board, Secretary of State, and Privy Council, have no field force to contend with, while four more have a relatively small proportion of their staff in the field. At the opposite extreme, the Post Office and the Fisheries Department each has over 90 per cent of its staff working outside the head-quarters' area. Almost equally widely dispersed are the staffs of Veterans Affairs, National Revenue, and Transport. The Departments of Agriculture, National Defence, Indian Affairs and Northern Development, and Public Works have between two-thirds to three-quarters of their staffs in regional outposts. It is also worth noting that External Affairs is not the only department with a field force located outside of Canada: more than half the departments have at least a few employees located abroad.

Why is it that half the departments find it necessary to station between 50 to 90 per cent of their staffs out of headquarters? The most obvious reason, as previously noted, is the need to adapt to the practical problem of administering across a continent and even beyond the country's boundaries. This phenomenon is not new: some of the long-standing depart-ments are those with the largest percentage of employees posted outside the Ottawa-Hull area, an arrangement that has prevailed from their beginnings.

It was customary in earlier days to refer to the Inside and the Outside Service, and even for civil servants at headquarters it was easy to forget about the existence of the Outside Service. In 1907, for example, a deputy minister with over forty years' service reported that 'he had no idea of what constituted the outside service until he visited the several localities.'[1] And, in a similar vein, a royal commission of 1891 felt it necessary to emphasize that 'a considerable part of the work in Ottawa consists of supervising, checking, and directing the work done by officers of the Government in connection with the Post Offices, Customs Houses, Harbours, Fisheries, and numerous other establishments in all parts of the Dominion.'[2]

Much of the work of these early outposts of the public service was concerned with the direct operation of particular services which had to be performed on the spot because a particular port, custom house, lighthouse, post office, or public work was physically planted in the locality. But even then another type of activity had to be performed which involved the provision of protective or regulatory services. The appearance so long ago of the Fisheries Protective Service is a good illustration, but it can also be said that the revenue-collecting services of Customs and Excise were

1 'Civil Service Commission, 1908, Report of the Commissioners,' *Sessional Papers*, 1907–8, no 29c, p. 27.
2 'Report of the Royal Commission Appointed to Enquire into Certain Matters Relating to the Civil Service of Canada,' *Sessional Papers*, 1892, no 16c, p. xv.

essentially 'control' operations, as was the early immigration service. Such direct operating and regulating responsibilities have grown apace, particularly in relation to the production and marketing of agricultural products and all forms of public transportation. In all such cases it was necessary to bring the administrator out of headquarters and place him close to the points where regulation or service was required.

A third type of activity, growing in importance with the advance of the welfare state, has also necessitated a physical dispersal of staff in order to maintain intimate contact with the beneficiaries. So far as the federal government is concerned, one should not exaggerate the significance of this factor. The vast proportion of these welfare services and benefits is handled by provincial or local authorities. The federal government involvement is in the main restricted to the making of grants to other authorities to enable them to provide the services and benefits. The administration of grants can be carried out from headquarters, the only field staff being those required to inspect or audit accounts. There are two important exceptions to this generalization: the Department of Veterans Affairs does concern itself with the direct provision of services and sundry benefits to its clients under the Veterans Charter and, to this end, has had to create an elaborate field apparatus. The other exception is the Indian Affairs Branch where again the location of specified beneficiaries on fixed reservations necessitates a dispersed operation.

Probably more important, from the standpoint of regional dispersal of activities, is the rapid advance of the federal government into various research and developmental enterprises. Some research can, of course, be conducted without any significant dispersal of staff. The centralized laboratories of the National Research Council are one example. In the Department of Mines and Technical Surveys less than 4 per cent of the permanent staff worked out of headquarters, but this figure underestimates the degree of dispersal which occurs where survey work is conducted in the field by seasonal employees who do not figure in Table I. Much of the government's research work has to be located in an appropriate area where special soils, climatic, geological, or other conditions are the determining factors. The extensive spread of the research activities undertaken by the Department of Agriculture is attributable to such considerations.

A fifth and most obvious factor contributing to the need for a far-flung field establishment has been the growth of Canadian interests abroad. Beginning with the immigration service and followed by the trade commissioner service, Canada moved into possession of fully sovereign powers exemplified in a slowly maturing Department of External Affairs, with an extensive array of foreign posts. As previously noted, many other departments have had occasion to follow suit, although their posts abroad are much more modest.

Thus, to summarize, there are at least five practical reasons for the present extensive dispersion of departmental staffs. First, certain direct operating functions, connected with specific programmes, may necessitate the transplanting of the administrative organization to the relevant locale. Second, there are numerous regulatory or protective responsibilities that can be assumed only by planting administrators at the crucial control points. Third, some direct services and benefits – both for the general public and more particularly for specified groups such as ex-servicemen and Indians – can best be dispensed by being brought close to the clients. Fourth, certain research activities can only be undertaken at particular locations that offer the environment or raw materials necessary for the study. Finally, the growth of Canadian interests abroad has been accompanied by a proliferation of foreign postings for many departments.

Turning now to the organizational patterns that have evolved in response to these factors, several variations quickly become apparent. Some departments have adopted the simple expedient of developing a single level of local outposts. The Customs and Excise Division of National Revenue, until recently reorganized, was a notable example, with over 280 customs ports reporting back to headquarters. Most departments, however, find it advisable to achieve physical dispersal in stages rather than at one fell swoop. Thus, the Health Services Branch of the Health Division under the Department of National Health and Welfare is dispersed to four regions, each region in turn having one or more district offices; similarly, the Indian and Northern Health Services has five regions and a varying number of 'zones' under each regional head. The same pattern appears in the Department of Veterans Affairs where the initial breakdown is to five regional administrators, each region having district offices and some of the districts having subdistrict offices – altogether three levels of organization in the field. The Post Office has the most refined regional breakdown for within each of the four regions there are districts, each district has area superintendents, and these in turn have several ranks of post offices and revenue post offices under them. Obviously, the more levels in the field structure the more complex the problems of establishing communication, co-ordination, and control from headquarters.

If, as the common practice of many departments testifies, the front line units of the field establishment have to be grouped in districts and districts in turn brought together by areas or regions, an important consideration is the criteria to be used in selecting the areas and districts. No detailed survey exists of the guiding considerations deemed most relevant in achieving this progressive deployment of staff. In general, it can be said that no two departments appear to have adopted the same bases. Sometimes only three regions are used, for example, the Western, Central, and Eastern Regions of the Citizenship Branch of the former Department of Citizenship and Immigration. The Air Services Branch of the Department of Transport uses six regions, while the Marine Services Branch of the same department has twelve regional marine service agencies. Thus, not only do the number and jurisdictional boundaries of the areas differ from department to department, they may also vary as between branches within the same department.

Normally, provincial boundaries provide a convenient historical basis for areas or regions of federal administration, but in most instances several provinces will be grouped together to form one area. Thus, there may be a western area embracing British Columbia and the prairie provinces and a maritime area taking in the four eastern provinces. Even here, however, certain concessions may have to be made to geographic factors: the projection of the Laurentian Shield into northern Ontario will place the Lakehead in a prairie region or the somewhat fluid boundary of the Gaspé region may place portions of Quebec in the maritime area.

The siting of regional headquarters also tends to follow provincial jurisdictions, with provincial capitals being the most favoured locations. However, here again the pattern varies, for even the regional units of branches of the same department may select different cities in the same area as their regional headquarters.

In short, the whole subject of 'regionalization' for administrative purposes is worthy of a separate detailed study that cannot be pursued here.[3] In view of the current popularity of regionalism it is surprising that our geographers, demographers, and administrative organizers have for so long neglected this outstanding feature of our public services. Clearly,

3 A first class study of the federal field structure is James G. Bowland's MA thesis, Carleton University, extensively reproduced in 'Geographical Decentralization in the Canadian Federal Public Service,' Canadian Public Administration 10 (Sept. 1967), pp. 323–64. The subject has been studied in some detail for the province of Ontario in a MA thesis, Queen's University, by C.R. Tindal, 'Regional Administration: A Study of Ontario Government Department Field Offices,' ibid. 11 (Summer 1968), pp. 186–249. It is also a problem common to the many efforts now being made to merge traditional local government units into larger regional administrative groupings for special functions; at the other end of the scale, it is also a subject of great concern to federal departments vested with responsibility for generating regional development. The lack of coherence in the approach to regional area administration is developed in my 'Regional Interests and Policy in a Federal Structure,' Canadian Journal of Economics and Political Science 32 (Feb. 1966), pp. 3–14.

there are a number of variables involved in selecting the most appropriate administrative areas, and their relevance will vary from department to department. For example, the amount of business will determine the siting of postal districts and post offices; but the activity of a particular postal district is dependent on the concentration of population, its position with respect to transportation facilities, the commercial or industrial concentration, and so on. Parenthetically, it is interesting to observe that eighty of the eleven thousand individual post offices account for four-fifths of all mail, while annual revenues range from a high of $46 million to a low of eleven dollars.[4] For an agency like the Indian Affairs Branch, obviously the areas have to be geared to the points of concentration of Indian reserves; Veterans Affairs will be guided by the vital statistics of the veteran population; while the Department of Fisheries will look to the physical location of the resource which it is concerned to promote and conserve.

Whatever criteria are used to justify the selection of the particular centres for regional administration, the implications of the present diversity of organizational patterns are quite apparent. Since departments have not adopted the same standard pattern of regions, interdepartmental co-ordination at the field level is not readily achieved. Similarly, because separate branches within the same department have developed entirely different regions, they tend to operate autonomously and again the problem of co-ordination is accentuated. By the same token, planting numerous isolated field units of different branches in one centre may lead to excessive duplication and inefficiency. Meanwhile, in general terms, as the resort to regionalization grows apace and as each department develops its own organizational solutions to the problems of work dispersal, the administrative map becomes increasingly confused and incoherent.

The decisions to adopt one or more levels of regional organization and to group field units into different areas raise a number of complex issues that have received far less attention than their importance deserves. Yet beyond these issues lies another range of critical problems associated with designing the most effective working relations between the region and its headquarters. In developing these relationships two important guiding considerations are relevant. The first consideration is how headquarters should be organized to cope with its regional outposts. There are two possible answers here: the regions may all report to a single central authority such as the deputy minister or an assistant; alternatively, they may report severally and separately to each of the relevant divisions at

4 See Royal Commission on Government Organization, *Report*, III, *Services for the Public* (Ottawa, 1962), report no 17: 'The Post Office,' p. 311.

1. INTEGRATED-UNITARY MODEL

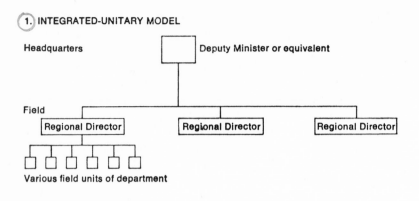

Headquarters — Deputy Minister or equivalent

Field — Regional Director | Regional Director | Regional Director

Various field units of department

2. INTEGRATED-MULTIPLE MODEL

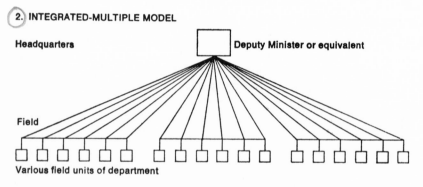

Headquarters — Deputy Minister or equivalent

Field

Various field units of department

headquarters. For purposes of convenient future reference, the first type of arrangement can be described as integrated and the second as dispersed headquarters' supervision and control.

The second consideration is to observe the manner in which the field units are organized for purposes of reporting back to headquarters. Here, again, there are two possible answers: on the one hand, each functional unit in the field may report back independently to headquarters; on the other hand, the supervisors of each such functional unit may report to a regional director who then acts as a single channel of communication to headquarters. The first type of arrangement may be designated as multiple and the second as unitary field direction and control.[5]

The permutations and combinations of these two sets of criteria give

5 This schemata is borrowed (but much adapted) from John M. Pfiffner, *Public Administration* (rev. ed., New York, 1946), p. 147 ff.

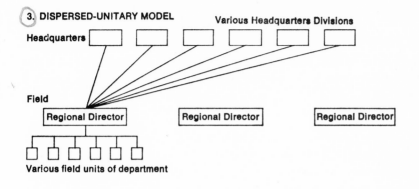

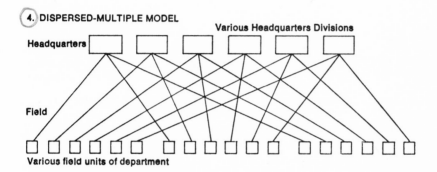

us four methods of organizing the headquarters-to-field relationship, as seen in the charts presented here. The choice of one or other of the four typical structures for maintaining headquarters-to-field relationships depends in part on the special characteristics of each department's programmes. Type number (2) integrated-multiple model would appear to be the least viable organizational solution, for the obvious and practical reason that the span of control of the headquarters' supervisor would normally be overextended. In a situation where it is essential to preserve a high degree of uniformity and consistency at all the local levels there are obvious merits in having each unit report directly to one senior official at headquarters. But if there happen to be a very large number of such local units scattered throughout the country this particular arrangement is likely to overwhelm the headquarters' supervisor. This was clearly the case with the Customs and Excise Division of the Department of National

Revenue where no less than 281 individual customs ports reported directly to the deputy minister.[6] Now the separate ports have been grouped into regions and each region reports to the assistant deputy minister (operations), thereby qualifying for inclusion in the integrated-unitary category.

Much the same observations applied to the units found in the Taxation Division of National Revenue where, before rearrangement, twenty-nine district offices reported directly to the deputy – obviously more than the number of units conventionally regarded as being within the competence of one man to supervise. Although many of the operations have become so routinized that they lend themselves to machine processes, many difficult decisions must come back to the minister, and thus the only change here has been to provide the deputy minister with an assistant deputy (operations) who supervises both the district offices and the data centre.

Rather different considerations apply to a more limited version of the same organizational pattern that developed in the Research Branch of the Department of Agriculture. Reporting to the director general of this branch were more than seventy distinctive research units scattered across Canada. When these were added to the other headquarters' units that reported to the director general, the span of control was clearly beyond the reach of one man. In this case, a solution comparable to that developed for National Revenue was recently adopted: headquarters' co-ordination of research is achieved by grouping research operations into two regions with assistant directors general in charge of each region and a separate assistant director general placed in charge of institutes that are regionally based but specialized as to function, for example, animal, entomology, food, plant, soil, etc.

The organizational patterns considered above have all been undergoing recent alterations that lead to the adoption of what is now the most common arrangement developed in other departments, that is, some approximation to type (1) integrated-unitary model. On paper, the pattern of relationships established by this arrangement appears to be the most coherent and logical. At the same time, it is a pattern that can be maintained only by resisting what might be called the 'natural pressures' based on the psychic needs of experts to deal with their own kind. Experts and technicians in the field want to deal directly with their counterparts at headquarters; they rebel against a system that forces them to negotiate

6 The following paragraphs reflect, once again, the hazards of commiting to print descriptions of structures that, particularly since 1966, have been changing very rapidly. Even repeated revisions to the text could not capture every change; consequently, this descriptive material should be viewed only as examples of the various models. In retrospect, all changes appear to be moving, at least on paper, towards the integrated-unitary model.

through intermediaries – both in the field and at headquarters – whom they may have due cause to believe have neither sufficient sympathy for nor understanding of the specialists' subject to urge these claims on their behalf. It follows, then, that the pattern of headquarters-to-field relationships that is most likely to assert itself (whatever the formal charts may depict) is that found in type (4) dispersed-multiple model. This arrangement most nearly meets the alleged need of experts to deal on a one-to-one basis with their fellows. Recognizing this natural proclivity of experts to consort together, it is not surprising to find that Canadian departments are predisposed – informally if not formally – towards the dispersed-multiple model. This predisposition may be accounted for by the need of so many departments to employ various types of scientists and technicians in the field to undertake research, or doctors, veterinarians, engineers and architects, biologists, and 'civilizing' educators for all the varied operating and protective functions demanded of government in so many different localities. It may also be related to the need to disperse specialized auxiliary services in order to bring them closer to the operating client divisions.

These generalizations may be reinforced by illustrations drawn from several departments. One of the most clear-cut examples of the integrated-unitary model is to be found in the Department of Veterans Affairs. At headquarters, the lines of supervision for the five regions are brought together in the hands of the deputy minister. In the field, each regional administrator acts as the focal point for the district and subdistrict offices, that is, in our terms, unitary supervision and co-ordination in the field. This formal structure for communication, subordination, and command is obviously dedicated to the need to ensure tight co-ordination and close supervision of the activities of a widespread field force. Like the organization of the Armed Services, from which most of this department's staff have come and whose ex-members it exists to serve, the Department of Veterans Affairs probably gave too much emphasis to co-ordination and top control at the risk of sacrificing prompt and sympathetic service to its clients. Nor was this merely a matter of slavishly imitating the military model: for the first two or three years after it was brought into being the department faced an explosive tenfold expansion of staff and had to develop a whole new array of servicing functions. In these circumstances it was essential to have a system that could ensure the utmost consistency in the development and application of regulations by an untried staff administering new programmes far from headquarters. As the department matured this initial preoccupation with co-ordination and control was supplanted by a set body of rules; more attention could then be directed to the provision of prompt and efficient service geared to local conditions and needs. Thus, while the formal structure remained virtually unchanged, informal channels developed which suggested a response to those 'natural pressures' mentioned above: the model moved closer to meeting the requirements of direct expert-to-expert communication between the several functional units under the regional director and their headquarters' counterparts.[7]

The same formal integrated-unitary pattern was found in the Department of Fisheries (before its combination with Forestry) in which five area directors acted as the single centres for all district supervisors and reported back to one official, an assistant deputy minister, at headquarters. But the fact that each district had functional units that were mirror-images of the units under the area director and that these, in turn, were almost exact counterparts of equivalent headquarters' divisions, strongly suggests that the normal method of communication did not rigorously follow the formal chain of command but was carried out by straight-line links between the relevant experts located at each level. Thus, in practice, the dispersed-multiple model tends to reassert itself in defiance of the formal structure.

Nearly all the other departments have to be considered branch by branch rather than as single entities. Each major branch or division has evolved its own regional apparatus and there is no question of melding these separate field structures, either at headquarters or in the local area. If we examine each of these branch or divisional arrangements we encounter the same variations in the pattern of headquarters-to-field relationships.

One of the most dispersed patterns is displayed by the Department of Agriculture, where we find a separate and distinct field structure attached to each of the headquarters' divisions. There are, for example, a variable number of district inspection offices located in different places for each of the dairy products, livestock, plant protection, and fruit and vegetable divisions; the headquarters' units concerned with research and protection (for example, soils, animal pathology, contagious diseases) also each have their own special field establishments. This department, even taken one branch at a time, offers a striking illustration of the dispersed-multiple model; however, in the past few years, Agriculture has been striving to secure a semblance of the integrated headquarters structure. No doubt the highly dispersed character of these arrangements gives emphasis to what has been said above about the natural instinct of experts to deal with

7 The chart of the department for 1967 does in fact reflect these trends and it would now appear to fit the dispersed-unitary model.

colleagues on a direct communication line rather than through any co-ordinating intermediary (see Figure 4 in chapter 8).

In the Health Division of the Department of National Health and Welfare one finds the same separation of field units attached to particular headquarters' services, but in these cases the picture is one of integration and unitary direction for each service. Thus, Health Services has its Public Health Engineering Division which in turn has four regional directors reporting to it, even as the district officers are co-ordinated by the regional heads. The same is true for Indian and Northern Health Services and its five regions, food and drugs, quarantine and immigrant health, and the division concerned with sick mariners.

The two operating divisions of the Department of Transport – Air Services and Marine Services – each follows the integrated-unitary model. Air Services, with its six regional directors reporting to the assistant deputy minister (air services), is a particularly clear-cut example of this type. In the field under each regional director are regional controllers for civil aviation, engineering, telecommunications and electronics, a regional meteorologist, and a regional administrator. Once again, however, the formal pattern of unitary control in the field must be set against the fact that each of the specialist units under the regional director has its counterpart at head office: thus, it is fair to assume – especially when so many technical skills are involved – that the informal man-to-man relationship will assert itself in the daily working of the system, thereby cutting through the formal integrative structure (see Figure 6 in chapter 8).

The separate components of the Department of Citizenship and Immigration followed a similar pattern of an integrated headquarters' control and a unitary overhead direction by the regional directors in the field. The Department of Public Works offers an interesting illustration of an organization that has recently evolved from a highly dispersed-multiple model to the integrated-unitary model. The emerging pattern shows new regional directors reporting to the senior assistant deputy minister (operations), each of these in turn being placed in charge of the key functional divisions in the region, that is, architecture and engineering. This pattern contrasts with a system in which each discrete functional unit in the field reported directly back to its functional counterpart at headquarters. At the same time, however, the district officers in charge of specific field functions and ostensibly under the wing of the regional director are also expected to report in their own right to the senior assistant deputy minister. This double-channelled arrangement is a clear acknowledgment of the potency of that natural pressure to which repeated reference has been made: the desire of the specialists to escape from a formal structure of co-ordination that forces them to communicate or negotiate with one another through 'lay' intermediaries.

At an early stage in this chapter it was emphasized that geographic dispersal of staff should not be confused with decentralization. The former can be readily ascertained by mere external inspection of organization charts and the vital statistics of staff. Decentralization, which refers to the actual authority or power devolved on the field force, is not as susceptible to such factual analysis. We know from previous discussion that all authority converges at the top in the ministerial head and his deputy. We also know that, as a practical matter, the head cannot exercise powers by himself: ways must be found to convey them down through the structure to the action stations. The hierarchical structure provides the initial means by which this transfer takes place. But, in the Canadian context especially, a further devolution out from headquarters' branches into field units is a necessary supplementary device for bringing power to the points where decisions and actions have to be taken. In both instances there is an important element of contingency in the process, for powers so delegated can at any time be brought back to their ministerial source – just as parliament in the exercise of its prerogative can at any time theoretically retract powers that it has conferred on a minister. This does not necessarily mean that the whole administrative situation is fluid and unstable; it does mean that in seeking to determine how decentralized an operation may be, we confront a dynamic process in which stability may be achieved by institutionalizing relationships but where shifts can occur in the centres of power.

A number of factors will influence the decision to concentrate or devolve power within a department.[8] One of the most important is the maturity of the organization. Organizations, like individuals, have to pass through a learning process. As experience or knowledge accumulates in the process of implementing programmes, issues which at an early stage would have required the thought and direct attention of senior people can at a later stage be treated as routine matters, probably fully covered by departmental regulations built on precedent. This evolution, as previously noted, characterized the development of the Department of Veterans Affairs: rapid growth, inexperienced staff, and the novelty of programmes necessitated an initial firm control at the top, a modicum of decentralization to the field, and a consequent constant referral of problems up the

8 The following paragraphs are much indebted to the work of James W. Fesler, 'Field Organization,' in *Elements of Public Administration*, ed. F.M. Marx (2nd ed., Englewood Cliffs, NJ, 1959), chap. 12.

line for final determination. Increased maturity brought relaxation of central controls and a devolution of decisive power (exercised within well-established precedents) to the field where service could be rendered promptly on the spot.

However, the relative stage of maturity of an organization is only one of the factors influencing the decision to decentralize: the character of the activity is as important. There is, for example, an obvious difference between the discretion to determine what shall travel by book post and the power to declare what the rate of postage on a book shall be: the first decision can safely be left to a clerk who knows the regulations, the second can only be settled at a high level of headquarters or by parliament itself. Thus, the 'policy content' of an activity has a marked effect on decentralization. In the Department of Finance, which is primarily concerned with policy issues, a high degree of centralization is imperative. Yet, there are other decisions with a rather low policy content which are nevertheless made at the centre rather than in the field. The letting of contracts would be a case in point, although the historical argument for centralizing such decisions has been that this is the best way to guard against improprieties. Another way of viewing the situation is that a decision with strong patronage overtones is preferably kept close to the minister and the cabinet. We shall see later, in examining the development of the Treasury Board, that such considerations tended to clutter up the top management machinery with administrative trivia, thereby prolonging the tendency to starve the extremities in the field.

A third factor having a bearing on the degree of decentralization that can be attained is the existence of a standard body of procedural rules and substantive regulations. Where such guides to the exercise of an official's duties exist it is obviously easier to decentralize, reserving only exceptional cases for higher consideration. In a sense this is rather the way law courts are structured, with a system of appeals to handle the more contentious cases. Departments that have extensive dealings with the public, either through the provision of services or the distribution of benefits or the performance of a regulatory function, are usually surrounded by a 'case law' of precedents and guides. These are designed to cover the vast majority of cases encountered at the local level; the remainder are amenable to the so-called 'exception principle,' that is, the few exceptions are singled out from the run-of-the-mill cases and redirected to special processing procedures at a higher level in the hierarchy. In those instances where local public servants may be required to make decisions on matters for which statutes, regulations, or rule books provide little or no guidance it is customary to find – as with the law courts – provision for appeals to the top of the hierarchy or even beyond the department itself. Administration of income tax returns provides an illustration of this procedure.

The quality and competence of the staff may have a strong bearing on the decision to decentralize. The temptation to treat field personnel as second-rate citizens, much on the lines by which a policeman may be 'rusticated' to the city's outskirts, has to be resisted if genuine decentralization is to become possible. A vicious circle is otherwise created in which headquarters is reluctant to devolve power on the field because it has no confidence in the competence of the staff, and local officials are never able to earn that confidence because they are not entrusted with sufficient power to display their resourcefulness and true capacities. The long-established system of central management controls, which will be examined in detail later, has been permeated with this philosophy.

There is a point, particularly in research activities or in operations demanding a high degree of professional competence, where the character of the work and the quality of the personnel combine to strengthen the case for decentralization. The scientific researcher with high professional qualifications presumably cannot be guided by regulations in the performance of his task, nor are these tasks fraught with discretionary policy components that require strict control of his actions. His is the field of the lone-wolf or the dedicated team, demanding high standards of professional competence and a sense of personal integrity or pride of profession. To a less marked degree, the engineer or technician must be relied on to employ as he sees fit the power that derives from his special knowledge or skill. His power, be it noted, does not depend on his legal status in a hierarchy of offices. In so far as the programmes of public departments have to rely on the training and capacities of scientists or technicians, power will have to be devolved on them to make those decisions which have to be based on complex or esoteric knowledge which his 'lay' superiors in the hierarchy cannot claim as their own. This concept of decentralization takes us beyond our immediate concerns into a new and growing range of problems associated with the interdependence of government and science.

For present purposes it is sufficient to establish that the extent of decentralization practised is a function of the relative maturity of an organization, the character of its work, and the quality and competence of its staff. This being said, we are still faced with the question of how one can gauge the actual degree of decentralization within a particular department. Such an estimate would require an elaborate analysis not only of the organizational pattern in each department but also the quantity and contents of the commands and instructions passing between headquarters and the field. Both a quantitative and a qualitative assessment would be required to secure an adequate impression of the actual decentralization achieved in each instance.

Probably the best indicator of the extent to which effective decentralization of authority has been achieved would be to determine whether the department prefers to issue detailed instructions or, alternatively, it is content to audit or inspect the performance of its field staff. In the first case, which could be called 'specification in advance,' little discretionary power would be devolved on the field force. Hedging a local desk officer with detailed manuals, regulations, instructions, and sundry other headquarters' communiqués accords with the preservation of a system in which uniformity and consistency are desired. On the other hand, the routinizing and codifying of what otherwise might be regarded as highly discretionary operations makes possible a devolution of decision-taking to field officers.

However, there can be little doubt that a department which relies on the alternative method of audit or inspection has taken a more positive step in the direction of outright decentralization. By the first method, one seeks to anticipate and provide for every eventuality; by the second, the local officer is much less confined by advance specifications and exercises his functions limited by the knowledge that he can be ultimately brought to account for inept decisions, abuse of power, or perhaps failure to detect the exceptional case which should have been referred immediately up the line.

Unfortunately, administrative historians have not studied organizations with a view to determining whether the Shakespearean 'ages of man' apply to them as well.[9] However, one might speculate that the life history of a department would reveal an evolution from a highly centralized power structure: at the learning stage, authority would be devolved into the field with many strings attached in the form of detailed instructions concerning the use of powers; advancing maturity would be signalized by the progressive reduction and cutting of the leading strings from headquarters; accompanying this stage would be the substitution of post audit and periodic reports upon which headquarters could gauge current performance and future needs. In this connection, it is possible that electronic communications and processing equipment, with its immense appetite for

9 Herbert A. Simon, *Administrative Behavior* (New York, 1947), and Philip Selznick, *Leadership in Administration* (Evanston, Ill., 1957), have some illuminating comments about the struggle for survival among administrative agencies that would provide a rewarding analytic framework for the administrative historian.

paper and its capacious memory, may hasten the maturing stage and thereby accelerate the trend towards genuine decentralization.[10]

The preoccupation in this chapter with the departments' response to the problems of dispersing work and authority to meet the challenge of geography should not be concluded without a passing reference to alternative solutions. As was suggested in chapter 2, the initial organizational response to continental politics was the adoption of the federal form of government. In the distribution of duties largely assigned under sections 91 and 92 of the British North America Act we find the initial attempt to decentralize administrative powers. Decentralization by means of a legally defined zoning of functions obviously produces rigidities which become more difficult to live with as the passing years witness great changes in governmental responsibilities. Necessary adjustments in the balance of functions can be made by resort to the cumbersome procedure of constitutional amendment, by *ad hoc* agreements reached by negotiation, or by the creation of joint programmes of administration and finance. In short, problems of control and co-ordination are enhanced when decentralization is achieved by a distribution of functions between separate legal entities in a federal system.[11] At the same time, if we visualize both federal and provincial departments each dispersing their operations into the field using their own pattern of regionalization, the likelihood of securing co-operation (let alone co-ordination) between field forces of two legally separate entities is not very great.

Apart from the federal solution to the problem of dispersing work, there is another possibility open to either the federal or provincial governments. They can create an agency outside the regular department and place it directly in the area with which its operations are concerned. There are several examples of such geographically based departmental 'camp followers' in the federal public service, notably the Prairie Farm Rehabilitation Administration, at first attached to the Department of Agriculture, then to Forestry and Regional Development, now to Regional Economic Expansion, but with headquarters in Regina, or the Maritime Marshland

10 The current popularity of such concepts as 'management reporting' and 'performance budgeting' or 'Planning-Programming-Budgeting' (PPB) is closely related to the generalized concepts of decentralization or devolution of management's functions, viewed in conjunction with improved communication technology. However, as Donald V. Fowke suggests, implementation of PPB concepts appears to entail a high degree of centralization because of the aggregative data that is used. See his 'PPB for Provinces,' in *Canadian Public Administration* 12 (Spring 1969), pp. 72–7.

11 For an interesting view of federalism from this perspective, see J. Stefan Dupré, 'Applied Areal Analysis: The Case of Canada,' in A. Maas, ed., *Area and Power* (Glencoe, 1959), pp. 89–109.

Rehabilitation Administration, now also attached to Regional Economic Expansion but operating out of Moncton. In addition, a few of the corporations examined in chapter 7 are set up outside the regular departmental structure in part because it was desirable to achieve the benefits of decentralized area administration. Polymer Corporation Limited in Sarnia, Eastern Rockies Forest Conservation Board in Edmonton and Calgary, and Atomic Energy of Canada Limited in Chalk River are three outstanding instances.

The use of such non-departmental administrative entities can be contemplated where there is no pressing need to co-ordinate their separate programmes with the operations of the parent department. Obviously, there is a limit to the number of programmes that can be properly left to relatively autonomous agencies whose operations are restricted to a single area. Although the amount of decentralization that can be achieved in this manner is likely to be 'spotty' the growth of interest in administration by regions (e.g., Cape Breton Development Corporation, the Atlantic Development Board, or the Area Development Agency), suggests that we may see a more extensive resort to this form of administrative decentralization.

Recognizing the possibilities of achieving decentralization by means of federalism and by means of non-departmental agencies, nevertheless the conventional solution to the problem of geographic dispersal of work will have to be found largely within the departmental hierarchy. Most of the material in this chapter has been devoted to identifying the various options open to departments when they seek to develop headquarters-to-field relationships. It is clear that, no matter what pattern is selected – and in many instances the pattern has not been a matter of self-conscious selection but a somewhat haphazard product of unplanned evolution – the internal hierarchy is stretched and strained. As the hierarchy seeks to accommodate itself to the problem of geographic work dispersal the capacity of the top command to co-ordinate and control its sprawling field structure is threatened. Thus, within any department there will always be a tension between the practical need to disperse authority to the extremities and the constitutional pressure to retain authority at the centre where the responsible minister can keep a tight rein on its applications.

The choice of means for preventing anaemia in the field offices and apoplexy at headquarters grows more difficult as the public service increases in size and complexity and as its contacts with clients in the field increase. A *responsive* bureaucracy clearly ought to be concentrating on transferring authority to the administrators down the hierarchy and out in the field; yet the historical claims for a *responsible* bureaucracy can best be met by retaining authority close to the top where it can be used by the minister and scrutinized by parliament. It is unlikely that the contradictory claims of centralization and decentralization can be resolved through adoption of a standard organizational formula; on the other hand, the quest for a satisfactory balance is too important for the ultimate operating efficiency of the departments to be left to chance. This conclusion holds true not only for the implementation of programmes but also for the management of the personnel and resources now required to achieve such programmes. The centralization-decentralization dichotomy of which we have been speaking in an operating context is even more pronounced when we turn our attention to the management of the public service. This theme pervades the history of the evolution of management agencies within the federal public service to which the following chapters are devoted.

PART THREE

Design for Management

A living organism consisting of many parts which may be physically remote from each other would not long survive if the activities of these parts were not co-ordinated. The price of specialization is dependence on others for performance of activities given up. The gain, if all goes well, is in terms of increased versatility, efficiency, power and elegance of performance for the organism as a whole.

'Physiology,' *Encyclopædia Britannica*

CHAPTER ELEVEN

The Treasury Board: cabinet's management arm

Concentration in the Canadian cabinet of collective responsibility for the initiation of major policies carries the related obligation to ensure the most efficient and economical use of all resources required for the implementation of such policies. For the proper performance of this general management function the cabinet relied, for nearly one hundred years, on an influential statutory committee drawn from its own members, headed by the Minister of Finance, served by a permanent staff which was part of his department, and designated from the outset 'The Treasury Board of Canada.' While the cabinet committee continues, it is now chaired by the ministerial head of a new portfolio, the President of the Treasury Board, and to this portfolio is now attached the small staff that was once part of the Department of Finance.

In the daily experience and working vocabulary of public servants 'Treasury Board' is customarily thought of as the staff who service the board rather than the formal committee of cabinet. The brooding presence of this omnicompetent arm of central management is a persistent, oft-times distasteful, but always essential fact of daily life for thousands of officers in regular departments and for many in non-departmental agencies; for them, Treasury Board is a power to be persuaded or placated. Yet, of all the instruments of government, the Treasury Board lives the most shadowy existence in the eyes of the general public; even the formal literature dealing with Canadian governmental institutions has paid scant attention to it;[1] its name crops up sporadically in the reports of early

1 The major encyclopædic textbook on Canadian government had to reach its fourth (1963) edition before finding it necessary to devote more than passing

investigations of the civil service; and, for earlier generations of civil servants, its powers and influence appear to have been much less pronounced than they have become in more recent times.

The legal foundation of the Treasury Board, as a committee of the cabinet, dates back to the second day following the birth of Confederation. Indeed, there are forerunners of this agency in the pre-Confederation service of the Province of Canada. The successful struggle for responsible government during the colonial period meant the absorption into the cabinet of the governor's prerogative powers, and the cabinet was compelled to adapt its structure to co-ordinate the increasing flow of business and public expenditures for which it had to assume collective responsibility. With this objective in mind, several subcommittees were struck, of which the clearest ancestors of the Treasury Board were the subcommittees on public works expenditures and on departmental appropriations.[2]

These earliest attempts to mould the cabinet into a more effective managerial agency were promptly recognized on 2 July 1867 when order in council PC 3 was approved to establish 'a Board of Treasury with such powers and duties as may from time to time be assigned to it' by the Governor in Council. Canadian statesmen, like Macdonald and Galt (the first Minister of Finance), were undoubtedly influenced in this decision by the model of the British Commissioners of the Treasury. Their belated though conscientious attempt to follow the practices of the mother country failed to take into account a peculiar institutional trait: in Britain, the substance frequently does not coincide with the form. In this instance Canadians adopted the form of the British Treasury commissioners without realizing that the commissioners had not met as a board since the 1820s.[3] Even so, to this day in the United Kingdom, there is still a First

reference to the Treasury Board. But see R. MacGregor Dawson, *The Government of Canada* (5th ed., Toronto, 1970), passim. The first detailed account of the Treasury Board at the height of its powers was given by Gordon W. Stead, 'The Treasury Board of Canada,' in Institute of Public Administration of Canada, Seventh Annual Conference, *Proceedings*, 1955, pp. 79–96. Most recently, Walter L. White and J.C. Strick have given detailed attention to the board in 'The Treasury Board and Parliament,' *Canadian Public Administration* 10 (June 1967), pp. 209–27; see also Walter L. White, 'The Treasury Board in Nineteenth Century Canada,' *Queen's Quarterly* 74 (Autumn 1967), pp. 492–505. Royal Commission on Government Organization, *Report*, I, *Management of the Public Service* (Ottawa, 1962), report no 2: 'Financial Management,' pp. 130–4, contains a description of organization and functions.
2 See my *Pioneer Public Service* (Toronto, 1955), chaps. 6 and 7, passim.
3 See F.A. Ogg, *English Government and Politics* (2nd ed., New York, 1936), pp.162–4.

Lord of the Treasury (the prime minister), a Second Lord (the chancellor of the Exchequer), and a number of junior lords. Thus, by the time Canadians saw fit to attach this collegial form to their own cabinet, Her Majesty's Commissioners of the Treasury had long since gone out of commission in Britain. Subsequent recognition of this disparity between form and substance has not resulted in any change in Canada: the top management functions have been retained, in substance as well as in form, as a collective responsibility of cabinet and its committee.

The slavish following of British forms demonstrated an unawareness of the realities of British practices which was underlined by an initial uncertainty among Canadian politicians about the proper functions to be performed by the Treasury Board.[4] However, in 1869, after the bill to give statutory life to the Treasury Board was approved, the uncertainty was disspelled.[5] By order in council PC 663, dated 18 September 1869, detailed rules and regulations governing the composition, organization, and functions of the board were promulgated. The board was to consist of all those cabinet ministers whose portfolios were concerned with the revenues – at that time the Receiver General and the Ministers of Customs and of Inland Revenue – together with the Minister of Finance as chairman and as the officer carrying the main responsibilities for expenditures. The board was to meet regularly on the 5th, 15th, and 25th day of each month, and at the call of the chairman. Reference was made to a secretary who was to prepare the agenda and keep records of the Treasury minutes.

The functions of the board, described in fine detail, fell into three categories, although all of them concerned financial matters pre-eminently within the jurisdiction of the Minister of Finance. First, the board was to keep under constant review the current inflow and outflow of money; second, the board was assigned an appellate function in reviewing submissions relating to such matters as remission of duties and other discretionary acts of the Departments of Customs, Excise, and Inland Revenue. Third, the board was empowered to approve departmental regulations affecting the revenue and the form of public accounts, as well as making decisions on 'all matters affecting the Income and Expenditure of the Dominion; all

4 *Can. H. of C. Debates*, 30 April 1869. Also Public Archives of Canada, Macdonald Papers, vol. 216, Sir Alexander Galt to Macdonald, July 1867: 'The question has arisen how we the Finance Treasury Board are to act as regards Revenue cases. I [Galt] propose to have ordered that they be referred to you as Attorney General of the Dominion ... I presume you will not at present desire to make any changes in the gentlemen who locally conduct the business, but it may be as well that they now take their instructions from you. In any case the Treasury must know who to apply to ...'
5 Stats Can. 32 & 33 Vict., c.4, s.6.

proposed changes in duties ... all matters of Financial Administration which do not by law appertain to one of the departments.' The final section of the order in council established a special relationship with the Board of Audit which was to prove in later years a source of much friction: 'At the meeting of the Board next after the regular monthly meeting of the Board of Audit [the] Secretary shall lay before the [Treasury] Board the special reports required by the Regulations of the Board of Audit from the several members as to the state of business in their respective Departments; and he shall report any deviations from such regulations or from the rules laid down by Order in Council respecting administration of the financial departments of the Government and the mode of receiving, disbursing and accounting for public money.'

It is important to realize that these regulations were in force at a time when the audit function was treated as an inseparable part of the total function of financial management. As long as this integration existed, no conflicts could arise. Indeed, the early convergence of all these significant powers of the Treasury Board can be attributed to the indiscriminate mingling of the function of internal financial control with what we today regard as the external function of audit. Until 1878 not only were these functions blended together but the several offices of deputy minister of Finance, secretary to the Treasury Board, and Auditor General were in the hands of one man, the renowned John Langton. Amendments to the Finance Act in 1878 clarified the Auditor General's position as an independent officer capable of asserting on behalf of parliament an *ex post facto* scrutiny of government spending. But his subsequent reports are filled with his resentful correspondence with the Treasury Board on decisions overruling his own, partly because the Auditor General himself had assumed that his functions also embraced the comptrol or check on the issuance of funds for expenditures.[6]

The files of the Treasury Board are not only replete with evidence of this tension between the board and the Auditor General; they are also filled with decisions bearing on the minutest details of expenditure and revenue matters assigned to it by the order in council of 1869. There are also scattered indications that, as time passed, the primary concern for financial matters inevitably came to embrace as well the whole spectrum of managerial issues relating to the staffing and organization of departments.

In the report of the Royal Commission on the Civil Service in 1881 we

6 Examples of this friction are scattered throughout Norman Ward's excellent study, *The Public Purse: A Study in Canadian Democracy* (Toronto, 1962).

find that little is said about the Treasury Board's role as financial manager; rather, the bulk of the board's work is described as dealing with problems of superannuation and the employment of 'extra' clerks.[7] An indication of the expanding role of the Treasury Board is provided in the amending legislation of 1885 by which the size of the board was increased and six ministers were specifically designated as members.[8] The enlargement was required in part to give better provincial representation but also because it seemed appropriate to add the Secretary of State, in view of his responsibility for the recently instituted scheme of entrance examinations for the public service, and the Minister of Justice, because of the number of legal references which arose in connection with the board's dealings with the departments and the Auditor General.[9] In this same period it was also common practice for the Treasury Board to approve departmental plans for reorganization before securing the concurrence of the cabinet. Unquestionably the most important extension of the board's jurisdiction occurred when order in council PC 3333, dated 5 October 1896, was approved. The order conferred sweeping powers on the board over 'all matters relating to appointment, employment or continuance of employment, promotion, increase or reduction of salary, granting or extension of leaves of absence, payment of travelling expenses, removal expenses, of permanent and temporary government employees.' All such matters were to be referred to the Treasury Board for decision before ultimate consideration and approval by cabinet.

It is curious that, despite this growth in the range of powers assigned the board, official investigations of the civil service in 1891–2 and in 1907–8 had nothing to say in their reports about this central managerial arm of the public service.[10] Only one sentence in a memorandum from the Secretary's Branch of the Post Office suggested to the royal commission of 1891–2 that the Treasury Board was a 'civil service death trap' for disposing of cases not supported politically and then went on to inveigh against the growing influence of the board.[11] Limited and cryptic as this reference to the Treasury Board was, it signalized the importance of

7 See 'First Report of the Civil Service Commission,' *Sessional Papers*, 1881, no 113, p. 54 ff.
8 Stats Can. 50 & 51 Vict., c.13.
9 See debates on the amending legislation, *Can. H. of C. Debates*, 1885, pp. 630, 631, 1670–1.
10 See 'Report of the Royal Commission Appointed to Enquire into Certain Matters Relating to the Civil Service of Canada,' *Sessional Papers*, 1892, no 16c. Also 'Civil Service Commission, 1908, Report of the Commissioners,' *Sessional Papers*, 1907–8, no 29a.
11 See *ibid.*, 1892, p. 410.

patronage in the management of the public service and further revealed that its dispensation could be undertaken only under collegial arrangements.

The royal commission to whom this memorandum was presented recommended a course of action which might have counteracted the influence of patronage in one management area. Unlike their investigatory predecessors, these royal commissioners refused to set out a detailed 'theoretical organization' for each department, declaring that this should be the task for a new Civil Service Commission.[12] In the terminology of the day 'theoretical organization' referred to what now would be called the fixed establishment of clerks and officers for each department. Thus, in today's parlance, the royal commission looked to a new Civil Service Commission as the agency responsible for establishment review and control. In fact, as reference to the terms of the order in council of 1896 (quoted above) indicates, Treasury Board was assigned this role. It was to be many years before the Civil Service Commission was placed in a position to exercise this function and when, in the years after the First World War, it attempted to do so – even though now sustained by a strong Civil Service Act – Treasury Board persistently and successfully claimed the right of ultimate approval of the commission's decisions. Thus, just as the separation after 1878 of the audit function from the function of internal financial management led to clashes between Treasury Board and Auditor General, so at a somewhat later date the efforts to place responsibility for personnel management in the hands of a similarly neutralized Civil Service Commission engendered the same kind of friction with the board.

The progressive extension of the range of public service issues dealt with by the board created friction in another direction as well. The official records of the cabinet contain sporadic evidence of the parent body's jealous protection of its own powers against their independent exercise by its management committee. The order in council of 1869, in defining the jurisdiction of the board, specified that its controlling powers over such matters as the public debt, interest payments, and new loans were to be subject to final approval by the cabinet. In other words, the committee of the cabinet might issue a formal decision – a minute of the board – but the decision still had to be ratified by the cabinet before it could take effect. As late as 1896 the cabinet is found rapping the knuckles of the Treasury Board and reminding itself of its own ultimate responsibility for a relatively minor decision: 'The Committee of the Privy Council have had their attention directed to a Minute of the Treasury Board, dated 29

12 *Ibid.*, p. xx ff.

November, 1895, respecting the payment of Department employees [here-after, all departmental employees at Ottawa were to be paid on pay lists certified by the Auditor General before payment]. The Committee upon reference to the Act constituting the Treasury Board (Chap. 289 the Revised Statutes) are of opinion that a Minute of the Treasury Board is inoperative until it receives the approval of His Excellency the Governor General in Council.'[13] It would appear, then, that even the protection against individual managerial decisions (with large patronage com-ponents) which the collegial Treasury Board provided was not deemed sufficient by a jealous and more widely representative cabinet. The latter had to give its stamp of approval or even overrule decisions made by a committee drawn from its own members.

The extent of the devolution of the general management function which was achieved by means of a committee of cabinet cannot be accurately determined, but we must infer from the position taken by the cabinet in 1896 that its refusal to devolve final authority on its committee resulted in a swamping of the cabinet in administrative trivia. This inference is strongly substantiated by the remarkable report on the public service prepared in 1912 by Sir George Murray at the invitation of the Canadian prime minister. With his knowledge of the British civil service, Sir George Murray was able to identify very quickly 'the important points which appear to require attention in connection with the organization of the public service.' Among these he listed: 'the amount of routine business transacted by Ministers both in Council and in their Departments; the necessity for a closer control over the expenditure; the practice of trans-acting business by oral discussion rather than by correspondence; the want of a proper classification of the duties and staff in the several Departments ...'[14]

The central management arm stood indicted, but the reasons lay in the original order in council of 1869 with its lengthy list containing both im-portant and trivial matters for the Treasury Board's attention. The conse-quent swamping of the board resulted in a corresponding submergence of the cabinet in the same trivia because of its determination to review and approve all Treasury Board decisions. In any event, Murray's strictures on the failings of top management were apparently taken to heart by the cabinet.

The first sign that the government was prepared to take the report seriously was provided in a memorandum of 16 September 1913, pre-

13 PC 447, Jan. 1896.
14 'Report on the Organization of the Public Service of Canada,' *Sessional Papers,* 1913, no 57a, para. 128.

pared by the Minister of Finance. After citing the key features of the report, the minister expressed agreement and went on to recommend: '... with a view to effecting an improvement in the administrative methods of the Government and affording relief to the Ministry in respect to the transaction of business of minor importance ... Treasury Board be authorized and instructed to review the whole of the duties now discharged by Your Excellency in Council and to report as to those which may be left to the discretion of individual Ministers or to a Committee of Ministers and that when such a report is made and adopted by Your Excellency the necessary legislation be introduced in Parliament to give effect thereto.'[15] In a further memorandum, dated two days after the first, the Minister of Finance again citing Murray's report recommended that: '... the Treasury Board be requested to give consideration [to Murray's report] and if deemed necessary to select a Committee of officials or to engage expert accountants outside the Public Service to examine the present system of keeping accounts in the several Departments with a view to its improvement and the establishing of uniformity of method.'[16]

The flurry of activity precipitated by Murray's report culminated in an order in council, PC 2402, dated 8 October 1913, in which after reciting the report's criticisms of the estimates procedures (paragraphs 31–46) the cabinet recommended the adoption of formal procedures which have since become the foundation for the present estimates review process – an operation that begins long before either the cabinet or parliament sees the estimates and that involves prolonged negotiations between departmental and Treasury Board officials.[17] Murray had complained in his report of the *ad hoc* informality of the estimates procedures and of the lack of any written records of decisions reached. The new dispensation, which emerged largely in the 1930s, erred on the side of excessive formality and time-consuming discussions between the staff of departments and of the Treasury Board.

The coming of the First World War directed the attention of the cabinet to more urgent problems of survival. A bureaucracy, growing in response to crises, provided little opportunity for the careful reappraisal of the management functions or the creation of more systematic procedures for reviewing the estimates. Nevertheless, in 1917–18, the cabinet once again found time to reopen the issues that had been raised by Murray in 1912 and were to have been scrutinized in detail by the Treasury Board according to the sequence of cabinet directives issued during 1913.

15 Formally endorsed by the cabinet in PC 2364, 24 Sept. 1913.
16 Formally endorsed by the cabinet in PC 2403, 24 Sept. 1913.
17 A comprehensive description of the procedures used by the board at the apex of its powers is to be found in Stead, 'The Treasury Board of Canada,' pp. 79–96.

The most significant indication that the Treasury Board had found time 'to review the whole of the duties now discharged by Your Excellency in Council' (the problem remitted to it by the cabinet in September 1913) was an order in council, PC 3061, of 26 October 1917. The preamble to this order declared: 'The Committee of the Privy Council have had before them a report, dated 24th October, 1917, from the President of the Privy Council, recommending that in order to relieve the Cabinet of as much purely routine business as possible, the following recommendations from the various Departments, be referred to the Treasury Board for consideration and report, before being finally dealt with by Council.' The order then goes on to list, by departments, an incredible miscellany of items to be processed initially by the Treasury Board. The list includes: appointments, confirmation of appointments, and resignations of veterinary officers and inspectors, and other inspectors under the Animals Contagious Diseases Act and the Meat and Canned Foods Act; compensation for animals slaughtered under the former act; authority for signing Letters of Credit cheques; licences for running local ferries; contracts for works under $5000 on Indian reserves, or by Public Works; right of way leases of all descriptions for railways and canals; inquiries into settlement duties, etc., on dominion lands by dominion lands inspectors; grants to Immigration Societies; and so on.

After examining this list, it is not surprising to discover that a memorandum outlining the activities of the Treasury Board, dated 23 July 1918, revealed that in the previous year (ending 30 June 1918) there had been sixty-six meetings of the board at which 7271 cases had been considered. Clearly, Sir George Murray's criticisms and recommendations had fallen on stony ground. There was, for example, no consideration given to diminishing the use of the phrase 'the Governor in Council shall determine' and substituting the minister as the final decision-taker. As long as the general phrase was used collegial action was required; and as long as the cabinet still insisted on approving all actions of its management committee, the Treasury Board was unable to make a final decision, even on the most trivial issues.

Perhaps the most damaging commentary on the inadequacy of the procedures promoted by the order in council of 1917 was a document describing the work of the Treasury Board as it existed at the end of the First World War.[18] The document begins by noting that the 'Board has a

18 Public Archives of Canada, RG 19, D 4, vol. 8, document, undated, headed 'Copy of a document made by Committee on Reorganization and Efficiency.' This was a committee of the Privy Council, chaired by A.K. MacLean, to maintain surveillance over the work of Griffenhagen and associates, a team of management consultants who undertook a study in 1920–1 comparable to that of the Glassco commission in the 1960s.

wide and varied field of activity. The law specifies numerous specific duties many of which are not important in connection with the work now done.' More precisely, as the document went on to indicate, the board by law is required:

To review monthly accounts submitted by the Accountant of Contingencies of sums paid in advance and remaining unaccounted for – this provision is inoperative.
To superintend the design of a plan of accounting books and accounts, and to act as a final authority in regard to what books shall be kept – no duties under this provision have arisen recently.
To purchase securities if the public debt exceeds the limit – this provision is inoperative.
To approve rules drawn by the Auditor General governing his work – this provision is practically inoperative.
To regulate methods of collecting revenue – no duties under this provision have arisen recently.
To receive twice yearly a list of the accounts passed by the Auditor General – this provision is inoperative.

As if to compensate for this strictly negative picture of the Treasury Board as the central financial management agency for the public service, the document hastens on to elaborate those inconsequential duties outlined in the 1917 order in council, from which a sample was presented above. The document concludes with the statement that 'The work of the Board is closely related to that of the Department of Finance and it acts in an advisory capacity to the Minister of Finance. Its relationship to the administration as a whole [it goes on to state with a burst of unwarranted optimism] is in some ways analogous to that of the British Treasury to the Departments.' And all this important activity, we are told at the conclusion of the document, is handled by a staff assigned to the Treasury Board from the Minister of Finance, numbering *five* employees!

Beyond this key piece of evidence, the files of both the Treasury Board and the cabinet indicate that the strictures on the central management system made by Murray in 1912 could have applied, with little change, to the situation that existed at the close of the First World War. The sorry conclusion from the evidence is that nearly all the time and energy of the Treasury Board was devoted to extricating itself from the mound of administrative detail, while the major tasks of central management went unattended.

Only one important exception to this generally lax situation may have partially redeemed the role of the Treasury Board: that fell in the area of expenditure control. As early as 20 September 1915 an order in Council, PC 2167, called attention to the need for immediate retrenchment of expenditure upon both ordinary and capital account and directed the Treasury Board 'to take the matter of our civil expenditures under advisement with a view to reducing or retarding them to such a degree as may be possible and advisable in the public interest.' Three years later a further order in council, PC 1962, dated 10 August 1918, directed that in order to enhance supervision and effect further economies where possible (both problems arising out of war conditions which had increased spending and made control more difficult) the Treasury be authorized:

(1) To make enquiry into the expenditures of the several Departments and of every Board, Commission or other administrative body acting under authority of the Government ...
(2) To consider and discuss with the heads of such Departments, Boards and Commissions the matter of economical administration and the restriction of expenditures so far as compatible with efficiency of service;
(3) To make from time to time to Your Excellency such reports or recommendations respecting the matters referred to as the Board may deem proper.

These directives are good examples of the central role assigned to and expected of the Treasury Board. On the other hand, the need to issue them would appear to suggest that the estimate control procedures designed in 1913 in response to the proddings of Sir George Murray had either failed to take effect or had broken down under wartime exigencies.

Thus, at war's end, though no one would question the formal status achieved by the Treasury Board as the central management arm of the cabinet, in practice it appeared to be something of a paper dragon fretting over detail at the expense of its major assignments. In this respect it was surely reflecting the proclivity of its parent body, the cabinet, to immerse itself in the same detail: the offspring obviously could not rise above the level achieved by its parent, particularly when the parent insisted on reviewing all decisions taken by the offspring.

During the 1920s the problem of organizing the personnel management function on a permanent and satisfactory footing took the spotlight away from the Treasury Board. A new Civil Service Commission, revitalized by a fresh statute in 1918, was armed with more comprehensive powers over all aspects of personnel administration than any of its counterparts in the United Kingdom or the United States. For the next decade the management battle lines were drawn between this new agency and the departments. The depression of the 1930s brought a new confrontation between the commission, armed with full statutory powers over personnel, and the

Treasury Board, armed with expenditure and establishment control powers which, as we have seen, had been delegated to it over the preceding years by the cabinet. In the uneven trial of strength that followed for the better part of the decade preceding the outbreak of the Second World War, the Treasury Board emerged the clear victor: its *de facto* control of the purse proved more than a match for the *de jure* powers (however omnibus they might be) conferred by parliament on the Civil Service Commission.

The depression also produced another new central control-cum-servicing agency, the Office of the Comptroller of the Treasury. Because of its attachment to the Minister of Finance, the emergence of the new agency further consolidated the minister's position as the official primarily responsible for the central management functions bearing on both financial and staffing problems. The explanation for the appearance of this unique office may be traced back to the somewhat imprecise separation between internal financial control and external audit which was achieved in the legislation of 1878.[19] The Auditor General, as an agent of parliament independent of the executive spending authorities, had nevertheless been expected to intervene at the time expenditures were made to testify as to their legality. The more independent Auditors General had been compelled, as a result, to carry on a running battle with the Treasury Board, arming themselves with constant rulings from the Department of Justice and always incurring the risk of being ignominiously overruled by the board. At the same time, as the record from 1913 to 1920 revealed, the Treasury Board had never attended to its mandate to prepare and supervise accounting procedures in the departments, nor had its control over estimates been very impressive. These factors combined – the awkward involvement of the auditor in the comptrol of expenditures and the lack of accounting and estimating controls provided by the Treasury Board – left the departments relatively free to overspend their parliamentary appropriations. Even if the controls exerted by means of annual estimates had been adequate, unchecked overspending tended to nullify the constraints imposed by the estimates.

Given these conditions and with the added incentive for seeking economies provided by the depression, R.B. Bennett, then prime minister, inaugurated the office of Comptroller of the Treasury.[20] The subsequent transfer of accounting personnel from the auditor's staff to the new comptroller indicated that the check on the outflow of funds was now to

19 Stats Can. 41 Vict., c.7.
20 A full account of the emergence and functioning of the Comptroller of the Treasury is to be found in R.D. Maclean, 'An Examination of the Role of the Comptroller of the Treasury,' *Canadian Public Administration* 7 (March 1964), pp. 1–136.

be undertaken by an agency of the executive rather than by an independent officer of parliament. This point was, in fact, the initial argument presented by Mr Bennett when he introduced the measure in 1931.[21] The further refinement of this new official's control by subdividing each appropriation into allotments and then checking the commitment of funds within each allotment before authorizing release of money for any expenditure are technically important matters which need not be elaborated at this point.[22] It is sufficient to note that, at this juncture, a central office with 'Treasury officers' planted in all spending departments and equipped with a voluminous manual of regulations quickly called a halt to the free-wheeling departmental spending habits of the 1920s.

Additional duties were also assigned to the new comptroller: he was given responsibility for ensuring that departmental accounts were maintained on a uniform basis; he had responsibility for and control over all issues of public money out of the Consolidated Revenue Fund, and thereby became in effect the paymaster general of the public service, ultimately equipped to issue millions of cheques a month. In the exercise of all these functions the Comptroller of the Treasury was made directly responsible to the Minister of Finance and his decisions could be appealed to the Treasury Board.

Thus, the decade of the thirties witnessed the culmination of a long process by which the Treasury Board was equipped to perform those functions which had been assigned to it in 1869. Chief among these functions were the control over departmental spending, central cheque issuance, and uniform accounting procedures in all departments. At the same time, the board gained a temporary ascendency over the Civil Service Commission which had emerged after the first war statutorily equipped to challenge the board's authority in staffing matters.

As the position of the Treasury Board was strengthened, the Department of Finance gained a corresponding ascendancy over the departments. The historical pre-eminence of the Minister of Finance as chairman of the Treasury Board had from the outset been underlined by using personnel from his department to provide the staff for the board. This position was further buttressed in the 1930s by making the new Comptroller of the Treasury responsible directly to him. This official, in turn, was now to perform control functions that had initially been conferred on the board but which, as the record reveals, it never satisfactorily performed.

In the same period before the war, that portion of the staff in Finance

21 *Can. H. of C. Debates*, 1931, p. 2936.
22 For a detailed description and criticism, see Royal Commission on Government Organization, *Report*, I, report no 2: 'Financial Management,' pp. 105–33, 141–61.

which serviced the board under a secretary (who also held the position of an assistant deputy minister of Finance) grew in influence though with little increase in size.[23] In particular, the formal procedures for negotiating the annual estimates, originally called for in the Murray report of 1912, began to function with a new stringency that drew cries of anguish from the departments, and for successive, beleaguered secretaries to the board created a position whose influence was matched only by the wear-and-tear on the persons involved. A new image of Treasury control appeared, to be summed up by the secretary of the board in the thirties with the blithely frank utterance: 'Yes, we're arbitrary, we're arbitrary.'[24]

The Second World War brought a radical transformation in the size and duties of the federal public service. Explosive growth and the pressure to get things done produced, as it did in other jurisdictions, an inevitable relaxation of central managerial controls and probably produced a temporary abatement of the strained relations between Treasury Board, Civil Service Commission, Comptroller of the Treasury, and the departments.

At this point the cabinet itself took some long overdue steps to accommodate itself to the mounting pressure of business.[25] In March 1940 it appointed the clerk of the Privy Council as secretary to the cabinet, and subsequently equipped the Privy Council Office with officers to provide secretariats for a number of cabinet committees. Almost as important was the creation of a special committee of council to deal with routine orders in council – a belated bow to Sir George Murray's plea for relieving a cabinet overwhelmed in detail of its own making.[26] Yet a further step in the direction first pointed out by Murray was taken in 1951 with the passage of the Financial Administration Act.[27] Section 5 of the act at last made provision for eliminating a good deal of the duplication of effort that arose, as previously noted, from cabinet's insistence on approving all decisions taken by Treasury Board. Now the board received by delegation

23 The then secretary of the board (C.K. Ronson) practised with his own parsimonious staffing of the Treasury Board what he so actively preached for other departments.
24 A strictly personal recollection of the author after a lengthy interview (but subsequently confirmed by even more colourful comments from associates in government who had had frequent occasion to bear the brunt of this power of negative thinking).
25 The story is vividly described by the chief participant in the new venture, A.D.P. Heeney, in his 'Cabinet Government in Canada: Some Recent Developments in the Machinery of the Central Executive,' *Canadian Journal of Economics and Political Science* 12 (Aug. 1946), pp. 282–301; see also his more recent analysis, 'Mackenzie King and the Canadian Cabinet,' *Canadian Public Administration* 10 (Sept. 1967), pp. 366–75.
26 The details are developed in J.R. Mallory's excellent article, 'Delegated Legislation in Canada: Recent Changes in Machinery,' *Canadian Journal of Economics and Political Science* 19 (Nov. 1953), pp. 462–71.
27 Stats Can. 1951 (2nd session), c.12.

from the cabinet the authority to make final decisions on a great variety of matters concerned with financing and staffing the public service. By a subsequent order in council, PC 3209, the cabinet devolved on the board its power to approve contracts, even as it raised the limits under which departments themselves could enter into contracts or leases or make purchases. 'In general,' as J.R. Mallory concludes, '[Treasury Board] has the power of final disposition over matters in which policy is already settled by statute, Order in Council, or Cabinet decision. The function of Treasury Board in substantive policy decisions remains essentially advisory rather than operative. In such matters it reports to the Governor in Council, by whom the final decision is made and action is taken.'[28]

Thus, by 1951–2 the cabinet had put its own administrative house in order by equipping itself with a secretary, shuffling off routine business to a special committee, and leaving the Treasury Board with final deciding powers in many areas. Meanwhile, the tension between the Civil Service Commission and the Treasury Board in the area of personnel management, which had developed into virtually a cold war in the thirties, had to be relieved. In 1945 a royal commission was set up to review the classification and pay of senior administrative grades.[29] In fact, the report of the commission went far beyond these specifics to make proposals for ironing out the ambiguities in the grey area of personnel management lying between the Civil Service Commission and the Treasury Board. Influenced, no doubt, by the presence of a senior British civil servant on the royal commission, the recommendations all tended in the direction of outright Treasury control on the model of the United Kingdom. The commission concluded that the *de facto* powers which had accrued to the Treasury Board ought to be legally recognized by openly transferring them from the Civil Service Commission. The latter would then have been left in much the same position as its British counterpart, its major responsibilities being confined to recruitment and review of departmental recommendations for promotion and transfer within certain categories.

In order to equip the Treasury Board for the performance of its enlarged duties, the royal commission proposed enlargment of its staff (partly by transfers from the Civil Service Commission) and appointment of a new official bearing the grandiose title of Director General of Establishments and Personnel. Ranked as a senior deputy minister, this official bore a strong family resemblance to the permanent secretary of the Treasury in Britain. As a concession to the firmly rooted tradition of collegial participation in management decisions, the commissioners pro-

28 'Delegated Legislation,' p. 471.
29 See Royal (Gordon) Commission on Administrative Classifications in the Public Service, *Report* (Ottawa, 1946).

posed an advisory committee for the director general, consisting of three or four deputy ministers and possibly the chairman of the Civil Service Commission. As a further offset to this plan for centralizing personnel management under the Treasury, the royal commission made a vigorous plea for upgrading and strengthening the position of personnel officers in the departments.

The major recommendations of the commission were not, in fact, adopted, although as late as 1954 a short-lived flutter in the dovecotes of the Civil Service Commission was precipitated by the rumour that a director general was to be appointed.[30] The government hastened to quash the rumour and none of the *de jure* powers possessed by the Civil Service Commission was transferred to the Treasury Board, let alone to a new director general.

In practice, an informal *modus vivendi* appears to have been reached which permitted commission and Treasury Board to settle down more amicably to work out a co-operative arrangement within their legally ambiguous and administratively dualistic setting. An exchange of personnel between their staffs reflected the new rapprochement between the two agencies, and a new programme of establishment review, undertaken in conjunction with the Treasury Board's annual estimates review, brought representatives of the Civil Service Commission into a direct working partnership with Treasury Board staff. Spurred on by the threat posed in the royal commission's report, the Civil Service Commission sought to improve its image with its departmental clients by taking a more positive approach to recruitment and other services, while quietly experimenting with the devolution to selected departments of certain of its functions, such as control over promotions. Associated with this selective devolution of the commission's legal powers to the departments came a gradual improvement in the status and qualifications of departmental personnel officers.

This uneasy, cumbersome, but workable balance of managerial forces characterized the system which had evolved by 1960. At this point, in September 1960, a massive inquest on the state of the public service was launched by the Royal Commission on Government Organization. The first four reports of this commission described, assessed, and made new prescriptions for the management of the public service. The details are laid out fully in these reports and need not be reproduced for present purposes.[31]

30 See *Globe and Mail*, Toronto, 10 Dec. 1954: an editorial, 'After Eight Years,' which was precipitated by a rumour in the *Ottawa Citizen* of previous date.
31 See especially the first three reports in vol. I, *Management of the Public Service*, 'A Plan for Management,' 'Financial Management,' and 'Personnel Management.'

The project groups who undertook the preliminary investigation of management in the public service overwhelmingly represented experts drawn from management consultant firms whose experience lay mainly in the field of private rather than public administration. It was subsequently alleged that the commission's appraisals and recommendations were, for this reason, unduly biased and tended to dismiss the essential differences between management operating in the private sector and in the public sector.[32] The allegation is probably borne out if one looks at many of the detailed proposals; but, in the broad context, the recommendations of the Glassco commission of 1960–3 were very much in line with Sir George Murray's report of 1912 and the report of the Gordon commission of 1946. Like Sir George Murray, the Glassco commission criticized the overcentralization which burdened the cabinet, the Treasury Board, and the ministerial head with unnecessary detail and, in turn, left little time to devote attention to the larger issues of management. Like the Gordon commission, the Glassco commission recognized that the management functions lacked a clear-cut and authoritative focal point in the public service. If Murray's plea for devolution had made sense in 1912, fifty years later in a public service swollen to ten times the size the plea was not only logical but irresistible. The result of imprecise lines of managerial authority was a time-consuming, often frustrating negotiation between an array of central control agencies and departmental managers, starved of authority to manage but held responsible for the effective operation of their departments. Moreover, given the postwar developments in management techniques, organizational theory, and electronic processing capacities, the need for a centre that could keep abreast of this advancing knowledge and this sophisticated technology was much more clearly apparent to the Glassco commission than it was even fifteen years before to the Gordon commission.

The essence of the Glassco commission proposals, as they related to the role of the Treasury Board, consisted of three propositions.[33] First, collective responsibility for the top managerial decisions should be retained by and should be confided to the Treasury Board, viewed essentially as the cabinet's management arm. Second, whatever merits could be claimed for the historical attachment of the Treasury Board to the Department of Finance through the provision of the minister as chairman and a staff from his own department, the central management role of the Treasury Board could be better performed by severing its direct attachment to the Department of Finance. Third, as an outgrowth of the second proposition,

32 See, for example, the vigorous critique by T.H. McLeod in 'Glassco Commission Report,' *Canadian Public Administration* 6 (Dec. 1963), pp. 386–406.
33 See especially the first report in vol. I, 'A Plan for Management.'

the Treasury Board ought to be assigned a minister of its own and its staff, provided with an upgraded secretary as director, transferred to the Office of the Privy Council.

The first proposition was based on a realistic appraisal of the federal pressures that had given rise to the long-standing tradition of collegial action on all matters of major policy, including as we have seen a determined effort to bring even the most trivial managerial issues to cabinet and Treasury Board.

The second proposition must be considered in the light of the commission's proposals for broadening the range of Treasury Board's concern from the purely financial components to a concern for co-ordination of programmes and an overall surveillance of the organizational or administrative needs of the public service. Hence, the commission recommended a reorganization of Treasury Board staff that would reflect these broadened managerial horizons in three major divisions: programme analysis, personnel, and administrative improvement. Obviously, money will always play an important part in all managerial decisions and for this reason the Minister of Finance should logically be a member (but not chairman) of the Treasury Board; similarly, liaison between the staff of the Treasury Board and the branches in the Department of Finance would have to be close and continuous but, again, not by retaining Treasury Board staff on the establishment of the Department of Finance. The assumption of the commission was that the financial aspects of managerial decisions were vital but not the only elements that had to be taken into account, and that these other elements would generally get short shrift in considering the broader range of management issues as long as the Treasury Board was chaired and staffed through the good offices of the Department of Finance.

The third proposition, calling for a separate Minister of Treasury Board and a relocation of the staff under its secretary in the Privy Council Office was defended by the royal commission on the score that: 'The ultimate authority lies with the Cabinet and is exercised by the Treasury Board only by delegation ... When Cabinet chooses to concern itself directly with these functions of central direction it must have at its disposal the staff support normally possessed by the Treasury Board. For this reason, the Treasury Board staff should be transferred from the Department of Finance to the Privy Council Office, where it would be more properly identified with the Cabinet and with the Treasury Board itself as a committee of Cabinet.'[34]

In the foregoing history of the evolution of the Treasury Board it will be recalled that the initial assumption was that the board existed essentially

34 *Ibid.*, pp. 55–6.

to advise the Minister of Finance in the performance of his functions but rather quickly began to act on behalf of the cabinet on such matters as pensions, salaries, organization, establishments, and appointments. Because the Minister of Finance chaired the board and reported to the cabinet on its behalf and because the staff of the Treasury Board were under his jurisdiction, progressive extensions of Treasury Board powers tended to become extensions of the powers of the Department of Finance. The key role played by estimates review and approval undertaken by the staff of the Treasury Board with the inevitable association of such estimates with the formulation of the budget by the Minister of Finance simply confirmed and consolidated the hold of this department over the public service in general.

The Glassco proposal to establish a formal connection between Treasury Board staff and the cabinet, and between the cabinet and the Treasury Board (as its management committee), was a logical and necessary affirmation of the need to achieve central focus and leadership for major managerial decisions affecting the public service as a whole. Ideally, that ultimate responsibility should come to rest in the prime minister himself; but, as the Glassco commission realistically admitted, 'other matters even more important than the general management of the machinery of government demand almost all the time and energy of any man in this office.'[35] At the same time, as the royal commission observed, the major responsibilities of the Minister of Finance leave him 'little time to devote to the day-to-day task of central administrative direction.' Accordingly, the commission recommended 'appointment of a presiding minister with no departmental responsibilities, who would give day-to-day guidance to its [the Treasury Board's] staff, provide the initiative needed within the Board itself, and ensure that general considerations of good management find adequate expression within the Cabinet on all matters to which they are relevant.'[36]

Anticipating the need to preserve 'a close relationship' between the responsibilities of the Minister of Finance and the Treasury Board, the commission suggested that 'the position of President [of the Treasury Board] might well be associated with the Department of Finance, comparable in status to the Minister but different in function.'[37] In the attempt to implement this somewhat involuted proposal of a separate ministerial head for the Treasury Board, who would at the same time not be severed from the historical link with Finance, the government began a complicated

35 *Ibid.*, p. 53.
36 *Ibid.*, pp. 53–4.
37 *Ibid.*, p. 54.

organizational manœuvre.[38] The sequence of steps initiated in November 1962 can be understood only if viewed as aspects of a two-stage operation, the first concerned with machinery to facilitate the analysis and ultimate implementation of the recommendations of the Glassco commission, the second concerned with a permanent structure to deal with the problems of top management.

The first stage began in 1962 when Senator Wallace McCutcheon, then minister without portfolio in the Diefenbaker cabinet, was made responsible for the fate of the recommendations still emanating from the Royal Commission on Government Organization. It was clear to all concerned that once the commission had closed its inquiries an extraordinarily large number of recommendations would be laid at the doorstep of the public service. Many of these recommendations, if accepted, would take a long time to implement and many of them would never get off the ground unless there was somewhere in the public service a 'ginger group' whose sole responsibility it would be to see that they were not neglected. Accordingly, Senator McCutcheon was given a tiny staff of facilitators, grouped together in a new Bureau of Government Organization, which in turn was rather loosely attached to the Privy Council Office. A senior deputy minister, George Davidson, was seconded to become the director of the bureau, while two members of his staff were drawn from the central group of researchers that had been associated with the royal commission. Although housed in the Privy Council Office, the bureau continued to report to Senator McCutcheon, despite the fact that he had switched from minister without portfolio to the Department of Trade and Commerce. Like the smile on the face of the Cheshire cat, the Bureau of Government Organization was eventually all that remained of the Glassco commission as the latter slowly faded from sight over the next few months. Uneasily housed, under somewhat indirect supervision, and with slender resources, the bureau nevertheless played the invaluable role of instigator, gadfly, and facilitator. At least it ensured that all the major recommendations of the commission were canvassed and, where agreements were secured, that action on them was initiated.

A change of government in the spring of 1963 produced a new allocation of portfolios in which the prime minister took the unusual step of placing the presidency of the Privy Council in hands other than his own. Since the Bureau of Government Organization was still attached to the

38 A good description of the various stages of this manœuvre is contained in G.V. Tunnoch, 'The Bureau of Government Organization: Improvement by Order-in-Council, Committee, and Anomaly,' *Canadian Public Administration* 8 (Dec. 1965), pp. 558–68.

Privy Council Office and the new president was not an overworked prime minister, it made sense to continue to have the bureau report to the president.

In May 1964 the second stage in this complicated manœuvre began with the transfer of the Bureau of Government Organization to the Department of Finance. Associated with this physical relocation was the appointment of the bureau's director to the position of secretary of the Treasury Board. Although the bureau continued to report back to the President of the Privy Council, its truncated staff was gradually dispersed to other departments or absorbed into the staff of the Treasury Board, thereby leaving only a faint smirk on the vanishing smile of the Cheshire cat. At this point, one is tempted to sum up the situation with the old adage: plus ça change, plus c'est la même chose!

However, it is not correct to suggest that we have come full circle, once the work of the bureau had been completed and its former director firmly entrenched as an upgraded secretary of the Treasury Board with a staff all back under the roof of the Department of Finance. There remained at least two significant departures from the old pattern, both of which reflected fairly precisely the original intentions of the Glassco commission. In the first place, the Treasury Board staff was gradually reconstructed around the three major divisions proposed by the royal commission to deal with programmes, personnel, and procedures. In the second place, the secretary to the Treasury Board no longer reported to the Minister of Finance but, following the practice that found him reporting to the President of the Privy Council, between 1963 and 1966, as of mid-1966 he reported to a newly designated ministerial portfolio, the President of the Treasury Board. This arrangement, including the very title of the new ministry itself, was precisely what the Glassco commission had in mind. It is probably irrelevant that the new position was at first occupied by a cabinet minister who also held the portfolio of National Revenue. What is significant is that the secretary and his staff came to be housed in close proximity to the staff of the Department of Finance but the chairman of the committee of cabinet to whom they now reported was given separate status as President of the Treasury Board and was no longer to be the Minister of Finance.

Even as the recommendations of the Glassco commission set up a train of repercussions that confirmed the Treasury Board as the major management arm of the cabinet, they also produced substantial reverberations throughout the other parts of the management apparatus. The Civil Service Commission, departmental management groups, and associations of public servants were all induced to pick their respective ways through those recommendations that most directly affected their participation in the tasks of management. The evolution of the role and tasks currently being assigned to these bodies is considered in the following chapters.

In retrospect, the story recounted in this chapter reveals a singular consistency in diagnosis of a problem and in the prescription for its cure. The problem was how to bring separate functioning entities into a co-ordinated, collaborative partnership that would bring real meaning to the term *the* civil service of Canada. The prescription proposed as early as 1867 was to inject a co-ordinating collegial body, the Treasury Board, into the top reaches of the system. For nearly one hundred years the prescription either did not 'take' or was so irritating that supplementary and often competing palliatives were prescribed. What is surprising is that in the mid-1960s, following a much more meticulous but nevertheless similar diagnosis, the system has responded very rapidly to a prescription for top co-ordination to achieve the long-deferred objective of a unified civil service. The reasons for this abrupt, positive systemic response, against a long history of rejection and opposing anti-bodies, will emerge in part in the narrative contained in the next three chapters.

CHAPTER TWELVE

The
Public Service
Commission:
the ambivalence of
central personnel
management

In the administration of private concerns it is considered axiomatic that management's responsibility for effective, economical performance carries with it full command over the manpower resources required for the assigned tasks. In public administration the situation is not nearly so clear-cut because employees, though allocated to and identified with a specific departmental establishment, are in fact members of a public service which embraces all departments. It is true that the doctrine of ministerial responsibility would appear to support the position taken by managers of private concerns: that is, full control within the department of all aspects of personnel management. On the other hand, the need to preserve a reasonably unified public service with standardized conditions of employment for employees scattered through two dozen departments, tends to impose restrictions on the freedom of departments to develop manpower policies and practices of their own. In addition, there is the historical constraint on departmental autonomy deriving from the prolonged struggle to eliminate political patronage. For this purpose a politically neutralized, central control agency has customarily been superimposed on departmental managers and frequently vested with nearly full authority to make all the vital decisions concerned with the staffing of departments.

Both these considerations – the need to preserve uniformity and the need to protect the so-called merit system – have encouraged the growth of an ambivalent attitude towards personnel management which has resulted in a confused sharing-out of this function among several agencies in the Canadian public service. Thus, while the doctrine of ministerial responsibility affirms the authority of the departmental head in assigning to him the care and management of his department, the claims of the merit system have resulted in the assignment of overriding powers in staffing matters to the Civil Service Commission.

A second source of ambiguity derives from the confusion over the precise status of the central personnel function, which in turn stems from uncertainty about the identity of the real 'employer' of public servants. When we say that the employer is the government of Canada, do we mean specifically the department, the executive in its collective capacity, or parliament? If the employer is deemed to be the executive – individual department head or collective cabinet – then the Civil Service Commission is to be viewed as an agent advisory to or servicing the needs of the executive; in practical terms, as the previous chapter has shown, cabinet's management arm, the Treasury Board, would be the supreme authority. On the other hand, if parliament is considered the employer then the Civil Service Commission is best viewed as an independent agent, deliberately set apart from management, reporting to parliament on the results of its exercise of vigilant controls over the sensitive area of personnel management. In this respect, the Civil Service Commission could best be viewed as the result of a self-denying ordinance on the part of members of parliament whereby they gave up their prescriptive rights to intervene, via the patronage route, in the field of personnel management. Thus, the Civil Service Commission, from its neutral vantage point, represents the institutionalized conscience of legislators, warding off the demon patronage rather like Alcoholics Anonymous wards off the demon rum on behalf of its membership.

As a result of these contradictory and confusing factors, the Civil Service Commission has been left with two roles which, in contemporary times, appear to have become increasingly incompatible. On the one hand it has been assigned personnel management functions which make it an integral part of the executive team largely responsible for service-wide conditions of employment that help to unify the public service. On the other hand, viewed in its traditional role as an independent agent, the commission is expected to serve as guarantor to parliament that the exercise of managerial prerogatives by the executive does no violence to the merit principle.

In recent times the tremendous expansion of staff coupled with the conviction that the merit system is no longer threatened by the dragon of patronage have fostered the view that parliament no longer needs this protective device. Nor is it felt that the negative control mentality induced by a guardian civil service commission is in the best interests of the public service. If these arguments are valid, then the commission is either outmoded and redundant or else ought to be merged into the executive team to provide common staffing services for departmental and central line managers. For the provision of such common personnel services, as other jurisdictions now appear to be assuming, there would seem to be little necessity for preserving a commission form of administration.[1]

It may still be argued in defence of the Civil Service Commission that there remains a need for an independent body to act as an umpire or arbitrator when management decisions affecting the rights or claims of employees are contested. However, the relatively recent and aggressive claims of staff associations to participate in management decisions affecting their membership, whether on grievances, appeals, or collective bargaining, may eliminate the necessity of retaining a commission vested with quasi-judicial powers for making determinations in such areas. The new machinery now being erected in the public service in response to staff pressures tends to be segregated from the Civil Service Commission rather than incorporated into it. It will be necessary to examine the role currently being assigned to staff associations in the realm of personnel management in a later chapter. In the following pages of this chapter we will deal with the key developments that brought the Civil Service Commission to the fore, created the anomalies which have been highlighted in the foregoing paragraphs, and have led to the major reforms of 1967.

Broadly speaking, until 1908 Canada maintained a system which stressed departmental autonomy in the management of all personnel matters, coupled as we have seen with a somewhat superficial though niggling control by the Treasury Board which was wedded to the accepted patronage practices of the day. The responsible minister at the head of each department exercised his managerial functions – especially in making appointments – in consultation with members of parliament, defeated candidates, or patronage committees of his own party. The minister's appointive power, it is true, had been slightly circumscribed by the provisions of the Civil Service Act of 1868 which imposed largely voluntary, simple pass examinations. These were administered by a board consisting of the deputy ministers from every department.[2] Subsequent changes in the act did not substantially alter this arrangement, other than to reduce the size

1 Compare, for example, the unquestioning acceptance of the traditional 'guardian' civil service commission, found in William E. Mosher and J. Donald Kingsley, *Public Personnel Administration* (New York and London, 1941), with a much-revised contemporary edition of the same text by O. Glenn Stahl (5th ed., New York and Evanston, 1962), p. 425 ff.

2 Stats Can. 1868, c.34. Orders in council PC 529, 27 May 1868, and PC 943, 19 Nov. 1868, set out in detail the membership, functions, and procedures to be followed by the first 'Civil Service Board.' Generally, on the evolution of the commission, see R. MacGregor Dawson, *The Civil Service of Canada* (London, 1929).

of the examining board and enable it to provide, when called upon, certain promotional examinations.[3]

Not until 1908, as a result of extensive and repeated inquiries into conditions in the service, did the locus of managerial authority shift from the political head. By the amending act of 1908 personnel management, at least so far as the headquarters' staff was concerned, was to be divided between a new, non-partisan Civil Service Commission and the permanent heads of each department.[4] Apparently, official policy now assumed that if the commission could eliminate patronage considerations from the recruitment stage, then the subsequent career of successful candidates could best be guided, in terms of merit and loyal service, by the deputy ministers and their senior assistants. At the same time, a simple, flexible scheme of classification and remuneration, modelled on British lines, gave the departmental officials a good deal of elbow room within which they could use their discretion in placing, transferring, and promoting staff. However, the break from previous patronage-dominated management practices was far from complete since the bulk of the service – the so-called Outside Service – was still subject to the old political rules of the game. With the coming of the First World War even the headquarters' staff tended to return to the traditional, free-and-easy, 'democratic' methods of recruitment and advancement.

In 1918 the Union Government pledged itself to sweeping civil service reform. Undoubtedly it was inspired by the enormous difficulty of administering patronage through the machinery of two parties which had historically been sworn enemies: loaves and fishes, in the absence of biblical miracles, are not infinitely divisible and their distribution through the good offices of a single party machine – let alone two competing machines – is difficult enough. In the event, an order in council dated 13 February 1918 inaugurated the third attempt to resolve the problem of centralizing managerial authority over manpower in the public service. The main feature of this new venture was the re-creation of the Civil Service Commission, no longer a weak adjunct to the departments but an all-powerful central personnel agency.[5]

3 Stats Can. 1882, c.4. The detailed annual reports of the Civil Service Board of Examiners, beginning with *Sessional Papers* 1883, no 13, are most illuminating. The dependence of the board on the cabinet is clearly revealed in an order in council, PC 302, 1887, which authorizes and prescribes a detailed curriculum for promotional examinations.
4 Stats Can. 1908, c.15, 'The Civil Service Amendment Act.'
5 PC 358, 13 Feb., and PC 548, 15 March 1918, formulated initial government policy and temporary measures pending preparation and approval of legislation (c12, 1918), which as amended in 1919 was to stand with relatively minor changes until major revisions were made in 1961 and 1967. The two orders in council are found in full in Stats Can. 1918, p. lxvii ff.

This decision, probably attributable to the prime minister, Sir Robert Borden, was made at a peculiarly disturbed period for the public service. The war was approaching a climax, the service was laden down with temporary employees, the influence and powers of the old Civil Service Commission were at a low ebb, already the claims of returning soldiers for preferred employment in the public service were becoming vociferous; in short, a major crisis was approaching. Suddenly, in these circumstances, the Civil Service Commission was instructed to take over the entire, war-swollen public service, including now the Outside as well as the Inside Service. 'History tells us,' said Clarence Jamieson, a civil service commissioner at the time, 'that about 5000 years ago Pharaoh of Egypt bade the chosen people that they were to make bricks without straw. If it may not be completely irreligious I think the task entrusted to them was little more difficult than that which was imposed upon the Commission in the handling of the public service of Canada, with an untrained staff of twelve. I think the only comparable thing,' he added significantly, 'would be the administering of patronage by a Union [that is, coalition] Government.'[6]

Two developments which left enduring marks on the civil service quickly transpired as a result of this almost disastrously sudden acquisition of authority by the commission. First, the commission was obviously ill-equipped to assume its new duties and promptly delegated its most urgent and important job, the reclassification of the service, to an outside firm of management consultants.[7] The ultimate outcome of this enterprise was the incorporation of a large schedule of classes which, lengthening with the years, served as the foundation of the classified civil service of Canada for nearly forty years.

The second lasting consequence of the sudden elevation of the Civil Service Commission to managerial pre-eminence was the departmental antagonism that was generated by the decision. Confined by the straight-jacket of the new classification plan whose subtleties frustrated them, the senior departmental officials began an immediate campaign to restore (literally) the *status quo ante bellum*. Appearing and speaking unreservedly before parliamentary committees in 1921 and 1923, the deputy ministers urged a restoration of their managerial prerogatives.[8] Some of

6 See his testimony before the special committee appointed to inquire into the operation of Chapter 12, 8–9 Geo. v, An Act Respecting the Civil Service of Canada, etc., *Can. H. of C. Journals*, 1923, appendix 5 (Ottawa, 1923), p. 896 ff.

7 *Ibid.*, pp. 895–6, 898–903.

8 See Special Committee of the House of Commons on Bill No. 122: An Act to Amend the Civil Service Act, 1918, *Proceedings* (Ottawa, 1921), passim; and the similar committee to inquire into the operation of Chapter 12, 8–9 Geo. v (1923), passim.

Just two years before, in 1919, the deputy minister of Agriculture,

the more elderly deputies, like Sir Joseph Pope and Thomas Mulvey, even argued for a restoration of the pre-1908 period, claiming that the maligned patronage system was in reality the only democratic way of managing the service. Without following them that far, it is clear that the deputies had a logical case for returning managerial responsibilities to the departments. Apart altogether from the early floundering efforts of the commission which drove unsympathetic departmental officials to rebellious sabotage, there was the constitutional position of the deputy. By statute he was held responsible to his ministerial head for the efficient conduct of the department's business. In turn, the ministerial head by custom was the only official whom parliament could hold responsible. The Civil Service Act of 1918, as amended in 1919, made the Civil Service Commission ultimately responsible for managerial decisions relating to appointments, promotions, transfers, salary scales, and classification. How could this alien agency be fitted into the traditional pattern of ministerial responsibility or, more important, how could the minister's deputy assume his statutory obligations for the efficient management of the department if he had to defer to the commission?

In the first bitterness at their abrupt loss of power some of the deputies took a gloomy view of the future. Sir Joseph Pope expressed himself most strongly on the point:

I do not see how a department is to be efficiently carried on if you introduce what I might call a foreign body into it. The man who is at the head of the department, the Statute says, has 'the duty under the minister to carry on the department.' It is his duty to do that. If you take away that duty – it makes no difference to me. I am an old man and approaching the end at any rate – but if you take away all or nearly all his powers from the deputy minister, how is the department to be carried on? Very largely the civil servants nowadays do not bother very much about the deputy. They know he cannot do anything much to them; he cannot dismiss them; he cannot do anything; and therefore

J.H. Grisdale, had been more optimistic before a Special Committee re the Working of the Staffs of the Inside Service, Minutes of Proceedings and Evidence, *Can. H. of C. Journals*, 1919, appendix 6: Q. 'Generally speaking, since the Civil Service Act came into effect ... has a deputy as good a hold over his department as he would have without the Act?' A. 'I do not know whether to attribute it to the acts or not, but the deputy can have very much more influence over his department now than he could, say fifteen years ago' (p. 49). But compare this statement with the story F.C.T. O'Hara, the deputy minister, Trade and Commerce, recounted to the same committee. His political chief, Sir George Foster, wishing to sign the appointment of a trade commissioner was told by O'Hara: 'you have nothing to do with it' now the applications have to go to the commission. 'That is extraordinary,' Sir George replied, 'I do not think there are ten members of the House of Commons know it' (p. 114).

they evince for him but slight regard. This is subversive of discipline, and that is bad.[9]

Dual and uncertain control of the public service inclined most of the deputies to take the milder view expressed by Thomas Mulvey, deputy under-secretary of state, before the 1923 parliamentary committee: 'To some extent I was glad that the responsibility of reorganization was not put upon my shoulders; I say it is the Civil Service Commission that does that; that is one of the bad effects of dual control. If I was called upon by my minister to say "Can you reorganize your department more efficiently," it would be up to me to do it; now I can say the Civil Service Commission should do that.' Joseph T. Shaw, one of the members of the parliamentary committee, summed up Mulvey's comments by pointing out the dilemma: 'So that it is a case I suppose of between the devil and the deep sea, patronage on the one hand and passing the buck on the other.'[10]

Yielding slightly to the arguments of these deputy ministers, the committee of 1923 recommended a partial restoration of the managerial responsibilities which the deputies had enjoyed after 1908, especially with respect to promotion and to discipline. The lurking devil of patronage was to be exorcised by a system of appeal boards representing the commission, departmental management, and staff. The apparently ambivalent claims of administrative purity and ministerial responsibility could be met, it would seem, only through this complicated managerial dualism. Acquiescing in the inevitability of shared responsibility for management, the committee of 1923 proposed a conference between the deputies and the Civil Service Commission to arrange a truce and attempt to establish some workable compromises.

There is no indication that the proposed peace conference was ever held,[11] but in fact throughout the twenties an uneasy balance was retained

9 Committee to inquire into the operation of Chapter 12, 8–9 Geo. v (1923), pp. 616–17.
10 *Ibid.*, pp. 626, 627.
11 In fact, the continuing recalcitrance of the deputies induced a Senate committee to intervene in 1924 with its own proposed *modus vivendi*. 'Senate Committee on Civil Service Efficiency, Second Report,' Senate of Canada, *Journals*, 1924. In a draft letter to the deputies (pp. 149–52) it proposed that the Civil Service Act be amended to give deputy ministers more control over staff and promotions, and a more elastic system for shifting excess employees to where they were needed. Then they proposed 'some kind of Board or Parliamentary Commission ... be established, with power to exercise the same control or check upon the growth of the staffs of departments, as is exercised by the Treasury Board in England.' (The proposal is significant evidence for the view expressed in the previous chapter that the Canadian Treasury Board was very much a cipher in this realm during the 1920s.) However, in their 'Third Report' (Senate, *Journals*

between the *de jure* omnicompetence of the commission and the traditional *de facto* privilege of the senior departmental officials to run their own show. Some relaxation of the tension came about as a result of the gradual strengthening of the commission's staff which improved its ability to fulfil the managerial mandates conferred by statute. But of greater importance were the practical adjustments to the system, largely imposed by parliamentary pressure: these may have departed from the rigorous – almost purist – spirit of the Civil Service Act, but they conformed more closely to the commission's capabilities and to the departments' own views of their managerial responsibilities.

In the first place, the act itself provided an escape hatch for the commission should it feel incapable of assuming jurisdiction over certain categories of civil servants. As early as 1921 a parliamentary committee had successfully recommended inclusion of such a loophole in the Civil Service Act.[12] This so-called 'Spinney Amendment' provided in section 59 that the Governor in Council, on recommendation of the Civil Service Commission, could exclude specified categories of officials from the provisions of the act. This amendment had its legitimate uses in enabling the commission to free itself, for example, from the petty, expensive, and almost impossible task of recruiting officials who would receive $200 or less per annum. But, unfortunately, it also gave members of parliament a lever with which to induce the commission to reopen parts of the service to patronage. By 1930 nearly one-third of the civil service was outside the jurisdiction of the commission and thus beyond the salutary influence of the merit principle. W.D. Euler, a confirmed supporter of that principle, was probably not exaggerating when in 1932 he contended that the 'Spinney Amendment' had been the 'coach and four' driven through the Civil Service Act.[13]

In other ways, too, the commission's jurisdiction was deliberately curtailed. Most new agencies created during the twenties and early thirties

1924, pp. 494–500), the senators came back to endorse the Civil Service Commission as 'the proper and authorized agency for this work,' and went on to suggest that the government issue an order in council 'enjoining the deputy heads to render the Commission the fullest co-operation and assistance. This order should further require the Commission to report to the Governor in Council and to Parliament all instances where their work is hampered or delayed by lack of co-operation upon the part of Deputy Ministers or their chief officials.'

12 Committee of 1921, *Proceedings, Report, etc.*, and Stats Can. 1921, c.22.
13 *Can. H. of C. Debates*, 1932, p. 541; see also R. MacGregor Dawson, 'The Canadian Civil Service,' *Canadian Journal of Economics and Political Science* 2 (Aug. 1936), pp. 288 ff.

went out of the way in their own founding acts to exclude themselves from the provisions of the Civil Service Act. The Soldiers' Settlement Board, Loan Board, Tariff Board, National Research Council, and the Radio Commission were all granted this immunity.[14] Moreover, the annual estimates were constantly being used by departments to legislate their way out of the act simply by incorporating with their request for sums of money to pay salaries the phrase, 'notwithstanding anything in the Civil Service Act to the contrary.'[15]

While these official and informal compromises with the merit principle embodied in the Civil Service Act were being countenanced, the future of the commission itself remained obscure and shaky. Beginning in the mid-twenties and reaching its climax about 1933, an attempt to abolish the commission gained momentum, with particularly prominent support from the Quebec members led by C.G. Power. The alleged inefficiency of two of the civil service commissioners which gave rise to a parliamentary committee's request that they be compulsorily retired; revelations of fraud in the examination branch of the commission; and frequent charges that the commission was merely rubber-stamping appointments actually made by permanent officials; all these weaknesses combined to make the critics' case more convincing.[16] However, the commission and the merit principle it was directed to uphold were not without vigorous supporters in the House. Members of the Progressive and Labour groups in parliament were particularly prominent in rising to the defence of the commission. Moreover, the series of parliamentary committees which reported to the House in 1932, 1934, 1938, and 1939 all reiterated their faith in the merit system and concentrated on detailed administrative problems arising in connection with the commission's responsibilities.

By the mid-thirties, then, the Civil Service Commission appeared to have won, once and for all, its battle for survival. But, it was at this particular point, as the previous chapter has shown, that the Treasury

14 During a debate on the bill to exclude the staff of the penitentiaries from the provisions of the Civil Service Act, Hugh Guthrie cited a lengthy list of exclusions. *Can. H. of C. Debates*, 1932–3, p. 3557.
15 See E.J. Garland's comments during the same debate at p. 3545.
16 John Vallance, a member of the 1932 parliamentary committee on the civil service contended that the evidence presented to the committee revealed that 'time after time an eligible list would be presented to the department and be torn up, that a second list would be presented and be torn up, and then the head of the department would write or suggest to somebody to make application, and that application would go through. The Civil Service Commission is not allowed to function.' *Can. H. of C. Debates*, 1932–3, p. 2746. For Power's attack, precipitated by the *proforma* motion to reduce the commission's estimates to $1.00, see *ibid.*, 1931, pp. 2990–3009.

Board appeared as the main contender for the commission's sweeping managerial powers over all personnel matters. It will be recalled that the vital question as to where managerial responsibility should be lodged had since Confederation received various answers. Managerial decisions with respect only to selection of staff (and, subsequently, their promotion) had shifted first from the political head to an advisory examining board – a glorified interdepartmental committee made up of deputy ministers. After 1908 managerial responsibilities had, in the main, devolved on the permanent heads of the departments and, in a limited sphere, the Civil Service Commission helped them select qualified candidates. At the end of the First World War the commission was vested with the most comprehensive managerial responsibilities, the permanent heads being effectively forced to the sidelines. However, the record of the twenties discloses that the commission was not, in reality, equipped or even permitted to exercise all its duties. As in the past, through a variety of expedients, they tended to be shared with both the political and permanent departmental heads. This was the situation at the time the first of a series of parliamentary committees reported in 1931–2. And it was precisely at this time that the Treasury Board began to throw its weight into the precarious balance of managerial agencies concerned with personnel administration.

With the emergence of the Treasury Board a three-cornered contest developed. To the historical tension between departmental officials and the Civil Service Commission which had been generated by the act of 1918, there was now added the voice of the supreme financial planning agency. And, since scarcely any managerial decision can be made without involving the purse, the Treasury Board appeared quite suddenly and dramatically as the focal point for nearly every decision involving the staffing and provisioning of government departments. The depression and the consequent need to tighten government purse strings were the factors that precipitated the confrontation beween Treasury Board and commission. Indeed, some of the decisions of the Treasury Board cut so deeply into the managerial preserves assigned by law to the Civil Service Commission that there was considerable questioning of the constitutional right of the board to intervene. However, the law officers of the Crown supported the board on the assumption that its general right to advise the cabinet on any problems connected with finance, revenue, and expenditures embraced as well the right to recommend detailed and general regulations covering all aspects of personnel management. When the decision of the law officers was announced, there were some close observers of the scene, like Lionel Chevrier, the member for Ottawa, who once more raised the question of the value of retaining an independent Civil Service Commission divested in practice of powers which parliament had deliberately conferred upon it.[17]

The Treasury Board's assumption of managerial rights over the civil service was not new, for since Confederation, as the previous chapter has made clear, it had constantly asserted itself on some of the most trivial aspects of personnel management. What was new was the changed legal condition under which the Treasury Board now laid claim to these managerial prerogatives. Up to 1918 the board had exercised managerial powers under authority conferred in general terms by its founding statute of 1869 and more explicitly conferred by statutes and regulations which dealt with the duties and responsibilities of separate administrative agencies. In part, it had also become a centre for making preliminary managerial decisions under authority of orders in council which the cabinet had passed in order to devolve its own responsibilities to the board. But this situation was altered by the terms of the Civil Service Act of 1918, which delegated comprehensive authority in the realm of personnel management to the Civil Service Commission. Presumably, until the onslaught of the depression, the Treasury Board was content to leave such managerial decisions to be worked out between the commission and the departments.[18] It was for this reason that its sudden and drastic interventions, beginning in 1931, seemed to introduce a new discordant note into a field of civil service management already resounding with dissonant chords.

17 *Can. H. of C. Debates*, 1935, p. 4107. In the early 1930s the civil service associations repeatedly expressed concern over the adverse impact of Treasury Board interventions, described in one article as 'Nibbling Away the Merit System' (*Civil Service Review*, March 1935). In the June 1935 issue of the *Civil Service Review* there is a particularly strong complaint: 'it is apparent that, continuing the trend of recent years, the authority of the Civil Service Commission is waning before the ascendancy of the Treasury. Under the Civil Service Act the approval of Treasury Board is required for reclassification involving increased expenditure, but promotions to vacancies may be made by the Civil Service Commission; while statutory increases may be made by the Deputy Ministers. In practice, however, Treasury Board has exercised authority over all staff expenditures since 1932 by its Staff Control Regulations formulated pursuant to special authority granted by the Governor in Council, P.C. 144/1367, June 14, 1932.' This was the order in council that the law officers in the Justice Department upheld in their decision. It would appear from these and other comments in a similar vein that this period witnessed the birth of the strong pro-commission attitude among staff associations which inclined them over the ensuing years to view the commission as their friend in court whenever the associations had to do battle with management.

18 The clearest confirmation of this point is the fact that all investigations during the first decade after the passing of the Civil Service Act concentrated on the relationship between departments (especially the deputy ministers) and the commission, while the Treasury Board received little mention.

Concluding a carefully reasoned appraisal of the managerial influence of the Treasury Board after a decade, George McIlraith, member for Ottawa West, remarked in the House in 1943 that the board had now extended its *de facto* control over the service to the point where, even if no expenditures were involved, the board was able to overrule the minister of a department. He concluded by observing that 'the present position is that in the House of Commons no minister is directly answerable as such for the administration of the public service.'[19] Mr McIlwraith might have added that the chief contender of the Treasury Board for the right to manage the service, the Civil Service Commission, was also without an adequate spokesman in parliament. Although the Secretary of State was technically responsible, there would be no incumbent of that office likely to quarrel with C.H. Cahan's view of his role when he told the House in 1935 that 'with regard to the Civil Service Commission, the Secretary of State occupies an irresponsible position. I think his sole responsibility is to place the estimates of the Commission before the House, and he is the medium through which the Commission reports to Parliament from year to year.'[20]

The comment of the Secretary of State sharpened the ambivalence of the central personnel function which the unresolved conflicts between departments, Treasury Board, and Civil Service Commission had been emphasizing for many years. In righteously denying itself the pleasures of patronage the legislature had created an independent agency, the Civil Service Commission, to act as its own conscience in applying the merit principle. But, parliament went much farther when it also conferred almost complete managerial functions on the commission, thereby setting up that debilitating competition between its own agency and departmental managers and the Treasury Board which predominated throughout the interwar years. The ancient rivalry between parliament and the executive over control of the public service was thus reconfirmed and kept alive by the internal struggle between the commission as the agent of parliament and the departments and the Treasury Board as agents of the executive. The commission's position as an agent of parliament required it to be insulated from the executive. But this independence, as we have seen, became a weakness when its active participation in the management of personnel drew it into the web of executive agencies equally concerned with similar issues. The latter were strongly represented in the cabinet and

19 *Can. H. of C. Debates*, 1943, p. 1243.
20 *Ibid.*, 1933, p. 4209. For much the same view of the relationship, twenty-five years later, see the comments of Secretary of State Henri Courtemanche, *ibid.*, 1958, p. 3251.

the Treasury Board, whereas the commission by deliberate design was deprived of all but the weakest of formal connecting links (the Secretary of State) with the executive. The commission's position was further weakened when, as noted, the law officers of the Crown gave legal sanction to Treasury Board interventions on the strength of its overriding power to recommend on all matters having financial implications.[21]

It would appear that the union of executive and legislative powers in parliament tended to conceal from the members of both branches the inherent ambiguities of a managerial system designed to give effect to two quite separate approaches to the problem of personnel administration in the public service. What was evident to all sides was the accumulation of hostility and frustration occasioned by the internal warfare generated by the contradictions of the system. Thus, when the government set up a royal commission in 1945 to investigate ways and means of recruiting and retaining senior administrative personnel, this broader issue was also brought before the inquiry.

The outcome of that inquiry has already been described in the previous chapter. Had the royal commission's proposals been adopted the Civil Service Commission would have been confined to recruitment and review of departmental recommendations for promotion and transfer within certain categories. The Treasury Board, strengthened by a new director general of establishments and personnel, would have assumed the remaining central personnel management functions, while the departments would have been encouraged to upgrade and strengthen their own personnel managers.

Although no formal changes were made in the arrangements for top management, perhaps the chief significance of the royal commission's report was that it underlined the need for a much more positive approach to personnel administration and brought into clearer focus the ambiguous position of the Civil Service Commission. As the institutionalized conscience of parliament standing guard over the portals to the public service, the commission had been compelled to stress the negative functions of 'keeping the rascals out'; to accomplish this task the commission had been organized outside the regular chain of ministerial command, for which (as we have just seen) it paid the price of insularity, that is, no effective spokesman in the cabinet, particularly when its decisions were being disputed by the Treasury Board. On the other hand, as the prime servicing

21 The reactions of the Civil Service Commission to the new situation created by the enlarged powers of the Treasury Board are to be found in *Twenty-fifth Annual Report* of the Civil Service Commission for the year 1933 (Ottawa, 1934).

agent devoted to the manifold tasks of building an efficient career service, the commission left much to be desired as an instrument of management. Nor, as long as the commission held the statutory powers over the major areas of personnel administration, could the departments seize the initiative. Moreover, the Treasury Board was not staffed for these purposes and its own bias was, like the commission's, control-oriented rather than positively oriented towards development. These points were made in the report of the royal commission in 1946, and under the obvious threat posed by its recommendations for a major reshuffling of managerial responsibilities, the opening chord was sounded for a theme that was not to be resolved until 1967.

The Civil Service Commission struggled to adjust to the threat by expanding greatly its search for the best qualified recruits in an increasingly competitive labour market – particularly with respect to the direct recruitment of university graduates on which a modest start had been made in the mid-1930s. Increased emphasis was placed on training and development courses, and conscientious efforts were made to improve and speed up the cumbersome machinery of promotions and appeals – partly by means of informal devolution to selected departments. The organization and methods work of the commission was expanded as a service facility to departments. A closer liaison between commission and Treasury Board was achieved in part by a change in top personnel and some interchange of staff. The Treasury Board, for its part, drew the commission into the preliminary negotiations involved in the preparations of the estimates by introducing an establishment review procedure. And, in the postwar period, departmental personnel work acquired a new dignity and a growing sense of professionalization. Last, but of increasing significance, organized staff associations became more vigorous in asserting their claims to influence management decisions that affected civil servants' working conditions.

In short, during the years following the Second World War there was a mounting self-consciousness within the public service, in both central agencies and departments, that gave rise to a ferment of ideas for self-improvement. The gigantic expansion in budgets and staff, the increasing number and complexity of programmes that either burdened the taxpayer or brought new services to his doorstep, all induced an increasing awareness of the significance of public administration. What went on within a government was no longer of marginal interest to the economy or to the citizen; the efficiency of the public organization was of vital concern to all groups devoted to nation-building in the emergent welfare state.

Outside the public service, stirred by the same forces of scientific and technological change, private administration refashioned and honed its managerial tools. Chartered accountancy firms found themselves drawn increasingly beyond the account books to examine the efficiency of procedures used to keep the ledgers balanced; many of them branched out into the expanding field of management consultancy, their services being in demand not only from private industry but from all levels of government.

These developments were instrumental in precipitating two major inquiries whose operations overlapped in time and subject matter. When their recommendations were cast into the far from placid waters of the public service, waves of change washed out in ever-broadening circles to cover the farthest shores of management. The period of the Sixties has, as a result, witnessed more profound alterations, more experimenting, more task force studies, more pilot projects in the various aspects of management than it is possible to keep up with, let alone recount in this chapter. However, the crests can be identified and, taken in conjunction with the developments traced in the following chapters at the departmental level and among organized civil servants, can provide some indication of the scope and direction of these reforms.

The first inquiry which was to have such a profound influence on the public service of the sixties was launched at the behest of the Liberal government in 1957 and wholeheartedly sustained by the Progressive Conservative government after it captured political power in the same year. The inquiry was initiated because of a decision to 'reopen' the Civil Service Act after nearly forty years during which it had served, with only minor amendments, as the major statutory base for personnel management. The Civil Service Commission was itself authorized to conduct the inquiry and, after exhaustive study of both Canadian and foreign experience as well as prolonged discussions with senior departmental officials, issued in 1958 what has become familiarly known as the 'Heeney report' on Personnel Administration in the Public Service.[22] A year and a half later Bill C-77 was introduced in the 1960 session of parliament to give effect to the Heeney report. However, the government acceded to a general request to postpone discussion in order to provide opportunity for fuller study.[23] In the 1961 session an altered Bill C-71 was given pro-

22 Civil Service Commission of Canada, (Heeney) *Report* (Ottawa, Dec. 1958).
23 The bill was given first reading only on 20 June 1960 (*Can. H. of C. Debates*, 1960, pp. 5128–61). By 3 July the government had acceded to requests to withdraw the legislation for fuller study (*ibid.*, p. 6177).

longed scrutiny by a special committee of the House of Commons and was ultimately approved by parliament.[24]

The significance of the revised Civil Service Act of 1961 is not so much in the changes made to the old act, for the comprehensive jurisdiction of the Civil Service Commission over all aspects of personnel management remained virtually intact. Its significance is to be found, rather, in the fact that for the first time systematic discussion between the central management agencies and the departments on the overall aspects of manpower management had been initiated and the debate, fed by the second and broader inquiry of the Royal Commission on Government Organization (created 16 September 1960), was not allowed to flicker out. Moreover, the opportunity given the staff associations to express their forceful reservations on the new sections in the act, which purported to accord them a broader range of influence in the field, equally promised a prolonged argument of which this was but the initial phase. These discussions were not concluded until the enactments of 1967 which granted organized civil servants bargaining rights and arbitration procedures for which they had been striving over the past decade.

The new Civil Service Act of 1961, then, was a valuable tidying up operation in that its amended terms caught up with forty years of practice. Nevertheless, the commission retained its exclusive rights to make appointments, to classify and police the classification system, and to make associated recommendations on the pay of the civil service. The most controversial clause – Clause 7 – of the act was deemed by the government to be the major concession to organized civil servants in that it authorized nominees of the Minister of Finance and the Civil Service Commission to consult with representatives of staff associations about pay and other terms and conditions of employment. The inconclusive debate over this clause stirred the associations to continue their agitation during the next few years for full collective bargaining privileges. There were two comparable concessions to departmental managers: the exclusive responsibility vested in the commission by the old act to initiate the organization or changes of organization in a department was reduced to an advisory power, thus leaving the departments greater freedom of action to deal with the Treasury Board in matters affecting establishments; the act also empowered the commission to delegate its personnel management functions to departments – thus confirming in law what the commission had been compelled to adopt in practice for a limited number of departments as an

24 Special Committee on the Civil Service Act (Bill C-71), *Minutes of Proceedings and Evidence* (Ottawa, 1961). See also *Can. H. of C. Debates*, 1960–1, pp. 2759 ff.; Stats Can. 1960–1, c.57.

expedient to meet war-swollen numbers. Finally, in its dealings with the Treasury Board (or, more accurately, the Governor in Council) on recommendations concerning pay, the Civil Service Commission was shorn of the absolute powers which had brought it so often in the past into head-on confrontations with the executive. Under the old legislation the Governor in Council was confined to accepting or rejecting *in toto* the commission's proposals on pay.[25] The new dispensation permitted the Governor in Council wider latitude in making such use as it deemed appropriate of the commission's recommendations.

There was much more in the act, including clarification of appeals procedures and the definition of the public service, which need not detain us here. The main points to be made are that the new act still left unchanged the ambivalent position of the central personnel agency – partly an arm of management, partly the instrument of parliament for preserving the merit system; and it opened up, rather than settled, a whole set of problems concerned with the commission's relations with departmental managers and with organized staff associations.

At that point in time when the government had drafted its 1960 bill based on the Heeney report, the second study of the public service was launched in September 1960 'to inquire and report upon the organization and methods of operation ... and to recommend the changes therein which they consider would best promote efficiency, economy and improved service ...' Commonly referred to as the Glassco commission, this investigation carried on for two and a half years, mounting an ambitious series of inquiries, modelled as to subject matter somewhat on the same lines as the two Hoover commissions in the United States.

The staff and the ultimate recommendations of the Royal Commission on Government Organization reflected the ferment in the field of management studies to which reference was made above. The project teams assigned to the major areas of management – manpower, finance, and administrative procedures – readily demonstrated that management practices and procedures in the public service had lagged behind the more progressive sectors of private corporate and industrial enterprises. The defects and deficiencies in the technical tools of management were identified and recommendations were made to update old procedures and intro-

25 After the creation in 1957 of the Pay Research Bureau, located in the commission, the government's disposition of the bureau's reports became a major bone of contention, renewing once again the old conundrum of an independent agency, ostensibly responsible to parliament, attempting to perform an executive function which in this particular instance always threatened to trespass on the preserves of the Treasury Board. See, particularly *Can. H. of C. Debates*, 1958, p. 3653.

duce new techniques and technicians. However, the commission encountered thornier issues when it faced up to the tasks which the revised Civil Service Act had nibbled at but had not bitten into decisively enough. One area, the relation between organized staff and management, was deliberately avoided by the Glassco commission. The easy path of omission was taken on the assumption that the problem was being disposed of by the special committee then (1961) considering the controversial Clause 7 of the new Civil Service Act. As noted, the act did not resolve the problem to the satisfaction of the staff associations, and the royal commission's avoidance of the problem forced the government, in August 1963, to appoint the Preparatory Committee on Collective Bargaining. The silence of the Glassco commission on this aspect of management did not prevent it from advancing recommendations on the locus of management responsibilities in the public service. These were not only at odds with the earlier proposals contained in the Civil Service Commission's Report on Personnel Administration and the discussions occurring in the special committee on the new civil service bill but were equally antagonistic to the staff associations' expressed loyalty to the centralization of manpower management in the Civil Service Commission.

As the foregoing analysis has shown, managerial functions and responsibilities had been somewhat indiscriminately assigned to and shifted among the departments and several central agencies. The ambivalent approach to the disposition of management functions was exemplified most clearly in the area of personnel management. Here, two conflicting values had been applied which created uncertainty as to function and tensions between the various participants. On the one hand, the historical path of reform had been marked by the introduction and preservation of the merit principle; this principle was asserted by developing a highly centralized but negative control apparatus, deliberately set up as an instrument of the legislature independent of the executive. Increasingly, however, as the federal work force became larger and more sophisticated, the management of men required more than this protective approach: efficient personnel management came to be viewed as one of the core responsibilities of the executive, requiring positive and imaginative direction.

It will be recalled that the Gordon commission report of 1946 had given explicit recognition to this new orientation in its insistence on transferring most of the statutory personnel functions of the Civil Service Commission to the Treasury Board and to an upgraded departmental personnel office. Subsequently, the Report on Personnel Administration of 1958 temporized by reasserting the central role of the Civil Service Commission, even as it made certain concessions noted above to the Treasury Board, departmental managers, and staff associations. The Glassco commission returned boldly to the Gordon commission's stance by vigorously espousing the executive's prime responsibility for manpower management and reinforcing the case for devolving on departments the key responsibilities in this area.[26] This shift in the locus of managerial responsibility was not to occur by grace and favour of a central personnel agency – the compromise proposed by the Civil Service Act of 1961. If departmental managers were, indeed, to manage, this fundamental element must be placed squarely within their range of responsibilities.

With this working principle as a guiding theme, the royal commission still had to reconcile the proposed departmental autonomy with the old but still relevant merit principle and with the equally important need to preserve a civil service that could still be viewed as an integrated whole. Accordingly, protection of the merit principle was to remain with the commission where it had been lodged since the act of 1918. But, to achieve this protection it was no longer deemed necessary to vest the sum total of personnel management decisions in the commission. Rather, its quasi-judicial position was to be the basis for emphasizing auditing, reviewing, and appellate functions which would arise in connection with such vital personnel decisions as those having to do with appointment, promotion, and disciplinary matters. In addition, viewed now as a central *servicing* agency rather than control body, the commission was to continue recruiting the large, service-wide categories of less specialized talent, assist departments with and operate its own training programmes, and, generally, to provide information, research data, and guidelines for departments as they sought to use their new-found managerial rights.

Through this reallocation the Glassco commission anticipated that it had not left the merit principle undefended, that the door had not been opened for complete disunity, nor was it proposed to waste the long experience and well-established organization of the commission in recruiting common categories of manpower required by most departments. At the same time, the notion of a civil service with uniform conditions of employment had to be further buttressed by a Treasury Board staff reconstituted into the three divisions described in the previous chapter. One of these, it will be recalled, was a Personnel Branch that would assume overall responsibility for conditions of service and generally deal with establishments as one of the components entering programmes on which a new budgeting system was to be based.

Official approval of the general philosophy of management delineated

26 See Royal Commission on Government Organization, *Report*, I, *Management of the Public Service* (Ottawa, 1962), report no 3 'Personnel Management,' especially pp. 254–75.

in the Glassco commission report came rather quickly. Departments and central agencies were induced to come to grips with the implications of this acceptance by the active presence of the small ginger group, the Bureau of Government Organization, which was created to facilitate implementation of the recommendations. But what precipitated the major measures of 1967 was the unanimous agreement of all political parties prior to the 1963 election to support the claims of the staff associations for collective bargaining and arbitration.[27] The Liberal government, confirmed in office by the election, was faithful to this promise and quickly set up the Preparatory Committee on Collective Bargaining to which reference has been previously made. As this committee discovered, before collective bargaining could be instituted a drastic simplification of the classification plan had to be achieved – a step which had been urged, for rather different reasons, by a succession of investigations going back to the Royal (Beatty) Commission on Scientific and Technical Services in 1930.

The competent job performed by this preparatory committee and implemented in stages over a period of three years by a newly created Bureau of Classification Revision in the Civil Service Commission, brought to fruition and clarified as never before the division of responsibilities for public personnel administration. In the course of designing units for collective bargaining purposes, the classification plan was reduced to six major occupational categories, incorporating sixty-seven occupational groups 'composed of employees with similar skills, performing similar kinds of work, bearing a relationship to an identifiable outside labour market.'[28] Not only was this move essential to a new scheme of collective bargaining, it was also simple enough to make possible for the first time a delegation to departments of responsibility for classifying their own employees (one of the recommendations urged by the Glassco commission).

The second major but indirect dividend from this preparatory action was the conclusive identification of the 'employer' for purposes of deter-

27 A good sketch of the build-up to the decision of 1967 is to be found in O.P. Dwivedi, 'Staff Relations in the Public Service of Canada,' in *Government Labor Relations in Transition*, ed. Keith Ocheltree for Public Personnel Association, Personnel report no 662. This is a slightly revised and updated version of an article originally appearing in *Public Administration* (Sydney) 24 (Dec. 1965), pp. 359–67.
28 I am grateful to J.J. Carson, chairman of the Public Service Commission, and to J.D. Love, who was at the time deeply involved with the analysis that lay behind the report on collective bargaining, for copies of papers prepared for delivery to various civil service groups that explain much of the background summarized here.

mining pay and other conditions of service. The Civil Service Commission was removed from its ambivalent position in this regard and the Treasury Board was declared to be the employer, except for certain agencies which were declared to be employers in their own right. Finally, in the effort to make collective bargaining procedures available on a relatively uniform basis to as wide a segment of public service employees as possible, the 'civil service' in its old and narrower sense was enlarged to accommodate some forty thousand prevailing rate employees in the global title 'Public Service of Canada' (a proposal strongly endorsed in the Report on Personnel Administration of 1958).

A measure of the scope and impact of these considerations can be taken from the three major pieces of legislation approved by parliament in 1967. The first of these, the Public Service Staff Relations Act,[29] is best left to a later chapter on staff associations for detailed comment, but there are two points in it which can be noted in confirmation of the generalizations offered above. First, there is the clear-cut definition of employer, that is, Her Majesty in right of Canada as represented by the Treasury Board for a long list of departments and agencies in Part I of Schedule A or by agencies themselves (listed in Part II of Schedule A) considered as employers. Second, the Civil Service Commission finds no place in this measure, ample testimony to the desire to relieve it of its ambiguous dual role as part of the management arm or as in any sense a representative of the employer. Rather than interpose the Civil Service Commission between employer and employee – which might have been possible in view of its judicial, politically neutralized status – a new Public Service Staff Relations Board and a separate Arbitration Board were created.

The second enactment of 1967 confirmed the new vision of a single public service in its very title: the Public Service Employment Act.[30] Effectively, this act displaced the 'new' Civil Service Act which had been approved as recently as 1961.[31] Apart from the meaningful change in title (which was also passed on even to the tradition-shrouded Civil Service Commission, converting it to the Public Service Commission), this act is remarkable for the brevity of section 5 which sets forth the 'General Powers and Duties of the Commission.' Appointments to and from within the public service still rest with the commission; responsibility for operating staff training and development programmes (either on their own or in conjunction with departments); establishing boards to render decisions on appeals; reporting to the Governor in Council 'upon such matters

29 Stats Can. 1966–7, c.72.
30 Ibid., c.71.
31 Ibid., 1960–1, c.57.

arising out of or relating to the administration or operation of this Act';
performing such other duties and functions with reference to the public
service as are assigned to it by the Governor in Council. This is the full
list of duties, apart from an important enabling section 6 which empowers
the commission to authorize a deputy head 'to exercise and perform ...
any of the powers, functions and duties of the Commission' (other than
those relating to appeals and investigations).

When we turn to the third piece of legislation, which completed the
package of reforms instituted in 1967, we find the explanation for the
brevity of the list of duties assigned to the Public Service Commission.
The amendments to the Financial Administration Act[32] spell out the
duties of the Treasury Board so as to leave little room for querying the
location of the ultimate repository of managerial authority over the public
service. The amended sections take particular care to define the board's
responsibilities with respect to personnel management and, in doing so,
reveal the significant transfer from the Civil Service Commission of those
responsibilities that had placed it in the ambiguous status to which repeated reference has been made above. By the amended terms of the
Financial Administration Act, the Treasury Board may *inter alia* act 'for
the Queen's Privy Council for Canada on all matters relating to ... the
organization of the public service or any portion thereof, and the determination and control of establishments therein ... personnel management
in the public service, including the determination of terms and conditions
of employment of persons employed therein.' To lend greater precision to
the general powers the board is specifically directed to determine requirements for manpower, training, and development of personnel; to provide
for classification of positions and employees; to determine and regulate
pay, hours of work, and leave, merit awards, standards of discipline and
penalties for breaches of discipline; standards governing physical working
conditions, health and safety; and generally 'such other matters, including
terms and conditions of employment not otherwise specified ... as the
Treasury Board considers necessary for effective personnel management
in the public service.' Any of these powers, at the discretion of the board
and accompanied by such conditions as it deems desirable, can be devolved on the deputy head of a department or the chief executive officer of
any portion of the public service.

The enactment of the Public Service Employment Act and the amended
Financial Administration Act eliminates many of the jurisdictional ambiguities that have plagued the relations between the two central agencies
concerned with personnel management in the public service. Lest there

32 *Ibid.*, 1966–7, c.74.

be any lingering doubts about jurisdictional boundary lines, the legislative draftsmen inserted a special section in the amendments to the Financial Administration Act, section 7(6): 'The powers and functions of the Treasury Board [in relation to personnel management] ... do not include or extend to any power or function specifically conferred on, or any process of personnel selection required or authorized to be employed by the Public Service Commission by or under the authority of the Public Service Employment Act.'

The net result of the legislative changes made in 1967 has been to relieve the Public Service Commission of many of its traditional responsibilities associated with classification, and the determination of rates of pay and conditions of employment. Basically, it is now required to concentrate its energies on staffing the public service – a task which involves in the mind of the commission's chairman 'continuous appraisal, inventorying of resources on a service-wide basis, early identification of needs, planned up-grading of programmes, planned rotations and planned long-range advice to the universities and other educational institutions as to our staffing requirements.'[33] Training and development is a second major responsibility with the commission, and one that, in the specific area of language training, has tended to assume unexpectedly large proportions as a massive programme develops to meet the objectives of a genuinely bilingual public service. Thirdly, as a residue of the formerly extensive quasi-adjudicative role, the commission retains its authority to handle appeals on all staffing decisions. This restricted adjudicative function is important to the commission as a device for determining whether departmental managers are respecting the merit principle in making staffing decisions. Moreover, because the new scheme of collective bargaining does not embrace the staffing function, policing of the merit system by the commission is necessary. Finally, under the general powers of the new legislation – though not explicitly stated – the commission planned to continue and expand its advisory services for organization and management problems encountered by departments and agencies. In 1968, however, these functions were transferred to a new Department of Supply and Services.[34]

This reassignment of responsibilities for performing the various tasks

33 From 'The New Role of the Civil Service Commission,' a paper by J.J. Carson prepared for presentation to the Federal Institute of Management, Ottawa, 1 Feb. 1966, mimeo.
34 By PC 1298, 12 July 1968, under the Public Services Rearrangement and Transfer of Duties Act, the transfer of the Bureau of Management Consulting Services was made to the Department of Defence Production (subsequently Supply and Services).

associated with the management of personnel appears to be eminently sensible in the light of the aggravations and tensions created by the arrangements that grew up between 1918 and 1967. Nevertheless, redefinition of responsibilities, necessary as it is, does not eliminate the old problems. Essentially, there remains the same need for a collaborative approach to the tasks of personnel administration, involving the traditional triumvirate (Treasury Board, commission, and departmental management). In the euphoric state generated by the prospect of advancing under more coherent marching orders, all three of the agencies concerned will still encounter many obstacles of which the creation of a new, positive role for a fourth party – organized civil servants – will constitute one of the greatest challenges to be met. The collaborative atmosphere now much in evidence gives rise to laudable intentions on the part of all concerned: the central agencies obviously mean to implement their promise to devolve the detailed decision-making to departmental personnel and financial officers and they are supported in this intention by the public commitment of the government.[35] Yet, for the commission and the Treasury Board there still remain many areas of potential conflict: where the former has to conduct a staffing operation according to classification and pay plans developed in the board, where the commission may be required to mount service-wide training and development schemes whose terms are set by the board, or where both agencies think of themselves as management consultants providing services to departmental managers. Hopefully, the collaborative note that is now being sounded will continue to prevail during the forthcoming period of adjustment and innovation, kept alive by the fortunate historical accident that the key people concerned have been working harmoniously together on the project since the Glassco commission first began the task of disentangling the management functions in the public service.

While the prospects for securing the long-delayed and highly desirable accommodation between the two central agencies appear to be most promising, the corresponding collaboration between these agencies and the departments will likely emerge in stages after prolonged and patient negotiation and education. The following chapter attempts to develop the context within which the new philosophy of managerial autonomy for departments has to evolve and highlights the contemporary measures being taken to equip the departments to become active partners in the management enterprise.

35 *Can. H. of C. Debates*, 1962–3, Mr Diefenbaker's statement on 29 Nov. 1962, at p. 2127 ff. See also *ibid.*, 11 Dec. 1963, the statement of Maurice Lamontagne, president of the Privy Council, at pp. 5705 ff. and 5714.

CHAPTER THIRTEEN

Departmental
management:
responsibility
without authority

The doctrine of ministerial responsibility is a long-standing heritage from
Britain and has been entrenched in every statute that has established a
Canadian government department by conferring on the ministerial head
the care and management of his department. But, as the two preceding
chapters demonstrate, the minister's statutory responsibility to manage his
own department has been curtailed in many of the most vital areas of
policy, finance, and personnel. The need of the executive to present a
united front to the legislature compelled each departmental head to meld
autonomous decisions on policy into an enforced collegial unity through
the cabinet. Similarly, the financing of a department's programmes was
brought, at the outset of Confederation, under the Treasury Board – the
cabinet's financial management committee. Admittedly, as the record
shows, it was not until the 1930s that the board became more than an
irritant to departments by imposing more stringent controls over their estimating and spending procedures. Coinciding with the advent of stronger
collegial Treasury Board control over departmental finances, a new office
of the Comptroller of the Treasury emerged in 1931. As his Treasury
officers spread throughout the departments a new era of centralized expenditure control was ushered in. Running a parallel course, the strenuous
efforts of reformers to dispel the spectre of patronage also eroded the
authority of departmental managers over their own personnel. These
efforts culminated in 1918 with a Civil Service Act which vested in a
central Civil Service Commission nearly all of the significant decisions
concerning employment, classification, promotion, and transfer of departmental employees. The anguished cries of certain deputy ministers, some

of which were quoted in the previous chapter, were a clear indication of their sense of grievance at the deprivation of their own managerial prerogatives. By a series of discrete withdrawals and a farming out of the initial task of classifying the civil service, the commission managed to survive its first decade only to find itself in the thirties in active conflict with a revived Treasury Board. Thus, departmental managers were now deprived not only of final authority for managing funds and personnel but also caught up in the in-fighting between two central control agencies struggling to escape from the internal contradictions of the system.

As long as departmental staff and budgets remained modest in size, departmental managers were just barely able to live with a situation in which, while held individually accountable for the efficient performance of their departments, they were in fact deprived of the necessary authority to make important managerial decisions. Even before the outbreak of war, however, the expansion of programmes and staff to meet the crisis of the depression began to call in question the wisdom of such a highly centralized managerial system with its accent, however well-founded in history, on restraints and controls. Criticism mounted as the frustration of living with the system increased in direct proportion to a quadrupling of staff and more than a fivefold increase in the budget in the decade or so after the outbreak of war.

Not only had the dimensions of the manager's jobs increased with growth in staff and expenditures and the increasing complexity of federal programmes, but also the concept of management itself underwent significant change under the pressure from the new electronic gadgetry and a more sophisticated approach to management generated in the realm of private administration. Equally relevant was the growing pressure on management by organized employees of the state.

The spread of collective bargaining in the private sector stimulated organization in the public service just at a time when the inflationary impact of the Korean War was making itself felt. The rapid upward trend of wages in the private sector accentuated the rigidity of classifications and related pay scales in the public service. Adding to staff unrest was the inability of pay determination machinery to keep up with these inflationary trends – even after the creation in 1957 of the Pay Research Bureau. All of these developments coincided with the return of a minority government which had the effect of sensitizing the executive to the pressures being generated within the public service.

This rapid review of the landmarks in the field of management as applied to the federal bureaucracy is sufficient to establish the major contention of this chapter: the elaboration and confirmation of the roles of departmental managers are contemporary issues whose solutions are only now being worked out within the public service. As a result, this chapter is concerned with current history and must inevitably suffer from the inconclusiveness that accompanies the description of a development whose end is not in sight and whose objectives may themselves be modified in the light of experiments with the new philosophy: 'let departmental managers manage.'

It would be incorrect, of course, to assume that this now popular slogan is confined to the management of personnel. However, even if management is 'money focused' as well as 'people focused' there is much truth in the cliché that the major key to successful management is to be found in the use it makes of human resources. Moreover, the developments in personnel administration are more visible, more readily traced, and probably more readily grasped than the highly technical aspects of management that bear on money, matériel, and procedures. Accordingly, this chapter presents first an extended survey of the recent efforts to devolve manpower management to the departments and offers a less detailed picture of what is occurring or in prospect for departmental managers in other relevant areas.

MANPOWER MANAGEMENT

The hostility towards enlarging the authority of departmental managers in the field of personnel, which pervaded the public service until recent times, is exemplified in exaggerated form by a comment attributed to Charles Bland, long-time officer and chairman of the Civil Service Commission. Speaking from his position in a central managerial agency and conditioned by years of experience with the negative philosophy of control, Mr Bland remarked in 1949: 'up to 10 or 15 years ago the title "Personnel Officer" or "Training Officer" would have been sufficient to have someone tried for witchcraft.[1] The accuracy of this pungent epitome is confirmed by the fact that just before the Second World War there were only three departmental personnel officers. Indeed, one of the strongest boosts to the embryonic profession occurred during the war when senior managers,

1 The attribution to Mr Bland is made by T.G. Morry in his keynote address to a personnel officers' training course conducted by the Departments of National Defence, Transport, and Veterans Affairs in May 1965. See 'Proceedings,' mimeo, p. 3. I have made extensive use of the wealth of material presented at this course because of the lack of published information in equally accessible form elsewhere. See also P.H. Dowdell, 'Personnel Administration in the Federal Public Service,' in *Public Administration in Canada: Selected Readings*, ed. A.M. Willms and W.D.K. Kernaghan (Toronto, 1968), pp. 360–88.

borrowed from industry, brought their own personnel specialists with them when they took over temporary wartime programmes in the public service.

The Royal (Gordon) Commission on Administrative Classifications in the Public Service considered these modest advances were inadequate to meet the prospective needs of an expanded postwar public service. Reporting in 1946, it made this critical appraisal: 'The existing machinery and procedures for the administration of personnel matters in departments are generally rudimentary in form and routine in operation. In some departments the duties relating to the control and administration of staff are combined ... In other departments, including some of the larger ones, there is no central organization of this work and the duties are widely dispersed among various officials and branches. Where this situation prevails much of the detailed responsibility falls directly upon the overburdened Deputy Minister.'[2]

The commission went on to recommend: '... The appointment in every department of an experienced and properly qualified Personnel Officer with adequate rank and power [to] promote general efficiency both by improving staff management and by affording relief to Deputy Ministers. Furthermore, the existence of such officers in all departments would enable, through appropriate co-operation with the central civil service authorities a better co-ordination of personnel policies through the service.'

Such an officer, the commission believed, could be full-time in larger departments and might, in smaller departments, combine his personnel duties with other administrative functions. These personnel officers would 'keep under constant review the personnel needs in the various branches of the department, the number and kinds of positions required, and the general efficiency of operation in the routine and clerical phases of the work. They should plan ahead ... and they should advise the Deputy Ministers on matters regarding promotion, transfer, discipline, etc. They should formulate and carry out programs for the improvement of morale and employee relations generally ...'

In brief, it was clear to the Gordon commission that if, at government urging, private employers were being induced to appoint personnel officers, the government itself had just as much reason to follow its own advice. The point was quickly taken, for almost immediately personnel officers began to appear in all departments. The promptness with which this recommendation was implemented is attributable not only to the urgent needs of an enlarging civil service but to the implied threat to the authority and powers of the Civil Service Commission which was contained in the Gordon commission's further recommendations for transferring many of

2 *Report* (Ottawa, 1946), pp. 21–2.

its duties to a proposed director general of establishments tied to the Department of Finance.

The ready acceptance by the Civil Service Commission of the need for developing a cadre of departmental personnel officers can best be understood as the reaction of an all-powerful central personnel agency having to maintain what amounted to a symbiotic relationship with client departments dependent on it for their staff. The very existence of such a central agency, vested with final decision-making powers over all major staffing questions, had virtually precluded the development of departmental personnel specialists. And, as long as the central agency was imbued with a negative, protective philosophy, personnel management could not become a vital, positive arm of general management. Accordingly, senior managers within many departments conditioned to this situation were not at all convinced that personnel administration amounted to more than a pedestrian maintenance of staff records or arranging for staff recreation. If an upgrading of status of personnel work was to be achieved, two things had to occur: first, the central agency (as by law it alone was empowered to do) would have to take the lead in developing the various, specialized aspects of a personnel programme and, second, much of this work would have to be devolved on departmental personnel officers.

This interdependence of the central agency and evolving departmental personnel specialists was readily substantiated by the sequence of measures taken in the wake of the Gordon commission's report. Because the Civil Service Commission had monopolized such expertise as existed in the field of personnel management, its own staff became the prime source of recruits for the new personnel divisions that were established in each department in response to the Gordon commission's prompting. Special training programmes, commenced by the Civil Service Commission in 1949, sought to fill the growing need for personnel officers and for the routine work connected with them.[3]

Perhaps of greatest significance to this development was the founding, in 1947, of the Public Personnel Institute which brought together the personnel directors of each department and agency and, as its constitution carefully declared, the 'Civil Service Commission may be privileged by representation of four members.'[4] It is clear from the records of the institute that the commission used this group as a sounding board in presenting new proposals for its critical appraisal, or in having its working

3 T.G. Morry, in 'Proceedings,' pp. 6–7.
4 Public Personnel Institute, Constitution and By-Laws, article IV, section I.
  Again I am indebted to various civil servants for making available a sample of the minutes, reports, etc., of the institute on which the following paragraphs are based.

committees recommend detailed revisions in the regulations to the Civil Service Act, or in carrying out surveys for the commission and the Treasury Board. Acting as a forum, clearing house, research body, or advisory committee, the institute over the years since its formation has dealt with every conceivable detail of personnel management, ranging from leave of absence and removal expenses, to training, veterans preference, appeals, rating procedures, service-wide standards of personnel administration, and so on.

The agenda of the Public Personnel Institute reflected the rapid accretion of tasks that were coming to be viewed as properly falling within the ambit of personnel managers. The addition of new tasks and programmes to the traditional protective functions of the Civil Service Commission led to corresponding recognition within departments of the need for specialized attention to such duties. The commission first directed its efforts to training programmes which in turn produced the need for liaison training groups in many departments; an efficiency rating scheme, introduced by the commission in 1947, again produced new tasks for departmental personnel managers; the following year a programmed review of establishments brought commission staff and deparmental personnel directors together; a selective devolution to departments of responsibility for certain promotions added yet another function; development of organization and methods surveys as a commission service to departments also necessitated collaboration with departmental managers. Thus, departmental personnel officers found their range of responsibilities extended with each fresh initiative taken by the commission.

However, the growth in functions of personnel administrators brought about by an apparent reciprocity of interest between central agency and departmental personnel managers failed to resolve one outstanding problem: should the balance of authority and responsibility be weighted in favour of the central agency or the departments? The first steps, noted immediately above, suggested that the Civil Service Commission, still operating within the monopoly framework established by the Civil Service Act of 1918, looked upon the new departmental personnel officers as outposts of the commission's empire. In this respect, departmental personnel managers, rather like the Treasury officers located in departments but acting as agents of the Comptroller of the Treasury, would have felt a primary allegiance to the commission rather than the department. No doubt this attitude was strengthened by the initial need to fill a number of the new departmental positions by drawing on senior staff members of the Civil Service Commission. Over time, this attitude changed and departmental personnel officers began to identify more with their own departments and with their fellow experts gathered in the Public Personnel Institute. Nevertheless, their own status in the departments depended, as we have just seen, on the expansion of the personnel management tasks which had to be initiated largely by the commission. Thus, if departmental personnel officers were to be entrusted with a share of these tasks, they had to remain *persona grata* with the commission.

The most significant indicator of this tension between the central agency and departmental personnel managers is to be found in the prolonged efforts to establish standards for the personnel officer class in the public service.[5] These efforts began in 1952 and could not be said to have been brought to anything approaching a successful conclusion until at least ten years later. The main hindrance to achieving appropriate classification standards for personnel work lay in the widespread confusion and disagreement over the functions and role of personnel officers. As late as 1962 a committee of the National Joint Council of the Public Service, reporting on 'The Role of the Departmental Personnel Officer,' commented that 'the application of a standard delineation of duties for a personnel officer was perhaps more difficult than is the case for any other officer in a government department.' The explanation for this difficulty, according to the committee, was that 'the duties of other departmental officers have to do with tangible, measurable, uniform or readily comparable things ... whereas the personnel officer has to do with people, whose attitudes and activities affect all parts of the organization and whose needs are extremely varied.'[6] The efforts of this committee to clarify the situation were commended by John Carson, chairman of the Civil Service Commission, in a paper prepared for the Public Personnel Institute in June 1965. But he went on to describe their report as a series of 'equivocal value judgments on the appropriateness and usefulness of various duties performed by existing personnel officers. In some ways it left me with the feeling that the job *could* be performed by any fairly bright administrative officer.'[7]

The confused conception of the role of the departmental personnel

5 The information on the ten-year struggle to develop the personnel officer classes is based primarily on an excellent study prepared by D.R. Cameron of the Civil Service Commission, as well as material scattered throughout the 'Proceedings' in n. 1 above.
6 National Joint Council of the Public Service, 'Report of the Committee on the Role of the Departmental Personnel Officer,' 28 Feb. 1962, mimeo.
7 'A Proposed Model for the Personnel Function at the Departmental Level,' 15 June 1965, mimeo.

officer was reflected in the wide range of tasks being performed by officials carrying this title and by the variety of classes engaged in personnel work, often as a subordinate adjunct to their main duties. The reason for the confusion must be laid at the doorstep of the Civil Service Act: as long as the act conferred monopoly powers on the commission departmental personnel officers simply grasped such functions as lay close to hand, without benefit of any guiding standards. It is significant, in this context, to observe that the first listing of a personnel officer class in 1947 was for the Taxation Division of the Department of National Revenue – an agency that was not covered, at the time, by the Civil Service Act. And, it was upon the standards established in that agency that the Civil Service Commission relied in 1952 when it inaugurated for all departments the first service-wide class of personnel officers.

In the light of the rapid extension of personnel management tasks in the 1950s, this first attempt to achieve an appropriate classification proved abortive. Between 1955 and 1962 the commission and the Public Personnel Institute collaborated in further attempts to clarify and define the guiding standards. In this task the commission faced a predicament. Decentralization of its own operations as well as extensive decentralization in the operating departments made it imperative to upgrade departmental personnel work. On the other hand, always conscious of its statutory pre-eminence in the field, the commission was loath to encourage classification standards for departmental personnel officers that would threaten its central position. Meanwhile, as commission and institute grappled with this predicament, new personnel functions and a corresponding need for specialization were producing a more motley array of people engaged in various aspects of personnel management, wider variations in departmental performance, and everwidening gaps in pay scales – particularly between the salaries paid in the central agency and those paid to departmental officers.

A rapid resolution of the problem was precipitated by the report of the Heeney committee in 1958 which called for a much more extensive delegation to departmental personnel managers of the Civil Service Commission's functions. Three years later the urgency of the situation was underlined by foreknowledge of the findings and likely recommendations of the Glassco commission's task force on manpower management. Anticipating the consequences of the adoption of the philosophy 'let departmental managers manage,' the Civil Service Commission set up a committee to undertake the job evaluation required to bring order into the confused categories involved in departmental personnel work. The two commission officers placed on the committee had recently been re-cruited from outside the civil service, and the eight departmental personnel directors were chosen for the committee because they were known to be among the most advanced in their thinking on this problem.

The so-called 'Committee of Ten' rapidly produced agreed standards and secured approval of the departments for what was shortly to become the Personnel Administrator Class, divided into six levels, with the 'work-ing levels' set at grades 3 and 4. Then followed nearly two years of com-mittee work in which every personnel position was reviewed, an incum-bent review was prepared by each officer, and personal interviews took place. The final outcome was a somewhat depressing confirmation of the Glassco commission's surmise that there was a wide gap between existing performances and the standards of performance required by the new philosophy of management. In the appraisal of thirty-two senior depart-mental personnel officers, seven (22 per cent) failed to meet the new standards; of the 216 persons in junior positions, one-fifth balked at the hurdle and withdrew before appraisal, while less than half of the total qualified.

Despite the havoc created in the ranks of the personnel officer com-munity by the application of the new standards, the decisions remained firm. It was apparent that nothing less would serve the new needs imposed by acceptance of the Glassco commission's recommendations. Moreover, the entire operation had been mounted after full consultation with depart-mental personnel directors and implemented with their active participation and concurrence. Nevertheless, the new dispensation inevitably resulted in a noticeable reduction in morale and productivity.

In this depressed atmosphere and with the cadre of personnel officers reduced by about one-half, the call for more personnel people of higher quality became more insistent as the full weight of the Glassco commis-sion proposals came down on the public service. Simultaneously, the initial findings of an important committee set up to explore the prospects of introducing collective bargaining for the civil service confirmed the shortage of competent personnel officers, particularly those equipped to grapple with the complexities of a new classification plan. The internal competition for such scarce resources led to an unhealthy mobility as the few officers with the necessary competence moved, almost at will, and always upward, from department to department.

In January 1964 the Civil Service Commission issued to all departments its views on the steps to be taken, particularly to salvage those who had failed to meet the higher standards. Recruitment to the entrance levels of the now defunct Personnel Officer Class was to cease; retraining and transfer were proposed for those in the operating levels; and a new support class for more routine personnel tasks was envisaged.

These were stopgap measures which did little to remedy the acute shortage of competent personnel officers. And this shortage was further underlined after the creation in the fall of 1964 of a Bureau of Classification Revision in the commission. Prompted by the bureau and by the Preparatory Committee on Collective Bargaining, the commission in 1965 announced its intention of adapting its organization to the functional reallocation recommended in the Glassco commission report. To give immediate effect to one of its major assignments it proposed to establish 'a total staffing program ... to give coherent leadership and service in the phases of recruitment, selection, placement, classification, training, career development and transfer for personnel administration classes.'[8]

The launching of the commission's Personnel Administration Staffing Programme was preceded by the report of the Preparatory Committee on Collective Bargaining in the Public Service.[9] This report stressed the initial need for classification experts to provide the foundation for bargaining units as well as to develop a more simple classification plan that would ultimately permit extensive devolution of classification to departments. Consequently, the first task to which the programme directed its efforts was a thorough inventory of the groups engaged in classification work – organization and establishment, standards, pay research, pay determination, and conditions of employment. Following the procedure used by the Committee of Ten in 1962, standards were set, appraisal committees were formed, personnel interviewed and ultimately positioned in the new class. Similar procedures were employed for related classes of training officers, Civil Service Commission officers, finance officers in the personnel area, and personnel support classes. It was hoped to complete the whole of this operation as a 'centennial project' for 1967. Efforts to recruit specialists outside the public service to meet the needs identified by the programme at the raised standards were reasonably successful, if one can measure the results by the protests from private industry at the loss of some of their trained people. Obviously, the immediate future calls for major training programmes – departmental and service-wide – to develop the varied skills and knowledge required for the demanding tasks of personnel administration. The fact that the Public Service Employment Act of 1967 permits the Public Service Commission to delegate to deputy ministers (or to such

8 Letter from the chairman of the Civil Service Commission to deputy ministers, 6 Jan. 1965, quoted by Morry, 'Proceedings,' pp. 7–8.
9 *Report* (Ottawa, 1965).

senior officers as may be named) important managerial responsibilities for personnel should provide both the incentive and the challenge which departmental personnel work has so conspicuously lacked in the past.

In summary, the 1960s have witnessed the Civil Service Commission pressed into taking the lead in a collaborative effort to overcome the problems created for it a half century ago when parliament conferred on it virtually a monopoly of managerial authority over manpower in the civil service. For departments long resigned to working under a central control body which deprived them of authority to manage but left them with responsibility for the results, it will not be easy to adjust to the new challenges. Not only is it a matter of being unable to secure immediate access to the kind of expertise now required, it is also a matter of living down fifty years of a tradition that discouraged departmental initiatives. Summoned by the new philosophy to manage their own affairs, it will be as difficult for departmental managers to assume their new responsibilities as it will for the central personnel agency to shift from its traditional control orientation to new concepts of service, support, guidance, and audit.

FINANCIAL MANAGEMENT

What has been said, at considerable length, about the struggle of departments to achieve managerial emancipation in the field of personnel administration, may be more briefly transposed to the other major area of managerial concern – finance. In the case of personnel management it was fear of patronage that induced parliament to divest departments of their authority by entrusting major manpower decisions to a central, independent agency. The centralization of financial management stemmed, on the other hand, from the collective responsibility which the executive has always borne for raising and dispersing the funds allocated by parliament. The executive performs this task in trust, as it were, for the legislature, on the basis of what amounts to a legal contract annually renegotiated between the executive and the legislature. Thus, from the outset a committee of the cabinet, the Treasury Board, was created to help the chief financial officer of the country formulate the terms of the contract and subsequently to supervise the administration and expenditure of public funds.

On the revenue side, the early creation of a Consolidated Revenue Fund quickly dissuaded departmental managers from entertaining any notion that money earned from their own operations 'belonged to them.' Such 'earnings' were paid into the Consolidated Fund and could only be secured by the conventional route of a parliamentary appropriation.[10] Not until the advent of non-departmental agencies like the public corporations was any departure made in this arrangement. Thus, from the beginning, departmental managers had no control over autonomous funds not properly voted by the legislature, although they could be called to task for inefficient methods of collecting revenues. Since most departments – with the notable exception of the Post Office – were administering programmes from which little, if any, revenue was expected, departmental managers never looked on this limitation as interference with their prerogatives. Indeed, because of their reliance on appropriations they were accustomed to think of financial management almost entirely in terms of expenditures. What was essential to them was to be placed in a position to drive the best bargain they could with the legislature and then, within the restrictions imposed by the contract, have complete freedom to spend their appropriations in the most effective and economical manner they could design.

However, the freedom of departmental managers to negotiate their own financial terms with the legislature and then to get ahead with the task of spending the money so allocated was hedged about by constitutional and practical restrictions. In the first place, the constitutional responsibility vested in the executive to request, on behalf of the Crown, the monies required to support the Crown's public services, was viewed at the outset as a collective enterprise rather than a matter of competitive, piecemeal negotiations by each departmental head. The United States, which followed this latter practice for well over a century, was slow to recognize the merits of requesting funds from the legislature through a budget in which all departmental requests were combined: a unified, 'Presidential budget' did not appear until after 1921.[11]

In Canada, departmental expenditure programmes were early assembled in a unified budget, and it was natural to assign this task to the Department of Finance since it was also responsible for formulating the taxation and

10 An excellent history and description of the process as it had evolved prior to the Second World War is to be found in the article by one of the most influential civil servants, the deputy minister of Finance, W.C. Clark, 'Financial Administration of the Government of Canada,' *Canadian Journal of Economics and Political Science* 4 (Aug. 1938), pp. 391–419. The former comptroller of the Treasury, H.R. Balls, has also written extensively on the history and practice of financial control and audit: see, for example, his 'The Public Accounts, Their Purposes and Factors Affecting Their Forms: An Administrative View,' *Canadian Public Administration* 7 (Dec. 1964), pp. 422–41, and 'The Development of Government Expenditure Control: The Issue and Audit Phases,' *ibid.* 10 (Nov. 1944), p. 464 ff.

11 On the 'Presidential budget,' see Robert K. Carr, Marver H. Bernstein, and Donald H. Morrison, *American Democracy in Theory and Practice* (rev. ed., New York, 1961), chap. 16.

borrowing policies which would generate the counterbalancing revenues.[12] It was equally natural that a federation, whose varied interests were represented in the cabinet, should insist that the Minister of Finance should not perform this vital task of budget building without the advice and consent of a select group of his colleagues: hence, the early creation of the Treasury Board. However, as we have seen, in 1912 Sir George Murray was critical of the methods used to integrate separate departmental requests for funds and it was not until the 1930s that there was clear evidence of the development of an effective system. From that time on, departmental managers have had to embark on a six-month period of hard bargaining with a specialized staff serving the Treasury Board and (until 1966) attached to the Department of Finance. In essence, departments negotiate their contracts with the Treasury Board and ultimately the cabinet.[13] Once approved, they are moved forward in an integrated budget for which the executive as a whole assumes collective responsibility when presented for parliamentary approval. It is true that, for purposes of detailed legislative scrutiny and approval, the budget (that is, the estimates) is subsequently broken down into compartments or 'votes,' each vote representing the financial contract between the legislature and the relevant department. Each vote, nevertheless, is presented on the basis that refusal of the legislature to support it is tantamount to a vote of no confidence in the entire executive. Accordingly, the end result of the prolonged discussion in House Committee of Supply or in the committees of the House of Commons that now consider estimates is that the integrity of the original budget submission remains intact. Although this outcome is a foregone conclusion, the process of parliamentary scrutiny and approval should not be regarded as a futile exercise: only by such procedures can parliament and the public at large insist on the executive explaining and defending the expenditure contracts it is seeking to negotiate. And only by casting the contracts in relatively detailed terms can parliament ensure that the executive is directing the funds to objectives specifically approved by the legislature.

The development of the procedures just described is designed to give concrete meaning to the theory of responsible government. But at this point we must take note of conflicting objectives of the executive and legislature which somehow must be resolved within the traditional framework of a union of the two branches in which one is responsible to the

---

12 See my *Pioneer Public Service* (Toronto, 1955), chap. 7.
13 The detailed contemporary procedures are described in Royal Commission on Government Organization, *Report*, I, *Management of the Public Service* (Ottawa, 1962), report no 2: 'Financial Management,' pp. 102–7, 141–62.

other. To attain the objective of adequate legislative scrutiny and control, the financial contracts ('votes') should be numerous and rigorously descriptive of the purposes for which each vote can be spent. To achieve the equally desirable objective of effective management of the funds, departments would prefer contracts with global sums and a minimum of prescriptive detail constricting their spending decisions.[14]

Obviously, some half-way house must be found between these extremes, and in Canada, with an eye to ensuring responsibility of the executive to the legislature, there has been a tendency to strike the balance in favour of the legislative branch by resorting to a large number of detailed votes. It is not surprising that parliament should be insistent on preserving a relatively detailed vote structure for once the votes have been approved the legislature's capacity to influence the allocation of funds to departmental managers is severely curtailed. By means of the votes parliament places monetary limits on management and seeks to ensure that expenditures are related to the purposes stated in each vote. Within these legal financial fences parliament must trust the executive branch to develop internal procedures of fiscal control and accountability which will ensure the most effective application of the funds to the various services and operations.

The fact that funds are voted in many compartments in no way destroys the constitutional principle that all monies so voted are entrusted to the executive as a whole, and not directly placed at the disposal of each departmental manager. Thus it happens that the executive's need to preserve a united front when it approaches the legislature hat in hand for its annual appropriations also obliges the executive to impose central controls over the allocation of funds to individual departments and their subsequent expenditure. For this purpose the Treasury Board not only processes the original estimates of expenditures submitted by departments but also approves the subdivisions of parliamentary votes, called allotments. Further subdivisions of allotments into suballotments is carried out by senior departmental managers. Internally, financial accountability is based on the allotments and departments must seek approval of the Treasury Board for transfer of funds from one allotment to another. Until quite recently allotmentsc have been based on 'standard objects of expenditure,' such as salaries and wages, rent, postage, materials and supply, usually totalling in all twenty-two items under each vote.

14 For strictures on overelaboration of votes structure, see comments of the Auditor General (Watson Sellar) before the Public Accounts Committee in 1947 and again in 1949, *Proceedings, 1947*, pp. 429–33, 443–5; *Proceedings, 1949*, pp. 21–2, 42. Too many votes lead to undue multiplication of 'cushions,' or requests for funds that departments are not certain they will need.

The recasting and subdivision of votes in this fashion was strongly criticized by the Royal Commission on Government Organization for two closely related reasons.[15] First, from the viewpoint of departmental managers, the breakdown by standard objects of expenditure fails to provide a meaningful internal scheme of financial reporting. Second, parliamentary scrutiny of estimates and public accounts, couched in the same terms, is not particularly effective. Thus, the commission was led to one of its most fundamental recommendations – a recommendation that would simultaneously improve the capacity of departmental managers to obtain a running measure of the performance of their staff and also provide parliament with more meaningful data on which to make an informed judgment on the executive's use of funds entrusted to it. The recommendation was to subdivide each vote by programmes rather than standard objects of expenditure. The investigating staff of the commission had found that certain departments had already begun to move in this direction by translating the allotments by standard objects to allotments corresponding to their operating responsibilities. Accordingly, the commission proposed that this procedure be generalized and that the form of the estimates be altered to reflect this internal change. 'There is no vote,' said the investigating team, 'that cannot be adapted to this manner of presentation. Allotments for administrative votes should be broken down on the basis of organizational units in the department. Operation and maintenance votes should be controlled by geographical regions or individual operational units. Capital votes should be controlled on the basis of projects.' Clearly, once departmental managers were required to shift to allotments by programmes they would have to scrutinize closely the assignment of responsibility within the organization, identify their objectives, and seek to find measures of physical performance. The dividends from this transformation were neatly summarized by the task force: 'Programme control will provide concise information on the total estimated cost of an activity and, when compared on a year-to-year basis, will clearly show the increase or decrease in cost of the activity, and permit the costs to be related to benefits. Presenting programmes in the Estimates will highlight for Parliament the change in the cost of activities. Similarly, programmes properly related to activities will provide a better yardstick for assessing management within the department, and will enable Treasury Board to exercise more effective control over departmental expenditures.'[16]

The far-reaching implications of this proposal to shift to programme or performance budgeting have to be related to the royal commission's pri-

15 Report no 2 'Financial Management,' pp. 116 ff., 141 ff.
16 *Ibid.*, p. 151.

mary concern to devolve on departments the authority to take expenditure decisions that had come to be too highly centralized and to be held properly accountable for them. We have observed how the exigencies of a constitutional system that necessitated a collegial approach to the legislature by the executive to secure funds imposed a highly centralized form of control over departmental managers in estimating their requirements. We have also seen that the legislature's concern to preserve the collective responsibility of the executive to it for the expenditure of funds led to a multiplication of votes and an internal allocation of each vote that was increasingly unsatisfactory for departmental managers and not really providing parliament with meaningful figures on which to base its judgments on the executive's performance.

The restrictions imposed on departmental financial managers by the system which had been developed for allocating funds were reinforced by adding a central control over the expenditure of the allocations. Under the original Consolidated and Revenue Act of 1878 the Auditor General was required to give approval to all departmental expenditures by countersigning all cheques drawn on the Consolidated Revenue Fund. Over time the auditor's control tended to become *ex post facto* – an audit of the payment after it had been made. As a result, departmental control over expenditures led to varying and often slipshod practices which, in effect, subverted the intentions of parliament as expressed in the votes: departmental votes were overspent; liabilities were incurred that committed the department before the next appropriations had been approved; expenditures were charged to the wrong vote – or made out of revenues; and so on. The Auditor General would report to parliament, after the event, on such questionable practices, but it was difficult to take preventive action.[17]

In 1931 a major revision of the Consolidated Revenue and Audit Act inaugurated the new office of Comptroller of the Treasury, one of whose functions was to control departmental expenditures and to develop more uniform accounting procedures.[18] As an adjunct to these responsibilities the comptroller became, in effect, the paymaster of the public service as the central cheque-issuing agency. The new office was placed under the Minister of Finance and its staff was largely built up by transferring departmental accounting officers. Many of these 'Treasury officers' remained physically located in the various departments but they were seldom viewed as part of the department's management teams. The fact that the

---

17 Some startling examples are provided in R.D. Maclean's excellent MA thesis, 'An Examination of the Role of the Comptroller of the Treasury,' printed in full in *Canadian Public Administration* 7 (March 1964), especially p. 44ff.
18 Stats Can. 1931, c.27.

new office was created at a time when economy had become the key word for governments induced the Comptroller of the Treasury to interpret his statutory duties in the broadest terms. In performing his assigned task of verifying and approving every account before payment (the so-called 'pre-audit' function) he determined whether the expenditure fell within the legal terms of the vote as approved by parliament, whether funds were available to meet the expenditure, whether the account was accurate and properly coded, and whether the goods or services received had been in accordance with regulations. In order to check overexpenditure the comptroller inaugurated a system of commitment control, which in effect was superimposed on each allotment. 'In this manner, the Comptroller maintains running balances for each allotment, showing the uncommitted balance, the portion committed but unspent, and the expenditures to date.'[19] A transfer of funds between allotments (not between votes) must be authorized by the Treasury Board.

The task force of the Glassco commission, from whose thorough investigations the foregoing summary account of these procedures has been taken, found that many departments had created their own commitment control records which were not necessarily maintained or used in the same way as the comptroller's. As a result there was a duplication of detailed records, not always mutually consistent, and duplication of verification operations. After a lengthy analysis of the intricacies and results of such procedures, the royal commission argued persuasively for a simplification in the commitment control operation and for a restoration to departmental managers of the power to spend and to perform the pre-audit functions that had been long monopolized by the Comptroller of the Treasury. In passing they remarked that 'Neither the United Kingdom nor the United States places this responsibility in the hands of an external control agency.'

In extolling the virtues of delegation of financial control to departments the commission added the reassuring comment that 'This re-location of financial powers is in no sense intended to place departmental managers beyond the complete control of the Executive, including Treasury Board and ministerial heads.' However, 'the current method of ensuring accountability, by surrounding departmental managers with a hedge of detailed, negative controls and regulations, can only frustrate the aims of efficient, economical management.' The appropriate restraints on departmental managers would be provided by policy guidelines established by the Treasury Board and by having the board concern itself in the appointment and participate in the career development of the senior finance officers

19 Report no 2: 'Financial Management,' p. 156.

of each department. Such finance officers would in no way be considered agents or officers of the board but would be subject to their own deputy ministers, thereby placing responsibility for departmental expenditures 'squarely' where it belongs – on the shoulders of senior departmental officers, who are held personally accountable.'[20] The commission's main proposals for reform of financial management, like those for personnel management, were accepted in principle by the government. But the gap between enunciation of desired objectives and the effective implementation of the objectives was much wider in the area of finance than in personnel administration, as subsequent developments proved. The validity of the old adage 'easier said than done' was soon brought home to control agencies and departments as they began to grapple with the practical issues posed by such key proposals as programme budgeting, revision of the estimates, and devolution of spending powers to departments.

In 1963–4 four of the larger departments (Agriculture, Northern Affairs, Transport, and Veterans Affairs) were chosen as guinea pigs, and fresh teams of management consultants were set to work on them in an effort to prove the feasibility of the Glassco recommendations.[21] Working with the guidance of a co-ordinating committee, detailed reports were prepared, reviewed, and their major conclusions ultimately drawn together in a policy statement issued by the Treasury Board in April 1966. Shortly thereafter a more elaborate guide was produced for 'the official who needs to know what modern financial management is all about, what it can do for him in the performance of his duties, and what might be expected of him.' The document is, however, more than a layman's guide to instant financial management; it is also a central control agency's new management manifesto to departments: 'This guide describes new departures already made or contemplated to rid control of its frustrating associations and to express its positive modern meaning.' It is in addition a challenge to departmental managers to link hands with the Treasury Board to make a joint effort 'towards the common objective: the best financial management system our collective wisdom can devise.'

It is unnecessary to summarize the contents of this document, but two features should be mentioned. First, the function of the senior departmental financial officer is firmly identified as 'a staff function of service and advice to line management at all levels.' Thus financial management takes its place beside personnel management as a staff adjunct to the

20 *Ibid.*, pp. 106–7.
21 See the preface to 'Financial Management in Departments and Agencies of the Government of Canada,' June 1966, guide issued by the Management Improvement Branch, Treasury Board.

deputy minister. Second, in the list of duties assigned to the financial management staffs we confront the full implications of the Glassco commission's general proposals. The main duties are: financial planning, budget preparation and expenditure control, control and safekeeping of assets, liaison with central finance agencies, training for financial management staff.[22] The purity of the staff-advisory role assigned to the finance officer is rendered somewhat dubious by the detailed list of duties, some of which have control and even operating elements in them. Be that as it may, this document provides at least the essential preliminary guidelines within which departmental and central financial managers will gradually make the transition to the new dispensation.

That the government has no illusions about the complexity of the task and the time required to complete it is evinced in the remarks of the President of the Treasury Board in December 1966. Referring to the new system of 'goal-oriented controls' and to the 'much greater freedom to manage their own affairs' conferred on departments, the minister observed: 'You can see why we regard this as a five to ten year job.'[23]

Already there is visible evidence of progress: the estimates have now been recast to express departmental expenditure proposals in terms of programmes, even as the old 'standard objects of expenditure' pattern begins to be phased out. Departmental finance officers have expressed enthusiasm for the new procedure and speak in some astonishment of how valuable they find the exercise of having to identify, for the first time, their main programmes of activity and break them down into smaller units. Parliament, as yet, has not been alerted to the large dividends that have been placed in its hands by having more meaningful financial statistics which should permit more intelligent debate on the government's spending plans. The impact of the new dispensation is likely to take gradual effect, not only in parliament but among departmental financial officers who will need time to adjust to the new freedom – which carries with it, as well, a new responsibility.

PAPERWORK AND SYSTEMS MANAGEMENT

In its fourth report on management practices in the public service the Glassco commission cast a critical eye on a miscellany of managerial activities associated with what may loosely be called paperwork and sys-

22 *Ibid.*, pp. 4, 5–7.
23 'What Has Been Happening to the Organization of the Government of Canada,' an address by E.J. Benson, president of the Treasury Board, 5 Dec. 1966, mimeo., p. 7.

tems.[24] Government is the greatest generator of paper: partly because paper is a substitute for blood in the communication arteries of the bureaucracy, partly because government demands a multitude of forms from the public, and partly because accountability of the public service must be guaranteed by placing decisions 'on the record.' The floods of paper must be channelled systematically; forms must be properly designed and the temptation to multiply them unnecessarily kept in check; expert attention must be devoted to filing and retrieval of papers when required; and disposal of obsolete records must be taken in hand if the bureaucracy is not to drown in a paper sea of its own making. Improper or inept management of these tasks becomes all the more serious as the full impact of the new electronic gadgetry is felt in the public service. Automatic data processing equipment creates more paper but also enables us to process and store it; but these are not toys – they are expensive, sophisticated tools for managers that place new demands on new breeds of technicians. Their extreme costliness suggests that their installation must be carefully planned; their voracious appetites indicate, further, that careful scheduling is required to keep them operating at optimum capacity. In short, paperwork and systems management now assumes major dimensions and takes its place alongside the more traditional managerial concerns for staffing and financing.

When the Glassco commission initiated its inquiry the public service was just beginning to recognize the implications for management of the application of these new techniques. The report of the commission stressed the urgency of the need to upgrade the personnel connected with these historically low-level managerial concerns, and indicated the kind of organization that would be required to provide initiative and leadership in taking rapid and effective measures. Immediate attention to this area was urged because, without substantial improvements in systems and procedures, the major recommendations of the commission for devolution to departmental managers accompanied by programme budgeting, responsibility reporting, and the like could not take place.

With these considerations in mind the commission proposed a third division for the Treasury Board staff, a Management Improvement Branch, with centralized responsibility for advising the board among other matters on information systems, material management, operations research, and electronic data processing. The placing of this branch on a level with the Personnel Policy Branch and the Programme Branch signified the elevated status to be accorded these newer aspects of management and the anticipated close co-ordination between them and the

24 *Report*, I, report no 4: 'Paperwork and Systems Management.'

other main managerial tasks. Essentially, the Management Improvement Branch is responsible for developing or guiding the development of 'an integrated system of government information' that will be fed to the main decision-making points to assist them in managing and controlling total government expenditures.[25] To meet the need for central co-ordination of electronic data processing services, a Data Processing Service Bureau was incorporated within the Management Improvement Branch.[26] The bureau has been equipped with a sophisticated computer facility with which to serve the expanding needs of the departments and also undertakes feasibility studies and provides advice to other agencies to make the optimal use of their data processing facilities. This strengthening of the central co-ordinating and servicing apparatus in relation to these newer managerial functions has been accompanied by the development and upgrading of comparable departmental services.

There is a good chance that the prolonged struggle to clarify the role of central and departmental management in the areas of personnel and financial administration will not be repeated for this area of emerging managerial concern. The central agencies have not had time to build a monopoly of expertise, while departments have simultaneously and equally been exposed to the new management technology. Thus, prospects appear to be promising for a fairly rapid but balanced and co-ordinated development of these newer management concerns, drawing equally on the skills and resources of central agencies and departmental teams.

The most significant indicator of this marked change from the evolutionary paths followed for other management functions is to be found in the inauguration of the Federal Institute of Management.[27] Prompted, no doubt, by the investigations of the large group of experts employed by the Glassco commission on paperwork and systems management, 150 public servants held an exploratory meeting in mid-July of 1962. The secretary of the Treasury Board, in lending his vigorous support to the projected institute, stressed the intention to maintain an arm's length relationship with it: the institute was not to be an arm of the reconstituted Treasury Board staff. On the other hand, to dispel fears expressed by one or two senior officials, it was also made clear that the institute would in

25 Benson, 'What Has Been Happening,' p. 7.
26 In 1968 the bureau was transferred to the Department of Defence Production as, it will be recalled, was also the Bureau of Management Consulting Services (from the Public Service Commission).
27 The emergence of this institute has attracted little public attention and I am grateful to the late Roger Lavergne (Department of National Defence) for first calling my attention to it and making available information on which I have drawn for the remainder of this section.

no way impair the responsibility of senior management to direct these new services. It was admitted that the proposed institute might trespass on or even absorb activities hitherto conducted by such specialized associations as the Public Personnel Institute, the Records Management Association, or the Institute of Public Administration of Canada whose membership extends beyond the federal public service. However, it was agreed that these bodies should retain their identity and be brought into the new institute's orbit (if they so desired) through affiliation or looser liaison arrangements. Clearly, there was an immediate set of tasks for the proposed Federal Institute of Management in considering ways and means of implementing the many recommendations from the Glassco commission. These broke down into several separable components for which separate groups would be (or had already been) formed, for example, the Administrative Improvement Group, the Computer and Data Processing Group, and the Matériel Control Group.

The preliminary meeting resulted in the ultimate drafting of a temporary constitution for the Federal Institute of Management and by August 1962 the first issue of a *News Bulletin* was published, followed by group-sponsored forums. At the end of 1962 the new institute had enrolled over 460 members in its various groups. By 1963 the organizational arrangements had been clarified. Four groups were federated, adding to the three mentioned above a new Federal Financial Officers Institute. To cover a more scattered array of officers whose responsibilities were somewhat more peripheral to these central ones, provision was made for membership-at-large. The problem of physical dispersal was met by providing for regional groups, while the Public Personnel Institute and Records Management Association were affiliated. An advisory council of selected senior management officials was also created.

The enthusiastic response to the initiative taken in mid-1962 and subsequently followed up by every appearance of continuing active interest among all groups within the institute appears to substantiate the expectations of those who tentatively visualized the new organization providing a forum for the interchange of ideas and a medium for collecting, publishing, and distributing information concerning management practices among federal government departments and agencies. Like the Public Personnel Institute which preceded it, the Federal Institute of Management will undoubtedly provide a forum and filter for developing and improving techniques and standards, as well as promoting systematic training and making recommendations to or carrying on special studies on behalf of senior management.

The Federal Institute of Management represents the latest departmental response to the new challenges posed by increasingly sophisticated management tools and techniques. This brief account of its sudden emergence provides a fitting conclusion to a chapter that has recorded the prolonged attempt to devolve on departmental managers the authority commensurate with responsibilities which have legally been theirs to exercise but which have been confided historically to centralized control bodies. The collaborative atmosphere in which the institute was launched augurs well for an extension of the same oecumenical spirit to those older areas of management which have been plagued in the past by constant friction and sometimes outright hostility. But, if there is a need for spreading the soothing oils of oecumenism in these areas of management, the real testing point will be in the sensitive area of employee relations to which the next chapter is devoted.

CHAPTER FOURTEEN   # Employees of the
public service:
the neglected
managerial link

Parliamentary approval of the Public Service Staff Relations Act in 1967
marked the culmination of a prolonged, often frustrating, campaign on
the part of federal public servants to secure a voice and some measure of
influence over managerial decisions affecting their terms and conditions
of employment. Resistance to the claims of public employees for rights
long established in the private sector cannot be attributed to their radical
nature or to frequent breaches in the prevailing rigid codes of conduct
imposed on public servants. No employee organization has ever preached
syndicalism or 'workers' control' in the name of industrial democracy as
was the case during the 1920s in France and in the United Kingdom. Nor
(until the mid-1960s) have organized employees, with the outstanding
exception of the Winnipeg strike in 1919, shown any overt tendency to
throw over the restrictive traces or to mobilize as a pressure group.

Basically, there are three avenues by which civil servants have sought
to convey their ideas, opinions, and grievances to management. Political
action – both individual and collective – was the first route, and one that
was likely to be capitalized on during the early days when the public service was fighting its way clear of patronage. Internal grievance and appeal procedures constitute a second channel for carrying the protests of
employees to the ear of authoritarian managers. The third route on which
organized civil servants have increasingly been pressing to travel is conventional industrial action, with all its components of unionization, negotiation, collective bargaining, conciliation, arbitration, and the strike.

Looking back, it is possible to identify at least five important factors
that have thwarted or delayed the efforts of civil servants to pursue one or

the other of these avenues of access to management. The first of these, the doctrine of sovereignty, for years provided top management with what appeared to be an impregnable rationalization for refusing to concede even a modicum of the claims urged on them by employees. The mystique of the Austinian theory of sovereignty, even when applied to the 'split sovereign' of the federal state of Canada, provided strong enough grounds for stubborn refusal of management to recognize that while the King could do no wrong His Majesty as employer might well be treating his employees shabbily. As long as this doctrine remained unshaken, a strike of public employees was regarded as treason ('essential services could never be permitted to grind to a halt'), collective bargaining was unthinkable, and even modest internal provisions for hearing appeals and grievances were accorded by grace and favour of the sovereign. Thus, the notion that the sovereignty of the state somehow gave the state as employer peculiar prerogatives over its employees closed the doors both to effective internal avenues of access to management and to external avenues via industrial rights of organization and collective bargaining.[1]

A second obstacle to the ambitions of civil servants was the hierarchical structure of the public organization in which they worked. The pyramiding of authority and responsibility in a rigid hierarchical structure is almost by definition authoritarian, with commands emanating from the top being relayed to the bottom and obedience rising to the top in formal stages. In a sense, the hierarchical organization of the bureaucracy reinforced the doctrine of sovereignty and both taken together acted as a persuasive check on civil servants seeking to use any of the three optional routes to those wielding 'life and death' powers over them.

The effort to eliminate patronage and to create, through a centrally policed merit system, a politically neutralized bureaucracy was a third factor that tended to close off access to management. In particular, the need to 'depoliticize' the public service induced management to frown on individual efforts of civil servants to lobby for preferential treatment or to seek remedies for both individual or collective grievances by cultivating access to political channels or by using conventional political instruments of the vote, the lobby, or mass demonstrations. Regulations governing the political activities of civil servants were viewed as a necessary buffer for managers as well as a way of preserving the permanency of civil servants whenever a change of government occurred: if a public servant had made no open avowal of political allegiance he could be

1 On this point, see S.J. Frankel, 'Staff Relations in the Public Service: The Ghost of Sovereignty,' *Canadian Public Administration* 2 (Winter 1959), pp. 65–76.

expected to serve masters of all political faiths. Coupled with the authoritarian ethos created by the sovereign state as a specially privileged employer and the hierarchical structure of organization, the attempt to preserve a clear dividing line between politically neutralized (and therefore permanent) administrators and a political ministry placed additional obstacles in the path of civil servants seeking access to management.[2]

Emerging out of the early popularity of 'Taylorism,' or the efficiency management movement, there came the tendency to treat the labour force as one of the instruments of production. As a result, the dehumanization of labour, already implicit in the grouping of large numbers of employees in a hierarchical structure, found a philosophical rationalization. The impact of the efficiency movement was directly felt by the bureaucracy for it resulted in the introduction of a complex classification system into the civil service after the First World War. The new classification system, policed by the all-powerful Civil Service Commission, came to be viewed as the prime instrument for preserving the merit system. A legal description of a class of positions provided a statutory framework for recruiting the right man for the right job, and no room for political considerations. Confronted by the complexity of a detailed classification plan, civil servants found difficulty in organizing in sufficiently comprehensive groupings to prevent their forces from being scattered and dissipated. *Faute de mieux*, they were often obliged to organize around the department which, as the previous chapter has indicated, lacked most of the authority to deal with conditions of employment. Thus, until the 1960s organized civil servants were forced to speak with many tongues, or at least to seek solace in a series of loose confederacies of associations.[3] The problem of negotiating with management through a multiplicity of associations was aggravated by a physical dispersion of the public service, where only one-quarter was conveniently grouped in the Ottawa–Hull area. The detailed classification plan and extensive physical dispersion of the labour force divided employees and reinforced management's capacity to rule.

2 This issue was formally considered by two committees in the United Kingdom but has generally received marginal consideration by comparable Canadian inquiries. See *Report of the Committee on the Parliamentary etc. Candidature of Civil Servants*, Cmd 2408 (London, 1925), and *Report of the Committee on the Political Activities of Civil Servants*, Cmd 7718 (London, 1949), and the Conservative government's white paper on *The Political Activities of Civil Servants*, Cmd 8783 (London, 1953). The only mildly comparable examination of the question in Canada is found as recently as 1967 in the proceedings of the Special Joint Committee of the Senate and of the House of Commons on Employer–Employee Relations in the Public Service of Canada. See its *Minutes of Proceedings and Evidence* (Ottawa, 1967), pp. 1280–92 (the discussion on section 32 of the proposed bill).
3 Generally, on civil service associations, see S.J. Frankel, *Staff Relations in the Civil Service* (Montreal, 1962).

Confusion over the proper locus of managerial authority was a fifth inhibiting factor. In previous chapters the reasons for this confusion have been detailed; the practical consequences for civil servants were that they were never certain – even assuming they were granted access – whether their deputy minister, the Civil Service Commission, or the Treasury Board was the appropriately authorized managerial agency whom they should be attempting to solicit or convince.

It is also probably fair to add that the extensive reliance on central, though divided, management agencies inhibited the development of a departmental managerial tradition or at least provided an atmosphere in which supervisory and senior departmental officers tended to join forces with their staff against the outsiders, who had all the real power. In these circumstances, the call from the Glassco commission to 'let departmental managers manage' potentially gave organized employees a focal point around which to regroup their ranks if and when collective bargaining was inaugurated.

Now that the enactments of 1967 have invited the Treasury Board as the 'real' employer for most situations to stand up, organized civil servants have had to regroup their forces, thereby abandoning an assumption built up over the years that the Civil Service Commission was the representative of the employer with whom they would normally deal. In any event, the lengthy history of managerial ambivalence, which has previously been recounted, stultified the efforts of civil servants to achieve the bargaining rights so long cherished by employees of private concerns.

It is within the constricting framework of these general considerations that civil servants have sought over the years to establish their right to influence managerial decisions affecting their careers and working conditions. For the most part their concerns, both individual and through associations, have been of the 'bread and butter' variety espoused by employees in the private sector. Nevertheless, in establishing the general framework for collective action which has so recently been created and in their agitation of larger causes affecting the personnel management functions in particular, public servants have won a significant, though subordinate, stake in the management enterprise. The account of their efforts can best be summarized by returning to the three avenues of access and examining the progress achieved in each.

POLITICAL ACTION

The ability of federal public servants to influence managerial decisions affecting their terms and conditions of employment by means of political action has always been negligible. Their political rights and privileges have been hedged about by restrictions that reflect the traditional concern to segregate public servants from partisan politics. This concern received its most extreme legislative expression in the Province of Canada where customs and excise workers were disfranchised in 1844, most postal workers lost the vote in 1851, and the crown land agents were added to the proscribed list in 1855.[4] These restrictions were temporarily applied to the public servants of the new dominion until permanent legislation governing the conduct of federal elections removed the prohibitions in 1874, leaving the judiciary as the sole occupants of the category of politically underprivileged.[5] Some of the provinces continued to disfranchise federal public servants in provincial elections for many years: Quebec retained the proscription until 1892, Manitoba until 1901, and Ontario did not remove the barrier until 1917.[6]

Coupled with this short-lived policy of disfranchisement a more durable and significant method of 'depoliticizing' public office-holders was found in the legislation borrowed from early British statutes dating back to the reign of Queen Anne. In these so-called 'Place Acts' all officers holding 'places of profit or emolument' were debarred from parliament except those holding ministerial office.[7] The exceptions permitted the growth of a cabinet of ministerial office-holders whose seats in the legislature could be retained. The Province of Canada in 1844 emulated these acts by a measure to 'Secure the Independence of Parliament' which provided that 'no person holding an office of emolument at the nomination of the Crown in this Province shall ... be eligible as member of the Legislative Assembly,' with the exception of members of the executive council.[8] This legislative formula was incorporated into a federal statute in 1868 and is retained to this day.[9]

4 Stats Prov. Can. 7 Vict., c.65 (1844). This act was approved by the provincial legislature in 1843, reserved by the governor for reference to the imperial authorities, and was enacted in 1844. In England, between 1782 and 1868, postal employees and customs and excise officials were also disfranchised. In 1866 Gladstone unsuccessfully attempted to extend the prohibition to all civil servants. See *Brit. H. of C. Debates*, 3rd series, 1867, cols. 189, 747–8; 1868, cols. 193, 398.
5 Stats Can. 31 Vict., c.25 (1868). Two temporary measures for conducting federal elections were approved in 1871 (34 Vict., c.204) and 1873 (36 Vict., c.27) which continued the pre-Confederation arrangements. The measure of 1874 (37 Vict., c.9), disfranchising only the judiciary, has remained unchanged in this respect.
6 Stats Que. 1892, c.3; Stats Man. 1901, c.11; Stats Ont. 1917, c.6.
7 A first class historical account of this development in Britain is to be found in the memorandum from the clerk of the House of Commons and the Attorney General appended to the valuable *Report from the Select Committee on Offices or Places of Profit under the Crown*, H.C. 120, 1940–1.
8 Stats Prov. Can. 7 Vict., c.65.
9 Stats Can. 31 Vict., c.25.

This formal separation of the political ministry from the civil service proper was originally designed to prevent the legislature from being over-run by office-holders appointed by the executive, but in Canada (as later in Britain) it tended to protect the permanency of tenure of civil servants by divorcing them from the partisan arena of the legislature. Given the durable patronage proclivities of earlier days this formal statutory separating wall required constant reinforcement by additional buttresses. A civil servant who had found his way into office through political influence would automatically assume that the way to get ahead was to employ the same political leverage as he had used to get in. Use of this leverage had apparently become so common that the Treasury Board intervened in January 1879. The board observed 'with much regret a growing practice on the part of gentlemen in the Public Service to endeavour to influence the Ministry to accede to their applications for increase of salary or additional retiring allowance by means of the private solicitations of Members of Parliament and other persons of political influence.'[10] After explaining its practice of considering such questions on their own merits the board argued 'that any attempt on the part of any officer to approach them on these matters through the private intercessions of persons unconnected with his Department is virtually imputing to the Board either that it is likely to turn a deaf ear to a reasonable application unless supported by political influence or that it may be induced to accede to an unreasonable application if such influence be brought to bear upon it.' Declining either alternative the board then ruled 'that any attempt made by [a public officer] to obtain their sanction to his application by any such solicitation ... will be treated by them as an admission on the part of such officer that the case is not good upon its merits and such application will be dealt with by them accordingly.'

This early Treasury Board ruling was reaffirmed much later in the regulations passed in conjunction with the Civil Service Act. On matters of appointment, promotion, transfer, and salary increase no solicitation of the Civil Service Commission (as the final arbiter) is permitted; all communications relating to such issues have to be channelled through the administrative hierarchy to the deputy minister.[11]

While these regulations firmly close the door on individual use of politi-

10 'Extract from the minutes of a meeting of the Honourable the Treasury Board – held in Ottawa, on the twenty-eighth day of January, 1879,' copy provided, courtesy of Privy Council Office.
11 See *Civil Service Regulations: Office Consolidation* (Ottawa, 1954), para. 105 (1) and (2): '... no person shall, directly or indirectly, solicit, or endeavour to influence a member of the Commission or any officer thereof, with respect to the appointment of any person to the Service, or with respect to the promotion or transfer of, or an increase of salary to, any officer, clerk, or employee in the Service.'

cal leverages to influence managerial decisions affecting public servants, further restrictions were required to close off access to alternative political leverages. As was noted the early prohibition against voting was soon dropped, but still unsettled was the question of how much further a civil servant could go in openly identifying himself with a party or in seeking an elective public office. Partisan activity on behalf of the party in power could be interpreted as a form of job insurance for the public servant or his means of ingratiating himself with his political overlords, but at the same time such activity jeopardized the doctrine of political non-alignment of public servants that protected them against dismissal when a governing party was defeated. Accordingly, even at risk of transforming public servants into politically underprivileged citizens, draconian legislation and crushing penalities were imposed to prevent all civil servants from engaging in open partisan politics or for standing for elective public office.

The original Civil Service Act of 1918 enshrined this attitude in section 32 which stated in part that 'no such deputy head, officer, etc. shall engage on partisan work in connection with any election or contribute, receive or in any way deal with any money for any party funds.' An order in council, PC 1467, 22 July 1922, spelled out the arrangements for making charges in writing and authorizing the minister of the department concerned to refer the charge to a special commission of inquiry. If the charge was proven immediate dismissal was the penalty. Although the penalty is brutally clear, the experience with this provision reveals that the definition of political partisanship has been imprecise and, more important, the method of ascertaining guilt (despite the order of 1922) has been most unsatisfactory. In 1938, for example, when James Gardiner, then minister of agriculture, was called upon to defend a series of dismissals among departmental officials in Prince Edward Island, he explained how the traditional method of dealing with such cases (and the one invoked in the current cases) had continued despite the provisions of the order in council of 1922.[12] The standard procedure was that if a member of parliament rose in his place and stated that of his personal knowledge an official was guilty of political partisanship under the terms of the Civil Service Act, dismissal became automatic without any provision for inquiry or for appeal. 'I am not arguing,' Mr Gardiner hastened to add, 'that it is the proper practice. I am simply saying it is the practice that has been followed in dealing with matters of this kind.' No one in the House dis-

12 *Can. H. of C. Debates*, 1938, p. 1109 ff. The same issue was raised in 1937 in connection with the dismissal of a civil servant in the Veterans' Assistance administration. *Ibid.*, 1937, p. 2690 ff.

puted the accuracy of his description; indeed, cases were cited to prove a continued existence of the practice of trial by political denunciation.[13]

Under revised regulations (Regulation 118) of the Civil Service Commission approved on 7 January 1954, no dismissal, suspension, or demotion could take place without an opportunity of presenting the case to a senior officer of the department nominated by the deputy head. But it is apparent that this regulation was intended to apply to cases involving administrative ineptitude and not to cases involving political partisanship. For the latter, the old ground rules continued to apply, as a discussion in the House in October 1957 revealed.[14] Political partisanship continued to remain undefined, and the status and rights of civil servants languished in an insecure shadow realm until 1967. The new Public Service Employment Act of 1967 and the prolonged discussion of this particular issue by the joint parliamentary committee prior to approval of the act revealed that at long last clarification and some element of equity had been restored.[15]

The terms of the revised act can best be understood by a brief refer-

13 One example cited was of the son or nephew of a member of parliament testifying that he had seen an employee 'go into a hall where a public political meeting was being held and had seen him come out again.' This was evidence enough to enable the member to denounce the employee, and the automatic dismissal that followed was not reversed despite the pleas of the employee for a proper hearing. *Ibid.*, 1938, p. 1115.

14 See question addressed by Lionel Chevrier to George H. Hees (minister of transport):
'Chevrier: ... Is it the policy of this department to dismiss employees in the Department of Transport merely because of charges of political partisanship?
Hees: Mr. Speaker, according to the rules and regulations of parliament as I understand them, if a member of parliament over his signature states that a civil servant or somebody working for the government has actively participated in political activity during a campaign, that person can be dismissed.
Chevrier: Are such dismissals made without a hearing or without an investigation even on the part of your department, or without giving an opportunity to the person dismissed to be heard by the employer in the department?
Hees: Anybody who would be charged would definitely be given an opportunity to be heard.
Mr. Winch: Where is the regulation?
Mr. Coldwell: Is this laid down in the regulations, that there is an appeal for the employees?
Mr. Hees: I understand, Mr. Speaker, that has been the practice followed in the past, but I will check it up.
Mr. Chevrier: No, it is not.'
Ibid., 1957, pp. 508–10.

15 See Special Joint Committee of the Senate and of the House of Commons on Employer-Employee Relations in the Public Service of Canada, *Minutes of Proceedings and Evidence*, pp. 1280–92, also appendix I, 'Memorandum to the Special Joint Committee: ... on Political Activity of Public Servants,' prepared by the Civil Service Commission, dated 15 Aug. 1966, pp. 327–30.

ence to developments in the United Kingdom. British civil servants, like their Canadian counterparts, were long subjected to the same total prohibitions against political partisanship and political office-holding. The rationale was the same: as the Royal (MacDonnell) Commission on the Civil Service of 1912 reported, 'the Civil Service [otherwise] would cease to be in fact an impartial non-political body capable of loyal service to all ministers and parties alike.'[16] A parliamentary committee (the Blanesburgh committee) confirmed the same rigorous code of political neutralism when it specifically investigated the question of parliamentary candidature of Crown servants in 1924. However, in 1948 a major breach with tradition was achieved as a result of the recommendations of the Masterman committee on the political activities of civil servants. Virtually complete freedom was proposed for all industrial civil servants (the equivalent of the old Canadian category of 'prevailing rate employees') and manipulative grades in the post office – now generally grouped in the 'operational category,' about 650,000 out of a total of one million. In 1953 the United Kingdom government announced a new formula which extended full rights of political participation to 62 per cent of the staff, freed another 22 per cent (subject to a general requirement to maintain 'a proper discretion' and specifically ruling out parliamentary candidature), and left the remaining 16 per cent under the traditional restrictions.[17]

Section 32 of the Public Service Employment Act of 1967 marks a major advance for Canadian public servants in the same direction. It first of all spells out the meaning of political partisanship: engaging in work for, on behalf of, or against a candidate for a federal, provincial, or territorial council election or engaging in work for, on behalf of, or against a political party, and standing as a candidate for election. Political partisanship does *not* consist of attending a political meeting or contributing money for the funds of a candidate. Accompanying the clarifying definitions is a spelling out of procedures: all charges alleging political partisanship are to be referred to a board established by the Public Service Commission, and if the board affirms the charge the Governor in Council (if a deputy head) or the commission (for all other employees) dismisses the offender.

An important provision of section 32 is that which charges the Public Service Commission with responsibility for determining, on individual application, whether to grant an employee leave of absence without pay

16 *Fourth Report*, Cd 7339 (London, 1914), p. 97.
17 An excellent treatment of the situation in Britain is to be found in James B. Christoph, 'Political Rights and Administrative Impartiality in the British Civil Service,' *American Political Science Review* 51 (March 1957), pp. 67–87.

to seek nomination and to be a candidate for an election. The test the commission is to apply is whether 'the usefulness to the Public Service of the employee in the position he now occupies would not be impaired by reason of his having been a candidate.'[18] Judging from the special memorandum prepared by the commission for the joint parliamentary committee on the public service bill, in discharging this new responsibility the commission will seek to establish categories, as in the British system, for those who will receive automatic endorsement of their application, those who may need to have it qualified, and those – especially in the senior policy levels – to whom the prohibitions will apply in full.[19]

This tidying-up operation was overdue but is none the less welcome. In general, however, the liberalizing of political participating rights for civil servants will not have much affect in the area upon which this chapter is focused, that is, the improvement of the civil servant's capacity to share in management decisions affecting his employment. The cautious extension of political rights is consonant with the move to relieve civil servants of any stigma of second-class citizenship, but the rights to vote, to seek and hold political office, to contribute to election or party funds, or to participate in conventional political gatherings provide only the most indirect support for the participatory role which civil servants seek in the management decisions affecting their workaday world. To achieve these aims, the alternative avenues to management mentioned at the beginning of this chapter are by far the more meaningful.

INTERNAL GRIEVANCE AND APPEAL PROCEDURES

The positive pronouncement of the Treasury Board, quoted in the previous section and subsequently reinforced by additional regulations, was designed to forestall the routing of individual or collective grievances to members of parliament or to political parties. That these rulings were difficult to enforce and did not completely prohibit a civil servant with a grievance to air it with his member of parliament is revealed by the following exchange in the House of Commons in 1956. Stanley Knowles, questioning Roch Pinard, secretary of state, inquired: 'Are there any restrictions on the right of government employees to bring any grievances they may have to the attention of Members of Parliament.' To which Mr Pinard replied: 'There may be administrative rules in particular departments .. but I know of no statute or regulation of general application that would restrict the right of government employees to bring a grievance to the attention of a Member of Parliament.'[20] In the light of existing regula-

18 Stats Can. 1966–7, c.71, s.32(3–5).   19 See reference in n. 15 above.
20 *Can. H. of C. Debates*, 1956, pp. 1663–5.

tions, this reply must be interpreted as a very restricted means, open to any citizen, to approach his member, but in this instance running the risk that his case will, for that very reason, be regarded with a jaundiced eye by management.

In any case, civil servants have tended to seek internal means for redress of grievances and the creation of mechanisms to hear appeals on managerial decisions affecting their terms and conditions of employment. For years, the authoritarian structure of the bureaucracy, the dehumanized approach to employees grouped in rigidly defined classes, and the autocratic control granted the head of the department (as heir to the sovereign's prerogative power over his employees) all combined to leave civil servants at the mercy of arbitrary managerial decisions.

The advent of a powerful Civil Service Commission after 1918 subjected most vital managerial decisions concerning departmental employees to the final approval of the commission. From that point on, civil servants and their associations looked to the commission as their 'protector' against any possible abuse of the managerial prerogatives of departmental heads. In practice, the commission became an appeal court to uphold or reject the decisions of senior departmental managers with respect to such matters as dismissal, suspension, lay-off, probation, transfers, promotion, reclassification, and the like. The machinery for handling appeals within the commission was not properly instituted until the late 1930s, in response to a series of reports by parliamentary committees in which this issue had been thoroughly canvassed.[21] The special appeal boards set up at the time were specifically designed to deal with promotions, while appeals against other decisions were dealt with by the commission and its staff. Section 70 of the revised Civil Service Act of 1961 consolidated and confirmed these procedural devices but the *ad hoc* boards of three persons that the commission was authorized to nominate were to consider an appeal on any matter which by regulation or the act could be appealed to the commission.[22]

When the Royal Commission on Government Organization examined the internal mechanisms for disposing of employee appeals and grievances, they found substantial variation in and, for the most part, only a rudimentary development of departmental machinery.[23] Consistent with the royal commission's view that managerial prerogatives should be

21 There were committees of the House of Commons to consider the civil service in 1932, 1934, 1938, and 1939. See, especially, Special Committee on the Civil Service Act, *Minutes of Proceedings and Evidence* (Ottawa, 1939).
22 Stats Can. 1961, c.57, s.70(2–5).
23 Royal Commission on Government Organization, *Report*, I, *Management of the Public Service* (Ottawa, 1962), report no 3: 'Personnel Management,' pp. 282 ff., 388–90.

shifted back to the departments from the commission and the Treasury Board, there was an urgent plea to upgrade the departmental procedures for handling grievances, the appellate procedures to be retained in the Civil Service Commission.

This recommendation came too late to influence the revisions of the Civil Service Act made in 1961, but in its successor, the Public Service Employment Act of 1967, the necessary changes were made.[24] In section 5(d), under 'General Powers and Duties of the Commission,' the new Public Service Commission was to 'establish boards to make recommendations to the Commission on matters referred to such Boards' under subsequent sections of the act. These matters include: board inquiries into the exercise of managerial powers delegated (by section 6 of the act) to deputy heads relating to appointments to or from within the public service; appeals from unsuccessful candidates for appointments made from within the public service, by closed competition or without competition (section 21); appeals from employees whom the deputy minister proposed to demote or release for incompetence or incapacity (section 31); and appeals on proposed dismissal for political partisanship (section 32).

These provisions, like much in the new act, strengthened and systematized the more casual procedures of the past, but they must be read in conjunction with the other major measure approved in 1967 – the Public Service Staff Relations Act.[25] The main thrust of this act concerns the issues to be raised in the final section of this chapter, but 'Part IV Grievances' is relevant at this stage. This section assumes the development of formal internal grievance procedures within each department, as recommended by the Royal Commission on Government Organization, although it makes no effort to spell these out; rather, it is concerned with authorizing the newly created Public Service Staff Relations Board to recommend to the Governor in Council that it appoint adjudicators to hear and adjudicate upon grievances that have already been presented up to and including the final level in the grievance process. The decision of such an adjudicating board is final.

The intent of both pieces of legislation was to preserve a separation between the appellate functions of the Public Service Commission and the adjudicative functions envisaged by the Public Service Relations Act. The commission's appeal procedures are designed to cover actions taken under authority of the Public Service Employment Act that relate to policy governing release for incompetence or incapacity (that is, actions related to the appointing power ultimately vested in the Public Service Commission). The adjudicative procedures are designed to cover actions taken

24 Stats Can. 1966–7, c.71.   25 *Ibid.*, c.72.

by the Treasury Board as the employer: these involve the interpretation or application of a collective agreement or an arbitral award, or 'disciplinary action resulting in discharge, suspension or a financial penalty' (section 91, subsection 1(b) of the Staff Relations Act). Thus, it would appear that if the two distinctive procedural routes are to be maintained a clear distinction must be preserved between release for incompetence or incapacity (subject to the commission's appellate jurisdiction) and disciplinary actions involving discharge or suspension (under Treasury Board jurisdiction but subject to adjudicative procedures provided in the Staff Relations Act). In practice an employee may be faulted on both counts and management may be at a loss as to which route to follow. In the event, employees might well be placed in 'double jeopardy' and would then be forced to present their appeals to both sets of authorities. It is even conceivable that invoking a double jeopardy situation might enable a civil servant to escape scot-free simply because neither the appellate nor the adjudicating body would be in a position to consider all the relevant facts bearing on his case.

As matters now stand, civil servants possess an elaborate, and perhaps overlapping, apparatus for appealing most significant managerial decisions affecting their terms and conditions of employment. The legislation of 1967 also implies that each agency will now have to cultivate good personnel relations with its employees by establishing the grievance procedures which for so many years had been largely centralized in the Civil Service Commission as a court of last resort. What was still lacking and what the new legislation was especially devoted to supplying was an outright recognition of the third avenue of approach to management through unions, collective bargaining, and the whole panoply of techniques that had long been used by the labour force outside government employment. It is to this important series of developments that we turn in the closing section of this chapter.

INDUSTRIAL RIGHTS

A prerequisite for successful application of the conventional tools of industrial negotiation or bargaining with management is the creation and official recognition of associations or unions. The earliest associations of civil servants were largely created to sponsor social or recreational activities – one of the first of these to come to light was the Civil Service Rifle Association, created in 1861.[26] Associations modelled more closely on

26 For interesting historical material, see the special issue of the *Civilian*, Ottawa, 1914; back files of the *Civil Service Review*, the quarterly journal of the Civil

their industrial counterparts began to appear in the last decade of the nineteenth century, beginning (as seems to have been true for other countries such as the United Kingdom) in the Post Office with the Federal Association of Letter Carriers, chartered on 15 September 1891 by the Trades and Labour Congress.[27] As in England, at the same period, the autocratic control of the departmental head delayed official recognition and, again as in England, it was the decision of a liberally minded postmaster general (in the case of Canada, Sir William Mulock) that finally permitted the association to take grievances to the head of the department. The inside staff of the Post Office did not attain a national association until 1912 with the creation of the Dominion Postal Employees Association.[28]

Other associations first developed as locals, a Customs and Excise Association being formed, for example, in 1906 and achieving national status as the Dominion Customs and Excise Association only in 1917.[29] At Ottawa an organization for headquarters' staff in all departments was brought into being in 1907 as the Civil Service Association of Ottawa. The CSAO was instrumental in assembling a variety of local staff associations into a loose confederacy in 1909, resulting in the Civil Service Federation.[30]

Eleven years later, possibly inspired by the more radical west coast views on labour organization ('the Wobblies' and the One Big Union idea), the Amalgamated Civil Servants of Canada came into being in 1920.[31] The Amalgamated remained firm adherents of the oecumenical

Service Federation of Canada, contain frequent references to the origins of various federated associations.

27 Edna L. Inglis, 'Let Us Search the Record: The Part Played by Civil Service Organizations in Improving Public Administration,' *Civil Service Review*, March 1938; see also the article on the FALC in *ibid.*, Sept. 1938.

28 On the contribution of Sir William Mulock, see the article by J.J. Reaves on the FALC in *ibid.*, March 1940. On British developments for this period, see H.G. Swift, *A History of Postal Agitation* (Manchester and London, 1929).

29 Inglis, 'Let Us Search the Record.'

30 Special issue of the *Civilian*, 1914; also O.T. Robichaud, 'La Fédération du Service Civil du Canada,' *Civil Service News*, Dec. 1931. An obituary for R.H. Coats, 'Canada's Recording Angel' (Dominion Statistician), shows him to have been instrumental in founding the Civil Service Association of Ottawa in 1907 as part of the organized effort to acquire a pension plan. See *ibid.*, March 1942.

31 See Frankel, *Staff Relations in the Civil Service*, pp. 35–6. Vancouver was the original headquarters for the Amalgamated, and labour on the west coast generally was at the time attracted to the One Big Union concept. See 'Federation Means Security,' *Civil Service Review*, Dec. 1935, for the counter-claims against 'the 100 per cent Myth' and demonstrated growth in the Federation, despite a minority doggedly seeking 'to convert the Civil Service to the idea of a single organization.'

approach to association as opposed to the persistent confederacy policy of the Civil Service Federation. The former argued for organization across classification and departmental lines, the latter believed in separate organization by departmental function, class, or grade, or even by locality.

By the end of the first World War the major patterns of organization had emerged, but the stress was on 'blue-collar' workers. However, in 1919 the Professional Institute was brought into being to represent the growing group of professional, technical, and scientific personnel that was achieving increasing importance in the public service, especially at headquarters. This association was distinctive in representing a more senior level of personnel which cut across departmental lines and had more advanced educational attainments.[32]

The widespread dispersal of civil servants, coupled with the increasing fragmentation of its various components by the detailed classification plan of 1919, obviously fitted the Civil Service Federation's conception of a loose confederacy of staff associations built around particular functions. At the same time, where the number of employees in one functional category was small or where public servants were isolated in tiny, multifunctional working units scattered across the country, the Amalgamated approach seemed to have greater merit. Since associations in the Amalgamated crossed departmental and classification lines, stray pockets of civil servants – even lone individuals – could be swept in wherever they were or whatever they were doing.[33]

By December 1935 the Civil Service Federation counted forty-eight affiliated associations under its comprehensive umbrella[34] and, in the same year, as a way of discounting the counter-attractions of the Amalgamated, began to experiment with the device of district councils: 'a common assembly on Civil Service questions of an inter-departmental character.'[35] Beginning with Toronto, the district councils were expanded over the next few years to Hamilton, Victoria, Winnipeg, and Montreal. Basically recreational or social, the district councils were also used to stimulate organization of local groups, induce them to form national associations, and then have the nationals federate with the Civil Service Federation. The Federal Public Works Association and the Unemployment Insurance Commission employees were organized and brought in to wider federation in this manner in the late 1930s and early 1940s.

32 See a brief history in 'Membership Recruitment Number' of the Professional Institute's journal, *Professional Public Service* 37 (Aug. 1958), p. 2.
33 The Federation, however, sought to pick up isolated stragglers by offering individual memberships. See *Civil Service Review*, June 1933.
34 'Federation Means Security,' *ibid.*, Dec. 1935, p. 68 ff.
35 *Ibid.*, March 1935, March 1938, Dec. 1938, March 1939.

In 1954 the Civil Service Association of Ottawa, which had been instrumental in organizing the Civil Service Federation, withdrew from the federation and subsequently merged with the Amalgamated in 1958. The openly antagonistic organizational philosophies of the Federation and the Amalgamated – which, as has been argued exemplified the problems facing unionization of a public service geographically spread and fragmented into a multitude of functional or departmental classes – long prevented these two major groups from coming together. Beginning in 1942 and renewed sporadically for more than a generation thereafter, the Federation opened the door to negotiating a peace treaty with the Amalgamated.[36] The olive branch was persistently rejected until 1958, largely because each of the major groups insisted on a merger on its own terms. Not until collective bargaining became a real possibility was there a need for reconsideration by the existing associations and they quickly realized that to become viable bargaining units the long-held promise of a merger needed to be fulfilled. In November 1966 the Civil Service Federation and the smaller (thirty thousand–member) Civil Service Association of Canada – successor to the old Amalgamated – came together in the Public Service Alliance of Canada, embracing a total of 115,000 members, or roughly half of the public servants subject to the new legislation.[37]

While organized associations are prerequisites for any form of collective negotiation with management, there must also be established mechanisms and procedures for drawing the two groups together. Until the end of the Second World War, civil service staff associations were obliged to carry on their negotiations separately and, because there was no special machinery, had to work with the divided management apparatus that was the peculiar feature of the Canadian public service. Thus, an association might at one time make a presentation to the cabinet or the Minister of Finance and, after a courteous hearing, be obliged to withdraw to await announcement of the government's pleasure – a far cry from negotiation let alone collective bargaining. More frequently, representatives of an association carried their members' grievances and appeals (particularly with respect to promotions) or larger issues concerning the protection of the merit principle to the Civil Service Commission. Thus, for most issues,

36 'A Place for Unity and a Plan,' *ibid.*, Dec. 1942. Since the *Review* throughout the thirties had been constantly sniping at the Amalgamated, this plea from a regional vice-president of the Federation marked a new departure. In March 1943 the *Review* carried a further article, 'Concerning Unity,' in which was reported a meeting between the two groups on 15 February that failed to agree on a mutually satisfactory reallocation of members. The annual convention of the federation in 1943 renewed the discussion but made no greater progress towards an amicable settlement.
37 See *Globe and Mail*, Toronto, 17 May and 7 Nov. 1966.

the associations came to view the commission not so much as management but as their main intermediary in dealing with management or as a final court of appeal on management decisions affecting their members. The strength of the associations, under these circumstances, depended on the influence and prestige of the commission acting as their intermediary or appellate court. As was noted in an earlier chapter, the commission's influence in the early 1930s began to wane in proportion as the influence of the Treasury Board expanded. The outbreak of war pushed the commission more and more into the background and the associations found their mediator, always an uncertain friend at court, now a progressively frailer reed on which to lean. It was at this point, in the closing period of the war, that the associations were provided with an alternative mechanism which, potentially at least, offered them the first opportunity to discuss and negotiate their claims collectively with the triumvirate of management – commission, Treasury Board, and senior departmental officials.

A mechanism for this new venture in collective discussion emerged in 1944 as the National Joint Council of the Public Service. The idea was far from new, for the joint council plan had been bruited in Canada ever since the so-called Whitley Councils had been created for the British civil service in 1919.[38] Throughout the 1920s organized labour and civil service associations in Canada had pressed for the adoption of similar joint management–employee councils.[39] A royal commission reporting on strikes in Manitoba had recommended in 1921 that the joint council plans, much in vogue in a number of countries, be actively investigated and that a national industrial conference be convened to further this objective. This conference, at which representatives of the Trades and Labour Congress and the Civil Service Federation were present, established a special committee that ultimately reported favourably on the proposal to create joint industrial councils. The Department of Labour was invited to create a special bureau to assist, when called upon, in the task of organizing such councils.

38 See Leonard D. White, *Whitley Councils in the British Civil Service* (Chicago, 1933). By PC 1743, 11 July 1918, all employees were given the right to organize in trade unions, and this right was not to be denied or interfered with in any manner whatsoever. (See references in *Can. H. of C. Debates*, 1932, p. 608.) On 1 May 1919 part of this order was cancelled, clearly with a view to exploring the joint council plan. Thereafter, every year witnessed constant agitation in the House of Commons for action and a steady government response that the matter was under consideration. See, for example, *ibid.*, 1921, p. 2820; 1922, p. 1061; 1923, p. 1654; 1924, p. 2358; 1925, p. 4922.

39 The *Civil Service Review*, Sept. 1928, contains an excellent review of developments and frustrations to date over the joint council proposals. See also Department of Labour, *Annual Report, 1921*, and Supplement to *Labour Gazette*, Feb. 1921.

The department responded in 1922 by appointing one official to provide the recommended assistance, but interest appears to have waned, despite the diligent efforts of J.S. Woodsworth to induce the government to bring in a plan for the civil service. The government, through its official spokesman, James Murdock, the minister of labour, grew increasingly cool to the plan and by 1923 the old managerial complacency was being reasserted. 'There is no employee,' said Mr Murdock, 'who has not had ample opportunity to present any views or representations he may wish to make to the Minister or to the Deputy Minister.' 'I take it,' retorted Mr Woodsworth, 'that merely the fact of making representations or having the right to make representations to the governing body does not constitute carrying out the principle of industrial councils.' Murdock's blunt rejoinder was that 'Parliament is maintaining industrial control here.'[40] Two years later, when Woodsworth renewed the attack, Murdock built his wall of objections higher by adding that the civil service was regulated by an act and 'there is nothing in the law which would specifically say to them [that is, the Civil Service Commission] "you shall give civil servants an opportunity for a voice and a vote in the determination of those questions".'[41]

Undeterred by the government's use of the Civil Service Act to prove that civil servants were amply protected as employees of the state, Woodsworth persistently reintroduced his proposal for a joint council plan in the civil service. In his view, not only would government be setting a good example for private employers but the morale of the civil service itself would be vastly improved.[42] In 1927 Woodsworth sought an amendment to the act itself providing 'for the setting up of machinery for consultation between Civil Service employees and the officials of the Government.' He fortified his argument by quoting from a recent statement of the prime minister which indicated his approval of the principle of staff representa-

40 *Can. H. of C. Debates*, 1923, pp. 1654–5.
41 *Ibid.*, 1924, p. 2358 ff.
42 *Ibid.*, 1924, p. 2710. Woodsworth, quoting from a policy document of the Liberal party in 1921 that indicated support for a policy of representing labour, community, and capital, concluded: 'And if that was true of private concerns how much more important is it that the principle should be carried out in connection with our governmental institutions.' And, again in *ibid.*, 1926, p. 4491: 'since we are an employer of labour we might become a model employer ... If we take the position that the civil servants are in a somewhat different position from other employees and ought not to resort to a strike or anything of that kind, then there should be the most adequate provision for councils by which they could bring their grievances to the proper authority.' The previous year, E.R.E. Chevrier had become Woodsworth's ally on much the same grounds: 'civil servants themselves are not represented in these [salary] deliberations that concern themselves most' (*ibid.*, 1925, p. 2447).

tion on a council.[43] Woodsworth's trial balloon was shot down, but when he sent it up again in the following session it received second reading and was referred for further study to the Standing Committee on Industrial and International Relations. The committee reported favourably on the principle of the measure but argued that no legislation would be required to effect the change.[44] It further recommended that the government set up a joint drafting committee to devise a constitution for the proposed national council and that, once drafted, the constitution be confirmed by order in council.

The government quickly met the committee's proposals; Peter Heenan, then minister of labour, invited the major civil service associations to name representatives to a drafting committee, and in May 1930 the committee was formally constituted by an order in council.[45] Unfortunately, the electoral defeat of the incumbent Liberal administration forced the postponement of the drafting committee's meeting scheduled in October. However, late in 1930 and again in 1931 the Conservative Minister of Labour, Gideon Robertson, convened meetings of the committee. The promise of bipartisan support for the committee's work augured well for an early creation of a National Joint Council. But apparently action was brought to a full halt when the new minister held out for the creation of departmental joint councils prior to the formation of a national council. The breakdown in negotiations did not come to light until 1932 when a 10 per cent flat cut of civil service salaries was made. The opposition, through W.L. Mackenzie King, asked why the government had acted arbitrarily and unilaterally rather than use the machinery of joint consultation established when he was in office. R.B. Bennett, leader of the government, quite properly checked up the poor memory of his predecessor by reminding him that no such councils had been bequeathed to him: 'The matter stands just where it was left by the Honourable gentleman. He passed his Order-in-Council and stopped. The top still stands.'[46]

Thus did Mr Bennett provide a pungent epilogue for the first prolonged effort to achieve a formal arena for the collective consideration of personnel issues by representatives of employee associations and of management. The abrupt termination of negotiations that had looked so promis-

43 *Ibid.*, 1927, p. 594.   44 *Ibid.*, 1927–8, pp. 13, 362.
45 *Ibid.*, 1929, p. 3255; 1930, pp. 61, 871. See also 'That National Civil Service Council,' *Civil Service Review*, March 1931; also June 1931, where the federation opposes departmental councils in small and scattered departments but sees the Post Office as a good candidate for such a council. The Minister of Labour, Gideon Robertson, is reported in *ibid.*, Dec. 1931, as being opposed to a departmental council for the Post Office because its organization was not adequate and because (obviously the real reason) such a council was not to be viewed as an instrument for considering salaries.
46 *Can. H. of C. Debates*, 1932, pp. 810, 3425.

ing and so over-ripe for settlement was followed by a decade of virtual silence so far as the joint council plan was concerned. The Civil Service Federation raised the issue perfunctorily before four parliamentary committees that examined the civil service during the 1930s, but it is clear that its attention and the interests of other associations were confined to survival and internal organizational problems during these fretful years. Direct lobbying of the executive tended to displace reliance on the Civil Service Commission as intermediary, while much effort in the late 1930s was also devoted to making good the associations' claims to direct representation on the promotion appeals boards of the Civil Service Commission.[47]

It is not altogether clear why, after ten years of quiet burial, the joint council was suddenly exhumed and new vigour pumped into it by both management and employee associations.[48] The government's decision in 1943 to make collective bargaining compulsory in defined circumstances for employees in the private sector may well have forced attention to the lack of joint consultation for the government's own work force. Possibly the prime precipitating factor was the associations' reactions to the creation of the Coon committee, which had been set up on 23 January 1943 by order in council to report to the Treasury Board on problems of administering personnel, with particular reference to salary issues created by wartime *ad hoc* regulations. While the associations were invited to appear before the committee the government rejected their claim for direct representation on it. After learning of the cabinet's rejection of their claim, the associations were induced to re-examine the rather meagre results of their efforts to date to secure representation on other bodies; the best they had been able to achieve was representation on the board for regulating the civil service hostel and the committee on luncheon facilities. Thus, they were left in their traditional posture of having their views heard, patiently awaiting the decision of Treasury Board through a press release, and then seeking further interviews with the board to re-open their case – and then to be told that the Coon committee report would not be published (which meant that the associations would have no idea how far Treasury Board decisions had departed from the committee report).[49]

47 Judging from a careful scanning of the *Civil Service Review* during the 1930s.
48 After 1932 the next significant reference in the Federation's journal to the joint council plan does not occur until December 1943 when C.W. Rump's 'The Establishment of National Civil Service Council' appeared.
49 See *Civil Service Review*, March 1943. Mr King's reply after the cabinet decision was taken was to the effect that the government was agreed on the desirability of representation but the distinction between government as employer and other employers 'is that representatives appointed by the government to act on its behalf as an employer are in most cases themselves civil servants.'

Clearly this unilateral form of decision-making could not continue to be accepted by the associations, and even from management's point of view the inevitable aftermath of such procedures was a flood of petitions, visitations, and endless dissatisfaction.[50]

The experience with the Coon committee could readily be seen as a prelude to what would inevitably be a series of battles to readjust a war-swollen service in a not unexpected state of disorganized shock. In the event, at its annual fall conference of 1943, the Civil Service Federation resurrected the National Joint Council plan which it had strongly supported in the previous decade. The cabinet also reacted by creating its own subcommittee in November 1943 to deal with the four major civil service organizations on personnel and salary issues and to consider anew the national council plan.[51] On 24 February 1944 J.L. Ilsley, the minister of finance, was able to announce to the House of Commons that the National Joint Council was at long last about to be launched.[52] By order in council PC 3676, 16 May 1944, a tentative constitution for the National Joint Council of the Public Service of Canada was framed and on 8 March of the following year a permanent constitution developed by the representatives of both sides was enshrined as well in a Treasury Board minute.

Both in purpose and structure the National Joint Council followed closely the model of the National Whitley Council for the British civil service. Designed 'to secure a greater measure of co-operation between the State in its capacity as employer and the general body of civil servants,' the council was 'to provide machinery for dealing with grievances; and generally to bring together the experience, and different points of view of representatives of the administrative, technical, clerical and manipulative branches of the Civil Service.' Management, represented by the 'official side,' was given nine members on the council of the rank of deputy or assistant deputy minister, named by the Governor in Council. The employees were represented on the 'staff side' by ten (subsequently twelve) specified associations, each of which named its own member to the council. The chairman of the council was to be separately appointed by the Governor in Council and was specified as a member on the official side; the vice-chairman was selected by the staff side representatives.

Reflecting the division of managerial responsibility, the council was directed to make its recommendations 'to the Governor General in Council, the Treasury Board and/or the Civil Service Commission.' No rec-

50 As witness successive issues of *Civil Service Review*, June and Dec. 1943.
51 *Ibid.*, Dec. 1943.
52 *Can. H. of C. Debates*, 1944, pp. 778–9.

ommendation could go forward unless it had the endorsement of both sides and 'only statements issued under the authority of the National Joint Council shall be published.' The matters on which the council could deliberate and offer recommendations covered a wide range, extending from general principles governing conditions of employment (for example, 'recruitment, training, hours of work, promotion, discipline, tenure, regular and over-time remuneration, welfare and seniority') to employee suggestion plans, office procedure, other appeal machinery, encouragement of further education and training, and so on.

In the somewhat eulogistic pamphlet issued to commemorate the tenth anniversary of the council in 1954 it is clear that in the seventy-five regular and special meetings held during the decade the council did in fact make recommendations on both minor and general issues relating to every area of their terms of reference.[53] However, with respect to one of its assignments, the consideration of 'the advisability of providing for the establishment of various departmental and regional Joint Councils,' the national council appears to have taken little initiative. As the Whitley Council plan has evolved in Britain, the departmental councils have come to play an increasingly important role and the national body has reached the point where it never meets as a whole but only in its various committees. In the light of this development in a system which had been the model for Canada it is difficult to explain why departmental councils failed to proliferate and, in the one or two departments and agencies where they did emerge, seemed to have attracted little interest. This failure to extend the joint council plan to the departments is surprising because their potential value for handling internal grievances, in a system notoriously deficient in such machinery, seems self-evident. The constraint may have been imposed by the reluctance of a highly centralized management apparatus to devolve to the departmental level and by the inability of a thinly staffed group of associations to cope with more than this centralized group of managerial agencies.

Now that the legislation of 1967 has moved well beyond the philosophy of joint discussion and negotiation enshrined in the national joint council plan to the activist role envisaged in outright collective bargaining, the future role of the National Joint Council has had to be reassessed. The need for joint consultation on matters that concern and affect employers in *all* bargaining units and that are not readily dealt with in individual

53 *The National Joint Council of the Public Service of Canada, 1944–1954* (Ottawa, 1954). C.W. Rump carries the factual story another ten years along in his article on the National Joint Council, 1944–63, prepared for the *Civil Service Review*, March 1963, pp. 41–7.

collective agreements may well be met by a modified National Joint Council.[54]

It is possible to point to many positive achievements of the council: it obviously filled a serious gap in communication between employees and management, improved relations, and boosted employee morale. Nevertheless, the council did not supplant the traditional routes of direct action previously used by civil service associations nor did it supervene in those areas where the Civil Service Commission had developed appellate procedures in which representatives of staff associations played the role of attorney and (paradoxically) of judge in cases involving their 'clients.'

In retrospect we can see that the machinery created in 1944 was the result of a belated decision which if taken, as appeared likely, in the late twenties would have been viewed as a magnanimous liberal reform. But, fifteen years later the climate of opinion within organized labour had shifted to sponsor more radical measures and the joint council plan soon came to be viewed as a reflection of old-fashioned 'enlightened' managerial benevolence. Even officials of the associations, who were almost all seconded civil servants retaining their pension rights, could not evade the suspicion that they were working as 'kept' men in company unions. Indeed, their participation on the national council, given its peculiar *modus operandi*, tended to create problems in preserving the confidence of their members in them and in the contributions of their associations.

This problem – perhaps the most critical for the staff side – arose from the confidential character of all discussions within the council and, more important, the constitutional requirement to publish only those decisions which were unanimous. In obeying these procedural requirements neither the staff side as a whole nor individual associations were in a position to take credit for the published collective recommendation. Even more serious, if there was disagreement and consequently no decision the requirement of secrecy prevented the associations' representatives from reporting back to their members. Under the circumstances, the representatives were put in an awkward position with respect to preserving the loyalty of their members; the associations' contributions were buried so that members remained uneasy about the persuasiveness of their representatives and generally apathetic to the work of the council as a whole.

In addition to this major problem the council was weakened by other

54 On 29 April 1966 the council remitted to a committee the question of its changing role. A report was presented in May 1966 suggesting minor modifications and including a proposal to have the council report to bodies other than the Treasury Board, Governor in Council, and Civil Service Commission because of the imminent prospect of new bodies emerging to deal with staff problems.

procedural difficulties. It was not surprising that the official side tended to be passive, leaving the initiative to the staff side in raising items for the agenda. To assume this initiative, the staff side needed access to full information as well as adequate research staff; during the heyday of the joint council it was by no means certain that either of these requirements was met (although the deficiency of research resources has been so thoroughly rectified that the Public Service Alliance now is reputed to have a larger professional research staff than any other union in Canada). Even if ideal conditions had prevailed, the initiatives taken by the staff side tended to come up *seriatim* and were fed into the consultative machinery in a disjointed fashion, leading to individual, unconnected recommendations. Obviously, no 'package deal' was possible, comparable to that which can be achieved through collective bargaining where the separate elements can be harmonized.[55]

Given the defects of piecemeal negotiation and the lack of provision for resolving a disagreement – where all reported decisions had to be unanimous – the growing demand for outright collective bargaining which emerged in the mid-fifties can be understood. Thus, while the belated inauguration of joint negotiating procedures through the national council met an immediate need, it failed to placate a more militant movement among the associations led by the postal unions. The stage was thereby set for the final decade of agitation which culminated in the Public Service Staff Relations Act of 1967.

Pressure from the staff associations to develop full-scale collective bargaining procedures appeared rather late in the day but then gathered strength very rapidly.[56] As late as 1948, when the Industrial Relations and Disputes Investigation Act was passed, civil servants were excluded

55 An excellent critique of the joint council procedures is to be found in Victor Johnston, 'The Effectiveness of Staff Associations in Employer-Employee Relations in the Public Service of Canada,' a paper presented 30 March 1955 to the Industrial Relations Study Group, Ottawa Chapter, Canadian Political Science Association. See also 'Negotiating Procedures in the Public Service of Canada,' 3 May 1955, prepared for Civil Service Association of Ottawa, mimeo. See also S.J. Frankel, 'Staff Relations in the Canadian Federal Public Service: Experience with Joint Consultation,' *Canadian Journal of Economics and Political Science* 22 (Nov. 1956), pp. 509–22.
56 For a quick review of the background and detailed discussion of developments emerging from the report of the preparatory committee, see O.P. Dwivedi, 'Recent Developments in Staff Relationships in the Public Service of Canada,' *Public Administration* (Sydney) 24 (Dec. 1965), pp. 359–67. In 1957 the Professional Institute was actively canvassing the issue of collective bargaining for its members and elected to await the outcome of the proposals for staff negotiation that were to be advanced in the Civil Service Commission's report on personnel administration in 1958. See *Professional Public Service* 36 (Oct. 1957).

from its provisions and apparently expressed no desire to be included. The provisions of the act were extended to a limited number of public corporations but it was not until the mid-fifties that the associations began to take up the issue. By the time that the Civil Service Act was brought forward in 1960 for its first major revision in over forty years, the associations were well prepared with their case. However, they were left totally dissatisfied with the formulation ultimately approved, after bitter debate, in the revised bill which became law on 29 September 1961.[57] In section 7 ('Consultation with Staff Organizations'), which was the main bone of contention, there were the following modest provisions: (1) the Minister of Finance or such members of the public service as he may designate shall from time to time consult with representatives of appropriate organizations and associations of employees with respect to remuneration, at the request of such representatives or whenever in the opinion of the Minister of Finance such consultation is necessary or desirable; (2) the Civil Service Commission and such members of the public service as the Minister of Finance may designate shall from time to time consult with representatives of appropriate organizations with respect to terms and conditions of employment over which the commission is empowered to propose regulations for approval of the Governor in Council; (3) again, the commission shall consult with respect to terms and conditions over which it has exclusive jurisdiction.

There was little new in these provisions apart from a formal statutory acknowledgment of a right of access that had long been exercised, however sporadically, in practice. The Civil Service Federation responded by circulating to all party leaders prior to the spring general election of 1963 a request for their views on collective bargaining rights for civil servants. All responded favourably, and when the Liberal party succeeded to office the new cabinet appointed the Preparatory Committee on Collective Bargaining in the Public Service. It was chaired by A.D. Heeney who had also headed the committee which produced the report of 1958 that had been a prelude to the revision of the Civil Service Act of 1961.

The committee took two years to prepare its report, consulting fully with organized labour as well as various staff associations during the course of its study. With one or two major changes, the draft proposals of the committee were confirmed in the Public Service Staff Relations Act which, along with a new Public Service Employment Act and a revised Financial Administration Act, came into force in 1967. For public servants, the Public Service Staff Relations Act of 1967 provided a fitting

57 Stats Can. 1961, c.57. See Special Committee on the Civil Service Act, *Minutes of Proceedings and Evidence* (Ottawa, 1961).

centennial achievement, marking the culmination of a long up-hill struggle to attain the most effective methods of permitting them to face an historically authoritarian management team on a more realistic, egalitarian footing.

Not only did the new measure constitute a charter of industrial rights for organized public servants, it also brought about a revolutionary transformation of the old classification system inaugurated after the First World War. As the Heeney committee of 1963 discovered, the necessary prelude to collective bargaining was the establishment of bargaining units, and for this purpose the detailed job classification plan was singularly inappropriate. Accordingly, the committee recommended six major occupational categories subdivided into sixty-seven occupational groups which were to provide the new bases for bargaining units. By the same token, the major civil service associations which, as we have observed, had been plagued by the complexities of the old classification plan, now found it possible to achieve the alliance which had been unsuccessfully promoted for many years. The new alliance should make possible the development as bargaining agents not only the existing separate associations but also (as the act envisages) 'councils' of employee organizations.[58] Recognition of the councils as bargaining agents should reduce the problem of organizational adjustment for various associations with independent historical roots now confronting a comprehensive and much simplified classification plan.

In the long section (Part II) of the act which spells out collective bargaining procedures, three general restrictive features are worth noting. First, in order to preserve a clear line between management and employees, some civil servants have had to be deprived of the right to belong to an association and thereby are excluded from collective agreements. Section 8 (1) states: 'no person who is employed in a managerial or confidential capacity, whether or not he is acting on behalf of the employer, shall participate in or interfere with the formation or administration of an employee organization or the representation of employees by such an organization.' The meaning to be attached to the phrase 'managerial or confidential capacity' is developed in the 'Interpretation' section (u) and includes not only deputy heads of departments and legal officers in the Department of Justice but also a 'person who has executive duties and responsibilities in relation to the development and administration of governmental programmes,' a personnel administrator, or any officer whose duties involve him in the process of collective bargaining or grievances on behalf of the employer and others to be specified by the new Public Ser-

58 Stats Can. 1966–7, c.72, ss. 28 and 29.

vice Staff Relations Board. The preservation of the line dividing management and employees is essential but offers a wide range of discretionary judgment to the board.

The second restrictive feature is found in section 39(2): the board shall not certify as bargaining agent for a bargaining unit any employee organization that receives, handles, or pays in its own name or requires as a condition of membership the payment by any of its members of any money for activities carried on, by, or on behalf of any political party. This prohibition is apparently directed to civil service associations that might affiliate with an outside trade union which in turn has a policy of making contributions to a party. In this respect the legislation is more restrictive than the new provisions in the Public Service Act which, as previously noted, no longer defines *individual* contributions to parties as an act of political partisanship.

The third and most important restriction applies to the collective agreement itself and is double-barrelled. Obviously there has to be a saving clause to preserve the sovereign right of parliament to control the purse strings: thus, section 56 (1) states that the terms of a collective agreement shall, subject to the appropriation by or under authority of parliament of any moneys that may be required by the employer therefore, be implemented by the parties. This conditional clause is obvious and is not likely to be a great impediment to fair bargaining. However, section 56 (2) adds a further substantive restriction: no collective agreement can result in the alteration or elimination of any existing term or condition of employment or the establishment of any new term or condition of employment which would require the enactment or amendment of any legislation by parliament (except for money bills as under section 56(1) above) or any conditions laid down in four specified acts – the Government Employees Compensation Act, Government Vessels Discipline Act, Public Service Employment Act, and the Public Service Superannuation Act. In the absence of concrete evidence one can only speculate that these rather extensive prohibitions may constitute a serious impediment to collective bargaining. On the surface they may be a source of future friction, unless possible difficulties can be overcome by broad authority conferred on the Treasury Board by the revised Financial Administration Act (1967) to deal with conditions of employment or anything required to improve personnel management in the public service.[59]

59 *Ibid.*, c.74, s.1. There is clear indication from the representatives of the staff associations that the exclusion from collective bargaining of matters that fall under the merit system (and hence under the Public Service Commission) is regarded as a major defect; see, for example, Navin Parekh, 'Collective Bargaining Legislation in the Federal Public Service,' *Civil Service Review* 44 (June 1971), pp. 4, 6, 28.

Part III of the act details 'the provisions applicable to resolution of disputes' arising out of the collective bargaining procedures or from interpretation of the agreements themselves. Here, the government faced divided opinions among the staff associations. Most were content with the formulation provided by the preparatory committee, namely, a provision for compulsory arbitration. But the postal unions, perennially the more radical in their approach, were insistent on the alternative method which entailed preliminary conciliation procedures backed by the right to strike should conciliation result in deadlock. The legislation moved beyond the preparatory committee's draft by offering the bargaining agent a choice of arbitration or of conciliation together with the strike.

Again it is important to single out the restrictive conditions imposed on these alternative approaches to resolving disputes. In the case of arbitration an award may deal 'with rates of pay, hours of work, leave entitlements, standards of discipline and other terms and conditions of employment directly related thereto.' But, as with collective bargaining itself, 'no arbitral award can require or have the effect of requiring the enactment or amendment of any legislation by Parliament' and no award 'shall deal with the standards, procedures or processes governing the appointment, appraisal, promotion, demotion, transfer, lay-off or release of employees' (section 70, subsections i, ii, iii). This array of personnel procedures presumably remains where it always has, in the custody and under the protection of the Public Service Commission. Within these restrictions an arbitral award is binding on the employer and the bargaining agent (section 72[1]) and, 'subject to the appropriation by or under the authority of Parliament of any moneys that may be required by the employer' is to be implemented within ninety days of the award (section 74). This clause goes further than the preparatory committee was prepared to go, for it eliminates the committee's proposal to give the cabinet the power to set aside an arbitral award in what it might decide to be abnormal circumstances.

Where conciliation has been chosen as the preferred optional method of settling a dispute, the restrictions on what can be reported on are exactly the same as those outlned for arbitration (section 86, subsections i, ii, iii) but in recognition of the accompanying right to resort to the strike as the ultimate mode of settlement, a special restrictive clause was inserted (section 79). Before a conciliation board is established the Public Service Staff Relations Board must be satisfied that certain so-called 'designated employees' in the bargaining unit have been identified. These are employees 'whose duties consist in whole or in part of duties the performance of which at any particular time or after any specified period of time is or will be necessary in the interest of the safety or security of the public.' Thus, if conciliation proves unsuccessful and a strike is legitimately the next step, services essential to the safety and security of the public will presumably continue to be performed.

It is difficult to visualize how meaningful this compromise clause will be. If we take the case of postal workers who have opted for the conciliation-cum-strike route, it is hard to imagine the board identifying 'designated employees' whose services are essential to the safety and security of the public, although after a 'specified period of time' they might become so – then it is too late for the board to insist on designating such employees. In these circumstances, one is presumably forced back to the procedure adopted occasionally in the past, that is, summoning parliament to deal with the issue outside the complex framework which the new act has so carefully designed.

Completing the charter of rights for organized civil servants is the section of the act dealing with grievances to which reference has been made in the previous part of this chapter. Attention was there directed to one potential area of overlapping and confusion: the possibility of placing an employee, so to speak, in double jeopardy, under both the appellate board created by the Public Service Commission or an adjudicator set up under the Public Service Staff Relations Act. No additional commentary on grievance procedures is called for here.

As may be surmised, the range of matters brought within this large and complex statute calls for an elaborate administrative apparatus. Perhaps it is a reflection on the past neglect of this whole area by the long-standing management groups that none of them was selected to deal with any of these issues. Rather, a whole new array of agencies had to be created, deliberately divorced from the Treasury Board as the now clearly identified representative of the employer, and also distinct from the new Public Service Commission which might have been regarded as the logical repository for such duties in view of its historical independence and its quasi-judicial role in hearing appeals. Given the new orientation of the Public Service Commission, with the stress on its servicing and auditing roles, it was probably wise to make a clean break and start with a new apparatus that could not, in any event, have been very conveniently absorbed in the commission. In fact, the only existing entity that had to be transferred from the commission to the new PSSRB was the Pay Research Bureau.

The new board is constituted like other regulatory agencies vested with judicial and discretionary powers. Its chairman and its vice-chairman are appointed by the Governor in Council to hold office during good behaviour for a period not exceeding ten years and can be removed only on joint address of the Senate and House of Commons (a provision comparable to that for the judiciary). The other four to eight members are appointed by the Governor in Council for periods up to seven years but may be removed 'for cause' by the same authority. In its administration of the act the board is given wide powers to make regulations and to issue orders requiring compliance with the act or the regulations. Where compliance is not secured the board reports the situation to parliament, although nothing is said about how parliament is to dispose of the issue once it has been placed before it (see sections 20 and 21).

For arbitration cases there is a Public Service Arbitration Tribunal consisting of a chairman appointed, on recommendation of the chairman of the PSSRB, by the Governor in Council and two panels of three persons each, appointed by the PSSRB, representing the employers and employees. A tribunal comprises the chairman or an associate chairman and one representative from each of the two panels. Decisions are by majority vote but the chairman has the deciding vote; reports are sent to the chairman of the PSSRB and the respective parties to the dispute.

For conciliation cases, the chairman of the PSSRB is authorized to establish boards if they 'serve the purpose of assisting the parties in reaching agreement' – though he has the power, if he does not consider conciliation will further agreement, to refuse to establish a board (section 78). The parties to the dispute each nominate one person to the board who in turn choose a third person as chairman. The chairman of the PSSRB makes any one of these appointments if either or both parties fail to provide candidates. The report of the conciliation board goes to the chairman who distributes copies to both parties and 'may publish in such manner as he sees fit' (section 87).

For the final stage of grievance hearings there is provision for appointment of adjudicators. Adjudicators are appointed by the Governor in Council on recommendation of the PSSRB, one of them being designated chief adjudicator. Where the grievance is one arising out of a collective agreement which names the adjudicator, the chief adjudicator refers the matter to him. When a board is requested the chief adjudicator names the chairman and appoints two members named by each of the respective parties. In practice, it has been customary to rely not on a board but on a single adjudicator named in the collective agreement or by the chief adjudicator. Decisions of an adjudicator or a board of adjudicators, like every order, award, direction, decision, declaration, or ruling of the board or the arbitration tribunal, are 'final and shall not be questioned in any court' (section 100).

This extended analysis of the legislation of 1967 is warranted by the scope and significance of a measure which marks a fitting climax to a century of agitation for improved employer-employee relations in the public service. Civil servants have now won a clear and more liberal statement of their political rights, although these, as has been said, are more symbolic of an improved status as citizens than of direct benefit to them in the struggle to achieve a voice in managerial decisions. To this end the belated development of joint negotiating machinery in the 1940s and its slow but inexorable extension in the measure of 1967 to collective bargaining, arbitration, conciliation, and a modified right to strike, represent the real shift in management attitudes and employee rights.

For management, in the short run, the test will be whether it can divorce itself from the old shibboleths of the sovereign employer and the authoritarian unilateralism of the past. For employee organizations the test will be whether they can stand on their own feet, no longer relying on a Civil Service Commission to intercede for them but compelled to fight their own battles within a new, complex, highly judicialized machinery. It is one thing to be given one's independence and rights but it is always an open question whether the recipients geared to an older and more hostile order will mature overnight in the responsible exercise of these rights. In any event, the experiment cannot be postponed, and only time and experience will prove the capacity of employees to make their positive contribution to 'the new management' of the public service. In exercising the new rights conferred by the wholesale application of collective bargaining to the public service the temptation will be great for employees to strengthen their position by moving to a single monolithic union – possibly on the pattern of an expanded Public Service Alliance. If this is indeed the likely response on the employees' side, then one could anticipate counter-organization by management to consolidate its forces at the centre – presumably in the Treasury Board. The extent to which these centralizing pressures may frustrate all the recent efforts to implement the devolution of managerial functions must remain at this stage a hypothetical cloud, but one that may become the real and present danger for the public service of tomorrow.

CHAPTER FIFTEEN

Conclusion

There is a paradox in the fact that the administrative branch of government is by far the largest of our public and private institutions and yet, even to the informed members of the general public, it is the least visible. The arcanum in which the civil service resides is attributable in part to the traditional protection of its public flank provided by ministers and cabinet and in part to its own structural complexity in which even the participants, let alone the outside observers, can rapidly become bemused or lost. Perhaps there was a time when it was possible to see the public service whole and to see it clear; but, as the foregoing pages of this study reveal, such an attempt today is an ambitious undertaking for which the venturer may at best expect an 'A' for effort. And yet, it would be unwise to accept defeat, leaving the public service as a source of mystification to grow and proliferate in accord with some internal law of momentum of its own making. It is far too important to the lives and livelihood of all citizens to be abandoned by students or written off by the popular press in a few clichés that only enlarge public misunderstandings.

This study was undertaken as a rescue operation, to revivify interest and to encourage others to join the expedition into the virtually uncharted terrain of the public service. It is admittedly only a beginning and as such has been confined to an historical-analytical survey, mapping the profile and physiology of the public service. Employing the physiological metaphor, Part One has attempted to set the public service in the broadest possible environmental context in order to observe how the organism has adapted to the peculiar features of Canada's physical, economic, technological, and cultural setting. From this broad perspective the focus is narrowed to include only the essential features of the political system that have had the most influence in shaping the public service as an interacting subsystem. And, finally, we explore the impact of law as a germinal and containing force for organizations and the powers they wield.

Parts Two and Three concentrate on design or anatomy. Organizational design is (or should be) a reflection of functions, and functions in this study have been divided broadly into those relating to the substantive operating programmes of the public service and those relating to the management of the public service. Dissection of the organizational anatomy has been undertaken in stages, from the gross subdivisions to which the major functions have been assigned to the more refined organs which have been created to handle the detailed division of labour. What has been divided and subdivided for practical operating purposes must somehow be kept in phase and in unison; hence the need for the co-ordinating, controlling, and supervisory structures, at the supradepartmental and departmental levels, whose roles and interrelationships are examined in Part Three.

The durable reader who has persisted through the foregoing pages should emerge with a profile of the structural elements of the Canadian public service and a reasonably clear impression of how environmental influences have helped to shape its salient features to form a unique administrative culture. What is notably missing is the human dimension: the powerful play of personalities in ubiquitous committees; the personal whirlpools of power and influence; the day-to-day drain on the psyche from living in a pyramided beehive; the struggle to achieve status, a self-respecting career, the recognition of one's peers in a formal hierarchy wedded to anonymity; the blunting of initiative and the tamping down of ambition that comes when a project is thwarted or disappears up the line into silence; the imbalance of a highly formalized system of work distribution that leaves a few at the top with too much to do while many are never afforded the chance to realize their full potential. But all this (and much more) would require another study for which the skills of the sociologist, the psychologist, the pathologist, and perhaps even the psychiatrist would be indispensable. The most illuminating studies of this genre have thus far been produced by novelists who, as in the case of C.P. Snow, possess the unusual combination of bureaucratic experience and literary imagination.

Acknowledging the existence of other dimensions left unprobed by this study, we may nevertheless extract from this more mundane analysis certain trends in structural design and hazard some hypotheses concerning their broader implications for the liberal democratic state.

Liberal democratic institutions have evolved slowly and painfully over the last century, responding to the forces of change largely at the same pace and in step with the communities they were authorized to serve. Representative institutions, competing parties, free elections, and independent media of information and education could see to it that public policy would so respond to society's expectations and demands that a sufficiently equitable balance could be achieved, thereby leaving few genuine dissidents for whom the community had no meaning. When disequilibrium developed it was not because our domestic institutions were faulty but because external pressures on our political system, particularly those promoted by other states professing alien philosophies of government, disrupted the even tenor of our ways.

Today, these optimistic (and, some would add, complacent) assumptions of the liberal democrat are everywhere under attack; but now the attack is largely launched from within. The critics see a mounting array of social, economic, and ecological issues crowding the public agenda, the solutions to which require more rapid response than can be expected from the piecemeal, time-consuming procedures of the liberal's consensual politics. In their view these problems threaten to overrun us, making human existence more precarious than in Hobbes' state of nature (nasty, brutish, and short). The polarized responses of the critics are either to invoke a neo-anarchistic individualism under the slogan of doing one's own thing (while yet there is time and while living off the surplus of the Affluent Society they profess to despise); or, to mount an all-out attack on existing social institutions – educational, economic, and governmental – on the grounds that they are all mindlessly and self-interestedly conniving in a gigantic conspiracy to deprive each human being of his birthrights to pure air and water, unpolluted cities, green and fruitful countrysides, and a self-respecting standard of living, including a meaningful liberating education.

In considering how those responsible for the fabric of our social institutions react to the mounting tide of increasingly articulate criticism, the response of the dissident drop-outs is not nearly so relevant as the response of the anxious, impatient activists. News travels fast in the electronic age of the global village. Although the media do not excel in sifting fact from fiction, the general public are content to rest their case on the old adage that where there's smoke (and the media see to it that there is lots of that!) there must be fire – and the cry goes out for the fire brigade. When the brigade responds sluggishly or even fails to show while we argue over whose brigade should be sent, impatience is inflamed or we are swept into deflated apathy, enveloped in a sense of helplessness.

Those who paint this morbid but not unrealistic picture of contemporary society are not convinced that our conventional liberal democratic institutions are capable of coping with the public agenda and are tending to despair of achieving the transformations that would make the institutions more effective. This study has concentrated on only one of these institutions but it is the one which in the public mind has usually been considered to be the most set in its ways, the least adaptable to the shifting demands of a society in change. Yet, in retrospect and in comparison, the public service more than any other institution has shown itself to be the barometer of societal pressures and the innovator of structural and procedural devices for meeting these changing demands. Organized interest groups, political parties, legislatures, and courts have, in comparison, undergone surprisingly slight transformations both with respect to their conception of purposes and the organization and procedures for implementing them. Sheer numerical growth in the public service, which has far exceeded that of any other institution, is but one piece of evidence bolstering the claim for its greater adaptability; another is the shift in the balance of power among institutions – for bureaucracy abhors a power vacuum, and many of the discretionary powers it now wields have been acquired by default from other institutions that have not proved as capable of adapting their structures and procedures to the specific requirements of the decision or action contemplated. Hence, the aggrandizement of the powers of the public service may be viewed as a reflection of the superior ability of this institution to make the adaptations or develop the innovations which have led to the bypassing of other public institutions, like parties, parliaments, or courts.

For present purposes it is not necessary to debate the question whether the public service has had this role thrust upon it or has assumed the role by dint of bureaucratic self-aggrandizement. Was it pushed or did it jump? We can disengage ourselves from this provocative query by simply asserting that a good deal of both has occurred. What is more pertinent to ask is whether the pressures placed on the public service, as the front-line, adaptative, and innovative public institution, may not be overtaxing its structures and diverting it from a single-minded pursuit of its operational goals? There may well be a limit to the innovative and adaptive ingenuity of the organization's members; there may also be a limit to the members' tolerance level when called upon to live in a perpetual state of organizational unease and fluidity. But, even if neither of these limits has been reached, there can be no doubt that the diversion of thought and energy to structural and procedural issues seriously impairs the capacity of the institution to accomplish its assigned objectives.

It is not irrelevant to observe that Canadian universities (the only other social institutions displaying a comparable concern for adapting structures to contemporary change) are confronted by precisely the same consequences stemming from intensive, introverted concern for self-improvement. In the universities there is also organizational uneasiness; the tolerance level (particularly of their permanent members) has been strained close to the breaking point with a consequent impairment of morale; structural reforms are seen to have their limits established by historical rigidities grounded in the 'departmentation' of knowledge; and, above all, learning, teaching, and research have undoubtedly suffered from the contemporary involvement in the 'how' rather than the 'what' of university government.

Of course, for all those concerned for the future of the universities the sustaining faith is found in the expectation that all this upheaval is temporary, that once new structures and procedural reforms are established things will settle down to permit each member to get on with his rightful business. Whether or not there are grounds for such optimism will very much depend on the stability of purposes imputed to the university. If structures and procedures are reflections of purposes, it follows that, once purposes of the university can be established that are widely accepted by the community at large as well as by the members of the institution, organizational uneasiness and tensions among the members should be alleviated.

For the public service there is less certainty about the prospects of attaining organizational equilibrium because the public agenda that reflects its purposes continues to lengthen and to become more fluid in response to the accelerated and variable tempo of mass demands on the state. As a result the public service cannot count on any surcease in its organizational uneasiness or in its intense preoccupation with managerial 'how to' techniques.

It is true that in a not insubstantial way the public service exercises a degree of influence over the content and the ordering of the items placed on the public agenda – and to a greater degree determines the timing for inclusion on the agenda. The liberal democratic convention is that political parties, legislatures, and responsible political executives are responsible for formulating the public agenda; but, as has been frequently observed throughout this study, the bureaucracy makes its own vigorous 'inputs' to the agenda. To the extent that this influence is present we might anticipate that it would have a conservative and stabilizing effect on the public agenda which in turn would be a constraint on the organizational uneasiness of the public service.

This conclusion should, however, be countered by another consideration. Accepting the fact that the bureaucracy plays an important role in
influencing the contents of the agenda it is important that it be as sensitive
to environmenal demands as are parties, legislatures, and political executives. We have no detailed studies of this phenomenon of bureaucratic
'exchange' with the environment or of what the military would call its
'intelligence services'; but the visible evidence points to an increase in the
direct exchanges between the public service and its clients (whether the
clients are receiving services or being regulated) that supplants or supplements the conventional, indirect methods of routing demands through
the more visible, representative institutions. In some fields, such as area
and community development, the bureaucracy frequently initiates the organization of its anticipated clientele, both to establish a stable communication linkage and to build an articulate interest group that will bolster
the agency's competitive position in the bureaucracy. This is an innovation
that sees the role of the civil servant changing from the neutral 'reacting'
official to a positive initiator with an 'out-reach' mission. While this role
is as yet far from the norm, the nature of many programmes now being
mounted by the liberal democratic state suggests that it will become much
more common. This being so, we could conclude that the public service
will become an increasingly vigorous sponsor (in the name of its clients)
for items to be included on the public agenda. The consequent expansion
of items and the competitive jostling for high priority positions on the
agenda will perpetuate in exaggerated form the currently heavy pressure
to make organizational and procedural adjustments in the public service.

These shifts in emphasis and priority are nowhere more clearly evident
than at the top level of the public service where the initial allocation of
functions to departments takes place. As the material in Part Two indicates, the last half dozen years of the sixties have witnessed more juggling
with portfolios than has occurred in the previous century. In the early
years after Confederation there were more departments than the limited
public agenda of the period required; accordingly, for a time as the agenda
grew, existing departments could easily absorb the added duties. When
'spill-overs' began to develop new portfolios were added but only to the
extent of a modest doubling of their original number. Since the notion of
a British ministry with a selected group making up a smaller cabinet was
rejected a practical limit to the number of ministerial portfolios was soon
established. There then remained no other option but to move outside the
departmental form to establish 'quasi-departments,' statutory executives,
public corporations, crown companies, and numerous commissions. The
resultant organizational mix may be a testimony to our inventive (and

imitative) genius but it is also a reflection of our *ad hoc* response to the increasingly crowded public agenda.

It is probable that no new forms of structure – departmental or non-departmental – remain to be exploited. Thus, unless we re-examine our present method of departmentation, we shall probably have to continue multiplying the non-departmental entities to meet the expansion of programmes on the public agenda. The problem of preserving a cabinet of workable size could be solved by adopting the British system, where a large number of departments can still be accommodated in a ministry with a selected group of these given cabinet status. In the past the barrier to such a move in Canada has been the political necessity of preserving a cabinet representing the major components of a federation: to ensure that all regional, ethnic, economic, and political interests had a voice, all ministerial portfolios had to be given cabinet rank. Moreover, the reluctance to confer discretion on an individual minister, coupled with the corresponding desire to preserve collegial decision-making in the cabinet (the Governor in Council), has further entrenched this practice. Even though these considerations are still weighty, practical exigencies may leave us no choice but to move in the direction of the British model. Currently (as of 1972), the 'ministry,' including parliamentary secretaries, numbers nearly sixty and the cabinet itself contains approximately half that number.

However, the problem to be met is now not merely that of coping with a growing number of organizations within the constraints of a cabinet kept to workable size; the real problem is to be discerned in the juggling of departmental portfolios that has been especially endemic since the mid-sixties. Implicit in these rapid and repeated reallocations is the recognition that the items now claiming high priority on the public agenda (such as poverty, pollution, consumer protection, regional, urban, or community development) require knowledge for policies and skills for operation and implementation that have to be combined and then recombined in a variety of patterns which constantly requires the assembly and reassembly of contemporary departmental containers.

Thus, while a measure such as the Organization Act of 1966 may make global readjustments and reassignments that may accurately reflect the state of the public agenda for that year, soon new items and shifting priorities will require further changes in programme assignments (as, indeed, was shown by subsequent global reorganization acts for 1969 and 1971). The vision of perpetual organizational fluidity conjured up by this prognosis will confuse the bureaucracy's relations with its publics and seriously undermine the civil servant's *esprit de corps* deriving from a reasonably stable identification with his department. Thus, we confront a task of preparing an organizational design for decision-making such that it can be accommodated to both a lengthening and a varying public agenda without those undue disruptions of structure which bemuse the client public and the guardian legislature and which alienate the loyalties of civil servants.

Diagnosis of a problem is often said to provide its own cure. In this case the diagnosis is sufficiently speculative and the physiology of the patient so complex that no such self-evident prescription for cure suggests itself. Nevertheless, there are scattered and as yet unrelated developments and proposals afoot that may help us to discern the general prescription we should be seeking. Some of these straws in the wind have already been noted: the strengthening of policy ('staff') arms at the centre and in the departments; the adoption of programme budgeting; the restructuring of the Department of Transport to make it a looser consortium of regulatory, operating and corporate entities or the proposed combination of agencies responsible for Canada's affairs abroad, under the aegis of the Department of External Affairs. To these developments, one should add the recent provision for ministers of state; certain recommendations of the Royal Commission on Bilingualism and Biculturalism; the concepts of regional administration that overlie and permeate many organizational adjustments now being undertaken by both dominion and provincial jurisdictions; and the proposals for constitutional reform, such as the arrangements for mutual devolution between the provinces and the federal government found in the so-called Fulton–Favreau formula.

What makes it reasonable to group these several developments together is their common concern with the perennial dichotomy between centralization and decentralization in a federal state. The relevant issue is not whether one or other line of departure leads to greater or less centralization. The essential issue is whether, whatever lines are being pursued, they are leading to a common acceptance of those functions that are best centralized and those that are best decentralized. We have long grasped the theoretical answer to this question: decisions affecting policy and coordination should be made at the centre; decisions relating to implementation (operations) are best left to the organization manning the front line close to the clients or area served. Obviously, the distinction is not always easy to make and we have been living for a century with structural rigidities that have made it difficult to adjust our organizations to more nearly reflect the distinction.

One of these rigidities is the legally compartmentalized assignment of programme areas to the dominion and provinces which is found in the British North America Act (especially but not exclusively in sections 91 and 92) and dutifully upheld by the courts. The Fulton–Favreau formula in part attempts to formulate a legally acceptable way of importing a needed flexibility into these containers by its proposals for two-way devolution of programmes.

The other important rigidity is found in the tradition of allocating operating programmes to departments with consequences that have been outlined above. One of the most serious of these is that at the ministerial level a programme for which a department is responsible is increasingly seen to rely on a policy that cuts athwart the programmes of several other departments. The response, as noted, is to try to reassemble all the related programme components under one roof – a response that may resolve that issue but only create a situation where the process has to be repeated with other combinations to meet yet another policy priority. By the same token, a cabinet made up of ministerial heads of equal status, carrying responsibility for operating programmes, is itself inclined to spend more time arbitrating jurisdictional squabbles and settling operational decisions rather than confining its attention to larger issues of policy. And, even when attention is given to policy, it is in the context of placating each individual minister's concern for preserving his department's operating programmes intact, letting 'policy' emerge as a resultant of balancing conflicting claims for operational jurisdiction.

If we are to escape the consequences of this structural block a real venture in organizational innovation lies before us. The current roster of programme-oriented departments would have to be supplanted by ministries, each concerned with a broad policy area, the refinement of policy into programmes, and the co-ordination of those operating agencies to whom the programmes were assigned. Such ministries would be quite small, being divested of their direct operating personnel and equipped with appropriate staff officers for investigating and advising on policy, making programme analyses, and digesting the 'feed-back' from the operating satellites.

In broad outline the proposal is not new – a Senate committee of 1919, following closely the report of the Haldane committee in Britain, made a not dissimilar recommendation. The proposal foundered (as it did in Britain) when the term 'super-ministry' was attached to it. Nevertheless, today there are isolated exemplars to be used as a basis for the reorganization proposed. The Department of Finance comes close to fitting the model, were the present Department of National Revenue relegated to non-cabinet rank to perform, as it now in fact does, as an agency responsible for implementing the tax policies conceived in the main in Finance. In another area, as an earlier chapter has noted, the Department of the

Secretary of State has become a holding company for a mixed group of cultural agencies, though its impact as a centre for policy formation would appear to be much less developed than in the case of Finance. The new Ministry of Transport appears to be hovering on the brink of a similar metamorphosis to a policy agency, with a galaxy of operating satellites (erstwhile branches, crown corporations, and regulatory tribunals) orbiting it in varying states of dependency. It is not unlikely that the Department of External Affairs will end up in much the same form, with its operating appendages abroad combined with those of Trade and Industry and with the less extensive operating staff abroad of other departments. Even more clearly, the introduction of two new categories of cabinet ministers – ministers of state for designated purposes and ministers of state to assist departmental ministers – reflects the government's concern to find more flexible and adaptable mechanisms at the top to cope with long-run co-ordinating problems and urgent short-run policy problems.[1]

The precedents for organizational change in the direction proposed appear, then, to have been established or are rapidly in process. The advantage for the cabinet is that it need not be threatened, as it now is, by

1 In introducing Bill C-207, the Government Organization Act, C.M. Drury, President of the Treasury Board, summed up the government's intentions with respect to the new concept of cabinet ministers as follows:
'With the enactment of the ministries and ministries of state act, there would be four categories of ministers of the Crown. Ministers in all four categories would be appointed on the advice of the prime minister by commission under the Great Seal of Canada, to serve at pleasure, and be responsible to Parliament as members of the government of the day and for any responsibility which might be assigned to them by law or otherwise.
'Departmental ministers would occupy an office created by statute to which are attached powers, duties and functions defined by statute; have supervision and control over a portion of the public service known as a department; be limited by the number of statutory ministerial offices; have salaries provided for by title in the Salaries Act; and seek appropriations on their own from Parliament to cover the costs of the activities for which they are responsible.
'Ministers of state for designated purposes would occupy an office created by proclamation on the advice of the prime minister; be limited in number by statute to five; be charged with responsibility for developing new and comprehensive policies in areas where the development of such policies is of particular urgency and importance; have a mandate effectively determined by the prime minister ... They would have a "secretary" who would have the status and authority of a deputy minister ... and would preside over ministries which would eventually either become parts of new or existing departments or whose existence would be terminated.
'Ministers of state would be appointed to assist a departmental minister in the discharge of his responsibilities ... receive the same salary as a minister without portfolio provided for them in the estimates of the minister with whom they were to be associated. Finally, ministers without portfolio would have responsibilities assigned by the prime minister and would not normally exercise statutory powers, duties and functions.'

pressure to increase its size (for reformation of departments into policy ministries would far from exhaust the two dozen and more seats now occupied in the cabinet). Moreover, a cabinet so constituted could concentrate, as it should, on being the supreme policy board for the country. The fluidity and intermeshing of policies required by changing priorities on the public agenda could be readily accommodated through a cabinet committee system, without resorting to the present dismantling and reassembling of departmental portfolios tied to programmes.

At the level of the individual minister of a policy ministry the distinction between policy and operations may prove difficult to maintain. It is unrealistic to assume that policy (and particularly its refinement into programmes) can be formulated in olympian detachment from operations. But, the normal consequences of the attempt to keep policy decision-makers in touch with the reality of operations is that they become so enmeshed in the day-to-day managerial concerns that policy-making gets short shrift. A possible way out of this impasse is to conceive of the ministerial head as presiding over a policy board made up of senior staff from his ministry and the heads of the agencies to whom the specific programmes have been assigned for implementation. This would provide the input of operational experience to the policy centre without involving the latter in excessive managerial detail. In addition, if the policy board had available to it an advisory committee, widely representative of the outside expertise in its various programme areas, the ministry would have formalized in structure that innovative picture of direct communication with its publics to which reference was previously made.[2]

2 The government's proposals for reorganizing the cabinet did not include this sort of provision but Mr Drury tied in his proposals with the concept of 'participatory democracy' in this way:

'In the last election there was a prevalent demand for greater sensitivity in government to be accompanied at the same time by more government activity and less government intrusion or, at least, less "big" government. As I implied, Mr. Speaker, the best answer to this apparent riddle lies in the strengthening of parliamentary institutions and in this context, among other things, in an increase in the number of Members of Parliament acting within the public service to develop policy, and generally to provide a nexus between the people and the public service.

'The primary concern should not be that cabinets are too large but rather that too few ministers are charged with so many urgent matters that they have to abdicate the task of policy development or at least its control, entirely to experts who do not have to be directly responsive to changing popular feelings. It is well to remember that however big a cabinet, all ministers are accountable to Parliament individually. Distribute all the burdens of government across a smaller ministry, and you generalize the grasp that each minister has over his larger area of responsibility ...

'Mr. Stanfield: Did you say grasp or graft?
'Mr. Drury: Grasp.
'Mr. Stanfield: I wasn't sure.'

At the level of what we have been calling operations, or programme implementation, we must be prepared to contemplate a somewhat looser hierarchical structure than that to which we have become accustomed. The operating agencies may be departments in their own right or they may take any or all the non-departmental forms which have been described in this study. They might, in fact, be provincial, regional, or even municipal operating agencies from whom the policy ministry could contract services. This suggestion seems well suited to the current emphasis on area or community development and would certainly be relevant for any forthcoming programmes for poverty or pollution. These will all require a collaborative effort – both at the policy level and, more particularly, at the implementation level. The concept of 'make or buy' as adumbrated in the report with this title by the Royal Commission on Government Organization was couched largely in terms of government contracting out to the private sector. Is there any reason why the concept should not be extended to contracting out to another level of government? (The precedent is the contracts which several provinces have with the Royal Canadian Mounted Police.) Much duplication and many jurisdictional wrangles could be avoided if this practice were broadly extended. At the same time, it would reduce intergovernmental competition for scarce, highly trained managerial, scientific, and technical manpower.

Not unrelated to the organizational alterations envisaged above is the recommendation from the Royal Commission on Bilingualism and Biculturalism for French-language units 'as a basic organizational and management principle,' 'in a variety of locations and [with] different sizes and functions.' It is certainly true, as the commissioners admit, that 'this sweeping proposal will present a unique and difficult challenge to the Public Service'; it is likely to be more acceptable and workable in the context of the general scheme of reform which has been suggested here, for the separation of operations from policy-making and programming implies the loosening up of hierarchy and the decentralization of operations which the commissioners' proposal would necessitate.

Reference to the 'loosening up of hierarchy' may suggest that the argument has led full circle back to the undesirable state of organizational unease from which the suggested reforms were supposed to free the public service. On the contrary, it is the relief from structural rigidities afforded by the scheme that should make constant reshaping of present programme-oriented departments much less necessary. The 'packaging' of the components relevant to the implementation of a programme could, under the proposed scheme, be accomplished by the policy ministry relying not only on its own operating satellites but on contracting for the services, knowledge, and skills possessed by operating units (and some of these could be the French-language units envisaged by the royal commission) at whatever level of government was most relevant.

In the last analysis, the mortar holding these various building bricks together is money. And, in this context, the emergence of programme budgeting – whatever exaggerated claims are made for it in its present partially developed form – may be the management tool that will provide the co-ordination that must accompany the decentralization of operations implied by the foregoing analysis. But, even with the greater sophistication in retention, retrieval, and manipulation of data afforded by the computer, programme budgeting is still far from providing ready answers to the problems of co-ordinating policies for the Canadian political system.

Description rather than prescription has been the intention of this book. By venturing into prescription this concluding chapter has taken liberties with the intention; it may also have left the impression that the answers to all our major social policy problems are to be found in giving unremitting, single-minded attention to reform of our bureaucratic structures and procedures. This bias springs naturally from the focus of this study and from the thesis of this concluding chapter that among our major political institutions the public service has given more attention to and shown the greatest willingness to experiment with adaptations in form and procedure.

Other institutions must make their own adaptations to cope with the changing balance of functions brought about by highly mobile public demands and what appears to be the readier response of the public service to such demands. From the foregoing analysis it is not unfair to conclude that the public service may have been compelled, *faute de mieux*, to carry too much of the burden of adjustment. Both for the sake of retaining its own internal operating efficiency and for the preservation of that historical balance of countervailing power possessed by other institutions the pressures from an enlarging and shifting public agenda ought to be more evenly distributed. A responsive bureaucracy, operating in a context where other components of the political system show no disposition to change, may well turn on its head the master-to-servant relationship which has been the essence of responsible government and of the liberal democratic state.

Index

Housekeeping agencies, *see* Auxiliary agencies
Howe, Joseph, 99n

Ilsley, J.L., 330
Immigration, administration of, 19, 41n, 105–6, 132
Immigration Appeal Board, 72n, 146
Immigration and Colonization, Department of, 106; *see also* Citizenship and Immigration, Department of; Manpower, Department of
Indian affairs, 94, 99; administration of, 104–5, 131, 222
Indian Affairs and Northern Development, Department of, 28, 99, 105, 125, 129, 131, 203
Industrial Development Bank, 151
Industrial Relations and Disputes Investigation Act, 333–4
Industry, Department of, 103, 178–9, 194
Information Canada, 66n
Innis, Harold A., 20n
Inside Service, 37, 221
Insurance, Department of, 89, 140
Interest groups, representation on advisory committees, 148–9
Interior, Department of, 18, 61, 99–100, 105, 125
International Boundary Commission, 144
International Joint Commission, 102, 144
Interpretation Act, 75, 80

Jamison, Clarence, 267
Jennings, Sir Ivor, 47
Johnston, Victor, 333n
Joy, Richard J., 37n
Justice, Department of, 46, 49–50, 90–1, 95–6, 116, 166, 194, 245

Kernaghan, W.D.K., 289n
King, W.L.M., 108, 216n, 328
Kingsley, J. Donald, 265n
Knowles, Stanley, 319

Labour: administration of, 42, 108;

Department of, 108, 129, 167, 194, 202, 326; distribution of in departments, 157–95
Laflamme, R., 50
Lalande, Gilles, 38n
Lamontagne, Maurice, 286n
Land, administration of, 19, 98–9, 125
Langton, John, 244
Lanphier, C. Michael, 93n, 216n, 218n
Lapointe, Ernest, 60
Laurier, Sir Wilfrid, 61, 65, 91
Lavergne, Roger, 307n
Lawyers, in administration, 116–7, 166
Leiserson, Avery, 161n
Line organization, *see* Hierarchy
Lloyd, Trevor, 218n
Love, J.D., 282n
Lower, A.R.M., 20n

Maas, A., 236n
Macdonald, Sir John A., 31, 33, 44, 46n, 49–50, 139, 242
Macdonald, John B., 28n
Macdonald, Sandfield, 209
Mackenzie, Alexander, 49
Mackenzie, W.J.M., 56n, 212n
Mackintosh, W.A., 20n
Maclean, R.D., 252n, 302n
Mallory, J.R., 213n, 254n, 255
Management of civil service: and civil servants, 310–40; by departments, 287–309; legal base for, 79–83, 264–5, 283–4; by minister and deputy minister, 207–8; by Treasury Board, 241–62
Management, scientific, 22–6, 276–7, 312
Manpower and Immigration, Department of, 106, 129
Mansfield, Harvey C., 4n
Marine and Fisheries, Department of, 23, 91, 98, 100, 102
Maritime Marshland Administration, 175, 236
Maritime Provinces, and public service, 35–6
Masterman Committee (UK), 318
McCutcheon, Wallace, 260n
McIlraith, George, 274
McLeod, Jack, 218n